Toward Critical Multimodality

A volume in
Contemporary Perspectives on Semiotics in Education:
Signs, Meanings, and Multimodality
Rachel J. Pinnow, Lynn E. Shanahan, Katarina N. Silvestri,
and Mary B. McVee, *Series Editors*

Toward Critical Multimodality

Theory, Research, and Practice in Transformative Educational Spaces

edited by

Katarina N. Silvestri
SUNY Cortland

Nichole Barrett
The Rural Outreach Center

Tiffany M. Nyachae
The Pennsylvania State University

INFORMATION AGE PUBLISHING, INC.
Charlotte, NC • www.infoagepub.com

Library of Congress Cataloging-in-Publication Data

A CIP record for this book is available from the Library of Congress
http://www.loc.gov

ISBN: 979-8-88730-248-5 (Paperback)
    979-8-88730-249-2 (Hardcover)
    979-8-88730-250-8 (E-Book)

Copyright © 2023 Information Age Publishing Inc.

All rights reserved. No part of this publication may be reproduced, stored in a retrieval system, or transmitted, in any form or by any means, electronic, mechanical, photocopying, microfilming, recording or otherwise, without written permission from the publisher.

Printed in the United States of America

CONTENTS

Prologue: AERA Chairs Introductory Remarks April 22, 2022
in Session Toward Critical Multimodality: Exploring Theory,
Research, and Practice in Transformative Educational Spaces ix
Katarina N. Silvestri, Nichole Barrett, Tiffany M. Nyachae

Acknowledgments xv

1 Troubling, Disrupting, and Reimagining Educational Spaces:
   The Need for Critical Multimodality Now... 1
   Katarina N. Silvestri, Nichole Barrett, and Tiffany M. Nyachae

SECTION I
THEORIZING FOR CRITICAL MULTIMODALITY

2 Multimodal Meaning Making in a Pandemic: Visions From
  the Multilingual Periphery as Epicenter.. 33
  Eunjeong Lee, Sara P. Alvarez, Laura Gonzales, and Amy J. Wan

3 Proceduralized Ideologies in Video Games and Playable Media 53
  *Earl Aguilera, Jeffrey B. Holmes, Kelly M. Tran,
  and Lynette D. Guzmán*

4 Meet Me in Outer Space: Theorizing Fugitive Spaces
   of Creation and Joy With Girls of Color 79
   Autumn A. Griffin and Grace D. Player

5 Multimodality as Accessibility: A Critical Perspective
   of Universal Design in Theory, Research, and Practice 103
   Kyesha M. Isadore and Angélica Galván

SECTION II

CRITICAL MULTIMODALITY AND STORYTELLING FOR AGENCY AND REVISIONING

6 All the Stars Are Closer: Black Girl Multimodal Practices
   for Time Traveling in a Dystopian World 123
   *ThedaMarie Gibbs Grey, Jennifer D. Turner,
   and Alexis Morgan Young*

7 Black Joy, Love, and Resistance: Using Digital Storytelling
   to Center Black Students' Full Humanity 147
   Davena Jackson

8 It Starts With a (Digital) Story: Agentive Inquiry Through
   Digital Storytelling 171
   Andrea N. Franyutti-Boyles, Sara Cooper, and Gregory Ramírez

SECTION III

CRITICAL MULTIMODALITY FOR REIMAGINING CURRICULUM

9 "Don't Tell Me It's Not Research": Using Multimodal Critical
   Inquiry Projects to Disrupt the Deficits in the Traditional
   ELA Paper 201
   Sarah M. Fleming

10 The Plat and the Gavel: Multimodal Critical Family History
   in Rural Teacher Education 219
   William S. Davis and Vicki Mokuria

11 Critical Multimodality at the Museum: How a Community–
   University Partnership Supports Transformative Praxis 241
   Matthew R. Deroo

SECTION IV

CRITICAL MULTIMODALITY IN PROTESTS AND SOCIAL MOVEMENTS

12 Bordados: A Feminist Collective Practice of Resistance and Solidarity in the Chilean Estallido 269
    Romina S. Peña-Pincheira, M. Isidora Bilbao-Nieva, and Lau Romero-Quintana

13 Post-it, Milk Tea, and Mini-Stonehenge: Making Sense of the Multimodality of Protest Artifacts in 2019–2020 Hong Kong Protest Movement 291
    Jason Man-Bo Ho

14 Disrupting Discourses in Place: Youth, Space, and Activism 325
    Amy Walker

15 Epilogue 355
    Mary B. McVee

About the Editors 359

About the Contributors 361

PROLOGUE

AERA Chairs Introductory Remarks April 22, 2022 in Session *Toward Critical Multimodality: Exploring Theory, Research, and Practice in Transformative Educational Spaces*

Katarina N. Silvestri
State University of New York, Cortland

Nichole Barrett
University at Buffalo, State University of New York

Tiffany M. Nyachae
The Pennsylvania State University

Welcome to our workshop, *Toward Critical Multimodality: Exploring Theory, Research, and Practice in Transformative Educational Spaces*. We first want to recognize that today, we are attending this AERA conference and learning on the ancestral and current lands of the Kumiyaay people.

Our group represents a collective of scholars committed to engaging with critical theories and foregrounding criticality in their work as researchers and educators through the theories and methodological tools afforded by social semiotics and multimodal perspectives.

As critical scholars and practitioners, we strive to consistently

- bring into clarity how power, privilege, and oppression are present in learning spaces and how these relate to ours and our students' social identities through space and time (Muhammad, 2018);
- question and de-center dominant narratives found in learning spaces (McVee & Boyd, 2015);
- center the varieties of language and meaning making that we and our students bring into learning spaces (Baker-Bell, 2020);
- critique "what counts" as meaning making and how students show they know (Muhammad, 2020); and
- reimagine and reenvision how these learning spaces can be transformed towards spaces that are rooted in equity and justice.

In this workshop, we contend that the theory of social semiotics and its associated multimodal perspectives are tools that can coordinate with critical theories and criticality, both instrumentally and purposefully, in our work to de-center "dominant" (i.e., White, patriarchal, colonizing, ableist, and heteronormative—among others) ideas of power and what counts as purposeful meaning making among scholars from diverse perspectives and educational contexts.

Specifically, social semiotics and multimodal perspectives are theoretical-analytical tools for broadening scope and critiquing what counts as meaning making across various communicative modalities (Kress, 2010), including different visual modalities (such as image, writing, color, layout, and more) as well as embodied modalities (such as gesture, haptics or touch, facial expressions, speech and intonation, body positioning, and more) in interaction with one another (Norris, 2004, 2019). Even more importantly, we strive to learn how signs across these modes are orchestrated by the signmaker, with all of their histories, identities, and complexities. Scholars *have* taken up tools of social semiotics and multimodality to both transcend meaning making and transform theorizing, analysis, and literacy practices in educational spaces towards criticality. We argue that the folks in this room are critical multimodal scholars who seek to "change [their] frame of reference" (Anzaldúa, 2009, p. 114) and honor the ways that educators and students see their worlds through their experiences, histories, and cultures; such scholars make meaning of power dynamics within interactions, texts, institutions, and societies using social semiotics and multimodality towards critical ends.

At this time, we are going to introduce our breakout groups and ask each authorship team—two per breakout group—to briefly describe their portion of the breakout group session. This time can also be used to describe what will be accomplished in the breakout group overall.

Critical Multimodality/Social Semiotics Theorizing Protest

- "Post-it, Milk Tea, and Mini-Stonehenge: Making Sense of the Multimodality of Protest Artifacts in 2019–2020 Hong Kong Protest Movement" (Jason Ho, Chapter 13)
- "Disrupting Discourses in Place: Youth, Space, and Activism" (Amy Walker, Chapter 14)

Critical Multimodality/Social Semiotics and Digital Storytelling

- "Black Joy, Love, and Resistance: Using Digital Storytelling to Center Black Students' Full Humanity" (Davena Jackson, Chapter 7)
- "It Starts With a (Digital) Story: Agentive Inquiry Through Digital Storytelling" (Sara Cooper, Andrea Franyutti Boyles, & Gregory Ramírez, Chapter 8)

Critical Multimodality/Social Semiotics Across Time, Place, and Space

- "All the Stars Are Closer: Black Girl Multimodal Practices for Time Traveling in a Dystopian World" (Jennifer Danridge Turner, Alexis Morgan Young, & Theda Gibbs Grey, Chapter 6)
- "The Plat and the Gavel: Multimodal Critical Family History in Rural Teacher Education" (William S. Davis & Vicki Mokuria, Chapter 10)

Critical Multimodality/Social Semiotics in Built Learning Environments

- Critical Multimodality at the Museum: How a Community–University Partnership Supports Transformative Praxis (Matthew R. Deroo, Chapter 11)
- Multimodality as Accessibility: A Critical Perspective on Universal Design in Theory, Research, and Practice (Kyesha Isadore & Angélica Galván, Chapter 5)

[At this point in the session, attendees selected their breakout groups and engaged with the research and ideas discussed within each.]

REFLECTING ON THE SESSION WITH A CRITICAL MULTIMODAL STANCE

The purpose of including these remarks as an introduction to this book is to situate parts of this work materially—in a place and time—a portion of the journey illustrating how this volume came to be. The session itself was the first time a great many of the authors and editors within this edited volume met one another in person or virtually on a screen. We were putting faces and ideas and names together in a way that was precluded by long distances and an ongoing, worldwide pandemic that required us to forgo in-person conferences. There is a different kind of energy that manifests when a group of people you've been working with virtually through email for months come together in the same space. It gave our endeavor of co-constructing a volume exploring the theoretical, analytical, and practical applications of critically-minded social semiotics and multimodality a tangibility and form that it did not previously possess. Perhaps this feeling was amplified by the overwhelming isolation that many of us felt from our academic friends due to the pandemic. For whatever reasons, *Toward Critical Multimodality* came into a greater degree of vibrancy and focus in this session.

When we walked into the room where our workshop would be held (which could be found down a dimly lit, long hallway), we found a large converted ballroom filled with rows of chairs and high ceilings. This would be a fine setup for a single presenter sharing their work one at a time, but this was slated as a workshop session, with multiple presenters sharing at the same time with attendees choosing where they'd like to go. Knowing that our session would require us to get into groups, the author teams presenting and I brainstormed solutions to our dilemma. We created four sections of chairs for each of the four breakout groups outlined above. Additionally, each group had pieces of paper with 1, 2, 3, and 4 printed upon them so that we could direct attendees easily to the breakout groups they'd like to attend. From a multimodal standpoint, our group recognized the need to modify the spatiality of the room to the best of our ability to support the interactive goals of our session.

Our session also had presenters that were presenting entirely virtually, given that in-person conference attendance can be prohibitively expensive, especially for folks who are required to travel internationally, and/or do not receive adequate funding from their institutions, and/or were prohibited from traveling due to COVID-19 necessitated restrictions. One of our workarounds was to use a computer and bluetooth speaker to project the voices of the two chapter authors who were slated to present virtually. While this has been a solution that worked in the past for me at conferences, it ultimately did not work very well in the conference space due to the high ceilings and the sound getting lost above. We adapted the best we could, passing the bluetooth speaker around and moving the computer towards attendees that wanted to ask specific questions.

Importantly, we can use critical multimodality and social semiotics to analyze this particular situation with respect to the critical issues of accessibility to the conference (e.g., reducing or eliminating barriers for participation from a financial standpoint) and accessibility within the sessions (i.e., providing more sign-language interpreters for workshops and other alternative sessions with multiple groups working simultaneously, captioning for any breakout sessions using video within roundtables, etc.). As the chapters within this volume demonstrate, reflecting on the specific intersectional axes of power, oppression, and privilege within the work that we do as scholars—and then changing our practice and the practices of our institutions in ways revealed by such reflection—is necessary if we are to engage in this work as critical multimodal scholars.

REFERENCES

Anzaldúa, G. (2009). *The Gloria Anzaldúa reader* (A. Keating, Ed.). Duke University Press.

Baker-Bell, A. (2020). *Linguistic justice: Black language, literacy, identity, and pedagogy.* Routledge.

Kress, G. R. (2010). *Multimodality: A social semiotic approach to contemporary communication.* Taylor & Francis.

McVee, M. B., & Boyd, F. B. (2015). *Exploring diversity through multimodality, narrative, and dialogue: A framework for teacher reflection.* Routledge.

Muhammad, G. E. (2018). A plea for identity and criticality: Reframing literacy learning standards through a four-layered equity model. *Journal of Adolescent & Adult Literacy, 62*(2), 137–142.

Muhammad, G. (2020). *Cultivating genius: An equity framework for culturally and historically responsive literacy.* Scholastic Incorporated.

Norris, S. (2004). *Analyzing multimodal interaction: A methodological framework.* Routledge.

Norris, S. (2019). *Systematically working with multimodal data: Research methods in multimodal discourse analysis.* John Wiley & Sons.

ACKNOWLEDGMENTS

To all the authors who have contributed their voices and stories to this work, thank you. Your contributions brought our intense vision for this book to fruition; that is, urgent calls for just experiences, educational or otherwise, that we wanted to see happen in the world. We would not have been able to do this without your stories, voices, honesty, and willingness to work with us throughout this process. We want to especially shout out our workshop about this book that took place during the 2022 American Educational Research Association (AERA) annual meeting; it drew a huge crowd, and there was authentic, generative engagement with critical multimodality amongst our contributors and attendees, revealing the need for this work. Overall, this was a learning experience for us—we learned from all of the authors and from each other.

Mary McVee, Rachel Pinnow, and Lynn Shanahan of the Information Age Publishing Semiotics in Education series editors, thank you for trusting us. We appreciate the opportunity to contribute to this book series and share the incredible work of those in our field. We also thank Marissa Baugh for her efforts checking the many, many references found throughout this book.

Mary, thank you for your endless support and guidance throughout this process. We continue to learn a great deal from you, most importantly how to purposefully trust the process. We thank you for bringing us together as co-editors for this book.

What we found during our work together as co-editors was something emergent and beautiful and built with trust. We entered as three friends who shared intersecting scholarly interests around criticality and multimodality; since then, we have grown together through this process, deepening our trust and care for one another in ways that fundamentally mattered to us during some of the most challenging times of our lives, collectively and individually. We worked entirely virtually through the COVID-19 pandemic (except the one time Nichole ran into Tiffany at Chipotle in Buffalo). We laughed, we cried, we vented, and we leaned on each other when we needed it; co-editing this book has gone far beyond the acts of theorizing, writing, and editing. As co-editors, we cultivated a trusting space where our personal *and* professional needs were met. Time and time again, over the three years we worked together, we were drawn to the book because we got to do work that matters to us with people we enjoy and who make us laugh during challenging times. In short, we are grateful for each other.

—**Katie, Nichole, and Tiffany**

CHAPTER 1

TROUBLING, DISRUPTING, AND REIMAGINING EDUCATIONAL SPACES

The Need for Critical Multimodality Now

Katarina N. Silvestri
State University of New York, Cortland

Nichole Barrett
*The Rural Outreach Center,
University at Buffalo, State University of New York*

Tiffany M. Nyachae
The Pennsylvania State University

ABSTRACT

In this introductory chapter, we, the co-editors of this book, begin by defining the social semiotic perspective of multimodality as well as criticality. We then use vignettes to consider these theoretical connections through our own experiences with criticality and a social semiotic perspective of multimodality in our research, teaching, and lives in general. These narrative vignettes act as springboards for our conversation regarding critical multimodal social semiotics and a call for criticality in multimodal research. We then provide a brief illustration of how these theories can work together to support arguments seeking to expand and transform educational spaces. The chapter concludes with an overview of the four sections in this edited volume and several provocations for readers to consider.

What Do We Mean by Multimodality?

As a part of this first volume in the series Contemporary Perspectives on Semiotics in Education: Signs, Meanings, and Multimodality we seek to answer the question, "What does it mean to be a critical multimodal scholar in educational spaces?" By highlighting the ways that choices made throughout multimodal design processes are "circumscribed by power" and reflect the "politics of choice" (Kress, 2010, p. 28), this book aims to draw attention to the ways that social semiotics and multimodality can be used to inform how scholars question dominant narratives in research, theory, method, and practice. As Hull and Nelson (2005) noted, "Multimodal text can create a different system of signification, one that transcends the collective contribution of its constituent parts. More simply put, multimodality can afford, not just a new way to make meaning, but a different kind of meaning" (p. 225). As both researchers and educators, we as co-editors assume that texts involve multiple modalities (e.g., image, writing, color, spatiality), and that social semiotics can be used to "say something about the *function* of each of the *modes*... about the *relation* of these *modes* to each other; and about the main entities" in a given text (Kress, 2010, p. 59, emphasis in original). A social semiotics perspective of multimodality is also positioned as a tool to support criticality. As Jewitt and Oyama (2001) observed, "Social semiotics is not an end in itself. It is meant as a tool for use in critical research" (p. 136). As such a tool, it is essential to consider what we mean by such terms as "critical" or "criticality" and the relationship between critical social semiotics and multimodality.

What Do We Mean by Criticality?

We, the co-editors of this volume, draw on Chicana feminist, Black feminist, and ethnic and culturally based frameworks to conceptualize criticality as foregrounded by a "criticality of self" (Anzaldúa, 2009, p. 116) that seeks to "change our frame of reference" (Anzaldúa, 2009, p. 114) and honor the ways that individuals and communities see their worlds through the lens of their experiences, histories, and cultures—those that are predetermined and/or thrust upon them through historical institutional systems of oppression. We seek understandings of criticality that explore the relationships between self and space. In particular, we draw upon those that emphasize the importance of individual truths. We seek to highlight how these truths are constructed as a part of multimodal layering and composition while individuals navigate the tensions that arise as a part of reframing what is familiar, problematic, and expected. We believe that changing our frame of reference requires a commitment to decentering the dominant White gaze and honoring the voices, experiences, and truths that come from within our individual selves and informed by our communities. To do so, we must investigate the ways that individual lenses and voices are manipulated as a result of an overt emphasis on a universal White truth.

Criticality speaks to being able to intuit, read, interpret, and work to shift power dynamics within interactions, texts, institutions, and societies. Importantly, criticality assumes that where there are hierarchical power structures, there is oppression and privilege, and that to enact criticality one must have a "lens of understanding how power, oppression, and privilege are present" (Muhammad, 2018, p. 139). In our world, oppression and privilege are historically forced and bestowed upon (respectively) people based on identities which they are born into, including race, gender, class, sexual orientation, region of the world, language, religious upbringing, and more. As Gholdy Muhammad (2020) writes, "Criticality enables us to question both the world and texts within it to better understand the truth in history, power, and equity" (p. 117). Criticality implies action, one key action grounded in criticality in the field of education involves naming and disrupting deficit narratives in favor of supporting learners' funds of knowledge (Moll et al., 1992). With respect to texts specifically, actions grounded in criticality involve naming and disrupting dominant ideologies, hierarchies, and extant power dynamics represented and reconstructed in texts in favor of creating multimodal texts that both take an extended view of texts and are anti-oppressive—that is, anti-racist, anti-sexist, anti-ableist, anti-homophobic, anti-transphobic, anti-classist, and against other forms of hierarchical oppression.

In this introductory chapter, we begin by considering some of these theoretical connections through our own experiences with criticality and a social semiotic perspective of multimodality in our research, teaching, and lives in general. These narrative vignettes act as springboards for our conversation regarding critical multimodal social semiotics and a call for criticality in multimodal research. We then provide a brief illustration of how these theories can work together to support arguments seeking to expand and transform educational spaces. The chapter concludes with an overview of the four sections in this edited volume and several provocations for readers to consider.

JOURNEYING TOWARD CRITICAL MULTIMODALITY

In the sections that follow, we share our stories and journeys as the co-editors of this volume and detail how critical multimodality reveals itself in our lives, how critical multimodality informs our teaching and learning, and how we came to be (and are continuing to become) critical multimodal scholars.

Determined to Humanize the Researcher Through Multimodal Composition: Nichole's Story

Different Ways of Knowing

There is a shared space at the University at Buffalo where I completed my doctoral work and later became an adjunct. This space, while I believe it was intended as a quiet workspace for planning and research, became a space for conversation, discussion, collaboration, and camaraderie. Having a space like this gave me the chance to get to know people beyond my specific program, eavesdrop on their conversations, and learn from them. I often found myself engaging in conversation and bouncing ideas off of those who also occupied this space, and I became familiar with their research and learning processes. Over time, we often leaned on each other for new, alternative perspectives. We pushed the boundaries of meaning making by visually, physically, and orally representing our thoughts and research. It was here that I began to realize how all the pieces of the puzzle fit together. There were drawings and diagrams all over the room—on the whiteboard, on giant Post-its, and sprawled across the many workspaces. The more people that entered the space, the more diversified voices I heard and the more I began to develop the courage to explore my own voice.

My Journey

I was a theater major in undergrad. I spent a lot of time trying to figure out both my physical and metaphorical voices. I went through a personal transformation as I learned to exist in my own body and trust my mind; it was here that I first found my embodied voice. As my path changed, I found myself enrolled in an English literature program that placed emphasis on the voices of others. The years that I spent working toward my master's degree required me to separate my voice and my being from the work that I was doing. Those that I looked to for guidance kept telling me that my voice didn't belong in academia, and I believed them. I taught myself how to speak and write in third person and transformed my writing into discourse that pleased my professors and reflected my academic knowledge. It felt cold and disconnected from the person behind the words. I learned to split my voice between personal and academic and I learned when each was appropriate—or at least I thought I did. When I graduated from my master's program, I had an understanding of academic writing that was print based and, in my opinion, lacked any real emotion or personal reflection. I had a style, but I didn't recognize it as my own. I accepted it as part of academia; I had to learn how to separate who I was in life from who I was in school. I had come to believe that they couldn't be the same person.

Eventually, I found myself working toward a degree in education, which was somewhere I never thought I would be, and I once again found myself struggling to find my voice. I was trying to navigate a doctoral program that wanted me to be both academic and authentic, two things that I wasn't sure I could be at the same time. I struggled to find the balance between my aesthetic reactions and my academic reflections and wondered if it was possible for them to exist in the same space. In my English education courses, I was encouraged to draw on my background in the performing arts. I was encouraged to "play around" with visuals and modes beyond print texts. I made collages, dioramas, drew body biographies, made movies, recorded podcasts, and performed in order to reflect. I read research and theory that positioned the aesthetic and emphasized the arts in English language arts. I highlighted passages that reframed academic writing as multimodal and dynamic but more importantly, the voice that I worked to suppress during my master's program was fighting its way back into my very being. My education classes were breathing life back into a part of myself that I thought I had lost.

Except, I didn't feel the same way during my research methods courses.

How Multimodality Changed My Research

Something happens when you become a doctoral student at a research university. I don't think it's intentional, it's just a part of the culture. But I also think that's the challenge. For whatever reason, being a researcher means you often think of things in the third person and focus on the results rather than the process it takes to get there. You observe, take notes, and create and collect data with the intention of proving something. Conducting research, writing research, and presenting research all focus on the result. But what about the process? We spend a lot of time talking about the process during our classes, but the second we sit down to write the methods section, our involvement in the process seems to disappear when we begin talking about participants and analysis. We give details about our research site, our participants, the methods and theories we used as a part of analysis, and we identify our biases. This is what we think of when we think of methods because this is what we are conditioned to expect. We are taught to expect the why, where, who, what, when, and how. We share the experiences of our participants, but how often do we talk about the experiences of the person who decided the why, identified the who, did the what, when, and how? How often do we look at the experience of the researcher alongside their collection and analysis? How often do we think about the embodied nature of the research process and how each decision and each step of the process has an impact on the researcher and the way they see their data? There are ethnographic and narrative research methods that help breathe life into educational research, but what happens when we challenge the expectations more broadly? What happens when we pull back the curtain, open the black box, and expose the researcher?

I had never considered myself to be a researcher. I didn't even know how to be a researcher, but I knew that part of being in my doctoral program was learning to be one. In fact, that is part of why I chose the program I did and I fell in love with the process. I was excited about figuring out and exploring my role in education from this perspective. I had a supportive advisor and honest support system, but there was no way that I could anticipate the personal struggle that would ensue. I knew that earning your PhD was challenging, but I did not foresee that I would have to once again navigate two different voices. As I entered into the dissertation phase of my program, it didn't take me very long to question why I was continuing to compartmentalize my voice.

Finding My Researcher Voice

My researcher voice began to evolve during the year and a half I spent exploring the transformative nature of digital video composition and identity with the members of a rural high school film club. As I began data analysis and the process of composing their individual stories, I felt it was impossible to give voice to these students without embodying the very argument I was making, and without highlighting my own transformation. As Moje and Luke (2009) argue, researchers need to remember that people "are constantly in the process of identifying and making meaning of identifications" (p. 433). My process included documenting each step of data collection and analysis in order to draw attention to the multimodal aspects of each part of my journey. I recorded myself after every data collection session. I recorded myself throughout every aspect of the analysis process. I captured my notes, my doodles, the highlighting, the transcription process, and all the writing (Figure 1.1).

When I began recording snippets of my research process I had no idea how valuable these videos would be. My original plan was to document my experiences in order to create a short film that would tell my dissertation story for no other reason than my belief that reflection is a catalyst for growth. I thought that composing this film would simply allow me to reflect on an experience that I anticipated I would never fully understand. This video was supposed to be just for me. What I discovered, however, was that the more I watched those snippets the more I began to understand my own experience alongside the experiences and stories of those voices

Figure 1.1 Examples of documented data collection and analysis.

I was choosing to share. I began to reflect on how much I had grown as a researcher and how important my relationship to this research was. This wasn't just about participants and data anymore; this was about all of us.

As I worked to articulate my experience as a part of my methods chapter, I discovered I could not give voice to my research without embodying my beliefs about its value. I could not talk about the impact video composition had upon student identities if I did not allow myself the opportunity to be transformed. These elements all became a part of my digital story. As I began to compose this video, I turned to the videos I had recorded throughout the year and a half in which I collected and analyzed my data. I relived all the highlighting, the transcribing, the writing, and the tiredness. I didn't set out to create a motion picture worthy of an Oscar; I set out to capture my experience. I set out to record life as it happened and document how my dissertation became a part of my very being. During editing, I was able to relive moments of inspiration and frustration. I was able to look at my data from a different and humble perspective. Composing this video helped me to conceptualize my experience and bring my data to life.

Educational researchers continue to advocate for educators to embrace and adopt digital and multimodal forms of composition as a part of everyday learning (e.g., Alexander, 2015; Jocius, 2013; Smith, 2016), yet these practices do not always extend to those pursuing postsecondary education. In fact, in many instances the deeper into academia you travel, the farther away multimodal and creative compositions seem. Hull (2003) argues for a focus on "the full range of communicative tools, modes, and media, plus an awareness of and a sensitivity to the power and importance of representation of self and others" (p. 230). My story aims to highlight the significance of the human experience in conjunction with changing notions of learning, research, and writing. While my experience focuses on my journey through higher education, my hope is that others find their own courage and voice and see the power and purpose of multimodality and social semiotics as a part of storytelling across a broad range of educational spaces.

The dissertation journey is both physical and emotional, and the more I engaged in conversation with those around me, the more I felt it was important to humanize the research I was conducting. I found it necessary to speak to what I believe are antiquated definitions of academic research. As a result, I committed myself to highlighting the importance of multimodal composition as a part of every aspect of my research. I embodied the nature of writing and gave meaning to the process of data collection, analysis, and narration. Composing this video (see Figure 1.2) helped me

Figure 1.2 QR code linking to https://youtu.be/isUeLtSMLdM.

to conceptualize my experience and share the cacophony of voices who contributed to the story. I would love to share my experience with you.

Supporting the Multimodal, Multilingual, and Critical Realities of Literacy Learning: Katarina's Story

Journeying Into Social Semiotics, Multimodality, and Criticality

Growing up, my two public-school teacher aunts made it their mission to support my education with respect to literacy and language learning; I believe that this is in large part due to their lived experiences, growing up bilingual with a first language of Italian spoken in the home and learning a new language of English once they got to school. As such, my aunts had a personal understanding of the variety and importance of the ways we come to make meaning and communicate in the world. My Aunt Loretta taught elementary school and was a state-certified reading teacher. My Aunt Linda, who has her doctorate in applied linguistics, taught within an English as a second language (ESL; the nomenclature at the time of her teaching) classroom in K–12 settings. Both taught for decades, and both helped me learn why it was important to teach across multiple modalities by having me sit in on their classrooms while I was on breaks during middle school and high school growing up. Loretta helped me understand the literacy side of it (e.g., explaining how pictures and graphs in texts support meaning making, which in turn can support how we figure out the unknown words on the page) and Linda—a polyglot five times over—helped me understand how important it is to use modalities aside from linguistics when learning and teaching a new language. My aunts helped me understand that learning and living (and the meaning making supporting these) are inherently multimodal and multilingual acts.

It was also here that my aunts planted the seeds of criticality in my own thinking and theorizing—especially my Aunt Linda. I remember how she was a staunch advocate for her multilingual students and their families, imploring that the educational system did not equitably support students who were essentially required to learn English in U.S. schools. Importantly, she explained how the policies in place did not support the actual timelines of language development (Abedi & Gandara, 2006; Collier 1987, 1989; Solórzano, 2008) and often tested students in ways that did not accurately represent students' academic abilities (Solórzano, 2008). As an ESL teacher, my aunt often felt as though she was one of the few voices advocating for her multilingual students in her schools. She sought to empower her students in a system that disempowered them, and I wanted to do the same as a future teacher.

It is, then, unsurprising that I remained skeptical when I entered my undergraduate education within the time period Alexander and Fox (2019) termed the *Era of Performance-Oriented Learning (2006–2015)*. I was thrust into a world of data analysis, standardized testing, and a seeming obsession with quantifiable modalities of assessment of reading print-based texts. I could see the kinds of demonstrated learning that was prioritized (i.e., written-responses to text, grammar, the ability to read words accurately and fluently, basic print-based comprehension). I did not see modalities outside of this assessed frequently. However, as I began my early teaching experiences, especially teaching both Kindergarten and first-grade, I could see that instruction and assessment were necessarily multimodal in part because most children are still learning printed letters and their sounds. I remember the importance placed on play, on sensing and developing an experiential knowledge across multiple modalities. Being able to make meaning across modalities is foundational. We do not initially make meaning from printed text but instead from the naturally multimodal world around us and as such, print modes cannot be the only modalities emphasized. And yet, in those same schools where I taught young children multimodally, we teachers still foregrounded printed text as the eventual primary mode for meaning making and school learning. I wondered why we lost that multimodal focus after around Grade 1 or Grade 2 in schools.

Another seed of criticality was planted during my time as a graduate student by a professor and mentor of mine, Dr. Hunter. It's troubling (and probably expected at this point, as a straight-passing White woman in the field of education in the United States) to say that my first real reckoning with my White privilege and general deficit ways of thinking about students happened in my literacy master's program. However, I can recall that disruption clearly even though nearly a decade has passed since that day in my Literacy for Culturally and Linguistically Diverse Learners course, when Dr. Hunter (the first Black professor I'd learned from) explicitly and overtly challenged my deeply held and problematic assumptions about schooling, especially with respect to race, ethnicity, language, and class. He specifically made clear how students of color and students who did not speak English in U.S. schools (among more minoritized groups) have historically experienced oppression. Subsequently, he demonstrated how this transferred into school settings. Dr. Hunter asked us to journal about our learning throughout his class, and I found this journaling to be space and time to reflect deeply on my own implicit biases, where they came from, and how my own current teaching practices upheld systems of oppression. Such spaces for reflection led to after-class conversations with Dr. Hunter and others within the course; this eventually grew into a mentorship that is strong to this day.

This critical learning experience opened my eyes to my own privilege, and I needed to keep my eyes open and (un)learn so that I could be a more critically-oriented person committed to deep examinations of power, privilege, and oppression. The fact that my eyes had opened this late in the game (as someone already teaching and a graduate student) is an example of such privilege. Not only did this disruption make me aware of my Whiteness and the privilege this carried, it also helped to disrupt another problematic discourse—that of the perfectionist, dutiful student. Later on, I'd learn enough about the theoretical connection between White supremacy and perfectionism (Okun & Jones, 2016), especially in White cis-women with respect to their proximity to the privileges of White patriarchy. Importantly, this disruption was uncomfortable and imbued with feelings, and this discomfort is not a bad thing. In fact, I do theorize, along with numerous learning theorists (e.g., Vygotsky, Bakhtin), that some amount of discomfort is required for deep learning shifts. Further, it is clear from an affective neuroscience standpoint that our emotions are deeply entwined with our learning (Immordino-Yang & Damasio, 2007). This instance of learning was no different. This was where criticality became a part of my everyday thinking explicitly, recognizing inequities as they exist in the current and throughout history entwined with power as well as persisting in fighting for equity and justice in school spaces and beyond.

Critical Social Semiotics and Multimodality in my Teaching and Research

Critical social semiotics and multimodality became a clear part of my teaching and my research as I progressed through my doctoral work and into my current position as an associate professor of literacy education. It began when initially working as a doctoral student and graduate assistant with both Dr. Fenice Boyd and Dr. Mary McVee who mentored me into teaching a graduate level course called Language, Literacy, and Culture. These professors and advisors used their courses addressing critical perspectives in literacy and language education as a way to introduce multimodal teaching and assessment methods while also teaching about the merits of the perspective of multimodality (McVee & Boyd, 2015). For example, graduate students crafted multimodal representations to support their discussions around narrative texts read in class relating to critical matters in education (e.g., race/Whiteness, language, socioeconomic status, disability, etc.). Teaching this necessarily critical and multimodal course solidified my commitment to helping current and future teachers embody the principle that there are multiple ways of showing what one knows, what one learns, no matter the content being taught. In the courses I currently teach, I continue to support students in showing what they know multimodally while also striving to provide both print-based and multimodal texts to support students' learning. To this end, I created a series of multimodal "explainer" videos about literacy theories, which I use when I teach my literacy theories-focused class, Language and Literacy Foundations (see Figures 1.3 and 1.4).

Figure 1.3 Title card for all about literacy theories! Multimodal explainer video.

Figure 1.4 QR code for video, *All About Literacy Theories: Why Are Theories Important to Understanding Literacy Learning and Instruction?* (Silvestri, McVee, & Barrett, 2021).

From a research standpoint, I also began my exploration into multimodal discourse analysis (Kress & van Leeuwen, 2001) early in my doctoral program during a course focused on discourse analysis writ large, where I conducted an analysis on a concept album across its music, print/lyrics, images, and artifacts found within the deluxe edition of the album—a passion project that combined my love of analysis with my love of music and the arts. This is also a course that I took with Tiffany (co-editor of this book), who will elaborate on her own project from this course in the following section. Interestingly, Tiffany and I were the only two students who engaged in multimodal discourse analysis within that particular course and were paired together to begin unpacking these analytical tools to support our respective projects.

Eventually, I took a 15-week course on social semiotics and multimodality, and this is where I began engaging in research relating to multimodal interactional analysis. This course is where I started to feel a sense of deep cohesion between my experiential understandings of multimodal and embodied ways of knowledge and how that manifested academically. It felt like coming home. A pivotal theoretical-analytical text for me was *Analyzing Multimodal Interaction* (Norris, 2004); it was foundational to my understanding as a multimodal scholar, as it helped me find clearer analytical paths and methods for aggregating analyzed data across modes with respect to modal density, complexity, and intensity. These multimodal analytical frameworks helped me theoretically and analytically bolster my arguments of what I knew to be true, especially when it came to analyzing data with respect to multilingual students: linguistic and print modalities were less frequently used and nonetheless communication was accomplished successfully through gesture, gaze, proximity, and artifact-handling.

My research during this time involved co-constructing an engineering and literacies after-school club in a nearby elementary school with literacy education and engineering faculty, as well as teachers from the local school. I analyzed data from this engineering and literacies club using Norris' (2004) multimodal interactional analysis as well as principles of multimodal discourse analysis and social semiotics writ large (Kress & van Leeuwen, 2001; Kress, 2010).

This analysis tended to focus on multilingual learners of varying "proficiency levels" as determined by assessments in their first language(s) as well as English communicating across multiple modalities (McVee, Silvestri, Shanahan, & English, 2017; Shanahan et al., 2018, 2022) as well as about interpersonal communication on an engineering design team focused on how the artifact itself impacts that communication (Silvestri, McVee, Jarmark et al., 2021). Finally, several of these analytical examples function as illustrations of theory-in-action in numerous chapters and articles pertaining to positioning theory and multimodality (McVee, Haq et al., 2019; McVee, Silvestri, Barrett, & Haq, 2019); positioning theory, multimodality, and embodiment (McVee, Silvestri, Schucker, & Cun, 2021); multiliteracies (McVee, Schucker et al., 2022); and opportunities for learning (McVee, Silvestri, & Shanahan, 2023). Co-creating these publications involved an immersion in deep theoretical readings, multimodal analysis, and commitments to foregrounding criticality in my work. Ultimately, these writings from my doctoral studies and early career are what led to the genesis of this edited book and to work with Tiffany, Nichole, and the chapter authors to co-construct this very book on criticality and multimodality that we needed. We cannot continue to privilege print-based or even linguistic modes when we are considering the teaching and learning of all learners, especially students who foreground the use of nonlinguistic modalities during their learning. We must instead embrace a multimodal, multilingual, and embodied approach to (literacy) learning.

Intentionally Merging Identity, Criticality, and Multimodality Within and Without: Tiffany's Story

Although I would not have named it as such, multimodality that was intentional, agentic, and at times critical, has always been present in my life. A community of artists existed within the small working-class Black church I attended from birth until young adulthood. Various church members, including my mother and several of her paternal first cousins (each of whom I called "aunt" because they were older than Mommy) made up this community. I would often find Mommy, a fashion illustrator and designer, sitting at her sewing machine working on wedding gowns, prom dresses, or hemming a pair of slacks after her day job. Yet, the excitement of the hustle and bustle of Mommy running up against her sewing deadlines was no comparison to one of my greatest childhood discoveries: a box full of her dope drawings of 1980s fashion models.

The burgeoning artistic community within my church also included cartoonists, drawing/sketch artists, hatmakers, decorators, songwriters, choir directors, psalmists, soloists, singers, organists/pianists, playwrights/directors, actors/actresses, poets, and more. Without a doubt, being surrounded by artists influenced my own creation and use of multimodal texts. As a young Black girl, I would go on to write and direct plays for my church and write songs for the gospel youth singing group I started, which also included my sister, Alicia, and cousin, Jolanda. One play highlighted the experiences of a Black single mother struggling to pay bills while being employed full time. I believe that a rigorous analysis of the performed play would have reflected critical multimodality. For example, an analysis of the multimodal interaction (Norris, 2004) between different communicative modes (e.g., language, gesture, gaze, material objects, etc.) merged with data analysis methods guided by critical theories (e.g., BlackCrit) could attend to the play's subliminal commentary of how upward mobility rhetoric fails the Black working class.

Given my lived experiences, it can be argued that I have always engaged critical multimodality. However, my work in creating social justice literacy workshops (SJLW) for youth of color who are labeled "struggling" readers and writers in schools (Nyachae, 2019) spurred my scholarly understanding of critical multimodality. Specifically, my research inquiry on meaning making within SJLW directed me to multimodality and my need for multimodality to offer more insight on how youth read multimodal texts through a critical literacy lens ushered me towards critical multimodality. In the summer of 2014, when I conducted my first SJLW with adolescents, I had just finished up the first year of my doctoral program and had only been out of the classroom for 1 year. Prior, I taught social studies and literacy for 7 years to seventh and eighth grade students, many of whom shared my race, ethnicity, and nationality as ascendants of enslaved African peoples in the United States. My entry into the doctoral program was the result of what felt like a pushout of critical Black teachers at the school and my refusal to make myself small while enduring intimidation tactics and the devaluing of my expertise from administration. Furthermore, I would come to see myself as a Black feminist pedagogue during my doctoral program. Even though I would not have named myself as such while in the classroom, I would argue that I had developed the sensibilities, stances, and practices then. As a Black feminist pedagogue, I was concerned about—and responsible to—the political, material, and academic realities of my students within the classroom and beyond (Dillard, 2006; Henry, 2005; Ladson-Billings, 1995; Omolade, 1987). Therefore, I found tensions in the mismatch between the school's claims of being invested in the lives of Black students and their disinterest in critical approaches to education.

The first year of my doctoral program allowed me to engage in deep thinking, reflection, and critique around my prior 7 years of teaching in schools and all I had believed about the best ways to support the literacy development and learning of students. Moreover, it called me to consider the true purpose of education; that is, to liberate and transform the world for justice.

SJLW was my opportunity to do school differently and better. This out-of-school space was meant to challenge traditional approaches to literacy support and to reposition students as capable of high-level literacy engagements and critical dialogue. Since many of the students participating in the workshop were "reading below grade level" and at varying reading levels, it was important that I found alternative ways for these students to enter a shared text. Students who are often marginalized in traditional classroom settings, and who rarely receive meaningful and high-quality literacy support, may have internalized harmful messaging about their literacy capacity and abilities. I was interested in how students labeled as struggling readers/writers in schools use a variety of tools beyond print-based texts to engage in meaning making within young adult literature (YAL) that highlighted themes of structural oppression and injustice.

In preparation for SJLW, I sought out texts that offered more than print for students who are often made to feel as if they are illiterate simply because their independent reading levels are below grade level according to various assessments. I wanted students to be able to enter texts—whether at their independent reading levels or not—and engage in meaning making in ways that incited critical dialogue; that is, when students "of varying and shared social identities...examin[e] issues of power, privilege, and oppression toward a goal of individual and social change" (Laman et al., 2012, p. 198) through talk. Unfortunately, non-graphic novel multimodal texts within YAL are often difficult to find. I wanted texts with significant amounts of print to be used as a tool to support reading development while not being so print heavy that students would be unable to find other ways to engage in meaning making. In SJLW, the text also needed to fall under the category of culturally diverse literature, or texts that highlight race, ethnicity, language, various family structures, religion, physical and mental disabilities, and/or social class (Boyd et al., 2015). *The Diary of a Part-Time Indian* by Sherman Alexie (2007) offered all these components in its showcasing of the complicated story of a Spokane boy navigating family life, school, racism, and classism via print and drawings with labels/captions. It is important to note that I used this text in 2014 before Alexie's sexual harassment allegations were well known to the general public. As a critical scholar, I must acknowledge how many educators and researchers may find using this text today problematic to say the least. As SJLW progressed, I noticed that even in cases where the book was beyond their independent reading level, students used the drawings and labels/captions to make meaning of the print. Thus, when the critical dialogue appeared to be stifled, I conducted a gallery walk of enlarged drawings from the text for students to slow down and use visual and print cues to unpack critical themes.

In the following spring semester, I took a course on discourse analysis that prompted me to relook at galley walk data collected during SJLW. I noted several dialogic interactions where students were supported to make meaning of multimodal texts and engage in critical dialogue. The course provided me with a plethora of methods and methodologies for analyzing talk and print-based text. However, to fully examine the multimodal text itself, the dialogue, and how they mutually informed each other for student meaning making, I needed to also conduct a multimodal analysis. Thus, I began to realize that my creation and use of multimodal texts was not only an aspect of my pedagogical approach, but that multimodality was crucial to many facets of my research methods. To illustrate, multimodal representations of how I saw distinct theories synergizing would help me to better articulate my theoretical framework and guide my data analysis during the dissertation process (Nyachae, 2018). In fact, the co-editors of this book, Katarina and Nichole, and I were graduate students in the same department, and often came together to share varied multimodal representations of our research as we supported each other to finish writing our dissertations.

Katarina, also enrolled in the course at the time, and I were paired together by the instructor due to our shared interest in multimodality. Together we geeked out over multimodality literature and often came together to share how it was pushing our understanding of data analysis within our individual research projects. It was an exciting time indeed! While I benefited greatly from the learning about various approaches to engaging in multimodal analysis (e.g., Callow, 2013; Jewitt, 2009), I soon realized that I wanted to do something different with multimodality; what I wanted to do and say about multimodality—or dialogically organized instruction and discourse for that matter—was not being said and discussed in classes.

Moreover, as the only Black woman in the class and one who believed research should challenge oppressive systems, I often felt like an outsider, not only to the class, but to the way the multimodal and discourse analysis scholarship and ideas were taken up in the class. My lived realities as a Black woman in the United States and my research interests at that point all had a critical bend, so when I did not see the criticality, I did not see myself. I was trying to find/make a place within multimodality, dialogic teaching, and discourse analysis. Even the ways in which certain professors would (dis)engage with the ideas I presented that often critiqued racism sent a clear message to me of where I did and did not belong. Again, I refused to make myself or my research small to fit into the narrow parameters of how discourse analysis and multimodality was taken up in the course. I was also looking for guidance around multimodal analysis and I did not find it in this course.

During that spring semester in 2015, I did not read scholarship that explicitly merged theories of multimodality with critical theories, such as, critical race theory, Black feminism, and so forth. Moreover, after a deep reading of the seminal text, *Social Semiotics* by Robert Hodge and Gunther Kress (1988), I soon realized that many multimodality scholars used this text to ground their work while failing to unpack, apply, or even mention how, as the authors argue, "modality points to the social construction or contestation of knowledge-systems... [and] is one of the critical indicators of political struggle... through sheer 'imposition' of meaning by the more powerful on the less powerful participant" (p. 123). Additionally, I quickly learned that although academics discuss the work of Paulo Freire to situate their perspectives on dialogue and discourse, many failed to engage the oppressor and oppressed nonmetaphorically; thereby, thoroughly negating a major theme of the text. Sitting in doctoral courses where the criticality is not there even though the course texts engage with critical ideas like liberation and justice is baffling. Moreover, in 2015, much of the scholarship that engaged multimodality critically was unavailable although they were on the way (e.g., Cappello et al., 2019; Griffin & Turner, 2021; Turner & Griffin, 2020). To clarify, I mean work that explicitly addressed the power and sociopolitical realities of oppressed groups (Cappello et al., 2019), specifically among students of color. In essence, in 2015, I was looking for a book like this one and I am excited that future generations of scholars will be able to use this text as a guide for explicitly merging criticality and multimodality in transformative ways.

WHY CRITICAL SOCIAL SEMIOTICS AND MULTIMODALITY?

This volume explores the need for theories that help explain the modalities in which we make meaning *and* analyze how those methods of meaning making intersect with power, especially in the realm of education. Social semiotics and the perspective of multimodality can be a powerful analytical tool when intersected with critical theories. Additionally, social semiotics can be interpreted as a critical-learning theory with early roots in critical linguistics (Hodge & Kress, 1993) before branching into theorizing and analyzing about modalities other than the linguistic (Kress & van Leeuwen, 2006). A recent retrospective panel regarding the work of Gunther Kress (AERA SIG: Semiotics in Education, 2022) agreed that power, ideology, and the development of tools to "render visible what often remains invisible and make audible what remains inaudible" have been interwoven through social semiotics and multimodality from the outset. However, pairing social semiotics and multimodality with an overtly critical framework can not only strengthen analysis—more importantly, it can help bring to the center cultural groups whose lived experiences and practices historically are thrust to the margins in educational spaces. Next, we illustrate the integration of one critical framework (i.e., anti-racist Black language pedagogy, Baker-Bell, 2020) with multimodal social semiotics in the field of literacy and language education in our (the co-editors) shared geographical context of the United States.

A Brief Illustration Integrating Critical and Multimodal Social Semiotic Frameworks

It is clear that schools prioritize the teaching and learning of print-based texts (Kress, 2010) and in the United States, these print-based texts are almost always written in White mainstream English (Baker-Bell, 2020). However, print-based modalities are simply not the only way that we communicate; even in the earliest classrooms, humans have used linguistic and nonlinguistic modalities to interact and learn meaningfully (Gaudin, 2019), and the ongoing development of digital technologies has made affordances of multimodal communication increasingly mainstream and accessible in learning environments (Jewitt, 2013). In spite of this, because print-based communication (i.e., traditionally what is viewed as "reading" and "writing" in schools) is the main modality of meaning making assessed on major state standardized tests in education, this is the kind of communication that is prioritized in terms of instruction (Moore-Russo & Shanahan, 2014). Thus, print-based communicative abilities are privileged in schools. So, children who can and prefer to communicate and learn in modalities that are not print-based are often positioned at a disadvantage in school settings, whereas children who communicate and learn successfully using mainly print-based modalities have a better chance at school success. It is important to reiterate that along with the print-based communicative abilities prioritized in schools, print is almost always representative of White mainstream English, often giving White native English users an enormous advantage in U.S. school settings while disadvantaging students who do not use White mainstream English as their home language (Smitherman, 2017). How can social semiotic perspectives of multimodality and critical theories interweave to support arguments for change in educational policy, curriculum, and instructional practice with respect to literacy education? And, in support of this particular case, how can we strive to decenter "the White gaze itself that sees, hears, and frames students of color in every which way as marginal and deficient" (Paris & Alim, 2017, p. 3) with respect to language and literacy practices in schools?

First, social semiotics and its perspective of modality already have criticality imbued within the theory itself. In *Multimodal Communication*, Kress (2010) specifically discusses how power is implicated in the modes we use, especially with respect to linguistic modalities and their "persistent" print-based counterparts being leveraged for social control, in part, by determining "what should count as official knowledge" (p. 25). Kress (2010) defines this as *canonicity*. It follows that where there is canonical knowledge and preferred modes for making sense of that canonical knowledge, any knowledge and modalities outside of that would be considered noncanonical. That noncanonical knowledge would be excluded (or at least not privileged) and certain modes would be elevated over others. In the example here, the canonical knowledge of White mainstream English and associated print-based modality in schools tends to privilege only certain kinds of learners. To use one critical framework, anti-racist Black language pedagogy, Baker-Bell (2020) similarly theorizes that not only do major institutions like U.S. schools often privilege print-based texts, but they also privilege the teaching and learning of White mainstream English. As such, children who grow up living, speaking, and using varieties of English such as Black language or a language other than English (as two examples) will not have the same advantages at school compared to those children who grow up using White mainstream English in both their home lives and school from the start. Bringing these theoretical stances together (in this case, the social semiotic perspective of multimodality and critical Black language pedagogies), we demonstrate one way to construct and theoretically support an argument that schools require a radical expansion in literacy education practices to centralize the instruction and assessment of learning and communication across multiple modalities and languages.

CRITICAL MULTIMODALITY IN THIS BOOK

In the subsections that follow, we will detail the four sections of this volume and outline the contributions of each authorship team with respect to the theme of the section.

Theorizing for Critical Multimodality

According to hooks (1994), "We need new theories rooted in an attempt to understand both the nature of our contemporary predicament and the means by which we might collectively engage in resistance that would transform our current reality" (p. 67). The chapters in this section are theory generating and demonstrate where critical perspectives, social semiotics, and multimodality can work together to recognize existing and often ignored multimodal practices, explain current educational inequities, and uncover opportunities for transformation in educational spaces. To illustrate, in Chapter 2, Lee, Alvarez, Gonzales, and Wan provide multiple critiques of monolingual ideologies with respect to current conceptions of social semiotics, multimodality, and multiliteracies, which frequently neglect the lived experiences, realities, and existing multimodal communicative practices of racialized communities—those who live on the periphery. The authors argue, "(Re)conceptualizing and (re)doing critical multimodality calls educators to centralize the very multilingual and multimodal practices of spaces in the periphery" (Lee, Alvarez, Gonzales, & Wan, Chapter 2). Additionally, through a dialogic exchange between woman of color authors in Chapter 4, Griffin, who is Black and Player, who is Asian, highlight the multimodal practices of girls of color by speaking through and across their personal histories and work with youth. They show how girls of color create their own spaces that welcome identity and experiential affirming multimodal rendings when traditional literacy classrooms often reject them. Furthermore, they see the space-making practices of girls of color, evident in multimodal artifacts, as a resistance and disruption to racialized gendered violence and White supremacy.

As the authors in this section theorize, they do so by shedding light on what their theory-making "affords analytically...backgrounds, to what effect, how this has played out in historical trajectories of citation and reputation, [and] what and whose voices have been silenced" (Patel, 2016, p. 60). In Chapter 3, Aguilera, Holmes, Tran, and Guzmán uncover the hegemonic ideologies present in video games and playable media by challenging the false notion that the procedures for using technologies are apolitical and neutral. Instead, in their understanding of video games as transformative educational spaces, they call us to attend to the *proceduralized ideologies* that are present and consumed by players because "games are fundamentally composed of, and express meaning through the enactment of processes" (Aguilera, Holmes, Tran, & Guzmán, Chapter 3). In essence, the procedural dimension of games strongly shape the meaning making of the players. Equally important, through a critical disability lens, Isadore and Galván argue in Chapter 5 for the importance of multiple modalities as a part of universal design within educational spaces. Weaving together theories of multimodality with universal design learning principles, they detail how multimodal spaces of inclusion are integral to the success of students with disabilities (Isadore & Galván, Chapter 5).

Critical Multimodality and Storytelling for Agency and Revisioning

Investigating critical multimodal approaches to storytelling draws our attention to the ways that critical multimodal storytelling offers spaces for individuals to explore identity, develop agency, and envision what is possible as they construct meaningful understandings of themselves, others, and the world. We build and transform identities in order to reflect a sense of self and share with others the things that matter most to us. Our perceptions of self-development through participation in multiple cultural and social worlds, and this participation impacts the degree to which we develop agency in respect to our actions. When we define identity as "the imaginings of self in worlds of action" (Holland et al., 1998, p. 5), we can see the ways identities are formed through, and are a direct reflection of, participation in and across multiple contexts and may be reflected in the stories that we choose to share with the world. In considering the ways that this identity transformation occurs as a part of critical multimodal storytelling, we must also take notice of the identities, histories, and beliefs that individuals bring with them to their processes and how those identities are negotiated and developed as a part of critical approaches to multimodal composition.

Each of the chapters in this section highlight the ways that critical multimodal storytelling provided opportunities for self-reflection and identity development alongside the creation of agentive narratives of self. In Chapter 6, Gibbs Grey, Turner, and Young detail the ways that Black girls employ multimodal practices not only to resist, but to "define and manifest their own ways of being and temporalities" (p. 125). Solely understanding the carnal purposes of Black girl multimodal practices limits their "other-worldly" manifestations and creations of themselves (Gibbs Grey, Turner, & Young, Chapter 6). Moreover, Black girls are everywhere and their multimodal practices reveal that they see themselves here, there, now, then, and in the future. In Chapter 7, Jackson highlights how the centering of Blackness in the digital storytelling of Black students welcomed their full humanity while prompting justice-oriented solidarity. The solidarity that developed in their Black space led to collective digital storytelling about Black joy, love, and resistance. This process allowed for the raising of critical consciousness and critically conscious talk (Jackson, Chapter 7). Finally, Chapter 8 explores how digital storytelling as a part of establishing teacher identity and perspective in teacher education can be a purposeful step in critically examining what and who counts in research and education. By sharing their personal experiences with a digital storytelling project, Boyles, Cooper, and Ramirez note how they gained a deeper awareness of their own subjectivity and reframed dominative narratives of research and education.

Critical Multimodality for Reimagining Curriculum

Reimagining curriculum with respect to critical multimodality means pushing back against traditional notions of "what counts as learning" and showing what one knows. It means taking an expanded view of text to include multiple modalities as well as leveraging the power of digital tools (New London Group, 1996) to engage students in student-directed inquiry. Chapter 9 seeks to disrupt the primacy of the research paper in high school spaces through student-directed, digital multimodal critical inquiry projects (Fleming, Chapter 9). Fleming argues that using social semiotics and multimodality to reframe dominant ideas of power and what "counts" as purposeful meaning making must happen first, and then students need to be repositioned as intentional, multimodal sign makers and orchestrators.

Using critical multimodality to reimagine curriculum also supports practices of teacher identity and criticality development. In Chapter 10, Davis and Mokuria argue for the importance of developing critical and structural consciousness among pre-service teachers. Utilizing critical multimodal and social semiotic frameworks, the authors detail how engaging in a critical family history (Sleeter, 2020) led to a deeper understanding of how ancestral history influences present day circumstance. Critical family histories support pre-service teachers in their exploration of (and challenges to) their ideologies as teachers to purposefully design their classrooms as spaces for justice (Davis & Mokuria, Chapter 10).

Finally, this section explores how critical multimodal frameworks may lead learners and teachers out of the classroom and into collaboration with community spaces. In Chapter 11, Deroo details his teacher's work with preservice teachers, sharing their collective experience working with an art museum to hack and remix art objects to explore and address issues of marginalization in their disciplines (Deroo, Chapter 11). Importantly, Deroo embodies reflective practice, sharing his successes, challenges, and tensions as a way to illustrate opportunities for growth through reflection. Ultimately, reimagining educational spaces with critical multimodality as a framework means using pedagogies which disrupt deficit models of teaching, learning, and assessment that pervade school systems through institutionalized systems of oppression relating to students' identities, standardized testing, and one-size-fits-all curricula.

Critical Multimodality in Protests and Social Movements

Using critical multimodality as a framework through which to view education opens up the possibilities of what "counts" as sites of education and learning. In our view, social movements of the 21st century, including protest movements in place-based and digital environments, can be a source of deep learning, community, and solidarity. Chapter 12 illustrates how *bordados* [embroidery] is used as a form of political protest by Chilean women. Circulated via social media, Peña-Pincheira, Bilbao-Nieva, and Romero-Quintana argue that bordados serve to recontextualize social and economic injustice, police violence, as well as the legitimacy of social protest in Chile. Along similar lines, Chapter 13 also shares the protest actions, this time carried out in the Hong Kong protest movement beginning in 2019. Ho uses critical social semiotics analysis of various kinds of protest artefacts [*sic*] used in the anti-extradition bill movement in Hong Kong in 2019–2020, including Post-it notes, images, graffiti, and other means that filled the streets, shopping malls, and social media during this point in time. Finally, Chapter 14 brings us to the rural, Midwestern United States where youth disrupted typified social discourses and demonstrated adeptness across multiple, critical literacies as a part of protests during Black Lives Matter protests. Walker uses geosemiotics and social geography analysis to highlight how protest materials relied on multimodal and semiotic representations in conjunction with spatial positioning to establish youths' agency (Walker, Chapter 14).

PROVOCATIONS FOR READERS

As you journey through this text amplifying critical multimodal theories, frameworks, methodologies, and pedagogies, we ask you to consider the following provocations:

- How can critical multimodality encourage self-reflection and agency? We encourage all readers to ask themselves and wonder:

- How have you examined (and continue to examine) your positionalities with respect to power, privilege, and oppression?
- How do you engage in self-reflection in your work as a student, scholar, researcher, educator, and other positionalities?
- How regularly do you engage in this self-reflection, and what modalities do you find yourself working within when you do so?
- How do you notice, intentionally (and specifically) name, and disrupt power structures like racism and White supremacy, cisheteropatriarchy, colonialism, classism, ableism, and xenophobia within your life (e.g., personally, professionally, in your communities, in society writ large)?
- How can your self-reflection push you towards agentive action towards anti-oppressive and just educational futures? Some examples: imbuing your pedagogical approaches and curricular content with criticality and asset-based, culturally sustaining approaches; engaging in social and political activism, imagining and realizing humanizing paths forward in support of your communities (e.g., mutual aid networks).

We prompt those who position themselves as multimodal scholars to engage with the following provocations:

- How are you pushing yourself and holding yourself accountable to notice and name the power structures inherent in your line(s) of research? How are your theoretical and analytical approaches informed by current narratives within the field of education, social movements, and scholars whose voices have been historically silenced or unacknowledged in educational spaces (i.e., Black, Indigenous scholars and practitioners of color; scholars and practitioners of the LGBTQIAP+ community; disabled and neurodivergent practitioners and scholars; perspectives informed by people experiencing poverty and unhoused members of the community; and more groups who tend to be minoritized in educational settings at all levels). Consider whose voices are and are not heard in your literature reviews. Consider the methodologies you use and how they frame the people involved in your research.
- How do you consider your research as troubling and disrupting oppression within your field, if at all? If not, how could you reimagine your work towards more critical and just ends?
- How do you see your research benefiting historically underserved communities, if at all? If not, how could your research become more impactful, accessible, and/or useful for these communities?

If you already position yourself as a critical multimodal scholar and/or practitioner, we encourage you to use this text to push you further on your journey while also examining this text with a critical eye, considering:

- Whose work are you drawing on to support your scholarship? What work did you discover that is new to you by reading this volume? What work do you wish would have been considered amongst the authors in this volume?
- How do you see your own work situated amongst the critical multimodal scholars and practitioners here? How are you pushing yourself and the field using critical multimodal and social semiotic frameworks?
- How are you being responsive to the changing nature of education (e.g., cultural, social, economic, digital landscapes) within your research?
- How are you working within your community? How is your work continuing to show up and support your community toward critical and just aims?
- If you are also a curriculum designer, how is your approach centering the lived experiences, inquiries, and multimodal practices of your students? How are you enabling your students' stories to not only be told, heard, and seen but also to be a part of shaping the curriculum?

REFERENCES

Abedi, J., & Gandara, P. (2006). Performance of English language learners as a subgroup in a large-scale assessment: Interaction of research and policy. *Educational Measurement: Issues & Practice, 26*(5), 36–46. https://doi.org/10.1111/j.1745-3992.2006.00077.x

AERA SIG: Semiotics in Education. (2022, September 12). *The scholarly impact of Gunther Kress panel (2022)– AERA Semiotics in Education SIG* [YouTube video]. Youtube. https://www.youtube.com/watch?v=RDsBLaC_SIE

Alexander, K. P. (with DePalma, M.-J.). (2015). A bag full of snakes: Negotiating the challenges of multimodal composition. *Computers and Composition, 37,* 182–200.

Alexander, P. A., & Fox, E. (2019). Reading research and practice over the decades: A historical analysis. In D. E. Alvermann, N. J. Unrau, M. Sailors, & R. B. Ruddell (Eds.), *Theoretical models and processes of literacy* (7th ed.; pp. 35–64). Routledge.

Alexie, S. (2007). *The diary of a part-time Indian.* Little Brown and Company.

Anzaldúa, G. (2009). *The Gloria Anzaldúa reader* (A. Keating, Ed.). Duke University Press.

Baker-Bell, A. (2020). *Linguistic justice: Black language, literacy, identity, and pedagogy*. Routledge.

Boyd, F. B., Causey, L. L., & Galda, L. (2015). Culturally diverse literature: Enriching variety in an era of Common Core State Standards. *The Reading Teacher, 68*(5), 378–387. https://doi.org/10.1002/trtr.1326

Callow, J. (2013). *The shape of text to come*. Primary English Teaching Association Australia. https://www.petaa.edu.au/w/Publications/PETAA_book_extras/tsottc.aspx

Cappello, M., Wiseman, A. M., & Turner, J. D. (2019). Framing equitable classroom practices: Potentials of critical multimodal literacy research. *Literacy Research: Theory, Method, and Practice, 68*(1), 205–225. https://journals.sagepub.com/doi/abs/10.1177/2381336919870274

Collier, V. (1987). Age and rate of acquisition of second language for academic purposes. *TESOL Quarterly, 21*(4), 617–641. https://doi.org/10.2307/3586986

Collier, V. (1989). How long? A synthesis of research on academic achievement in a second language. *TESOL Quarterly, 23*(3), 509–531. https://doi.org/10.2307/3586923

Dillard, C. B. (2006). *On spiritual strivings: Transforming an African American woman's academic life*. State University of New York Press.

Gaudin, J. (2019). A history of the multimodal classroom from antiquity to the nineteenth century. In H. de Silva Joyce & S. Feez (Eds.), *Multimodality across classrooms: Learning about and through different modalities* (pp. 7–29). Routledge.

Griffin, A. A., & Turner, J. D. (2021). Toward a pedagogy of Black livingness: Black students' creative multimodal renderings of resistance to anti-Blackness. *English Teaching: Practice & Critique, 20*(4), 440–453. https://doi.org/10.1108/ETPC-09-2020-0123

Henry, A. (2005). Black feminist pedagogy: Critiques and contributions. In W. H. Watkins (Ed.), *Black protest thought and education* (pp. 89–105). Peter Lang.

Hodge, R., & Kress, G. (1988). *Social semiotics*. Cornell University Press.

Hodge, R., & Kress, G. (1993). *Language as ideology* (2nd ed.). Routledge.

Holland, D., Lachicotte, W., Jr., Skinner, D., & Cain, C. (1998). *Identity and agency in cultural worlds*. Harvard University Press.

hooks, b. (1994). *Teaching to transgress: Education as the practice of freedom*. Routledge.

Hull, G. A. (2003). At last: Youth culture and digital media: New literacies for new times. *Research in the Teaching of English, 38*(2), 229–233.

Hull, G. A., & Nelson, M. E. (2005). Locating the semiotic power of multimodality. *Written Communication, 22*(2), 224–261.

Immordino-Yang, M. H., & Damasio, A. (2007). We feel, therefore we learn: The relevance of affective and social neuroscience to education. *Mind, Brain, and Education, 1*(1), 3–10. https://doi.org/10.1111/j.1751-228X.2007.00004.x

Jewitt, C. (2009). An introduction to multimodality. In C. Jewitt (Ed.), *The Routledge handbook of multimodal analysis* (pp. 14–27). Routledge.

Jewitt, C. (2013). Multimodality and digital technologies in the classroom. In I. de Saint-Georges & J. J. Weber (Eds.), *Multilingualism and multimodality: Current challenges for educational studies* (pp. 141–152). SensePublishers.

Jewitt, C., & Oyama, R. (2001). Visual meaning: A social semiotic. In T. van Leeuwen & C. Jewitt (Eds.), *The handbook of visual analysis* (pp. 134–157). SAGE Publications.

Jocius, R. (2013). Exploring adolescents' multimodal responses to *The Kite Runner*: Understanding how students use digital media for academic purposes. *Journal of Media Literacy Education, 5*(1), 310–325. https://doi.org/10.23860/jmle-5-1-4

Kress, G. (2010). *Multimodality: A social semiotic approach to contemporary communication.* Routledge.

Kress, G., & van Leeuwen, T. (2001). *Multimodal discourse: The modes and media of contemporary communication.* Oxford University Press.

Kress, G., & van Leeuwen, T. (2006). *Reading images: The grammar of visual design* (2nd ed.). Routledge.

Ladson-Billings, G. (1995). Toward a theory of culturally relevant pedagogy. *American Educational Research Journal, 32*(3), 465–491. https://doi.org/10.2307/1163320

Laman, T. T., Jewett, P., Jennings, L. B., Wilson, J. L., & Souto-Manning, M. (2012). Supporting critical dialogue across educational contexts. *Equity & Excellence in Education, 45*(1), 197–216. https://doi.org/10.1080/10665684.2012.641871

McVee, M. B., & Boyd, F. B. (2015). *Exploring diversity through multimodality, narrative, and dialogue: A framework for teacher reflection.* Routledge.

McVee, M. B., Haq, K. S., Barrett, N., Silvestri, K. N., & Shanahan, L. E. (2019). The positioning theory diamond as an analytic tool to examine multimodal social interaction in an engineering club. *Papers on Social Representations, 28*(1), 7.1–7.23. https://psr.iscte-iul.pt/index.php/PSR/article/view/495

McVee, M. B., Schucker, K. A., Silvestri, K. N., & Tripp, J. N. (2022). Using multiliteracies and multimodality to explore engineering literacies and problem-scoping for multilingual learners: A perspective on multiliteracies for STEM learning. In R. Tierney, F. Rizvi, & K. Ercikan (Eds.), *International Encyclopedia of Education* (4th ed.; pp. 50–63). Elsevier Science.

McVee, M. B., Silvestri, K. N., Shanahan, L. E., & English, K. (2017). Productive communication in an engineering afterschool club with girls who are English language learners. *Theory Into Practice, 56*(4), 246–254. https://doi.org/10.1080/00405841.2017.1350490

McVee, M. B., Silvestri, K. N., Barrett, N., & Haq, K. S. (2019). Positioning theory. In D. E. Alvermann, N. J. Unrau, M. Sailors, R. B. Ruddell (Eds.), *Theoretical models and processes of literacy* (7th ed., pp. 397–416). Routledge.

McVee, M. B., Silvestri, K. N., Schucker, K., & Cun, A. (2021). Positioning theory, embodiment, and the moral orders of objects in social dynamics: How psychology has neglected the body and artifactual knowing. *Journal for the Theory of Social Behaviour,* 1–23. https://doi.org/10.1111/jtsb.12289

McVee, M. B., Silvestri, K. N., & Shanahan, L. E. (2023). Opportunities for learning disciplinary literacies in an engineering club (Grades 3–5). In C. Brock, B. Exley, & I. Rigney (Eds.) *International perspectives on literacies, diversities, and opportunities for learning: Critical conversations* (Chapter 5). Routledge.

Moje, E. B., & Luke, A. (2009). Literacy and identity: Examining the metaphors in history and contemporary research. *Reading Research Quarterly, 44*(4), 415–437. https://www.jstor.org/stable/25655467

Moll, L. C., Amanti, C., Neff, D., & Gonzalez, N. (1992). Funds of knowledge for teaching: Using a qualitative approach to connect homes and classrooms. *Theory Into Practice, 31*(2), 132–141. https://www.jstor.org/stable/1476399?origin=JSTOR-pdf

Moore-Russo, D., & Shanahan, L. E. (2014). A broader vision of literacy: Including the visual with the linguistic. *Journal of Adolescent & Adult Literacy, 57*(7), 527–532. https://doi.org/10.1002/jaal.282

Muhammad, G. E. (2018). A plea for identity and criticality: Reframing literacy learning standards through a four-layered equity model. *Journal of Adolescent & Adult Literacy, 62*(2), 137–142. https://doi.org/10.1002/jaal.869

Muhammad, G. E. (2020). *Cultivating genius: An equity framework for culturally and historically responsive literacy*. Scholastic Incorporated.

New London Group. (1996). A pedagogy of multiliteracies: Designing social futures. *Harvard Educational Review, 66*(1), 60–92. https://doi.org/10.17763/haer.66.1.17370n67v22j160u

Norris, S. (2004). *Analyzing multimodal interaction: A methodological framework*. Routledge.

Nyachae, T. M. (2018). *'Race space' critical professional development as Third Space: Cultivating racial literacy, ideological becoming, and social justice teaching with/in urban teachers* (Publication No. 10816448) [Doctoral dissertation, State University of New York at Buffalo]. Proquest Dissertations and Theses Global. https://www.proquest.com/openview/85ebffa31b981210c38b9832d8132435/1?pq-origsite=gscholar&cbl=18750

Nyachae, T. M. (2019). Social justice literacy workshop for critical dialogue. *Journal of Adolescent & Adult Literacy, 63*(1), 106–110. https://doi.org/10.1002/jaal.977

Okun, T., & Jones, K. (2016). White supremacy culture. *Dismantling racism: 2016 workbook*. https://resourcegeneration.org/wp-content/uploads/2018/01/2016-dRworks-workbook.pdf

Omolade, B. (1987). A Black feminist pedagogy. *Women's Studies Quarterly, 15*(3/4), 32–39. https://www.proquest.com/docview/1292049341

Paris, D., & Alim, H. S. (2017). *Culturally sustaining pedagogies: Teaching and learning for justice in a changing world*. Teachers College Press.

Patel, L. (2016). *Decolonizing educational research: From ownership to answerability*. Routledge.

Shanahan, L. E., McVee, M. B., & Silvestri, K. N. (2018). Digital engineering design team journals: Providing multimodal opportunities for English language learners to explain design choices. *Journal of Adolescent and Adult Literacy, 61*(4), 445–451.

Shanahan, L. E., McVee, M. B., & Silvestri, K. N. (2022). Elementary students' social interactions in the engineering design process across materials and modes. In A. A. Wilson-Lopez, E. Tucker-Raymond, A. Esquinca, & J. Mejía (Eds.), *The literacies of design: Studies of equity and imagination with engineering and making*. Purdue University Press.

Silvestri, K. N., McVee, M. B., Jarmark, C. J., Shanahan, L. E., & English, K. E. (2021). Multimodal positioning of artifacts in interaction in a collaborative elementary engineering club. *Multimodal Communication, 10*(3), 1–21. https://doi.org/10.1515/mc-2020-0017

Silvestri, K. N., McVee, M. B., & Barrett, N. (2021, August 12). *All about literacy theories: Why are theories important to understanding literacy learning and instruction?* [Video]. https://video.cortland.edu/Watch/a2W4PnCf

Sleeter, C. (2020). Critical family history: An introduction. *Genealogy, 4*(2), 64–69. https://doi.org/10.3390/genealogy4020064

Smith, B. E. (2016). Composing across modes: A comparative analysis of adolescents' multimodal composing processes. *Learning, Media and Technology, 42*(3), 259–278. https://doi.org/10.1080/17439884.2016.1182924

Smitherman, G. (2017). Raciolinguistics, "mis-education," and language arts teaching in the 21st century. *Language Arts Journal of Michigan, 32*(2), 4–12. https://scholarworks.gvsu.edu/cgi/viewcontent.cgi?article=2164&context=lajm

Solórzano, R. W. (2008). High stakes testing: Issues, implications, and remedies for English language learners. *Review of Educational Research, 78*(2), 260–329. https://doi.org/10.3102/0034654308317845

Turner, J. D., & Griffin, A. A. (2020). Brown girls dreaming: Adolescent Black girls' futuremaking through multimodal representations of race, gender, and career aspirations. *Research in the Teaching of English, 55*(2), 109–133. https://library-ncte-org.ezproxy.lib.uconn.edu/journals/RTE/issues/v55-2/31020

SECTION I
THEORIZING FOR CRITICAL MULTIMODALITY

CHAPTER 2

MULTIMODAL MEANING MAKING IN A PANDEMIC

Visions From the Multilingual Periphery as Epicenter

Eunjeong Lee
University of Houston

Sara P. Alvarez
Queens College

Laura Gonzales
University of Florida

Amy J. Wan
Queens College and CUNY Graduate Center

ABSTRACT

When the world envisions New York City (NYC), Queens is but a periphery, in the hustle and bustle of the city. But this "periphery" is in fact the center of the very rich cultural, linguistic, and racioethnic diversity that often portrays NYC, and much of the world's rising multicultural sites. Yet, for Queens' predominantly immigrant-generation and non-U.S. born populations (U.S. Census), facing systemic and societal inequities is an everyday happening, including underfunded educational institutions and perpetual monolingual ideology that racializes our multilingual students' and their communities' ways of being, knowing, and meaning making.

In the backdrop of inequities exacerbated by the pandemic, how do language and literacy educators work to sustain and amplify the rich languaging and cultural practices of students in transnational epicenters—especially in the virtual learning context? This chapter examines how our pedagogical dispositions oriented by translingualism (Horner & Alvarez, 2019) at a public institution of tertiary education have guided us in languaging, and cultivating multimodalities to better answer to our multilingual students' meaning-making practices and the conditions they work in, while being attentive to the potential structural and technological constraints. We describe how we, as educators, have drawn on our criticality, in tandem with our students' labor and vision toward their own criticality, to resist dominant conceptualizations of meaning making. As recent research examining multilingualism has shown, to cultivate the full potential of racialized and language-minoritized students' practices, we must consider the multimodalities that rest on the bodies of people languaging in various contexts (San Pedro, 2017). We must also contend with the impact of linguistic injustice and harm done to students in the name of education (Baker-Bell, 2020), and we must take into account how professional settings and accessibility dynamically transform students' meaning-making in multimodal design (Gonzales, 2018).

In examining our translingual-informed pedagogy, we heed recent critiques on uncritical framing of multilingualism and multimodality that perpetuate neoliberalism and racism in education (Flores, 2013; Kubota, 2020). Therefore, our approach to transforming literacy learning spaces in relationship to translingualism focuses on material conditions and/of laboring language difference, ideology, and disposition to language (Horner & Alvarez, 2019) and recognizes multimodality as a critical part of multilingual students' meaning making. We argue that the integration of these orientations around translingualism, multimodality, labor, and materiality are essential in supporting and centralizing language-minoritized students, so that their practices and expertise move from the periphery to the center.

When the world envisions New York City (NYC), Queens is but a periphery, in the hustle and bustle of its imagination. But this "periphery" is in fact the center of the very rich cultural, linguistic, and racioethnic diversity that often portrays NYC, and much of the world's rising metropolitan sites. Yet, for Queens' predominantly immigrant-generation and non-U.S. born populations (U.S. Census, 2018), facing systemic and societal inequities is an everyday happening, including underfunded educational institutions and perpetual monolingual ideology that racializes our students and their communities' multilingual ways of being, knowing, and meaning making. Queens and its place, on the periphery of the city's imagination, represents what often happens to racialized communities—with the majority of the people who live there being pushed to the margins: Only when crisis and disaster strikes, such as when Queens became the first U.S. epicenter of the COVID-19 pandemic, do such communities temporarily gain the spotlight.

(Re)conceptualizing and (re)doing critical multimodality calls educators to centralize the very multilingual and multimodal practices of those in the periphery. Such centralization shifts away from celebratory frameworks that merely fetishize diversity, and often further blur structural inequities. In this chapter, focusing on the communicative practices of racialized multilingual communities, we contend with the following questions: "How do inequities, such as those exacerbated by the pandemic, challenge us educators to expand the notion of critical multimodality?"; "Why do the rich languaging and cultural practices of students in transnational epicenters need to be perceived as more than just at the 'periphery' when developing multimodal pedagogies?"; and "How can language and literacy educators work to sustain and amplify their language and cultural practices, and ways of seeing and (re)envisioning the world—especially in the remote learning context?" To begin unpacking these questions, we examine our own educator labor of languaging and cultivating multimodalities to better answer our multilingual students' meaning-making practices and the conditions they work in, while also being attentive to the potential structural and technological constraints.

At the core of this work is understanding how centralizing the embodied literacy and languaging practices of people at the periphery, like the majority of our students at Queens College, City University of New York (CUNY), is a matter of criticality and justice. On the one hand, this centralization, takes on the "resist, revitalize, and reimagine" stance called for in culturally sustaining pedagogies (CSP), so that we, as educators, may act in a way "that disrupts a schooling system centered on ideologies of White, middle-class, monolingual, cisheteropatriarchal, able-bodied superiority" (Alim & Paris, 2017, pp. 12–13). On the other hand, our attunement to the visions and languaging labor that racialized communities are already doing is a call to scholars to amplify how and what we mean by critical multimodality. Indeed, racialized and transnational communities' ways of doing language and literacies have long contributed to dominant discussions and research findings on critical literacies (Alvarez, 2018). But such contributions have been, and are, largely not made for "literacy consumption" or school-related practices, despite the fact that in many cases, these practices are the very life literacies sustaining "self" in a community (Alvarez, 2023; Kinloch, 2017; San Pedro, 2017).

In this manner, our vision sees students' embodied multilingual practices as a crucial form of multimodal labor that must be accounted for in our understanding and doing of critical multimodality. In examining this labor we highlight the importance of acknowledging the ongoing threads and historicities between language, embodiment, and land, especially as articulated by Indigenous scholars who advocate for the value of multilingualism and multimodality as survival strategies for marginalized communities (Driskill, 2016; Ríos, 2015). As recent research examining multilingualism has shown, to cultivate the full potential of racialized and language-minoritized people's practices, we must consider the multimodalities that rest on the bodies of people languaging in various contexts (San Pedro, 2017). We must also contend with the impact of linguistic injustice and harm done to students in the name of education (Baker-Bell, 2020; Kinloch et al., 2020), and we must consider how professional settings and accessibility dynamically transform students' meaning making in multimodal design (Gonzales, 2018).

Our chapter, then, begins with an examination of critical multimodality and its possibilities, centered on the perspective of racialized communities at the periphery. In this examination, we heed recent critiques on uncritical framing of multilingualism and multimodality that perpetuate neoliberalism and racism in education (Flores, 2013; Kubota, 2019). We work from a place and positionality that recognizes how literacies are constructed in everyday life, specific to a person's individual and communal ways of knowing and navigating the world, and yet are often overshadowed by disciplinary groundings that privilege White, monolingual, Western ways of knowing and being. Guided by translingualism, we then show how our approach to transforming literacy learning spaces focuses on material conditions of laboring language pluralism and disposition to language (Horner & Alvarez, 2019), while recognizing multimodality as a critical part of multilingual students' meaning making. We argue that the integration of these orientations around translingualism, multimodality, labor, and materiality are essential in honoring and centralizing racialized students and their communities' languaging practices and expertise, so that they move from the periphery to the center without being tokenized or fetishized in the name of education.

In forwarding a call for movement from the periphery to the center, we are considering both physical and epistemological grounds. We acknowledge our own positionalities as racialized, multilingual, immigrant-generation, full-time women faculty, and draw from our experiences working with students who are often racialized and pushed to the periphery in educational spaces, and whose labor and knowledge making go undervalued or unseen. Bringing the periphery to the center means understanding how waves of ideologies, structures, and material conditions constantly work to re-marginalize the periphery and center the dominant. This also means working against those waves to redefine the "critical" in multilingual and multimodal literacies. In centering the periphery, we labor purposefully to acknowledge the powerful vision our students have of their own experiences and expertise in navigating the world. As literacy educators, we need to be mindful of these waves and currents within the context of injustice, both internal and external to our institutions, if we intend to more expansively define multimodality.

REDEFINING CRITICAL MULTIMODALITY: BRINGING RACIALIZED MULTILINGUAL COMMUNITIES TO THE CENTER

Critical education and literacy scholars continue to demonstrate that disciplinary groundings and epistemological histories matter—the ways in which our fields and disciplines situate our foundations and definitional concepts consistently influence the people and practices we value, and by proxy, those we do not. As scholars such as Timothy San Pedro, Angela Haas, and Adam Banks continue to illustrate, when it comes to multimodality and digital literacy (more broadly), racialized communities continuously innovate multimodal digital practices, orientations, and knowledges. As Angela Haas (2007) emphasizes when drawing on Indigenous epistemologies in her definition of digital rhetoric, the term digital "refers to our fingers, our digits, one of the primary ways (along with our ears and eyes) through which we make sense of the world and with which we write into the world" (p. 84). As such, "digital" rhetoric, and the modalities through which humans make meaning, are always interconnected with the bodies and lands through and with which we navigate the world.

Yet, in academic scholarship across fields, when researchers define or theorize multimodality, we often rely on theoretical foundations stemming from predominantly White, Western, monolingual contexts (see, e.g., Kress, 2010; The New London Group, 1996). While these foundational texts on multimodality have value in their own right, the ideas in these texts are often taught and discussed as discrete skills necessary for the 21st century learning and global workforce, within the purview of the neoliberal ideologies (Mirra & Garcia, 2020). As many have critiqued, such uncritical framing of multimodality perpetuates the racist hegemonic view of language and literacies, and therefore, maintains the inequitable and unequal structures of learning and teaching (e.g., Kubota, 2020). Pointing out the relative lack of explicit and intentional concern for equity, justice, and humanity in research on multiliteracies, Mirra and Garcia (2020) importantly argue, "Instead of continuing to look aspirationally ahead in time to the next tool that will change society," we must "consider the tensions and values that endure and underlie education across the centuries" (p. 493). Stemming from this collection's emphasis on critical approaches to multimodality, our goal in this chapter is to illustrate the possibilities cultivated when we ground definitions of multimodality in the experiences of racialized and language-minoritized communities. We centralize definitions of multimodality that emerge from the lived experiences, visions, and innovation practices of racialized multilingual communities, in order to highlight how critical approaches to multimodality are already enacted, developed, and sustained in multilingual spaces. In framing our theorizations of critical multimodality, we thus draw from our experiences, the experiences of our students and communities, as well as scholarship about multimodality written for and by Black, Indigenous, and people of color (BIPOC). We prioritize this research in our framing to highlight how BIPOC communities have always envisioned multimodality in relation to embodied praxis, including but not limited to language.

Figure 2.1 represents traditional visualizations of multimodality as defined by The New London Group (1996). In this traditional model, multimodality is defined as encompassing visual, linguistic, aural, spatial, and gestural modes. While the modes represented in Figure 2.1 are an important part of multimodal praxis, what we want to highlight in this chapter is the fluid movement among modes, the labor of enacting multimodality, and the connections between digital and material modalities. Figure 2.2 represents our approach to critically engaging multimodality.

In Figure 2.2, discrete modalities such as the "visual" and "gestural" are still represented. However, the boundaries between modalities are less rigid, and the waves of motion among communicative practices and tools are represented through wave-like patterns. While critical multimodality does

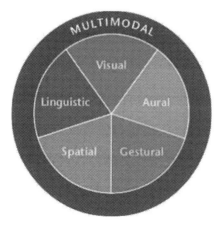

Figure 2.1 Traditional visualizations of multimodality.

Multimodal Meaning Making in a Pandemic • 39

Figure 2.2 Critical multimodality in action.

encompass the use of digital technologies (represented by the cell phone in Figure 2.2), the emphasis in this model is on connections—among people, their languages and words, and our surrounding lands and environments. While no image could fully encompass the communicative practices of racialized multilingual communities, what we are seeking to demonstrate in Figure 2.2, and in this chapter more broadly, is that centralizing the periphery in multimodal theories and pedagogies requires an attunement to the waves and/of interactions of communication, rather than just a recognition of discrete modes and their rhetorical impact.

Rather than focusing on multimodality as the layering of different modes (e.g., visual, gestural, spatial) as outlined in mainstream scholarship, we ask: "What can we recognize and center when we define multimodality through frameworks put forth by racialized multilingual communities, scholars, and students?"; "What could educators and researchers learn by centering the multimodal labor of racialized multilingual communities?" For example, instead of centralizing widely standardized definitions of multimodality, how could critical approaches to multimodality emerge from the work of Zapotec activist Janet Chavez Santiago? Santiago (2021) describes her Zapotec community's weaving practices in Teotitlán del Valle as multimodal. She notes,

> Our weaving tradition derives from ancestral knowledge, but this does not make the process static—the creativity of each weaver makes this art contemporary. Our traditions change and evolve as human beings innovate and incorporate influences from the world as we know it now. The wool fiber that we use to weave our rugs is never the same, for each rug we weave we can experience different feelings and struggles, each rug is one of a kind. (n.p.)

Surely, as academic researchers, we could trace Santiago's description of her community's weaving practices through Kress's *Multimodality: Semiotic Approach to Contemporary Communication*; we could also outline how Zapotec weavers combine the five modes as defined by The New London Group (1996): linguistic, visual, gestural, spatial, and aural. Through this process, we could help define, or even justify, a Zapotec community's weaving practices as "fitting" within academic approaches to multimodal practice. However, in tracing or framing Santiago's work only through White/Western definitions of multimodality, we limit our understanding of multimodal practice to the frameworks that have been previously outlined through the White gaze. Additionally, as Lopez-Gopar (2007) points out, we would be disregarding the important epistemological and ontological work of this cultural process of weaving. As Lopez-Gopar (2007) emphasizes, many Indigenous communities enact multimodality through the creation and building of "*códices andantes en los vestidos, la cerámica, las decoraciones florales y los tapetes*" (codices on clothing, ceramics, floral arrangements, and rugs) in addition to practices such as "*leer el clima y saber cuándo plantar*" (reading the weather and knowing when to plant [the soil]; p. 54). Thus, accounting for dynamic multimodal practices, such as those embraced and innovated by racialized multilingual students, requires an attunement to traditions and groundings beyond what is typically cited or accepted in the academy.

In line with the objectives of this collection, in this chapter, we re-center the experiences, imaginings, and expertise of racialized multilingual communities in the design and definition of multimodal practice. Through this process, we expand multimodality by highlighting the materialities and labor that minoritized communities draw from when engaging in multimodality, both in and outside the classroom. We ask: "What happens when minoritized communities are brought from the periphery to the center, particularly in discussions of multimodality in literacy and education?" Racialized and language-minoritized communities continue to be underserved and exploited in various societal domains, including spaces of our knowledge making and sharing and institutions where racialized communities are a significant part of the student population, such as many of the U.S. metropolitan sites. This necessitates work that acknowledges, legitimizes, centers, and amplifies multiple ways of being, living, and doing of minoritized communities. Below, we highlight the importance of recognizing the labor and vision of multimodality and further discuss what centralizing their multimodality can look like in classrooms.

BRINGING ATTENTION TO LABOR AND VISION OF MULTIMODALITY

As we seek to centralize students who are often viewed as in the periphery in our discussion of critical multimodality, we insist on bringing their labor to the forefront. As we have highlighted in our previous works, part of sustaining the plural ways of knowing, doing, and envisioning of our cultural and community practices, is acknowledging both their meaning-making labor and the very conditions and materialities by which such production takes place (Alvarez & Lee, 2020; Lee et al., 2021). This attention to labor is echoed by Indigenous scholars who make connections between land, labor, and literacy in theorizing multimodality. For example, in her discussion of land-based literacies as enacted by farmworkers affiliated with the Florida Coalition of Immokalee Workers (CIW), Gabriela Raquel Ríos (2015) explains that the physical labor involved in farm work is part of a multimodal practice that "1) recognizes the ways in which land can produce relations and 2) recognizes the value of embodied ways of knowing" (p. 60). Bringing attention to labor in the production of knowledge, Ríos emphasizes, helps to foster frameworks that "respect the rhetorical skills that farm workers have gained from their labor and experiences, if not from formal education" (p. 62).

The connection between embodied knowledge and multimodal and multilingual practices suggests that rethinking critical multimodality must follow questioning whose bodies are laboring, how, and under what conditions. As many critical scholar-educators' work shows, our language-minoritized students' lived experiences are at the core of their multimodal and multilingual practices, which in turn build and sustain their embodied knowledge (de los Ríos, 2020; Gonzales et al., 2020; San Pedro, 2017). At the same time, centering and building on students' dynamic, creative, and critical multilingual and multimodal practices also requires attention to the bodies, historicities of the bodies and language labor, and the conditions of such work in order not to flatten different ways that these students engage with multilingualism and multimodality (Gilyard, 2016; Lee & Alvarez, 2020). Foregrounding labor, in this sense, helps us to consider the very connection between different bodies and their meaning-making practices in ways that also intersect with the matters of equity and justice.

Centering multilingual and language-minoritized students' embodied multimodal labor and material conditions of their labor also makes it imperative that we view their multilingual and multimodal work as closely tied to and reflective of their own vision, voice, and lived experiences. As Rebecca Lorimer Leonard (2023) has highlighted, many of the discussions on multilingualism often seek to uplift the practices of multilingual students, dissociated from their own processes of identity and "mending" of conflict and complexity within their daily multilingual interactions. And less attended to is the imagination that multilingual students wish to envision, construct, and build on, in, and through their literacies. In this regard, Nelson Flores (2020) calls for the framework of language architecture. Flores emphasizes that language-minoritized students' language practices must be seen as legitimate in their own right that "reflect their own unique vision and voice" (p. 25), rather than deficient and/or in need of academic language. By foregrounding language-minoritized students' own language architecture work and the vision constructed and envisioned through such labor, we can move beyond raciolinguistic ideologies (Flores & Rosa, 2015) and the deficit thinking that frames students' multilingual and multimodal meaning-making. In line with this view, we propose that our understanding, exploration, and practice of critical multimodality must center the very language architecture work of our students, including their vision, voice, and the material conditions of their multilingual and multimodal labor.

CENTERING MOTIVATION OF COMMUNITIES' MULTIMODALITY FOR A JUSTICE-DRIVEN APPROACH

In centering definitions of multimodality in the experiences, expertise, and imaginations of racialized multilingual communities, educators should consider not only these communities' labor of enacting multimodal praxis, but also the motivations and reasons rhetorically guiding their multimodal communication. This requires an attunement to both how and why racialized multilingual communities enact multimodality in situated contexts for specific reasons. This also requires an understanding of how multimodality and multilingualism are intertwined in the communicative experiences and practices of racialized multilingual communities.

For example, some researchers focusing on multilingualism in rhetoric and composition point to the fact that "welcoming" or even "making space" for students' diverse languaging practices in the classroom is not enough to foster multilingual learning (e.g., Gonzales, 2018). The United States, in particular, has long histories (and present-day realities) of punishing multilingual students for speaking their heritage languages in classroom spaces. Thus, students may rightfully hesitate to bring their languages into classrooms and institutions that continuously privilege standardized White American English. A simple "invitation" or "encouragement" from teachers to bring in multilingual practice into classroom spaces may not result in multilingual students feeling comfortable enough to enact their multilingual languaging practices in the classroom.

In a similar vein, when situating definitions of multimodality in the experiences and imaginings of racialized multilingual students, it is important to consider the motivations for, the histories, and the consequences of multimodal communication for racialized multilingual communities. For some racialized multilingual communicators, enacting multimodality is far more than a classroom activity; multimodality can be a means for survival and survivance, as multilingual communities leverage multiple modes of communication when standardized language systems are unavailable or unnecessary. For example, racialized multilingual communities may use visuals, gestures, sounds, and other modes of expression simultaneously when trying to navigate communication in government agencies and offices that consistently break language access policies by providing standardized White American English-only communication. In these cases, multilingual communities learn to navigate digital technologies, multiple messaging apps and keyboards, as well as embodied practices of gesturing, pointing, and using as many senses as possible to convey information, often in very stressful situations with high stakes (e.g., completing a transaction in a government office, trying to communicate with a healthcare practitioner during a medical procedure). In these instances, multimodality becomes a rhetorical means for achieving a specific goal, for surviving, in White supremacist English dominant systems.

Thus, when researchers and educators introduce multimodality in classroom spaces, they should consider the material consequences and motivations that racialized multilingual communities carry in their rhetorical repertoires, where modes are not additive singular entities but part of a broader survival network. While mainstream approaches to multimodality have highlighted the fact that multimodal communication does not necessarily need to include the use of digital technologies (Shipka, 2011), centralizing definitions of multimodality on the experiences and practices of racialized multilingual communities pushes educators to further account for the previous contexts in which students have had to enact multimodal communication in community. For example, how do we teach students about the rhetorical impact of multimodal texts in a way that recognizes the high-stress situations in which multimodal praxis often happens for racialized multilingual communities? How do we model multimodal assignments, activities, and conversations that assume multilingualism is a critical, rather than an additive, component of multimodal communication? How do we create space for multilingual students to use multimodal communication and multimodal writing to not only be "rhetorically effective" for academic audiences, but to also reach the communities that have long-established approaches to multimodality? By moving definitions and foundations of multimodality away from Whitewashed representations and frameworks, we can work toward a reimagining of critical multimodality and what this framework can do to further respect and honor our students' lived experiences.

UNDERSTANDING THE WORKING OF STRUCTURES OF INJUSTICE

Recognizing critical multimodality means not only understanding the language and literacy labor of minoritized communities but also the structures in which such labor is valued. And while we have talked up to this point about this as an epistemological shift, critical multimodality is also one that is deeply intertwined with larger projects of justice, equity, and structural critique, and the material conditions under which such projects take place. Because even though, as we have just discussed, critical multimodality can be used to understand the linguistic practices of language-minoritized students, this process of minoritizing is directed and even cultivated by the structures of our institutions and other physical and material spaces that give value to certain kinds of knowledge over others. In order to center students' multimodal labor in understandings of critical multimodality, we must also acknowledge the structural inequities and material conditions that guide whose language and labor is legitimized and made easier and whose is pushed to the periphery.

For example, as we consider our educational context and its material and monolingual limitations (cf Canagarajah, 2002), we are reminded of classrooms that view and treat racialized and language-minoritized students through a deficit lens. As briefly discussed above, the dominant view in the educational structure that centers White, Western, and monolingual texts and values often determines what counts as "critical," "literacy," and "knowledge." Such deficit-oriented views push students' rich meaning making practices aside and erase the complexity and value of their varied multimodal labor. Bringing students' multimodal labor to the center, in this sense, must account for how different bodies and their knowledge-making and sharing as multimodal practices come to be (un)seen, (de)valorized, and/or (il)legitimized. Therefore, part of enacting critical multimodality that centers our racialized multilingual students must include interrogating the inequitable structures that oppress and harm our students and differentially impose labor on different bodies.

Building on Flores' (2020) approach to "language architecture," we take the time to acknowledge the material structures that often prevent language-minoritized students from being seen as language architects with agency and legitimate language practices or do not recognize the amount of labor they are doing. Because the practices of students are judged within the context of normative classroom spaces, the persistence of such spaces to define language work so narrowly plays a significant role in that process of marginalization, keeping the periphery in its place. And the re-marginalizing the periphery and re-centering of the dominant is enforced by the inequities that are embedded in the educational and economic structures shaping our classrooms. In the K–12 space, this re-marginalization and the necessity of legitimizing out-of-school literacy practices and contexts is evident in issues like the school-to-prison pipeline and inadequate funding for facilities and technology, particularly urban public schools with low-income students of color (Kinloch et al., 2020).

Similar funding gaps at publicly funded higher education institutions extend the structural inequities of the K–12 context. While public higher education like CUNY is often lauded as an engine of social mobility, the significant disinvestment of public higher education diminishes this path and makes it a more difficult one to take (Fabricant & Brier, 2016). In the context of literacy teaching, this often means students are taught by a significant number of contingent and part-time labor who might not have the time or compensation for faculty development to cultivate this shift in understanding students' language practices, as well as less access to resources and facilities. We do not mean state-of-the-art multimedia labs (although that would be nice). While, as we discussed above, the expansion of critical multimodality means weaving together what cannot be contained by linguistic, visual, gestural, spatial, and aural categories and the work that racialized and language-minoritized students are already doing, we recognize that classrooms with a questionable amount of ventilation or a constantly unstable WiFi signal or an uncomfortably small classroom space (or one infested with vermin or leaks) creates additional and unnecessary labor to students' composing process.

Yet classrooms or even educational systems do not exist on their own; they are part of larger writing ecologies (Syverson, 1999) that considers a "complex, constantly evolving system of relationships between the social and material" (Byrd, 2019, p. 32), including both micro- and macro-level forces like structural racism. And as Antonio Byrd argues, literacy and language scholars might better understand "how marginalized communities' interactions with people and the materials of writing systems are also interactions with white supremacy" (Byrd, 2019, p. 34). This means tracking both the local and systemic material conditions under which students are doing language and literacies.

Even physically, in their neighborhoods and at their underfunded institutions of public higher education, our students are often at the periphery, pushed to those spaces by structural inequities. Just as Queens is often seen at the periphery, the outer borough to the central point of Manhattan, Queens College, and other publicly funded and accessible colleges and universities, are at the periphery of higher education as an institution, in the shadow of its private counterparts in Manhattan. Yet, students and their communities in places like Queens are home to the service and essential workers, the periphery that allows the center to run.

Our students feel the effects of racial capitalism (Melamed, 2015) that our economic system is based on the "producing and moving through relations of severe inequality among human groups" (Melamed, 2015, p. 77). During the pandemic, they often continued to go to school and work, exposing themselves to the virus more so than their privileged counterparts—all the while technology and access to devices (the portal to school itself during virtual learning) has been limited. The building of transformative educational spaces can feel unattainable as a result of these funding gaps and the attendant effects on classroom and learning spaces. Our educational spaces are part of this larger system of racial capitalism in which racialization and capitalism are co-constitutive and that the inequities that we are left with are keenly felt within educational systems. While we attempt to use educational systems to get outside of racial capitalism or move up within it, we also need to recognize how educational systems are reflective of and replicate these practices. To this end, literacy educators must be mindful about how narrow understandings of literacy, as well as multilingualism and multimodality, can be used to determine certain kinds of success and enforce already existing inequities.

DOING CRITICAL MULTIMODALITY: BRINGING THE "PERIPHERY" TO THE "CENTER" IN CLASSROOMS

Given how a series of structural injustices—both material and ideological in its nature—pushes our students to the "periphery" in our institutions and beyond, we see the work of bringing them to the center as three-fold: cultivating a space to (a) contend the very structural means and ways that push them to the "periphery"; (b) explore and understand multimodality as rich, complex, and expansive meaning-making labor that is already part of students' own lived experiences, along with their vision; and (c) sustain their multilingual and multimodal practices at the center. In Queens, where our racialized multilingual students engage in varied language and literacy work on an everyday basis, doing critical multimodal praxis meant also exploring the ways our students' multimodal practices are dynamically weaved and layered onto their multilingual practices (Baker-Bell, 2020; Gonzales, 2018). In this regard, translingualism's tenet of seeing linguistic and cultural plurality as a communicative norm, and also understanding of such norms as multiple, ideological, and negotiated—can offer instructors and students a language to see their own communicative practices and norms away from the White, Western, and monolingual-centered view.

Such opportunities can begin by inviting students to reflect on what literacies mean to them and how they engage in a variety of literacies beyond what is institutionally understood as "fluent," "proficient," or "literate" practices, while questioning the assumptions behind the very terms. The reflection on and interrogation of how these terms are experienced, understood, and taken up to position and categorize our students is an important part of doing and rewriting critical multimodality. Beyond their practices to navigate and use different digital technologies or apps that are often tied to the way multimodality is understood and enacted in a pedagogical space, students can share different literacies they engage in and how such practices matter in their family and communities' lives. For instance, the class could start from discussing how our meaning-making takes place: bodies, sounds, movements, emotion, and how this "extra" stuff plays equally important, if not essential, roles. This discussion can offer a moment for students to think about what it means to be literate and what counts as "literacy" as they often question who gets to claim "bilingual." Building on this idea, students can share multimodal literacies that have been crucial for their own and their community members' life, as they investigate, examine, and reflect on different ways of making meaning. In our own classrooms, the reflections often have generated a wide range of multimodal work, from using body language and understanding and drawing on different gestures to reading facial expressions, having 눈치 (*nun-chi*, a Korean rhetorical sensitivity to interpersonal dynamics in a given setting), breaking bad news or asking sensitive information to the patients or customers, translating American Sign Language (ASL) to different languages, and realizing the moment of being racialized.

The conversations and different literacies students share can help students to see how their knowledge and practice of multilingual meaning making is always multimodal, embodied, and situated in their own lived experiences and realities, and therefore, cannot be understood apart from their positionalities and the vision. Our discussions then often lead to the point of how these varied experiences of multimodality are the very crucial literacies that shape and/or sustain their communities' well-being. At the same time, our students have crucially pointed out how the ideological underpinning that determines what are "valuable" literacies relies on the ableist, racist, and monolingual frameworks that privilege and erase certain bodies and embodied ways and experiences of meaning-making.

This point became even more apparent during the pandemic; as the majority of Eunjeong's students were working in essential businesses and services, or had family members who worked in these spaces, navigating, negotiating, and otherwise working—multimodality became a central part of our daily discussions and understanding of literacies. In addition to resourcefulness in how they learned to work with available technologies against the material constraints, students' literacies outside the classrooms in Queens were the very critical multimodal labor their communities could rely on to live through the pandemic. The discussions worked in tandem to define, find, and expand our understanding and appreciation of labor of multimodality—the embodied labor that matters to our racialized multilingual students and their communities yet does not often get credit that it deserves and gets pushed to the periphery.

Given the constant and varied ways that "push" our racialized multilingual students to the margin, one of the most crucial aspects of doing critical multimodality is how we sustain this work. And this sustaining work requires constant conscientious thinking and repositioning of ourselves from the center to the periphery—from the one with authority and legitimate knowledge in the classroom to a fellow community member and learner in our local communities. While we, language and literacy scholar educators, bring varied experiences of racialization and multilingual practices, we also occupy a privileged position of full-time faculty in the institutional space that determines the center and the periphery. In this sense, sustaining our students' critical multimodality in the center also demands both the epistemological shift in our thinking of language, literacy, and multimodality and in our own positioning away from the center. Gloria Ladson-Billings (2021) importantly situates the exigence of such an epistemological shift in the context of the ongoing pandemic. Ladson-Billing poses, "Learning to do a hard reset...challenges educators to engage and interrogate their own worldviews and develop the facility to move from the center to the margins" (p. 77). As much as our racialized multilingual students are forced to practice such "de-centering," we as educators must regularly de-center what we know and value in language and literacy and stand in the margin to bring our students' multimodal practices to the center.

FINAL OFFERINGS

Critical education scholars have called us to reimagine the "doings" and "ways of being" of our richly multilingual world. To some extent these calls have brought attention to multilingual practices as innovative and highly complex, but that has not shifted our historization or value of the communities at the heart of these productions. So what does it mean for language and literacy educators to critically bring language-minoritized students to the center? What might this mean in the context of multimodality in ways that are also cognizant of how little we have explored this practice from the perspective of those who engage it and produce it on an everyday basis?

While this chapter centered the context of Queens in our grappling with these questions, we hope our discussion offers an opportunity for other educators to think about racialized multilingual communities and their own labor of multimodality that sustain their vitality. As we have emphasized, doing so should start from students' lived experiences and thinking about the way that their writing and work upholds their communities. It is their critical multimodal practices that continue to challenge us to think about multimodality beyond the "traditional" Western view that defines and values construction of and other engagement with "text." This also means we, as educators, have to think about our own relationships with our communities and how we can amplify different languages and literacies, and by extension, vision of our communities in centering the shared space. This thinking and labor is an important part of doing critical multimodality.

At the same time, to bring "Queens" to the center, we need institutional support, infrastructure, and sustainable ways to keep the "periphery" in the center. While students and teachers in Queens have persisted in cultivating and sustaining their multimodality before and throughout the pandemic, relying on their extra labor in building worlds in which their critical multimodality could be fostered and valued itself is not just and equitable. As we have witnessed throughout the pandemic, it was our racialized multilingual communities, especially our Black and Latinx communities, who had to suffer from the impacts of the pandemic, making their labor conditions even more challenging. Without transforming the inequitable structure that already oppresses and harms racialized communities—both materially and epistemologically—our work to center racialized multilingual students' multimodal labor cannot be sustained.

REFERENCES

Alim, H. S., & Paris, D. (Eds.). (2017). What is culturally sustaining pedagogy and why does it matter? In D. Paris & H. S. Alim (Eds.), *Culturally sustaining pedagogies: Teaching and learning for justice in a changing world* (pp. 1–21). Teachers College Press.

Alvarez, S. P. (2023). Multilingualism beyond walls: Undocumented young adults subverting writing education. In D. S. Martins, B. R. Schreiber, & X. You (Eds.), *Writing on the wall: Writing education and resistance to isolationism* (pp. 106–128). The University Press of Colorado.

Alvarez, S. P. (2018). Multilingual writers in college contexts. *Journal of Adolescent & Adult Literacy, 62*(3), 342–345. https://doi.org/10.1002/jaal.903

Alvarez, S. P., & Lee, E. (2020). Ordinary difference, extraordinary dispositions: Sustaining multilingualism in the writing classroom. In J. W. Lee & S. Dovchin

(Eds.), *Translinguistics: Negotiating innovation and ordinariness* (pp. 61–72). Routledge.
Baker-Bell, A. (2020). *Linguistic justice, Black language, literacy, identity and pedagogy.* Routledge.
Byrd, A. (2019). Between learning and opportunity: A study of African American coders' networks of support. *Literacy in Composition Studies, 7*(2), 31–55.
Canagarajah, S. (2002). *A geopolitics of academic writing.* University of Pittsburgh Press.
de los Ríos, C. V. (2020). Writing oneself into the curriculum: Photovoice journaling in a secondary ethnic studies course. *Written Communication, 37*(4), 487–511. https://doi.org/10.1177/0741088320938794
Driskill, Q. L. (2016). *Asegi stories: Cherokee queer and two-spirit memory.* University of Arizona Press.
Fabricant, M., & Brier, S. (2016). *Austerity blues: Fighting for the soul of higher education.* John Hopkins University Press.
Flores, N. (2013). The unexamined relationship between neoliberalism and plurallingualism: A cautionary tale. *TESOL Quarterly, 47*(3), 500–520. https://doi.org/10.1002/tesq.114
Flores, N. (2020). From academic language to language architecture: Challenging raciolinguistic ideologies in research and practice. *Theory Into Practice, 59*(1), 22–31.
Flores, N., & Rosa, J. (2015). Undoing appropriateness: Raciolinguistic ideologies and language diversity in education. *Harvard Educational Review, 85*, 149–171. https://doi.org/10.17763/0017-8055.85.2.149
Gilyard, K. (2016). The rhetoric of translingualism. *College English, 78*(3), 284–289. https://www.jstor.org/stable/44075119
Gonzales, L. (2018). *Sites of translation: What multilinguals can teach us about digital writing and rhetoric.* University of Michigan Press.
Gonzales, L., González, M. Y., & The Fugitive Literacies Collective. (2020). Multimodal cuentos as fugitive literacies on the Mexico-U.S. borderlands. *English Education, 52*(3), 223–256. https://library.ncte.org/journals/EE/issues/v52-3/30597
Haas, A. (2007). Wampum as hypertext: An American Indian intellectual tradition of multimedia theory and practice. *Studies in American Indian Literatures, 19*(4), 77–100. https://doi.org/10.1353/ail.2008.0005
Horner, B., & Alvarez, S. P. (2019). Defining translinguality. *Literacy in Composition Studies, 7*(2), 1–30. https://doi.org/10.21623/1.7.2.2
Kinloch, V. (2017). "You ain't making me write": Culturally sustaining pedagogies and Black youths' performances of resistance. In D. Paris & H. S. Alim (Eds.), *Culturally sustaining pedagogies: Teaching and learning for justice in a changing world* (pp. 25–41). Teachers College Press.
Kinloch, V., Burkhard, T., & Penn, C. (2020). Race, justice, and activism in literacy instruction: An introduction. In V. Kinloch, T. Burkhard, & C. Penn (Eds.), *Race, justice, and activism in literacy* instruction (pp. 1–9). Teachers College Press.
Kress, G. (2010). *Multimodality: Semiotic approach to contemporary communication.* Routledge.

Kubota, R. (2019). Confronting epistemological racism, decolonizing scholarly knowledge: Race and gender in Applied Linguistics. *Applied Linguistics, 41*(5), 712–732. https://doi.org/10.1093/applin/amz033

Ladson-Billing, G. (2021). I'm here for the hard re-set: Post pandemic pedagogy to preserve our culture. *Equity & Excellence in Education, 54*(1), 68–78. https://doi.org/10.1080/10665684.2020.1863883

Lee, E., & Alvarez, S. P. (2020). World Englishes, translingualism, and racialization in the U.S. college composition classroom. *World Englishes, 39*(2), 263–274. https://doi.org/10.1111/weng.12459

Lee, E., Alvarez, S. P., & Wan, A. J. (2021). Cultivating multimodality from the multilingual epicenter: Queens, "the next America. *Journal of Global Literacies, Technologies, and Emerging Pedagogies, 7*(1), 1256–1281. http://jogltep.com/wp-content/uploads/2021/02/71_4_LeeWanAlvarez_final.pdf

Lopez-Gopar, M. E. (2007). El alfabeto marginante en la educacíon indígena: El potencial de las Multilectoescrituras [The marginalizing alphabet in indigenous education: The potential of the multiliteracy]. *Lectura y Vida, 28*(3), 49–57. http://www.lecturayvida.fahce.unlp.edu.ar/numeros/a28n3/28_03_Lopez.pdf

Lorimer Leonard, R. (2023). Writing to mend literate fragmentation. In D. S. Martins, B. R. Schreiber, & X. You (Eds.), *Writing on the wall: Writing education and resistance to isolationism* (pp. 89–105). The University Press of Colorado Press.

Melamed, J. (2015). Racial capitalism. *Critical Ethnic Studies, 1*(1), 76–85. https://www.jstor.org/stable/10.5749/jcritethnstud.1.1.0076

Mirra, N., & Garcia, A. (2020). In search of the meaning and purpose of 21st-century literacy learning: A critical review of research and practice. *Reading Research Quarterly, 56*(3), 463–496. https://doi.org/10.1002/rrq.313

Ríos, G. R. (2015). Cultivating land-based literacies and rhetoric. *Literacy in Composition Studies, 3*(1), 60–70. https://doi.org/10.21623/1.3.1.5

San Pedro, T. (2017). "This stuff interests me": Re-centering Indigenous paradigms in colonizing schooling spaces. In D. Paris & H. S. Alim (Eds.), *Culturally sustaining pedagogies: Teaching and learning for justice in a changing world* (pp. 99–116). Teachers College Press.

Santiago, J. C. (2021). Keynote: Tramando la palabra/Weaving the word. *Digital Scholarship in the Humanities, 36*, i4–i8. https://doi.org/10.1093/llc/fqaa038

Shipka, J. (2011). *Toward a composition made whole*. University of Pittsburgh Press.

Syverson, M. A. (1999). *The wealth of reality: An ecology of composition*. Southern Illinois University Press.

The New London Group. (1996). A pedagogy of multiliteracies: Designing social futures. *Harvard Educational Review, 66*(1), 60–93. https://doi.org/10.17763/haer.66.1.17370n67v22j160u

U.S. Census. (2018). "Quick Facts: Queens County, New York." https://www.census.gov/quickfacts/fact/table/queenscountyqueensboroughnewyork/POP645218

CHAPTER 3

PROCEDURALIZED IDEOLOGIES IN VIDEO GAMES AND PLAYABLE MEDIA

Earl Aguilera
California State University, Fresno

Jeffrey B. Holmes
Arizona State University

Kelly M. Tran
Evolved Play

Lynette D. Guzmán
California State University, Fresno

ABSTRACT

The purpose of this chapter is to demonstrate how video games can be understood as spaces of transformative education, along with the ways that we, as critical scholars of multimodality, might productively situate ourselves in the study of games as a semiotically rich, constantly evolving, and value-laden media form. While recognizing that video games are multimodal artifacts that represent meaning through visual, textual, auditory, and other perceptual elements, this chapter emphasizes the procedural dimension of games—that is, the fact that games are fundamentally composed of, and express meaning through the enactment of processes. These processes include the fundamental rules and rule systems that players engage with, coupled with the meaning potentials that develop at the intersection of game systems, player interaction, and sensory modes of representation—all informed by broader contexts of production, distribution, and reception. Building on this idea of procedurality as a semiotic mode of meaning making, we then discuss the nature of video games as ideologically constructed and contested spaces. Just as in more traditional media forms (books, television, film), perspectives, worldviews, and assumptions can be represented, enacted, and circulated through video games as players engage with their procedural design in a variety of contexts. Bringing these concepts together, we offer the term *proceduralized ideologies* as a way to describe this phenomenon, drawing from and extending scholarship on critical theory, computational studies, and social semiotics. To illustrate this conceptualization, and to invite further analysis, we explore examples of proceduralized ideologies across a range of video games, game genres, and related cultural artifacts, such as physical board games. Ultimately, we seek to demonstrate how the analysis of proceduralized ideologies can be an important vehicle for doing the work of critical multimodality as interactive digital media technologies become more and more entangled with ideology, representation, power relations, and the material realities of our everyday lives.

OVERVIEW OF THE ARGUMENT

This chapter argues that an essential part of how video games signify meaning can be understood through the ways they create and recruit participants into ideological worlds through features of computational design. We use the term *proceduralized ideologies* to describe this phenomenon, highlighting the perspectives, worldviews, and value systems that are embedded into and enacted through the processes represented in video games. Beyond simply making claims about the world, proceduralized ideologies serve to quite literally shape the experiences and meaning-making potentials of the shared virtual spaces that more and more people are coming to inhabit. Highlighting examples from a range of games and related interactive software applications, we demonstrate how the concept of proceduralized ideologies can be a generative tool for understanding the dialectic relationship between computational technologies and the human experience. Finally, by considering the transformative educational possibilities in games through their proceduralized ideological design, we emphasize gaming as a potential act of resistance to oppression and social injustice in a rapidly changing, digitally connected world.

BACKGROUND AND CONTEXT

Once dismissed as a childhood pastime, a venue for mindless entertainment, or a distraction from more productive life pursuits, video games and the social practices surrounding them are now being recognized as a globalized sociocultural phenomenon impacting entertainment, education, socializing, artistic creation, civic engagement, and even scientific research in the 21st century (Gray & Leonard, 2018). In a recent report entitled "2021 Essential Facts about the Video Game Industry," the Electronic Software Association reports that in the United States alone, nearly 227 million people play video games. Two-thirds of adults and three-quarters of children under 18 in the United States have been reported to play video games weekly. The average age of a video game player in the contemporary United States is 31 years old, with over 80% of U.S. players being older than 18 (Electronic Software Association [ESA], 2021). Across all age ranges, players are reported to be nearly half female (45%) and half male (55%). And while ESA report claims that 87% of players agree that video gamers comprise a diverse group of people, the same report identifies only 27% of gamers as Hispanic (9%), Black/African American (8%), Asian/Pacific Islander (6%), or "other" non-White (2%). According to the market research firm Newzoo (2021), the video game industry generated an estimated $144 billion in revenue worldwide, with $24.23 billion coming from the United States (ESA, 2021).

Adding to this ubiquity, academic interest in video games has broadened over the past several decades to encompass areas such as computer science, anthropology, sociology, psychology, philosophy, economics, the humanities, and education (Aguilera & de Roock, 2022). Within the field of education specifically, interest in video games can be traced at least as far back as Seymore Papert's (1980, 1988) writings on the potential of computer games to support children's learning, though scholars such as Johan Huizinga and Roger Callaiois had been conceptualizing the relationship of play, games, and meaning making in human cultures around the world long before then (Aguilera & de Roock, 2022). Educational technologist Mark Prensky (2003) is among those credited with popularizing the term *digital-game based learning*, while James Paul Gee (2007) is also credited with igniting scholarly interest in video games as they relate to language, literacy, and learning. In recent years, a variety of academic and popular texts have been published exploring game-based learning and related concepts, including McGonigal's (2011) *Reality Is Broken*, Schrier's (2016) *Knowledge Games*, and Gray and Leonard's (2018) *Woke Gaming*.

As Aguilera and de Roock (2022) summarize, educational research on the relationship between video games and learning has historically fallen into positivist, interpretivist, and critical traditions, roughly aligning with three established paradigms of social science research. *Positivist* approaches (All et al., 2014; Clark et al., 2016; e.g., Siew et al., 2016) in this area are typically concerned with understanding the effects of video games on outcomes such as academic achievement, behavior, skill development, or other variables. On the other hand, *interpretive* approaches to game studies (Hayes & Gee, 2010; Holmes, 2015; e.g., Steinkuehler & Duncan, 2008; Tran, 2018) tend to explore the ways players make meaning through gameplay, the social practices that occur within and around games, or issues more related to a more playful view of learning. Finally, *critical* scholarship on video games and learning (Bogost, 2014; e.g., Dyer-Witheford & De Peuter, 2009; Gray & Leonard, 2018) tends to examine issues of ideology, power, and agency, typically situating games and learning within the broader contexts of society and its institutions.

Critical Foundations

Like other contributions to this volume, our chapter takes as its starting point the ethical commitments that often animate Critical studies in the field of education. Following the logic of Muhammad (2020), we distinguish small "c" criticality as framed in through a positivist paradigm from big "C" Criticality. Positivist traditions of criticality tend to equate the concept with deep, analytic thinking, often linked to taxonomies of cognition. Big C Criticality—in Muhammad's framing—refers to traditions of teaching, organizing, and activisim actively challenging the social realities of entrenched power, structural oppression, and marginalization. Contemporary manifestations of such Critical work have roots in the Black radical tradition (Robinson, 1983), Chicana feminist approaches (Gonzales, 1980), and anti-colonial pedagogies (Freire, 1970). We name these antecedents specifically because while the Critical tradition is often traced to European thinkers, individuals like Marx and Engels did no more to "invent" this tradition than Newton did to invent gravity (Robinson, 1983). Summarizing the diverse theoretical and methodological roots of the contemporary Critical tradition, Allan Luke (2012) identifies three cross-cutting themes:

(a) a focus on ideology critique and cultural analysis as a key element of education against cultural exclusion and marginalization;

(b) a commitment to the inclusion of working class, cultural and linguistic minorities, indigenous learners, and others marginalized on the basis of gender, sexuality, or other forms of difference; and

(c) an engagement with the significance of text, ideology, and discourse in the construction of social and material relations, everyday cultural and political life (p. 6).

While Luke's summary does not address the construct of race and the process of racialization, scholars such as Robinson (1983), Crenshaw et al. (1995), hooks (2009), and Fields and Fields (2014) have demonstrated how these constructs are inextricable from the broad umbrella of Critical theory. Seeking to bridge these Critical traditions with the social and material realities of computational technology, this chapter approaches the concept of proceduralized ideologies as an analytic tool for understanding video games as transformative educational spaces.

Author Positionalities

As co-authors and collaborators on this chapter, we bring to this work our own lived experiences at the intersection of multiple axes of privilege and subordination—including our racialized, gendered, and classed identities (Muhammad, 2018). We recognize that such critical work often involves an inward turn to understand our own histories, identities, literacies, and impulses toward liberation (Mentor, 2021; Moraga & Anzaldúa, 2015). We hope it is informative for the argument to clarify some of this positionality. Earl, this chapter's first author, has long struggled with a hyphenated cultural identity born in the United States as the son of Philippine immigrants. His experiences teaching in racially and economically segregated high schools marked the beginnings of his professional work to dismantle racialized hierarchies and other oppressive legacies of colonialism. Jeff, this chapter's second author, is of mixed European heritage and has spent much of his academic and professional career examining the ways dominant hegemonic structures impact educational spaces, as well as spaces outside of formal institutions, such as video games. Kelly, the chapter's third author, is of mixed Vietnamese and European descent. Her work has focused on communities around gaming, and the out-of-school learning and knowledge practices within them. Finally, Lynette, this chapter's fourth author, is a Latinx woman who has continually grappled with imposed labels of being "underrepresented" in educational spaces. Her work focuses on reframing stories we recirculate in classrooms about students and their funds of knowledge. As individuals, we have experienced and worked within the interlocking socio-material systems that hooks (2009) collectively refers to as the "imperialist White supremacist capitalist heteropatriarchy" (p. 8). And in our collective authorship, we seek to draw attention to some of these broader issues as they go beyond our individual perspectives. But what do these broader societal issues have to do with our theorizing of proceduralized ideologies in video games? Before we address this question, we should first establish a shared conceptual understanding of video games as transformative educational spaces.

VIDEO GAMES AS TRANSFORMATIVE EDUCATIONAL SPACES

A central premise of our chapter is that video games, by their fundamental nature and relationship to teaching, learning, and society, constitute transformative educational spaces. To properly ground this claim, we need to explicate our own understandings of these concepts.

The Nature of Games

To center video games as a site of critical multimodal analysis, we must begin with a shared definition of games in general. In one of the most well-known books on the topic, Katie Salen Tekinbaş and Eric Zimmerman (2003) define a game as "a system in which players engage in an artificial conflict, defined by rules, that results in a quantifiable outcome" (p. 11). For Tekinbaş and Zimmerman, a game is a *system* because it involves a set of things (space, objects, players, etc.) that affect each other to form a larger pattern that is different from any of the individual parts. A game also involves *players*—active participants interacting with the system of the game in order to experience the play of the game. With regard to *conflict*, Tekinbaş and Zimmerman argue that all games involve a contest of powers—though not all games must be a contest between players. Games typically involve *rules* that provide the structure out of which gameplay emerges, by delimiting what a player can or cannot do. Finally, games involve some kind of *quantifiable outcome*—in its simplest form, a state of victory or defeat. Such a definition is helpful because it distinguishes games from less formalized experiences of play, though there are often edge-cases that challenge this definition.

Two examples of such edge-cases, according to Tekinbaş and Zimmerman, are puzzles and tabletop role-playing games (TTRPGs). The case of puzzles, at first glance, certainly seems to push the boundaries of the artificial conflict and quantifiable outcome portions of the above definition of games. However, in the example of something like a crossword puzzle, we might imagine the outcome of solved/unsolved as a binary state, similar to a win or a loss, a one or a zero. The concept of the conflict then becomes a representation of the mental challenge presented to players who have not yet solved the puzzle, that is, have not yet reached the solution designed by the puzzle's creator. Activities like crossword puzzles, for Tekinbaş and Zimmerman, constitute a special kind of game, in which the outcome is predetermined by the designer, and the challenge put to players is to attempt to reach this outcome within the constraints of a system.

On the other hand, TTRPG games such as *Dungeons & Dragons* appear at first to be more akin to open-ended storytelling activities with some of the trappings of games (dice, numerically defined character attributes, variable player powers, etc.). In *Dungeons & Dragons,* one player takes on the role of a lead storyteller (called a Dungeon Master or a Game Master), and narrates a scenario faced by the other players. These other players take on the role of characters within the narrative, oftentimes with their own background story, motivations, and special abilities. Taking turns, the players narrate how they address the scenario posed. When a conflict needs to be resolved, dice are rolled to simulate chance of success, with modifiers applied to the die rolls based on character traits (a warrior character may gain a bonus for engaging in a contest of strength) or contextual factors (crossing difficult terrain in harsh weather may come with a numerical penalty). The Dungeon Master then narrates the outcome, and these scenarios are repeated and chained together to form an adventure. Because of the open-ended nature of *Dungeons & Dragons* (and TTRPG in general), the definitional component of quantifiable outcome is called into question. Can one really "win" or "lose" such an open-ended activity? While Tekinbaş and Zimmerman certainly acknowledge the complexity of such an edge-case, another way to approach the situation is to identify the "family resemblance" between TTRPGs and video games like *World of Warcraft* and *The Sims.* Despite none of these having the same kind of clearly defined outcome, oftentimes it is up to the players to develop and pursue goals for their own play. As Tekinbaş and Zimmerman (2003) conclude, "Sometimes the answer to the question of whether or not a game is a game rests in the eye of the beholder." (p. 13).

In summary, for the purposes of this chapter, we are less interested in splitting hairs about what counts as a game and what doesn't, and more concerned with identifying the semiotic potentials that are shared by the many artifacts, experiences, and activities that can be framed as games.

Defining Video Games

When we use the term video games in this chapter, we refer broadly to games that are designed to be played on computational platforms, including personal computers, dedicated gaming platforms, and even smartphones. In a helpful theoretical move, Tekinbaş and Zimmerman (2003) suggest that it may be more generative to think about what video games *do* (beyond their analog counterparts), rather than what they are. These affordances include the following: First, video games can offer experiences of interactivity that are generally characterized by both immediacy and focus. This is mainly due to the fact that video games are programmed into computer consoles, thus providing both increased immediacy of feedback as the system is "triggered" to respond to player input, and narrowed range of interactivity, as possible player inputs and outcomes are limited by what a game developer has programmed into the software.

Secondly, video games (and digital media more broadly) make use of a computer's capacity for collecting, storing, retrieving, manipulating, revealing, or even concealing information in the form of images, text, animations, sound, and player behavioral data (Murray, 1997, 2017). Thirdly, due to their computational nature, video games have the potential to automate systems and procedures that may be far more complex for non-digital games to simulate. Examples of these complex systems can include simulated environmental features such as terrain-movement interactions, lines of sight, weather cycles, and even interactions with animals or non-player characters (NPCs) in the virtual game world (Dunnigan, 2000).

Finally, many (though not all) contemporary video games have the ability to facilitate interaction between players across networks, such as the online networks that connect players in multiplayer, internet-connected games. These multi-user features can include technologies that enable voice or text chat between players within a particular game. We will return to some of these technical features later in this argument.

Games and Learning

Our framing of video games as transformative educational spaces draws largely on the work of James Paul Gee (2007) who grounds his work in more situated and sociocultural perspectives on learning and technology. Gee argues that the pedagogical value of video games lies not necessarily in the accomplishment of external, formalized outcomes (e.g., increased performance on standardized achievement measures), but instead in the meaning-making experiences that occur within and around games. In Gee's view, good video games are inherently developed to encourage progressive, scaffolded, and meaningful learning within virtual game worlds themselves, which Gee refers to as "small g" games. At the same time, Gee argues that important social-learning experiences occur in settings where players gather to discuss issues around games—whether they be in-game strategies, procedural analysis of underlying game rules to improve player outcomes (i.e., "theorycrafting"), or simply developing camaraderie around the experience of playing the same game titles. Gee refers to these experiences as "meta-gaming," and can occur in affinity spaces such as online forums or physical gatherings at internet cafes and local game shops. Gee uses the term "Big G" Gaming to describe the totality of meaningful learning encompassing both "small g" games and "meta-gaming" experiences.

Because all of the above phenomena involve social practices, and because social practices necessarily involve "social relationships in which things like status, solidarity, or other social goods are potentially at stake" (Gee, 2004, p. 33), Gee describes this framing as a critical one. For Gee, critical approaches are not necessarily ones that impose predetermined (typically leftist) politics, but instead are ones that deal more broadly with the notion of politics as what happens when social goods, such as power, status, and resources, are at stake. Additional stakes in such critical work can also include "social bads," such as the increased risks to health, mortality, and freedom often faced by Black Americans and other marginalized peoples of the world (Gee & Aguilera, 2021). The question of education, for us, is fundamentally one rooted in Gee's definitions of politics and critical analysis.

This framing of video games as transformative educational spaces may suggest a view that centers schooling; however, a wide range of studies has demonstrated that much of the meaningful teaching and learning in games often occurs beyond formal institutions.

Anthropological accounts by Nardi (2010) and Chen (2012) explored the ways that the learning of complex systems, the development of cross-functional teams, and teaching through modeling and mentoring occurred within the massive multiplayer online role-playing game *World of Warcraft*. Holmes' (2015) work around the multiplayer online battle arena game *DOTA2* demonstrated the ways that teaching and learning were "distributed" across people, tools, and sites in ways not always anticipated by developers. Finally, Tran's (2018)'s work around the mobile phone game *Pokémon Go!* highlighted how families came together in experiences of intergenerational play, teaching, and learning in ways that centered collaboration, cooperation, and collective knowledge generation. While these approaches to game studies in education have formed the foundation of our own doctoral training and early career scholarship, it is also important to recognize that they are not the only ways to critically frame the social practice of games.

Woke Gaming

Another way to consider video games as transformative educational spaces is from the perspective of *woke gaming* (Gray & Leonard, 2018)—specifically, the ways that players, communities, and independent developers from historically marginalized backgrounds have been using video games themselves as a medium for exploring experiences of marginalization, resisting systems of oppression, and seeking to transform inequitable social conditions. For us, what sets this tradition of work apart are several breaks from dominant traditions of theorizing games. The foundational volume, *Woke Gaming: Digital Challenges to Oppression and Social Injustice*, edited by

Kishonna Gray and David Leonard (2018), is characterized by three such breaks: (a) explicit attention to issues of racialization as developed in the Black radical tradition, (b) a deliberate subversion of academic discourse that go beyond dominant (and often racialized) notions of "appropriateness," and (c) an approach to identity that recognizes the intersection of multiple areas of marginalization (e.g., gender, race, *and* social class).

In this foundational edited volume, Gray and Leonard (2018) map out a wide range of these experiences, including developer Momopixel's *Hair Nah*—a game that addresses issues such as the history of White supremacy, the fetishization of racialized bodies, and the daily social aggressions suffered by Black women, all through the lens of an avatar trying to "smack away as many White hands as possible," as they reach in from off-screen to "touch the character's locs, twists, braids, and relaxed Black hair" (Gray & Leonard, 2018, p. 3; cf. Seraaj & Zdanowicz, 2017).

Marginalized gender and sexual identities are explored in the book *Video Games Have Always Been Queer*, in which Bo Ruberg (2019) explicates how LGBTQ+ gamers and communities have engaged in agentive play experiences that center their own identities in a medium that has historically been associated with heteronormativity, toxic masculinity, and conservative framings of sexual and gender identity. As a final example, Maize Longboat (2019) outlines in his multimodal dissertation the ways in which Native, First-Nations, and Indigenous video game players, communities, and game developers have incorporated cultural storytelling practices, historical claims to land and treaty rights, and activism against environmental degradation in a digital age. To briefly summarize the argument so far, we have established the contemporary ubiquity of video games as a cultural phenomenon. We have discussed the growing interest in video games in academic and scholarly circles, particularly in educational research. We have situated ourselves within discourses around video gaming, highlighting the critical paradigms that inform our own work, including the cultural-historical, discursive, and anti-oppressive approaches outlined earlier. And we have explored three perspectives on video games as transformative educational spaces: One that grounded in the nature of games as cultural artifacts, one that emphasizes big "G" gaming as a meaningful and socially significant practice in and of itself, and a third that highlights woke gaming as an act of resistance to oppression and social injustice in a rapidly changing, digitally connected world. Having established these baseline understandings, we now turn to the question of how video games offer socially significant meaning potentials through certain features that overlap with more traditional texts, and others that distinguish video games as a unique venue for semiosis. We summarize the unique meaning potentials of games in what we call the "procedural dimension" of multimodality, a concept to which we now turn.

MULTIMODALITY, PROCEDURALITY, AND VIDEO GAMES

From a theoretical perspective that centers on socially situated meaning making—one of the core affordances of video games lies in their multimodal nature (Gee, 2007; Hawreliak, 2018). Akin to media forms that preceded them—books, film, and television—video games express meaning through visual, auditory, and textual channels, often grouped together under the label of *semiotic modes* (Kress & Van Leeuwen, 2001). And while the majority of research in the field of multimodality has organized semiotic modes from a perceptual perspective (cf. Serafini, 2010), game scholars have also begun to draw attention to the ways games signify meaning in a procedural dimension (Hawreliak, 2018; Pérez-Latorre et al., 2017; Wardrip-Fruin, 2020). While the semiotic resources in a visual mode may constitute things like color, shape, size, and composition, the semiotic resources in a procedural mode constitute elements of process that are represented in games—rules, logics, operations, attributes, states, space, actions—that give rise to the aesthetic experience of playing a game (Hunicke et al., 2004; Osborn, 2018; Schell, 2008).

Conceptualizing Procedurality

Central to our argument is the idea that games have meaning-making potential in their procedurality along with their perceptual dimensions. That is, the underlying rules and systems of games are an important mode to consider. This work builds on (and departs from) previous scholarly work on this notion.

The concept of a procedural dimension of computational media such as video games is often traced back to the work of media scholar Janet Murray (1997, 2017). In her foundational text, *Hamlet on the Holodeck,* Murray (1997, 2017) outlines the procedural nature of computational media—that is, the fact that media such as video games are fundamentally composed of executable rules. In *Hair Nah,* a player presses the left and right directional arrows on a keyboard, for example, and the avatar swipes away disembodied white hands reaching in to invade the personal space and physical autonomy of a Black woman. Further, Murray argues it is this procedural affordance, combined with the nature of computational media as a participatory medium, that gives rise to the aesthetic experience of interactivity for users engaging with these media.

The idea of procedurality as a resource for expressing meaning was further developed by Ian Bogost's (2010) concept of procedural rhetoric, which builds on the foundations of rhetoric as the art of making (persuasive) claims about the world. Procedural rhetoric extends logocentric and perceptual multimodal traditions of rhetoric by addressing the art of persuasion through processes, such as the rule systems that govern a video game, a legal proceeding, or an economic transaction. Among a wide range of video games, Bogost highlighted the text-based, choose-your-own-adventure game *Tenure* as an example of a game using procedural systems (in this case, the day-to-day choices made by a new teacher and their sometimes unintended consequences) as a means for making claims about the pedagogical, bureaucratic, and political tensions that teachers have to navigate.

Taking these foundations even further into the world of multimodal semiotics, Hawreliak (2018) further argued for the recognition of the procedural mode as an essential aspect of video game analysis and critique. Drawing on Jewitt's (2009) definition of a mode as a means for meaning making, Hawreliak outlines case examples of the ways that procedural resources, such as a game's rule systems, meet several fundamental criteria for what "counts" as a mode:

1. Is it a material "means of making meaning"?
2. Does it have its own affordances or communicative advantages relative to other modes?
3. Does adding or subtracting the potential mode change the overall meaning of a multimodal artifact?

As part of his analysis, Hawreliak uses the example of the game *Mafia III*, highlighting the variations of speed in police response to crime depending on the relative affluence (and racialized makeup) of the city sectors in which a player is currently located. In this case, the procedural aspects of the game (e.g., the underlying variables that define police response time) offer a socially situated commentary about inequities in policing that are fundamentally different from the ways that a primarily textual or even image-based modes would offer. As we hope the examples of *Monopoly* and *The Landlord's Game* will demonstrate, highlighting a procedural dimension of multimodality that works in concert with the perceptual dimension can indeed demonstrate how the semiotic resources of a game's rules, logic, states, actions, space, operations provide essential contributions to the meaning potentials and aesthetic experience of gameplay.

Procedurality in Board Game Design: The Case of *Monopoly*

To illustrate the concept of procedurality as a dimension of multimodal meaning making, consider the rule system underlying the popular board game *Monopoly*—specifically, the rules that dictate the "win" condition of the game. In its current variants, the object of the game is ultimately to bankrupt other players by monopolizing property ownership on the game board. We should pause here to note that all of these rules are not simply abstracted logics—they are imbued with meaning in the context of the real-estate purchasing theme signified in the coordination of perceptual multimodal elements including the game's printed text, imagery, and visual design.

Players are incentivized to take actions in the game space in a winner-takes-all orientation. In Hunicke et al.'s (2004) framing, this competitive dynamic gives rise to an aesthetic experience of cutthroat domination, where even the formation of alliances with other players is typically positioned as a transitional step to later betrayal for one's own self-interest. We can conclude from this analysis that the ideological thrust of *Monopoly* is one that privileges free-market capitalism and neoliberal competition over all else.

Pilon (2015) traces the history of this popular game back to a very different design by Elizabeth Magpie, which was intended to teach players about the dangers of monopolistic land- grabbing that underlies even our present system of private land ownership. *The Landlord's Game*, as it was initially called, included a separate, collaborative win condition that was achieved when the player having the lowest monetary amount had doubled their original stake—rewarding all players for their shared role in wealth creation. This "anti-monopoly" procedural modification to the rules of the game shifts its multimodal meaning potentials in a stark contrast to the aesthetic experience generated in the play of the modern incarnation of the game.

As Pilon tells it, *The Landlord's Game* was developed by Magpie as a creative outlet for expressing her progressive political views. As the descendant of Scottish immigrants who bore witness to the extreme social inequality of the early 1900s, Magpie developed and patented her version of *The Landlord's Game* in 1903 with an original rule set that became popular among left-wing intellectuals and college students, spreading to multiple localities that customized it to the names of their local neighborhoods. However, after Charles Darrow and Parker Brothers bought the rights to the Landlord's Game and related properties, the new owners dropped the anti-monopoly rule set, paving the way for its modern incarnation. While Pilon (2015) concludes that the Monopoly case opens up questions about "who should get credit for an invention, and how" (n.p.), we argue that this case also highlights the role of cultural-historical context, dominant ideology, and political interests in shaping games as semiotic artifacts.

Procedurality in Video Game Design: The Case of *Undertale*

Carrying this concept into the world of video games, the game *Undertale*, by independent developer Toby Fox (2015), demonstrates a similar kind of procedural inversion of established conventions. This role-playing game (RPG) puts players in the role of a small child who becomes trapped in an underground world as they engage with "monsters" of all kinds on a journey toward the surface. Many seasoned RPG players picking up Undertale may initially find themselves familiar with the procedural gameplay tropes (sometimes referred to as game mechanics) that have often characterized the RPG genre—exploration of unknown areas, turn-based combat, and narrative-shifting player choice points (Seraphine, 2018). However, while the idea of engaging and defeating creatures (often positioned as "monsters") in combat has become a genre-standard way of reaching a given RPG's final win state, or ending, Fox uses the procedural and narrative design of Undertale to forward a critique of this convention. Players who engage in constant combat with the underground's denizens ultimately reach an ending that frames the player's actions as a genocide; the game offers an alternative "pacifist" ending that can only be reached if the player discovers nonviolent means for resolving conflicts. Now widely recognized for these conventional inversions, Fox's *Undertale* represents another example of how shift procedural designs, in concern with the rest of the perceptual multimodal ensemble through which a game signifies meaning, has the potential to dramatically change the meaning potentials and aesthetic experience of gameplay.

Proceduralized Ideologies in Video Games

At this point in the argument, our own conceptual framing of video games and meaning begins to depart from prior work on procedural rhetoric and procedural semiotics. We agree with Bogost (2010) that the procedural mode can be an integral part of how video games and related software make claims about the world. We also agree with Hawreliak (2018) that procedurality presents essential semiotic resources offered by video games and interactive media. However, we seek to extend these positions to argue that beyond making socially-significant, computational claims about the world, our framing of proceduralized ideologies argues that games and related media utilize semiotic resources to quite literally create and recruit their participants into ideological worlds to inhabit.

While not always computational in nature, these procedural systems also have the potential to shape our ideological understandings of the social, material, and virtual worlds that we inhabit. These social realities are not ontologically "real" objects waiting to be "discovered." Instead, they are constructed ideologically by groups, communities, institutions, or cultures. In our view, digital interactive software, including video games, does not solely make claims about the world, but utilize procedurality to construct ideological worlds of their own, enroll users into these worlds, and play a role in maintaining or transforming material conditions and power relations impacting our everyday lives (Holland et al., 2001).

Building on these concepts, Aguilera and de Roock (2022) have described *proceduralization* as the sociotechnical process through which aspects of our material and social worlds become represented in digital media (such as video games) and other computational technologies. Drawing on Murray's (1997, 2017) four-part characterization of computational media, they frame proceduralization as operating in at least four ways:

- *Repetition.* Unlike a book, which you only read once or a few times, regularly used software such as a popular video games or social networking platform do ideological work through repeated everyday use. The more often used, the more potential for circulating and shaping ideologies.
- *Scale.* In the same ways that mass media such as television and radio serve to circulate discourses and ideologies, so too can software have differential impacts at varying scales. The more people are exposed to a piece of software that does ideological work, the stronger the potential for influence.
- *Automaticity.* Like other computational software, video games rely on processes that are triggered automatically given certain human inputs, giving the feeling of "naturalness" when using digital technologies.
- *Invisibility.* Unlike perceptual multimodal representation, computational processes underlying video games and other software are usually imperceptible by humans. Rendering these processes invisible makes it difficult to understand, let alone resist or critique their influence.

While there are many things that can be proceduralized through computational means, we focus in this chapter on the ways that ideological constructions, such as cultural models, political views, and value systems, are embedded in and enacted through video games.

Even beyond discussions of procedurality, the concept of ideology can be a tricky one to pin down, as it is often weaponized as a way to frame oppositional arguments or perspectives—folks arguing the other side of an issue have ideological motivations, but our side does not. To address this issue, we find value in Hall's (1996) definition of ideology as "mental frameworks—the languages, the concepts, categories, imagery of thought, and the systems of representation—which different classes and social groups deploy in order to make sense of, define, figure out and render intelligible the way society works" (Hall, 1996, p. 29). Van Dijk's (1998) simplified definition feels even more appealing, as he frames ideology as "the basis of social representations shared by members of a social group" (p. 8). Like Hall and van Dijk, we are concerned with the connection between ideology, power, and hegemony, namely, the ways particular sets of ideologies come to dominate the thinking in a particular historical period that aid in the maintenance of power and material relations, in this case through procedurality in an increasingly digitized society (Abercrombie & Turner, 1978).

Bringing these ideas together, we now come to the central offering of this chapter: the concept of proceduralized ideologies as a way to describe the values, perspectives, and worldviews that are embedded in and enacted through procedural means. Given the ideas we have established so far in this chapter and in related research discussed elsewhere, we also offer the following preliminary observations about proceduralized ideologies in video games:

Firstly, given the computational nature of video games, understanding the properties of repetition, automaticity, invisibility, and scale can help us better frame proceduralized ideologies in relation to broader socio-technical contexts. The potential for independent games like *Undertale* and *Hair Nah*, depends in part on how popularized and widespread they become. In contrast, a game like *America's Army*, which was distributed by the U.S. military as a recruiting tool, is imbued with a very different potential for performing its ideological work (Aguilera & de Roock, 2022). As Dyer-Witheford and De Peuter (2009) explain the latter example:

> Downloaded over seven million times since its release on the Fourth of July, 2002, America's Army is an online first-person shooter intended to put into playable form the military service performed by some of the nearly three million active soldiers and reservists employed by the United States. Money is no matter in America's Army; it is free to play online, courtesy of a publicly funded, multi-million-dollar investment by the U.S. Department of Defense. A more recent addition to the America's Army Web site is "Real Heroes," which includes a list of the accomplishments of soldiers from Iraq and Afghanistan who have earned awards for valor, and gamers can read profiles or watch video interviews of soldiers talking about their childhood and military experiences. (p. xiii)

Since it was originally released in 2002, America's Army has evolved into a franchise of computer games, each composed largely of procedural tropes common to other games of its genre. A first-person camera perspective positions players as soldiers in the U.S. Army. The game's controls allow players to fire weapons and kill enemy combatants in simulated combat. Removing players from experiencing the horrors of war, however, such killing is done with the click of a mouse button, with players being rewarded for various performance metrics leading to victorious outcomes for their side.

In line with the game's emphasis on realism, the player can only take a few shots themselves before being unable to continue. And in a further break from these tropes, the U.S. Army's game also introduces features that invite players to explore real-world information, including a simulated medic exam based on a training module used by the military. But the gameplay itself is not meant to be a standalone experience. As Dyer-Witheford and De Peuter (2009) go on to explain:

> As you log in and out from your skirmish via the home page of America's Army, you have the opportunity to link directly to the Website goarmy.com. Twenty-eight percent of all visitors to America's Army's Web page click through. It is a major recruitment site for theU.S. Army, one that reportedly has a higher success rate in attracting enlistments than any other method. The battle you experienced as a cathartic bloodbath, a bit of fun, is for the world's undisputed armed superpower a serious public-relations device targeted at a generation of game players and intended to solve the crisis of a military struggling to meet its intake targets for the fatal front lines of the war on terror. (p. xiii)

Here, we can see an explicit example of procedural design working in the service of a broader ideological goal: the recruitment of young people into a world where military force is justified, valorized, and meaningful. Allowing players to carry their knowledge of other first-person shooter games into *America's Army* gives it a feeling of naturalness (automaticity). Not only are the computational processes that underpin the game hidden from players, but so too are the true horrors and costs of war (invisibility). Players are rewarded for completing training missions, progressing through campaigns, and building up experience through multiple sessions over time (repetition). And after having run on free-to-play online servers supported by the largest military branch of the U.S. Armed Forces for 20 years, the scale of the game has been recognized in world record books. On this final point of scale, the U.S. Army plans to discontinue support for the series in 2022, as it is already turning its attention to established and popular game franchises such as *Call of Duty* (Robson, 2022).

Secondly, while video games, like the media forms that came before them, are ideologically contested and value-laden artifacts, not all of the ideological work in games is performed through procedural means. For example, the ideological construction of native and indigenous peoples as bystanders to and instruments for American settler-colonizers in *The Oregon Trail* was largely expressed through linguistic and visual modes (Longboat, 2019). While players take on the role of White settler-colonists, one of the procedural choices they are faced with is how to cross a river in their wagon. One of the options presented is to "trade with an Indian to guide you," which positions indigenous peoples (whose tribes and communities go unnamed and unrecognized) as tools for the furthering of settler-colonial ends. Visually, the game illustrates indigenous peoples as bystanding villagers, or occasionally on horseback (but facing, and perhaps attendant to, the settler-character). In contrast, *When the Rivers Were Trails* (Indian Land Tenure Foundation, 2019) represents an indigenous-centered take on the same procedural tropes. *When the Rivers Were Trails* puts players in the shoes of an Anishinaabeg in the 1890s who has been displaced from their traditional territory in Minnesota by the U.S. government. The player-character, who can choose from one of four clans to change their gameplay experience, heads west to California, encountering Indian agents, meeting people from different nations, and otherwise acting agentically and intentionally to balance well-being and relations with those they meet along the trail. The procedural design of *When the Rivers Were Trails* takes on different meaning potentials altogether when combined with the artistic style, narrative dialogue, and sound design of the game, which features contributions from over 30 Indigenous creators (Aguilera, 2022).

A third and related observation is that proceduralized ideologies in video games cannot solely be understood through a complete abstraction and separation of procedural resources into logical structures, mathematical operations, and computer code. Instead, these resources integrate with perceptual elements—graphics, sound, and language—to produce meaning potentials evident only in the full ensemble of multimodality (Hawreliak, 2018). Returning to the example of police response time in *Mafia III*, the purely computational logic of a countdown timer cannot, by itself, be construed as creating or recruiting players into a particular ideological world. It is only when combined with other elements of the game, which semiotically attach this procedural design with the perceptual representation of police, that deeper meaning potentials emerge.

Finally, in line with prior principles fundamental to social semiotics, an analysis of proceduralized ideologies in video games should be informed by an understanding of the sites of production, reception, and dissemination which encompass the broader sociocultural context in which video games exist (Rose, 2012). An analysis of *America's Army*, as we have outlined above, is much more thoroughly informed by its context of use as a recruitment tool, rather than solely as a playable cultural artifact.

The Proceduralized Ideologies of *Monopoly* and *Undertale*

To illustrate the ways proceduralized ideologies operate in games writ large, we can begin by applying the concept to some of the examples we have already introduced in this chapter.

Returning to our board game examples, we can focus an analysis on the victory conditions of *Monopoly* and *The Landlord's Game* as representing opposing ideological worldviews about material wealth, social relations, and power. As we have established that the designed rule set of *Monopoly*, which emphasizes a victory condition of forcing all other players out of the game through bankruptcy, gives rise to dynamics of competition and an aesthetic experience of domination. Focusing our view on the proceduralized ideologies underlying this version of the game, we can see that Monopoly creates an ideological world inhabited by players where cutthroat competition, hoarding of resources, and exploitation of one's peers is paramount to one's success. Contrast this with the ideological world enacted through the procedural design of *The Landlord's Game*, which emphasizes mutual benefit as a shared victory condition among players. Rather than ideological worlds, Holland et al. (2001) use the term "figured world" to describe a "socially and culturally constructed realm[s] of interpretation in which particular characters and actors are recognized, significance is assigned to certain acts, and particular outcomes are valued over others" (p. 52). And in keeping with our focus on video games and digital media, we offer the idea of the "configured world" as an extension of Holland's ideas into the procedural domain. In the configured world of *Monopoly*, putting the good of all participants above one's own material enrichment is framed as the idealized pathway to success.

In our discussion of *Undertale* earlier in this chapter, we cited the procedural trope of resolving conflict through combat as a genre-defining feature of many role-playing video games. Whether the role-playing goal is protecting medieval villages in the *Witcher III*, demonstrating that you have become the very best *Pokémon* trainer there ever was, or surviving the harsh desert world of *Wild Arms*, combat is often framed as the primary, if not the only means toward resolution. This proceduralized ideology creates a configured world in which violence is normalized, even praised as an approach in conflict resolution—often without lasting and meaningful negative consequences. We can contrast this with the configured world constructed through the design of *Undertale*, where violence is not only one of several pathways to conflict resolution, but one whose negative impacts reverberate deeply throughout the world.

In related research developing this concept, we have been exploring the ways in which broader ideological systems, such as White supremacy, can also be represented and enacted through procedural means. For example, the genre of strategy games under the banner of "4x" (explore, expand, exploit, exterminate) can be characterized by the proceduralized ideologies of colonialism and imperialism as "default" states of human relations, and expansion and exploitation as the fundamental characterization of human relations with other beings in the natural world. In role-playing video games that borrow from the world-building conventions of the Western fantasy genre, the concept of differences in "race" are often procedurally paired with differences in physical or mental attributes or moral predilections. As Aguilera (2022) asserts:

> Taking the massively popular World of Warcraft (Blizzard Entertainment, 2004) as an example, we can see that the humans of the world are typically stylized according to medieval European tropes: knights in armor, castles of stone, and imperial monarchies. Contrast this with the portrayal of the Tauren, a non-human race of anthropomorphic bull-like creatures, which draws heavily from tropes that have been used to characterize the racialized Native and Indigenous peoples of the Americas—tepees, totems, and a spirituality centered on the natural world, etc. (Aguilera, 2022, n.p.)

Sturtevant (2017) further explains that, one of the original sins at the heart of these designs is the conflation of race, ability, and culture—a conflation that also underlies much White supremacist thinking. Even in game designs that appear to take inspiration from a diverse range of real-world ethnic and cultural experiences, aspects of non-White cultures are often misappropriated through both procedural and perceptual modes. Drawing heavily on inaccurate stereotypes about certain Native people's views of the spirit world, following the "Totem Warrior" character progression path in the game *Baldur's Gate III* comes complete with a spirit animal and the ability to gain supernatural might through this entity. Yikes.

Following the oppositional pairings presented in this chapter so far, we are also interested in the ways that procedural design can also offer a venue for resisting such oppressive and dominating systems, as in the example of indigenous and Native centered gaming spaces.

Contrasting the standard 4x mentality, games like Maize Longboat's *Terra Nova*, explores a nonviolent "First Contact" story set in the distant future. The brief, two-player platformer centers goals like exploration, cooperation, and survival without necessarily glorifying the goals of the empire or normalizing the logics of White settler-colonialism. In the game *When the Rivers Were Trails*, created in partnership with the Indian Land Tenure Foundation, players explore an Anishinaabe perspective on indigenous land displacement in the United States. At the beginning of the game, players are asked to choose a clan to represent their heritage, each of which offer procedural impact on gameplay, while avoiding the racialized procedural pitfalls of the Western RPG genre. As a final example, Upper One Games' *Never Alone*, which was developed in partnership with individuals and communities of Iñupiaq and Tlingit heritage, procedurally represents relationships with the spiritual and natural world as something beyond the control of people—a set of relations to be respected, not conquered.

An additional area we have not yet discussed is the concept of player agency in games. For instance, due in part to open-ended design of games like *World of Warcraft*, players have found success playing in ways that seem oppositional to a game's proceduralized ideologies; the story of a player who attained a high level of character experience by picking flowers, rather than engaging in combat, is a highly publicized example of this (Messner, 2020). Players can resist or negotiate the proceduralized ideologies present in games. While our focus in this chapter emphasizes the design of games and the proceduralized ideologies that shape such designs, player agency is a crucial lens for viewing games that is worth considering but is currently beyond the scope of this chapter.

To summarize, we have just offered the term proceduralized ideologies as a way to describe the values, perspectives, worldviews, and other ideological constructions that are embedded in and enacted through procedural (often computational) media. We have discussed that while this phenomenon can be observed in a range of software applications and digital media, video games represent a particularly generative medium for this kind of analysis. We outlined what we see as defining features of proceduralized ideologies, including how they are developed in the dialectic between procedural and perceptual modes of meaning making. Finally, we explicated several examples of proceduralized ideologies in video games, seeking to clarify these through contrasting approaches to social, material, political, and economic issues.

IMPLICATIONS FOR EDUCATORS

Just as the foundational work of the New Literacy Studies ushered in an expansion of research projects and inquiries exploring the myriad of constantly-shifting literacy practices adopted and developed by learners around the world, we hope this chapter serves as inspiration for further exploration of the range of proceduralized ideologies represented in video games and other digital media. Though we have asserted that the transformative educational potential of video games does not necessarily lie in their integration into formal schooling systems, we believe that the concept of proceduralized ideologies does have implications for professional educators. For example, as teachers continue to experiment with the possibilities of centering video games and other contemporary digital media as objects of study, we hope that the concept of proceduralized ideologies offers an additional critical lens for guiding students through these discussions. As educational technologies continue to be purchased by administrators and required in schools, we hope that the concept of proceduralized ideologies offers some language for highlighting the philosophies of surveillance, control, sorting, carcerality, and social stratification that underlie many of these platforms (Foucault,

1977). As Watters (2021) points out, so much of the "gamification" of educational apps, from badges, to leaderboards, to in-game economies, are built on principles of behavioral conditioning and social engineering. Finally, as tools for game making become increasingly accessible to a wider range of people, we hope that the concept of proceduralized ideologies offers a tool for critical engagement with creative multimodal design. While it may be beyond the scope of this chapter to address, important bodies of scholarship are developing around the ethics of the design of computational software designed specifically for children (Ito et al., 2021).

Additionally, video games are not the only computational artifacts that do ideological work through procedural means. Examples of proceduralized ideologies also include the settler-colonial nation-states (but not indigenous territories) that are recognized as "valid" locations in mapping software, the weighting of emoji-like "reactions" to influence social media algorithms, and the range of linguistic accents that are rendered intelligible within speech-to-text software. Within the realm of educational technology, proceduralized ideologies can include the positioning of the roles of teacher and student, as well as the philosophical nature of teaching itself (Aguilera & de Roock, 2022). As public education continues to be assailed by privatization, censorship, and standardization, proceduralized ideologies can serve as an additional framework for empowering teachers to engage agentically in the ideological struggle for the future of the teaching profession.

CLOSING THOUGHTS

This chapter has sought to demonstrate how the analysis of proceduralized ideologies can be an important vehicle for doing the work of critical multimodality as interactive digital media technologies become more and more entangled with discourses, social relations, power structures, and the material realities of our everyday lives. When these proceduralized ideologies are not critically examined, we run the risk of allowing the hegemonic cultural perspectives, political economies, and power relations that characterize the experiences of software developers to frame more and more of our technologically-mediated social practices in ways that maintain or exacerbate existing inequalities (Benjamin, 2019; de Roock, 2021). Conversely, when taken up as a means of resistance to systems of oppression, marginalization, and exploitation, proceduralized ideologies can also serve as tools for exploring (con)figured worlds of human and nonhuman relations that transcend our current realities. In this sense, what is perhaps most powerful about video games is not that they give us an escape from the world we live in; instead, they can offer us a reminder that other worlds are possible, if only we choose to create them together.

REFERENCES

Abercrombie, N., & Turner, B. S. (1978). The dominant ideology thesis. *British Journal of Sociology, 29*(2), 149–170. https://doi.org/10.2307/589886

Aguilera, E. (2022). Theorizing Whiteness as a proceduralized ideology in videogames. *Journal of Games Criticism, 5* (Bonus Issue A), 1–21. http://gamescriticism.org/articles/aguilera-5-a

Aguilera, E., & de Roock, R. (2022). Datafication, educational platforms, and proceduralized ideologies. In J. Sefton-Greene & L. Pangrazio (Eds.), *Learning to live with datafication: Educational case studies and initiatives from across the world* (pp. 17–34). Taylor and Francis.

All, A., Castellar, E. P. N., & Van Looy, J. (2014). Measuring effectiveness in digital game-based learning: A methodological review. *International Journal of Serious Games, 1*(2). https://doi.org/10.17083/ijsg.v1i2.18

Benjamin, R. (2019). *Race after technology: Abolitionist tools for the New Jim Code*. John Wiley & Sons.

Bogost, I. (2010). *Persuasive games: The expressive power of videogames*. MIT Press.

Bogost, I. (2014). Why gamification is bullshit. In S. P. Walz & S. Deterding (Eds.), *The gameful world: Approaches, issues, applications* (pp. 65–79). The MIT Press.

Chen, M. (2012). *Leet noobs: The life and death of an expert player group in World of Warcraft*. Peter Lang.

Clark, D. B., Tanner-Smith, E. E., & Killingsworth, S. S. (2016). Digital games, design, and learning: A systematic review and meta-analysis. *Review of Educational Research, 86*(1), 79–122. https://doi.org/10.3102/0034654315582065

Crenshaw, K., Gotanda, N., Peller, G., & Thomas, K. (1995). *Critical race theory: The key writings that formed the movement*. The New Press.

De Roock, R. S. (2021). On the material consequences of (digital) literacy: Digital writing with, for, and against racial capitalism. *Theory Into Practice, 60*(2), 183–193. https://doi.org/10.1080/00405841.2020.1857128

Dunnigan, J. F. (2000). *Wargames handbook: How to play and design commercial and professional wargames*. iUniverse.

Dyer-Witheford, N., & De Peuter, G. (2009). *Games of Empire: Global capitalism and video games*. University of Minnesota Press.

Electronic Software Association. (2021). *Video games in the 21st century: The 2020 economic impact report*. TEConomy Partners. https://www.theesa.com/wp-content/uploads/2019/02/Video-Games-in-the-21st-Century-2020-Economic-Impact-Report-Final.pdf

Fields, K. E., & Fields, B. J. (2014). *Racecraft: The soul of inequality in American life*. Verso Books.

Foucault, M. (1977). *Discipline and punish: The birth of the prison*. Vintage Books.

Fox, T. (2015). *Undertale* [Video game]. Toby Fox (independent developer).

Freire, P. (1970). *Pedagogy of the oppressed* (Myra Bergman Ramos, Trans.). Continuum.

Gee, E. R., & Aguilera, E. (2021). Bridging the analog-digital divide: Critical literacies and procedural design in young people's game-making practices. *Pedagogies an International Journal, 16*(2), 173–186. https://doi.org/10.1080/1544480X.2021.1914057

Gee, J. P. (2004). Discourse analysis: What makes it critical? In R. Rogers (Ed.), *An introduction to critical discourse analysis in education* (pp. 49–80). Routledge.

Gee, J. P. (2007). *What video games have to teach us about learning and literacy* (2nd ed.). St. Martin's Press.

Gonzales, S. (1980). Toward a feminist pedagogy for chicana self-actualization. *Frontiers: A Journal of Women Studies, 5*(2), 48–51. https://www.jstor.org/stable/3346035

Gray, K. L., & Leonard, D. J. (2018). *Woke gaming: Digital challenges to oppression and social injustice.* University of Washington Press.

Hall, S. (1996). The problem of ideology: Marxism without guarantees. In D. Morley & K.-H. Chen (Eds.), *Stuart Hall: Critical dialogues in cultural studies* (pp. 25–46). Routledge.

Hawreliak, J. (2018). *Multimodal semiotics and rhetoric in videogames.* Routledge.

Hayes, E. R., & Gee, J. P. (2010). No selling the genie lamp: A game literacy practice in The Sims. *E-Learning and Digital Media, 7*(1), 67–78. https://doi.org/10.2304/elea.2010.7.1.

Holland, D., Lachicotte, W. S., Jr., Skinner, D., & Cain, C. (2001). *Identity and agency in cultural worlds.* Harvard University Press.

Holmes, J. (2015). Distributed teaching and learning systems in Dota 2. *Well Played, 4*(2), 92–111. https://press.etc.cmu.edu/articles/distributed-teaching-and-learning-systems-dota-2-0

hooks, b. (2009). *Belonging: A culture of place.* Routledge.

Hunicke, R., LeBlanc, M., & Zubek, R. (2004). MDA: A formal approach to game design and game research. *Proceedings of the AAAI Workshop on Challenges in Game AI, 4.* https://users.cs.northwestern.edu/~hunicke/MDA.pdf

Indian Land Tenure Foundation. (2019). *When rivers were trails* [Video game]. Michigan State University's Games for Entertainment and Learning Lab.

Ito, M., Cross, R., Dinakar, K., & Odgers, C. (2021). *Algorithmic rights and protections for children.* MIT Works in Progress. https://wip.mitpress.mit.edu/algorithmic-rights-and-protections-for-children

Jewitt, C. (2009). An introduction to multimodality. In D. Jewitt (Ed.), *The Routledge Handbook of Multimodal Analysis* (pp. 14–27). Routledge.

Kress, G. R., & Van Leeuwen, T. (2001). *Multimodal discourse: The modes and media of contemporary communication* (Vol. 312). JSTOR.

Longboat, M. (2019). *Terra nova: Enacting vVideogame development through Indigenous-led creation* [Master's thesis, Concordia University]. https://spectrum.library.concordia.ca/985763/

Luke, A. (2012). Critical literacy: Foundational notes. *Theory Into Practice, 51*(1), 4–11. https://doi.org/10.1080/00405841.2012.636324

McGonigal, J. (2011). *Reality is broken: Why games make us better and how they can change the world.* Penguin.

Mentor, M. S.-R. (2021). Doing the deep work of antiracist pedagogy: Toward self-excavation for equitable classroom teaching. *Language Arts, 99*(1), 19–24. https://www.proquest.com/docview/2578205030

Messner, S. (2020, December 11). *World of warcraft's pacifist panda just hit level 60 by picking millions of flowers.* https://www.pcgamer.com/world-of-warcrafts-pacifist-panda-just-hit-level-60-by-picking-millions-of-flowers/

Moraga, C., & Anzaldúa, G. (2015). *This bridge called my back: Writings by radical women of color* (4th ed.). SUNY Press.
Muhammad, G. E. (2018). A plea for identity and criticality: Reframing literacy learning standards through a four-layered equity model. *Journal of Adolescent & Adult Literacy: A Journal From the International Reading Association, 62*(2), 137–142. https://doi.org/10.1002/jaal.869
Muhammad, G. (2020). *Cultivating genius: An equity framework for culturally and historically responsive literacy.* Scholastic.
Murray, J. H. (1997). *Hamlet on the holodeck: The future of narrative in cyberspace* (Vol. 1). MIT Press.
Murray, J. H. (2017). *Hamlet on the holodeck: The future of narrative in cyberspace* (Vol. 2). MIT Press.
Nardi, B. (2010). *My life as a night elf priest: An anthropological account of World of Warcraft.* University of Michigan Press.
Newzoo. (2021). *Global games market report 2021—free version.* https://newzoo.com/insights/trend-reports/newzoo-global-games-market-report-2021-free-version
Osborn, J. C. (2018). *Operationalizing operational logics* [Unpublished doctoral dissertation]. University of California, Santa Cruz.
Papert, S. (1980). *Mindstorms: Children, computers, and powerful ideas.* Basic Books.
Papert, S. (1988). Does easy do it? Children, games, and learning. *Game Developer Magazine,* 88. http://papert.org/articles/Doeseasydoit.html
Pérez-Latorre, Ó., Oliva, M., & Besalú, R. (2017). Videogame analysis: A social-semiotic approach. *Social Semiotics, 27*(5), 586–603. https://doi.org/10.1080/10350330.2016.1191146
Pilon, M. (2015). *The monopolists: Obsession, fury, and the scandal behind the world's favorite board game.* Bloomsbury Publishing.
Prensky, M. (2003). Digital game-based learning. *Computers and Entertainment, 1*(1), 21– 21. https://doi.org/10.1145/950566.950596
Robinson, C. J. (1983). *Black Marxism: The making of the Black radical tradition.* UNC Press Books.
Robson, C. (2022, February 9). *America's Army recruitment tool game shutting down.* Gamerant. https://gamerant.com/americas-army-game-shutting-down/
Rose, G. (2012). *Visual methodologies: An introduction to researching with visual materials.* SAGE Publications.
Ruberg, B. (2019). *Video games have always been queer.* NYU Press.
Schell, J. (2008). *The art of game design: A book of lenses.* CRC Press.
Schrier, K. (2016). *Knowledge games: How playing games can solve problems, create insight, and make change.* JHU Press.
Seraaj, I., & Zdanowicz, C. (2017, November 17). *A video game for Black women tired of people touching their hair.* CNN. https://www.cnn.com/2017/11/17/health/video-game-dont-touch-black-womens-hair-trnd/index.html
Serafini, F. (2010). Reading multimodal texts: Perceptual, structural and ideological perspectives. *Children's Literature in Education, 41*(2), 85–104. https://doi.org/10.1007/s10583-010-9100-5
Seraphine, F. (2018, July). Ethics at play in undertale: Rhetoric, identity and deconstruction. In *Proceedings of the 2018 DiGRA International Conference: The game*

is the message. http://www.digra.org/wp-content/uploads/digital-library/DIGRA_2018_paper_248.pdf

Siew, N. M., Geofrey, J., & Lee, B. N. (2016). Students' algebraic thinking and attitudes towards algebra: The effects of game-based learning using Dragonbox 12+ App. *The Research Journal of Mathematics and Technology, 5*(1), 66–79. https://www.academia.edu/22072893/Students_Algebraic_Thinking_and_Attitudes_towards_Algebra_The_Effects_of_Game_Based_Learning_using_Dragonbox_12_App

Steinkuehler, C., & Duncan, S. (2008). Scientific habits of mind in virtual worlds. *Journal of Science Education and Technology, 17*(6), 530–543. https://doi.org/10.1007/s10956-008-9120-8

Sturtevant, P. (2017, December 5). Race: The original sin of the fantasy genre. *The Public Medievalist, 5.* https://www.publicmedievalist.com/race-fantasy-genre/

Tekinbaş, K. S., & Zimmerman, E. (2003). *Rules of play: Game design fundamentals.* MIT Press.

Tran, K. M. (2018). Families, resources, and learning around Pokémon Go. *E-Learning and Digital Media, 15*(3), 113–127. https://doi.org/10.1177/2042753018761166

Wardrip-Fruin, N. (2020). *How Pac-Man eats.* MIT Press.

Watters, A. (2021). *Teaching machines.* MIT Press.

Van Dijk, T. A. (1998). *Ideology: A multidisciplinary approach.* SAGE.

CHAPTER 4

MEET ME IN OUTER SPACE

Theorizing Fugitive Spaces of Creation and Joy With Girls of Color

Autumn A. Griffin
Georgia State University

Grace D. Player
University of Connecticut

ABSTRACT

In a world fraught with physical, emotional, and academic violence steeped in racism and sexism directed towards girls and women of color, we believe there is no better time to build theories that center, honor, and uplift the ingenious critical multimodal literacies of girls of color. Importantly, we acknowledge that schools—and school-based spaces of literacy learning in particular—have seldom been places of refuge for girls of color, as they often work to contain, silence, and eradicate their multiple and brilliant literacies (Brown, 2013). However, like their foremothers, girls of color have historically and contemporarily built their own spaces—often outside of the classroom—that both honor their identities and allow them to take up creative, resistant, and disruptive acts of literacy (Muhammad, 2012; Ohito, 2020). In this chapter, we draw on the work of scholar activists who, through their work with girls of color seek to build, sustain, and protect spaces where girls of color can safely and collectively employ their multimodal literacies as they evoke joy, practice celebration, and (re)imagine possibilities for their futures (Griffin & Turner, 2023; Toliver, 2022; Turner & Griffin, 2020). Specifically, we take up notions of fugitivity (Player et al., 2020), outerspace (Coles & Kingsley, 2021) and youthtopias (Coles, 2021), geospatiality (Butler, 2018), hush harbors (Kynard, 2010), and homeplace (hooks, 1990; Player et al., 2022) to theorize the space-making practices girls of color employ in order to create arts-based literate renderings. Employing a critical multimodal analysis framework (Griffin, 2020), we first examine the ways their creations work to resist and disrupt violent gendered (Collins, 1991) and White supremacist (mis)representations of their personhood in the extant literature (Player et al., 2022). We then draw on that same literature to construct a framework for the active creation and sustenance of joyful fugitive spaces. To represent our implications for this chapter, we include a multimodal piece of art that serves as one example of depiction of the joyful fugitive spaces created by girls of color. We highlight the symbols within the artwork and briefly discuss how it can serve as a guide for educators interested in working with girls of color as co-conspirators in the construction of liberating and celebratory spaces of literacy learning.

> Meet me in outer space
> We could spend the night
> I've grown tired of this place
> We could start again
>
> When you look at me what do you see?
> What do you see in my place?
> I've been awake for 9,274 days
> Your plastic pictures, tinted mirrors
> Tell me nothing 'bout myself
> I've been complacent with the stories
> And the lies you tell my heart
>
> So, I'm leaving on a jet plane
> Don't know if I'll be back again
> —Jamila Woods, 2016

These beautiful words of Jamila Woods (2016), singer/songwriter and poet from Chicago, Illinois, are a call to Black girls to join her in her quest to find a land in outer space that not only welcomes them, but does so with open arms, allowing them to flee from the oppressive confines of this world and helping them to discover who they are and tell authentic stories about their experiences. Like Woods, we believe there are spaces, beyond those that currently exist, in which Black girls, and all girls of color, can cultivate through joy, celebration, and imagination. Those spaces do not exist in literacy classrooms in their current form; instead, girls of color seek out, build, and sustain those spaces in their varied creative and multimodal literate renderings. They exist in the art girls of color create and the stories they tell; they exist in the dances they dance and in the secrets they divulge in whispers between one another and to trusted adults; they exist. And only those whom girls of color understand to be unwavering in their commitment to their liberation are invited to travel with them.

Throughout this chapter, we draw on the work of scholar activists who, through their work with girls of color seek to build, sustain, and protect spaces where girls of color can safely and collectively employ their multimodal literacies as they evoke joy, practice celebration, and (re)imagine possibilities for their futures (Griffin & Turner, 2022; Toliver, 2021; Turner & Griffin, 2020) to catapult into what we call outer space (Coles & Kingsley, 2021; Toliver, 2022). We take up notions of fugitivity (Player et al., 2020), youthtopias (Coles, 2021), geospatiality (Butler, 2018), hush harbors (Kynard, 2010), and homeplace (hooks, 1990; Player & González Ybarra, 2021) to theorize the space-making practices girls of color employ in order to create arts-based literate renderings that depict the worlds they know to exist. Employing a discursive and critical multimodal analysis framework (Griffin, 2021), we examine the ways their creations work to resist and disrupt violent gendered (Collins, 1991) and White supremacist (mis)representations of their personhood in extant literature (Player et al., 2020). We then draw on that same literature to construct a framework for the active creation and sustenance of joyful outer spaces.

To conclude, we represent our implications for this chapter in a multimodal piece of art that serves as one example of the joyful spaces created by girls of color. We highlight the symbols within the artwork and briefly discuss how it can serve as a guide for educators interested in working with girls of color as co-conspirators in the construction of liberating and celebratory spaces of literacy learning.

INTERLUDE: POPSICLES AND PLACE MAKING

So one day these random girls are at my office, and one girl's like, "Y'all remember how to play Rockin' Robin?" And we all broke out into formation, and we were like "Popsicle, popsicle, a bang-bang me we was rockin' in the treetop..." And it was so great, it was like, these Black women that I did not know, had met that day, and we like all knew how to play Popsicle together. And then like all of the people who weren't Black were just looking at us like... "Did y'all go to elementary school together?" It was literally like the best inside secret that I felt like I had ever had. That's one of my favorite things about blackness.

—Jamila Woods, 2016

This bit of storytelling arises in an interlude, "Popsicle," on Woods's (2016) album, *Heavn*. The narrator describes an eruption of Black girl magic, a cracking of a White dominant workplace. This gorgeous rupturing of White space that transcends White understanding and imagination is the work girls of color and women of color do constantly as they navigate and build clandestine worlds—sometimes in plain sight—more beautiful than what whiteness can even dare to imagine. The girls we've worked with over the years engage in this same type of place making, disrupting their school spaces with their multimodal renderings of love, joy, and celebration.

In a world fraught with physical, emotional, and academic violence steeped in racism and sexism directed towards girls and women of color, we believe there is no better time to build theories that center, honor, and uplift the ingenious critical multimodal literacies of girls of color. Importantly, we acknowledge that schools—and school-based spaces of literacy learning in particular—have seldom been places of refuge for girls of color, as they often work to contain, silence, and eradicate their multiple and brilliant literacies (Brown, 2013). However, like their foremothers, girls of color have historically and contemporarily built their own spaces that both honor their identities and allow them to take up creative, resistant, and disruptive acts of literacy (Price-Dennis & Muhammad, 2021; Ohito, 2020) as they "play popsicle" and move toward joy, celebration, and healing. Like Jamila Woods, scholars who have chosen to stand beside girls of color in this work understand the oppressive nature of the current world and implore them to join them as they create outer spaces—those spaces outside the confines of a classroom, school building, or other liminal or carceral locales—together. Below we detail extant literature that investigates the world-building arts-based practices of youth of color and discuss the implications of this work for girls of color.

We build our understandings of liberatory spaces for girls of color as existing outside of the limitations and violence of Whiteness, as untethered to the inherently racist and misogynistic structures of American education. Coles and Kingsley (2021) explore the possibilities held by "Black English outer spaces...alternative, Black-centric and underground curricular spaces" that "exist beyond sites of curriculum violence" (para. 11). These are spaces which are envisioned through the lens of Black imagination which center on the healing, health, and joy of Black people and transcendence of settler colonialism, anti-Blackness, heteropatriarchy, and the various and intersecting forces of damage. The construction of these outer spaces relies on fugitive practices that radically reject the pain and violence of our nation in favor of loving, affirming, imaginative, future gazing, humanizing practices of celebrating girls of color (Player et al., 2020; Campt, 2017; Ohito, 2020; Lyiscott & the Fugitive Literacies Collective, 2020; Gonzalez et al., 2020; Patel, 2019). As Patel (2019) describes, it is in the act of fugitivity that those fleeing the carceral state build practices of truth seeking, truth teaching, truth telling, and truth building for themselves and each other.

We believe, then, it is possible for girls of color to collectively build utopias where they can safely practice and celebrate their literacies free of restraint and oppression. We therefore draw on the work of Coles (2021) who, in his work with Black high school students, conceptualized youthtopias as educational spaces where young people can work together to build locales of learning, resistance, and empowerment. Coles draws on the work of Akom et al. (2008) to define *youthtopias* as

> traditional and non-traditional educational spaces where young people depend on one another's skills, perspectives, and experiential knowledge, to generate original, multi-textual, youth-driven cultural products that embody a critique of oppression, a desire for social justice, and ultimately lay the foundation for community empowerment and social change. (p. 3)

Within this definition, we see the power of young people and the possibility for developing educational spaces rooted in resistance to oppression and celebration of self. We take up these notions and ground our own work on space creation with girls of color in the idea of youthtopias, as it creates space for imaginaries we have not yet seen, but aspire to build together.

These are practices that are creative and developed over time, necessarily because of the sustained everyday-ness of violence girls of color encounter as a product of White heteropatriarchy (Campt, 2017). Thus, the fugitive acts take form in continuous flight (Campt, 2017) and, we contend, show up in practices girls of color engage regularly in their multimodal creations on the page, in the digital space, and in their embodied encounters with one another. Building on various threads of women of color feminist theory, we argue here to consider the intersections of race and gender in the ways that girls of color have utilized their multimodal literacies to create outer spaces with and for one another.

Crucial to the understanding of girls of color outer spaces is a conceptualization of spatiality. Butler (2018) builds on earlier notions of a politics of spatiality (Dotson, 2013)—that which regards the theoretical and physical spaces Black women create and sustain—to examine "how Black girls unpack their relationships between race, gender, class, and geospatial location" (Butler, 2018, p. 36). She takes up the notion of Black girl cartography, interrogating the intersections of race, gender, dis/ability, sexuality, and location to understand the ways Black girls are excluded—both epistemically and physically—from notions of girlhood. Her work highlights the ways schools and the disciplinary actions they uphold build and sustain worlds dedicated to White femininity and limit Black girls' ways of being. Black girl cartographers, however, she argues, "highlight how Black girls carve out spaces in urban schools to engage in sustainable practices of teaching and caring for one another" (Butler, 2018, p. 37), allowing for listening, healing, and love to flourish.

Importantly, such practices are often developed in homeplace, theorized by hooks (1990), as communal spaces of resistance to White dominance, where knowledge and practices are shared intergenerationally and amongst peers as means for healing and survival upon encounters with a violent world. As literacy scholars have explored, these are spaces that girls of color and women of color creatively develop both on the periphery as well as in the midst of White dominated spaces (Kelly, 2020; Player & Ybarra, 2021). We believe these spaces to be the coveted secrets of girls of color, hidden in plain sight. We draw on the work of Kynard (2010) who takes up the notion of hush harbors, "African American sites of resistance that functioned as 'hidey' spaces for multiple literacies that were officially banned via institutional and state structures that prohibited African American humanity during slavery" (p. 33). These spaces, these sites of memory, served as a strategic layer of protection from the White gaze and White violence.

As scholars of multimodal literacies, we have noted the specific ways girls of color engage and employ their multimodal literacies to create spaces of joy, celebration, and love. Griffin (2021) points out the spatiality of multimodal depictions of Black girlhood, noting that of particular importance to what Black girls choose to create, is *where* they choose to create. She draws on the work of scholars of Black theory (Davis, 2020; McKittrick & Woods, 2007) to explain that given the history of the United States, where and how Black folks choose to take up space is inherently racialized, and for Black girls, also gendered. She analyzes the work of several Black girls, centering their imaginative world-making practices that create space for possibility and the refusal of death. Similarly, Flores (2021) describes the work of Latina mothers and daughters in Somos Escritoras, a creative space in which members of the group could write and perform their own stories. Together, the group created artwork, crafted writing, and performed narratives in order to express and define self. Likewise, Player (2021a) employs narrative portraiture to inquire how two Asian American girls channel their multiple literacies within a multiracial collaborative writing group to both explore and express their identities and political commitments. The girls evoke storytelling, drawing on survival, resistance, and joy as they engage in self-definition as an act of resistance against stereotypes. In another study, Player (2021b) conceptualizes the critical celebrations within a writing group of girls of color. She explores the varied ways their artistry, specifically the writing of poetry, assists them in building solidarity across difference. Through their words, they create a powerful coalition of self-affirmed girls of color, free from the confines, gaze, and terror of Whiteness.

It is our belief that the multimodal outer spaces girls of color build together have the potential not only to disrupt, but to be liberatory spaces of love, joy, and celebration; spaces they build for themselves alone. We are aligned with the scholars mentioned above who understand that school-based spaces of learning are often violent and exclusionary and thus recognize the dire necessity of these outer spaces, and take up a commitment to conspiring with girls of color to fiercely protect those spaces. We emphasize that it is not us as educators who build these spaces *for* girls of color, but rather we follow their lead and work alongside them to build spaces they desire to see come to life (Butler, 2018). Thus, throughout the remainder of this chapter we highlight the work of girls of color—exploring, through collaging and discursive multimodal analysis, the worlds they create.

VRY BLK. VRY ASN. VRY MUCH SISTERS: POSITIONALITY

> *You take my [sister, sister, sister]*
> *I fight back, back, back, back*
> —Jamila Woods, 2016

Throughout this chapter we put forth a unique perspective that is specifically built on the writing practices of women and girls of color across varying marginalized racialized identities. Autumn is a Black American woman whose ancestors were kidnapped from their homes and enslaved on stolen U.S. land. She was raised in the Northeastern region of the United States. Grace is a multiracial Japanese American woman with maternal roots in Brazil. We come together in this work as a Black woman and an Asian American woman and as co-conspirators (Love, 2019) to co-construct an image of outer spaces for girls of color, building on our own disparate but connected experiences as women, once girls, of color. Though both of us are linked through our experiences as raced-gendered people, we also contend with the very different forces of anti-Black and anti-Asian racism in our lives and in the United States generally, and thus bring very different lived experiences to this work. What's more, we both bring different lineages of ancestral, cultural, and familial knowledges, all of which contribute to the ways we experience/d and theorize girlhood (Brown, 2013) and practice women of color research and pedagogies.

It is significant that we write together from the positionality of women reaching across nondominant differences, and imperative that we acknowledge it in this chapter. We do not attempt to create a singular or monolithic depiction of our experiences as women of color.

Instead, we assert, as Morales (2001) does, that

> [this collective] called "Women of Color" is not an ethnicity. It is one of the inventions of solidarity, an alliance, a political necessity that is not the given

> name of every female with dark skin and a colonized tongue, but rather a choice about how to resist and with whom. (pp. 102–103)

We acknowledge the differences in our lived experiences as legitimate and commit to the practice of listening to and learning from one another as we partner in this work for the liberation of all girls of color.

Further, we draw on the historical practices of women of color and third world women (Collins, 1991) as we seek to build knowledge and power collectively rather than to hold power over or keep power from. As Lorde (2007) highlights,

> Within the interdependence of mutual (nondominant) differences lies that security which enables us to descend into the chaos of knowledge and return with true visions of our future, along with the concomitant power to effect those changes which can bring that future into being. Difference is that raw and powerful connection from which our personal power is forged. (pp. 111–112)

Thus, as does Lorde, we believe and proclaim that difference matters and can be a great source of intellectual and political power. We see our work together with girls of color as opportunities to create "true visions of our [futures]" and know that as we work together to co-construct worlds envisioned from a place of love and liberation, we can "bring [those futures] into being."

We do not diminish this work by claiming it to be easy, automatic, or uncritical. As Moraga (1983) teaches us, sisterhood

> is not a given. I keep wanting to repeat over and over again, the pain and shock of difference, the joy of commonness, the exhilaration of meeting through incredible odds against it. But the passage is *through*, not over, not by, not around, but through. (p. xiv)

We recognize that even as this work of co-conspiratorship and cross-racial collaboration is difficult, it is a choice, and can and should be done in the spirit of critical sisterhood, is ultimately a choice. The writing of this chapter, then, is an effort to work through our differences to reimagine education for girls of color. It puts forth a unique effort to more deeply understand girlhoods of color because it builds theory through a dialogic practice between women of color across both difference and connectedness. What follows in the section below is a dialogue between the two authors; a dialogic exchange between two women of color, sister scholars. Together we build towards co-conspiritorship (Love, 2019) with and alongside each other, with and alongside the girls with whom we work. "In outer space...On a jet plane" (Jamila Woods, 2016).

UP AND AWAY!: CREATING JOYFUL OUTER SPACES WITH AND FOR GIRLS OF COLOR

I wanna go
To my own private planet I've been dreaming of
Little moon in my head I be moving on
Up and away
Up and away

Just 'cause I'm born here
Don't mean I'm from here
I'm ready to run
And rocket to sun
I'm way up
I'm way up
Just 'cause I'm born here
Don't mean I'm from here
I'm ready to run
And rocket to sun
I'm way up
I'm way up
—Jamila Woods, 2016

Throughout our time working with girls of color, we have come to notice that almost all of them, like Woods states, desire to go to a world away from here; a world where they feel they belong, where they are from. We build this research from our own outer space—an outer space that centers art and girls of color/women of color talk. Below, we have composed a mosaic (Evans-Winters, 2019; Figure 4.1) of images compiled from the work of girls we've worked with and our own compositions.

We then include a transcript of our dialogic analysis of the collage. In an attempt to piece together various voices, modes of meaning making, and stories arising from our work with girls and our own multimodal analyses of that work, we have created a visual compilation of girls of color outer spaces. This visual and dialogic analysis we offer builds on the work of Evans-Winters (2019), who centers the idea of mosaic in research with girls of color, defining mosaic as "a piece of artwork composed of a combination of diverse elements, patterns, and forms...a gender- and race-based approach to qualitative inquiry and analysis" (p. 15). We take up this metaphor for women of color feminist research quite literally, and offer the outer space mosaic below. Further, we take up the practices of women of color who have gathered around kitchen tables to engage in laughter, joy, gossip, and healing (Haddix et al., 2016; Lyiscott et al., 2021), as a mode of

88 ▪ A. A. GRIFFIN and G. D. PLAYER

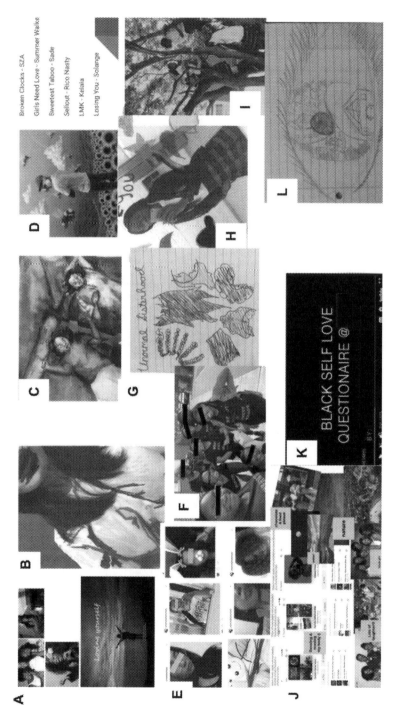

Figure 4.1 Visions of other worlds: The arts-based renderings of girls of color.

analysis. Given our work with and for girls of color, we found it most appropriate to take up an analytical frame most authentic to us and the girls with whom we work. We invite you to observe the image with the understanding that art, in and of itself, is analysis. As theorists and methodologists alike have studied, art is theory making (Anzaldúa, 2015; Rolling, 2013). We, like Lawrence-Lightfoot and Davis (1997), choose to "blur the boundaries of aesthetics and empiricism in an effort to capture the complexity, dynamics, and subtlety of human experience and organizational life" (p. xv) and present a mosaic of voices—girls of color and our own—that offers creative and relational theorization of outer space.

Autumn: So, as we look at this, what are some of the things that are sticking out to you?

Grace: Right now, I think the way that space and environment is incorporated into a lot of these things is really interesting. Some of the images your students picked with the sky and the horizon being a really significant thing with the cloud sky and the orangey glow I think is something, as well as things like the girls in the tree (see I in Figure 4.1), the girls outside (see C in Figure 4.1)—that was my painting—but girls outside, girls in trees, cityscapes (see L in Figure 4.1), all that. I feel like there's something about environment and taking claim over it.

Autumn: I agree. I think what stuck out to me initially was color. And just the uses of color throughout, like you said. Once I started looking closer, I think a lot of the color is in the form of environment. So even in this "loving yourself" picture on the side (see A in Figure 4.1), there's this yellowy glow, but she is outside. Even in the image you have here with the two girls laying down (see C in Figure 4.1). Is that your artwork?

Grace: That's my artwork, but it's of two of the girls who were in my club.

Autumn: That's so dope! So they're laying down and they are still outside, I'm assuming that's grass in the background. This picture of Tyler the Creator's album that one of my students chose to use for her album cover (see D in Figure 4.1), which I just can't get over! There's so much there, the sunflowers and the bees and also this glow and something is covering this person's face. Then even in this picture of Seraphina and the fact that she chose to use stars and clouds (Player et al., 2023; see H in Figure 4.1); she's indoors, but she's still adding color. She's choosing to represent this outdoor space, even within that. There is something here about the fact that they're taking claim over places and spaces. On the bottom left, there's this collage that some of the women I worked with did of music (see J in Figure 4.1) and things that bring them joy and healing. And you see glimpses of outside there too with this pinkish purple sky, you have the beach, you have the moon. So, it seems to me that part of what they're saying here is that these indoor spaces that we've been confined to just cannot contain who we are.

Grace: I was thinking too, in the piece that I'm writing, as well as the dialogue piece that we did for my special issue (Player et al., 2022), Tamara Butler, in the dialogue piece, she talks about futures being green. Futures for Black girls, girls of color being green. That has been sticking out to me so much, and the rebellion against being confined or being indoors, and it's like, "No, we're so much more than that." And with this eyeball picture (see L in Figure 4.1), I think one of the reasons it continues to resonate with me is this was her visioning of the future and it does kind of have a futuristic vibe to it, but it simultaneously is what she values about the future. What does she value about her environment and see projected into the future? And it is her cityscape, and it is families and it is homes, protection. I think that there's something there about how we, how girls and women of color, Black girls, Asian girls, how they're thinking about their claim over space and their love of space. Like the girls in the tree (see I in Figure 4.1). I love that picture so much. That was us on our last day of the club meeting. They just kind of took over the backyard and were climbing in trees and they all have their shirts that I had made them, the "Unnormal Sisterhood" shirts, on over their uniforms. They're just transforming space, transforming bodies.

And I love that picture because I think it's just so...

Autumn: It's so joyful!

Grace: There's just so much joy and they're playful and being kids in ways that they should be allowed to be kids all the time. I know when they're in school, they weren't allowed to be kids. And I think that claiming of girlhood is really beautiful. Having permission to be girls, having permission to be children, is something that they should have the right to.

Autumn: Listening to you talk makes me think of two things. One is the picture of the girls outside by their school against the wall (see F in Figure 4.1), because that picture stands out to me because they chose this brick wall, this rigidity as we were talking about love, and softness, and care (Griffin, 2021). And there's this clear dichotomy between what the school represents to them and who they are and how they see themselves. And that is so fascinating to me. And then also, there are so many platforms right now that are thinking about Black folks being outside. There's this Black girl hike and yoga program that happens in Philly and it's just Black women spending time outside with nature together. Even now, before we started the recording, we talked about the fact that we were both going for runs. And how there's this need to spend time outside, before sitting down and getting to work. There's something there!

Grace: No, I've been thinking about that a lot too, because since quarantine I've been foraging a little bit. I've been able to make multiple meals out of things I found in the woods. There's this account on Instagram, @blackforager (Nelson, n.d.), and she's this zany, fun woman who just knows all about her environment. She actually had a post that I was looking at the other day that talks about how food is so political and finding your food is built on traditions that we've had to build, as people of color, and in her case, as Black people, she's like we had to do this and we actually had this taken away and that's part of the confinement that was placed on people because we were outlawed from them. You know all these trespassing laws, a lot of them were established to prevent Black people from foraging. And I was like this is so fascinating. When we think about the ways that these myths about confinement or being indoors, those were things that were forced on people. So this rebellion and claiming of the outdoors, I think is really beautiful and important. Significant to who girls are and how they're able to be so full, and so beautiful, and feeling. Sun on skin is such a powerful feeling for me. So when I see the sunset picture, all the sunset pictures in here, it's feeling that glow and how beautiful skin is in the sun and that sunset glow. I just, it makes me feel just, I don't know. Happy.

Autumn: My dad has a garden that you may have seen me post on Instagram before, and I never feel closer to him, to the land, than when I'm in that space. And I feel like that's when he's also the most at peace. And my parents have some friends who have grandkids that came over this weekend, and there were two little girls and a boy, and they were three, four and five. And we went into the garden and just to see their joy and their inquisitiveness about, "We just picked this?" and "You can eat this?" There's this connection that we stomp out of children so early and teach them the outside is a bad thing. Even the myths around Black folks being scared of outside and being scared of the woods. That wasn't always true. Even if we think of Indigenous connections to the land, and when I say Indigenous, I mean yes, both here in the States, but also on the continent [of Africa]. Indigeneity is global. Black folks who were Indigenous to the continent were doing some of that outdoor work themselves before we were ever kidnapped and brought to this country.

There is this returning, that we can see even in the collage. We can see this practice of returning to the land and spending time outside. And it might not even be for physical nourishment, but it's clear that there's some type of spiritual nourishment happening here. We see that in the smiles, in the stances, even in this picture that's the album cover (see D in Figure 4.1), in the way this person is standing so confidently outside, right in the middle of nature and almost has become part of nature themselves. It makes me think of some of Jamila Woods' lyrics.

Somewhere on her album, she talks about Black skin glowing. I can't think of what song it is right now, but she talks about Black skin glowing and just this magic that there is to being outside. She even has a song about the lake and spending—and it's a manmade lake, but the point is that folks are outside and spending time in nature. That is for sure something that I'm thinking a lot about; literal outer spaces. Outside spaces.

Grace: I think that that's really beautiful. Because even thinking about Woods' lyrics and talking about going to the sun, going someplace and recalling Octavia Butler. I think one of the reasons why that resonates with me so much, why I keep thinking about it is because I see girls, I see us, I see women seeking the sun and these worlds, complete worlds, and I think they're dynamic and I think they blend so many different aspects of life that girls already have, but are also seeking. So even that talk about indigeneity and going backwards, those are things that are rooted in us. My family in Brazil are farmers. That was my mom, their family came from Japan to Brazil, in order to find farmland. Because of war in Japan, it wasn't sustainable for them to be there. So, they came to Brazil because they knew that's where the land was, from conversations with other people who had migrated. That migration was driven by seeking land, seeking sustenance, seeking a place that was livable. I think that, though my mom certainly was not a farmer in the United States, she rejected that part of her lineage. I think it still is something that builds us, and that we seek, and that allowed our families to survive is an attachment to the land.

Autumn: Yes! My family owns land in Alabama and I've learned recently that the way they acquired it was through enslavement. So, the slave owner had children with his White wife, in addition to my great, great, great, great, great grandmother through forced means. And when he died, he left land to all of his children. The Black folks got far less land, but it's still there. And part of the reason my family holds onto it is that it's a form of resistance. Because these White folks have been trying to get what they believe is their land back for decades. And so, I think that's even where my dad's love for and interest in gardening comes from. This idea that there's this connection to this land and he has a right to cultivate land, and to gain sustenance from it. But even seeing this image, again in the bottom left corner, the words, "nature," and "water," and "movement." That's so important. And I think what's starting to stick out about the colors to me is the fact that they are kind of this imagination of other worlds. A lot of the colors of outside, unless they are photographs, are not colors that we would expect to see every day, or if we do we marvel at them. This purplish pink sky is something that you would see in outer space (see J in Figure 4.1). This yellow sky, this orange and yellow sky (see D in Figure 4.1), and even this star with the rainbow coming from it (see H in Figure 4.1), this shooting star, they are clearly imagining spaces that are beyond what currently exists.

Grace: I created this art piece for one of my friends, a collage. It actually reminds me a lot of this, and now that you're saying that about the collage being otherworldly, I think this combination of the flowers and the flowers being a different, kind of oddness of it, the kind of twisting up, is beyond reality, beyond what we actually would find on the earth but still using these beautiful components of the earth to create it. So it's that remix.

Autumn: In this Unnormal Sisterhood picture in the middle (see G in Figure 4.1), what are these things that are on the wall?

Grace: Oh that's hair.

Autumn: That's what I thought. Okay.

Grace: Yeah. It's all hair. So we were creating logos, to represent us, and that's what one of them created. Seraphina actually created it as a symbol of us. I don't know where that blonde person came from (laughs). Do you see any blondes in here?

Autumn: I think the other thing that sticks out to me is just the joy across. The joy and the peace. The words "laughter" and "community," in this top left picture (see A in Figure 4.1), and the images of these Black women and their smiles and the care that they have for one another. In this painting that you have of the two girls (see C in Figure 4.1), where the one's arm is kind of reaching out and touching the other. There are these instances of care throughout. And then this Black "self-love questionnaire," (see K in Figure 4.1) they created a video where they interviewed their classmates about what they believe self-love is for Black folks. Even the care they put into developing the questions and spending time asking, and listening, and then putting together a video to say "your words are important." This is so rich.

Grace: When I was creating that piece, it was for a friend who was going through some stuff, I was like, "Let me put together something that is nature, is kind of flighty." It's kind of projecting her into a place that's beautiful, and colorful, and bright. On that note, thinking about care and the way that so many of these do represent care, touching, tenderness, being together, community, even with both the logo that we have right here with hair. The way that it's kind of reclining too, I feel like that is, reclining is relaxation, being at peace, being calm, being safe. So the fact that the hair looks like it's people lying down, like the hair out as being in recline, and then, the painting with the girls in recline and reaching to each other, that being able to be and respond, being able to relax is movement as well as relaxation. What do our bodies need? They need to rest. They also love to move; that combination and the juxtaposition of both climbing trees and relaxing. In this one in the corner, "dancing," "moving my body," as well as this feeling, the "loving yourself" picture (see A in Figure 4.1) of just being out there and just doing what your body needs to do, I think is another really important part of this. Both our environments, as well as what our bodies are able to do in those environments, is seeking what we need, whether it's rest, whether it's movement, whether it's joyful explosions, whether it's reaching to another person, I feel all of those are symbols of care, both for ourselves and for each other.

Autumn: And I think there's something, too, about how our bodies feel in those spaces, because like you said, the body language of reaching out to one another or being reclined, or even on the very bottom there's this picture of folks outside and dancing and on the playlist (see J in Figure 4.1), there is Beyonce's "My Power." As I think about the lyrics of that song, she says, "You'll never take my power." The images of the girls' selfies, where they're looking at themselves and they're clearly confident in doing so. There's something about the ways that when we feel community, when we feel nourished, when we feel at rest, we do feel powerful and we feel strong and capable of everything. And it makes me think of Halliday and Brown's (2018) piece about Nicki Minaj's "Feelin' Myself" and how that song is an anthem. The music throughout makes me think of soundtracks and the sounds that we hear when we're in these spaces. It's clear that there's laughter, but there's also music and joy and celebration in all of these things as well.

Grace: It's making me think there's something about being allowed to be full, being allowed to be complex, being allowed to be multiple things and naming and seeking, and being able to get what you need. Whether that is, thinking about these sounds and what music is and brings to us, or how it allows us to have this full range of emotions. This full, joyful, sad, angry, all of these things that we need and that we are. And I think that these spaces do that for us. We're allowed to experience a full range of emotions, of needs, of relationships within these spaces. Thinking about a soundtrack and what an arc of a soundtrack is, how that allows us to travel through such a range of things. So you have your slow jams but you also have your anthems.

Autumn: Yeah! I see India.Arie, and then I also see SZA, and Kalila, and Summer Walker on here (see J in Figure 4.1). So there's this past, this present-ness and this futurity of what music is and where the sound is going.

Grace: And the way music transports us to a time and place. Certain songs are always going to remind me of certain people, certain places. It allows you to have that connection, even if you're alone, you're still "Oh man, that song brings me back to that place." It's transportational through time and space, which I really, I think there's something there.

Autumn: So, if we're looking at this collage, what do we think it's telling us about what these joyful outer spaces that we create with girls of color *should* look like?

Grace: So I think they should be spaces that do take into consideration the full range of needs and desires of girls of color, spaces that allow for girls to name who they are, what they are, where they are, and what they need in any given moment without putting constraints on that.

Autumn: I think also they should be, like Tamara Butler says, green spaces (Player et al., 2022). And to add to that, colorful spaces and spaces that allow them to see all the brilliance in terms of intelligence, but also in terms of brightness of who they are. If I think about a classroom, and how often classrooms are these four walls and this dull color that is so antithetical to everything they've created here. So how do we transport them to spaces, whether outside of the building or even transform spaces, if we're talking about schools, inside of the building, and if not how do we bring those spaces to life together? I'm thinking a lot about physical space and how physical space often determines how I feel. If I think of some of the Black woman-owned yoga studios I've practiced at, my soul feels at peace. And it's because of the way the owners set up the physical space. Looking here, I think they're telling us a lot about the physical spaces that they need to feel seen, to feel safe, to feel nurtured, to be able to rest, to be able to show love and care for one another.

Grace: You're even making me think about how classrooms are set up. So many classrooms are set up as desks and rows, which is again such a confining, restrictive configuration of space.

Whereas, what if we had cozy corners and places where girls could recline, where they could also get up and dance, where they could move, where they weren't told you have to sit down, you have to be here, you have to be there, but they had choice about what their bodies needed, what their souls needed, what they needed to do in any given time. And also, noise. In so many classrooms, the teacher's voice is the dominant thing and everything else is punishable. So what if spaces were spaces where girls had the authority over when they wanted to make noise, when they wanted to be quiet, how they wanted to make noise, whether through music, through laughter, through talk, through gossip, or through purposeful silence. I think all of those things are such important parts of the sonic quality of a classroom or any space is so important. Thinking about that scene in *Pose* (Our Lady J., 2018–2021) when for the women, I think they're in Montauk, they're out in Long Island somewhere, in a little preppy beach town, and they're making noise, and laughing, and having joy, and this woman comes up and she's like, "You are disturbing our dinner." And the character, Elektra, tells her about herself. It's just such a claiming of space and claiming of being able to make the sound, share with laughter, and talk, and conversation. All of these things that we exude and that so many people try to take away from us. What if we just had the spaces where we could make all the noise or claim all the silence we needed.

Autumn: Something about what you just said, also made me think about the conferences we attend and the way silence and noise are politicized in those spaces. What would it even mean to disrupt those spaces and to present on something like this in a joyful way, in a way that is representative of the work that we're presenting, that includes music and color. Our experiences are sensory. They are multimodal in the most literal sense. I remember you talking about you having food for the girls when they would come in (Player, 2021b). My girls and I sat around the table with food each week (Griffin, 2020). What does it mean to disrupt the ways we gather? I remember both growing up and now observing schools seeing so many teachers reprimand kids for having food. There was this discussion at the beginning of the pandemic, you can't eat on camera. I'm in my house. You're going to tell me I can't eat? And so creating spaces means being able to also nourish our bodies in the way that we need when we need to, while we're doing this work.

Grace: When we think about things like the kitchen table or all of these spaces, these are spaces of nourishment. If we can nourish our bodies, we can nourish our minds. But if we are saying, "No, this is what we do in school," or "What we do when we learn is sit there and be quiet." How is that learning? Thinking about the food and back to that picture in the corner, I think it's dancing and moving my body, that's about health and taking care of your body, lots of laughter, let's center joy. Black girl community, let's be with one another. "Nature," "water," and then "chocolate and food please." These are all of the things that pretty much sums it up. Bodily nourishment, right to bodily movement, right

to being outdoors, right to water, water is life. I feel like this right there pretty much sums it up. That is the outer space.
Autumn: That is the outer space, that *is* the blueprint.
Grace: When you said colorful spaces, I think that's what that is. We are able to color our spaces and when we do that, that's joy.

YOU CAN'T BUST UP OUR BUBBLE

Black girl be in a bubble, bubble
Floating quietly out of trouble, trouble
They call you shy
Always ask why you listen before you speak
Black girl braids filled with bubbles, bubbles
Jump in puddles in double, double
How many different oils we know, we know?
To turn our skin from brown to gold

Na na na na na na na na na na na
You can't bust up my bubble busta
You can't bust up my bubble
You can't bust up my bubble
You can't bust up my bubble
You can't bust up my bubble
—Jamila Woods, 2016

Above, we drew upon collaging (Evans-Winters, 2019) and discursive multimodal analysis to explore the outer spaces girls of color create, choosing specifically to draw on the discursive practices of our own foremothers; the once girls of color—now women of color—who first taught us how to be and who we be. As we noted, these spaces are colorful and center joy, care, love, celebration, and healing. These spaces hold a type of literacy learning that exists within our varied homeplaces (hooks, 1990) and are often so much more than meets the eye. As girls of color transform their worlds, they meet one another in outer spaces of their own creation. The image below (Figure 4.2), created by Grace, depicts the hands of a Black girl, sitting outside, in the green, while creating a girls of color outer space on her device. The worlds girls of color create are layered, transportational, colorful, dynamic, and transport us through time, space, and dimension. The image below invokes color, peace, care, rest, and creation. It implies that the work of girls of color happens both in the spaces we create physically, and in the ones they choose to create virtually. It implies that our communities are boundless and that our work is always that of world building. This image

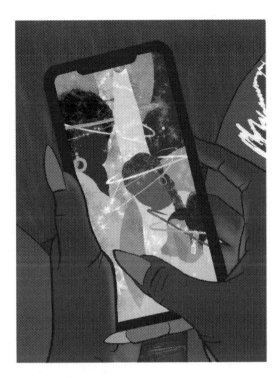

Figure 4.2 A Black girl creates an outer space.

beautifully summarizes the work of the girls with whom we've created and is just a glimpse of who they are.

Jamila Woods sings of Black girls creating bubbles that simply can't be busted by anyone. These are bubbles in which Black girls shine, play, listen, and float quietly away from worlds troubled by White heteronormative patriarchal violence to those that take up care, rest, and love. We call on educators, particularly women of color educators, to *continue* to build the spaces of protection, thriving, love, and joy that girls of color desire, create, and imagine. We can do this work by attending to the mosaics of girls of color genius they constantly create with their multimodal literate engagements with the world—the way they move, draw, speak, write, sing, build, and style. As they create these spaces, girls of color can engage in the work of future gazing to build and sustain futures and worlds in their own images; futures and worlds that not only include them, but are stylized by and for them (Campt, 2017; Jemison, 2013; Thomas, 2019). Thus, returning to the words of Woods, first called into conversation at the beginning of this chapter, we contend that our outer spaces exist, on jet planes, on private planets, and in our own bubbles. And you can't bust up our bubble. Na.

REFERENCES

Akom, A. A., Cammarota, J., & Ginwright, S. (2008). Youthtopias: Towards a new paradigm of critical youth studies. *Youth Media Reporter, 2*(4), 1–30. http://www.youthmediareporter.org/2008/08/15/youthtopias-towards-a-new-paradigm-of-critical-youth-studies/

Anzaldúa, G. (2015). *Light in the dark/luz en lo oscuro: Rewriting identity, spirituality, reality* (A. Keating, Ed.). Duke University Press.

Brown, R. N. (2013). *Hear our truths: The creative potential of Black girlhood.* University of Illinois Press.

Butler, T. (2018). Black girl cartography: Black girlhood and place-making in education research. *Review of Research in Education, 42*(1), 28–45. https://doi.org/10.3102/0091732X18762114

Campt, T. M. (2017). *Listening to images.* Duke University Press.

Coles, J. A. (2021). Black desire: Black-centric youthtopias as critical race educational praxis. *International Journal of Qualitative Studies in Education,* 1–22. https://doi.org/10.1080/09518398.2021.1888163

Coles, J. A., & Kingsley, M. (2021). Blackness as intervention: Black English outer spaces and the rupturing of antiblackness and/in English education. *English Teaching: Practice and Critique, 20*(4), 454–484. https://doi.org/10.1108/ETPC-10-2020-0135

Collins, P. H. (1991). *Black feminist thought: Knowledge, consciousness, and the politics of empowerment.* Routledge.

Davis, P. G. (2020). Spatiality at the cyber-margins: Black-oriented blogs and the production of territoriality online. *Social Media + Society, 6*(2), 1–10. https://doi.org/10.1177/2056305120928506

Dotson, K. (2013). Knowing in space: Three lessons from Black women's social theory [Unpublished manuscript]. http://ssrn.com/abstract=2270343

Evans-Winters, V. E. (2019). *Black feminism in qualitative inquiry: A mosaic for writing our daughter's body.* Routledge.

Flores, T. T. (2021). Somos escritoras/We are writers: Latina mothers and daughters writing and sharing "En convivencia." *Urban Education, 57*(10). https://doi.org/10.1177/0042085921100392

Gonzales, L., González Ybarra, M., & The Fugitive Literacies Collective. (2020). Multimodal cuentos as fugitive literacies on the Mexico-U.S. borderlands. *English Education, 52*(3), 223–255. https://www.proquest.com/openview/da410d6384a0aa6a5a8619ee73c7decc/1?pq-origsite=gscholar&cbl=34722

Griffin, A. (2020). *Finding love in a hopeless place: Black girls' twenty-first century self-love literacies* (UMI No. 20700) [Doctoral dissertation, University of Maryland–College Park]. ProQuest Dissertations and Theses Database.

Griffin, A. A. (2021). Black parade: Conceptualizing Black adolescent girls' multimodal renderings as parades. *Urban Education, 57*(10). https://doi.org/10.1177/00420859211003944

Griffin, A. A., & Turner, J. D. (2022). E-racing false narratives: A Black woman track star's multimodal counterstory of possible futures. *International Journal of Qualitative Studies in Education.* https://doi.org/10.1080/09518398.2022.2100506

Haddix, M., McArthur, S. A., Muhammad, G. E., Price-Dennis, D., & Sealey-Ruiz, Y. (2016). At the kitchen table: Black women English educators speaking our truths. *English Education, 48*(4), 380–395. https://www.proquest.com/docview/1808333798

Halliday, A. S., & Brown, N. E. (2018). The power of Black girl magic anthems: Nicki Minaj, Beyoncé, and "feeling myself" as political empowerment. *Souls: A Critical Journal of Black Politics, Culture, and Society, 20*(2), 222–238. https://doi.org/10.1080/10999949.2018.1520067

hooks, b. (1990). Homeplace (A site of resistance). In *Yearning: Race, gender, and cultural politics* (pp. 382–390). South End Press.

Jemison, N. K. (2013, September 30). *How long 'til Black future month?: The Toxins of speculative fiction, and the antidote that is Janelle Monae.* https://nkjemisin.com/2013/09/how-long-til-black-future-month/

Kelly, L. (2020). "I love us for real": Exploring homeplace as a site for healing and resistance for Black girls in schools. *Equity & Excellence in Schools, 53*(4), 450–465. https://doi.org/10.1080/10665684.2020.1791283

Kynard, C. (2010). From candy girls to cyber sista-cypher: Narrating Black females' color-consciousness and counterstories in and out of school. *Harvard Educational Review, 80*(1), 30–52. https://doi.org/10.17763/haer.80.1.4611255014427701

Lawrence-Lightfoot, S., & Davis, J. H. (1997). *The art and science of portraiture.* Jossey-Bass.

Lorde, A. (2007). *Sister outsider: Essays and speeches by Audre Lorde.* Crossing Press.

Love, B. (2019). *We want to do more than survive: Abolitionist teaching and the pursuit of educational freedom.* Beacon Press.

Lyiscott, J., & The Fugitive Literacies Collective. (2020). Fugitive literacies as inscriptions of freedom. *English Education, 52*(3), 256–263. https://library-ncte-org.ezproxy.lib.uconn.edu/journals/EE/issues/v52-3/30598

Lyiscott, J., Green, K. L., Ohito, E. O., & Coles, J. A. (2021). Call us by our names: Kitchen-table dialogue on doin' it for the culture. *Equity and Excellence in Education, 54*(1). https://doi.org/10.1080/10665684.2021.1877867

McKittrick, K., & Woods, C. (2007). No one knows the mysteries at the bottom of the ocean. In K. McKittrick & C. Woods (Eds.), *Black geographies and the politics of place* (pp. 1–13). South End Press.

Moraga, C. (1983). Refugees of a world on fire: Forward to the second edition. In C. Moraga & G. Anzaldúa (Eds.), *This bridge called my back: Writings by radical women of color* (2nd ed., n.p.). Third Woman Press.

Morales, A. L. (2001). My name is this story. In *Telling to live: Latina feminist testimonios* (pp. 88–103). Duke University Press.

Muhammad, G. E. (2012). Creating spaces for Black adolescent girls to "write it out!" *Journal of Adolescent & Adult Literacy, 56*(3), 203–211.

Nelson, A. N. [@blackforager] (n.d.). *Posts* [Instagram profile]. Retrieved October 4, 2021, from https://www.instagram.com/blackforager/

Ohito, E. (2020). "The creative aspect woke me up": Awakening to multimodal essay composition as a fugitive literacy practice. *English Education, 52*(3), 186–222. https://library-ncte-org.ezproxy.lib.uconn.edu/journals/EE/issues/v52-3/30596

Our Lady J. (Executive Producer). (2018–2021). *Pose* [TV series]. FX. https://www.fxnetworks.com/shows/pose/crew/our-lady-j-producer-writer

Patel, L. (2019). Fugitive practices: Learning in a settler colony. *Educational Studies, 55*(3), 253–261. https://doi.org/10.1080/00131946.2019.1605368

Player, G. D. (2021a). "People get mistaken": Asian American girls using multiple literacies to defy dominant imaginings of Asian American girlhood. *Reading Research Quarterly, 57*(2), 431–448. https://doi.org/10.1002/rrq.412

Player, G. D. (2021b). "My color of my name": Composing critical self-celebration with girls of color through a feminist of color writing pedagogy. *Research in the Teaching of English, 55*(3), 216–240. https://library-ncte-org.ezproxy.lib.uconn.edu/journals/RTE/issues/v55-3/31184

Player, G. D., Coles, J. A., González Ybarra, M. G., & The Fugitive Literacies Collective. (2020). Enacting educational fugitivity with youth of color: A statement/love letter from the Fugitive Literacies Collective. *The High School Journal, 103*(3), 140–156. https://doi.org/10.1353/hsj.2020.0009

Player, G. D., & González Ybarra, M. G (2021). Re-imagining literacy and language education for girls of color. *Urban Education, 57*(10). https://doi.org/10.1177/00420859211003924

Player, G. D., González Ybarra, M. G., Brochin, C., Brown, R. N., Butler, T. T., Cervantes-Soon, Gill, S. V. Kinloch, V., Price-Dennis, D., Saavedra, C. M., & Sealey-Ruiz, Y. (2022). "We are our only way forward": Dialogic re-imaginings and the cultivation of homeplace for girls, women, and femmes of color. *Urban Education, 57*(10), 1784–1804. https://doi.org/10.1177/00420859211003931

Price-Dennis, D., & Muhammad, G. E. (Eds.). (2021). *Black Girls' Literacies: Transforming Lives and Literacy Practices*. Routledge.

Rolling, J. H. (2013). *Arts-based research primer*. Peter Lang.

Thomas, E. E. (2019). *The dark fantastic: Race and the imagination from Harry Potter to the Hunger Games*. NYU Press.

Toliver, S. R. (2021). Afrocarnival: Celebrating Black bodies and critiquing oppressive bodies in Afrofuturist literature. *Children's Literature in Education, 52*, 132–148. https://doi.org/10.1007/s10583-020-09403-y

Toliver, S. R. (2022). "Dreamland": Black girls saying and creating space through fantasy worlds. *Girlhood Studies, 15*(1), 17–33. https://doi.org/10.3167/ghs.2022.150103

Turner, J. D., & Griffin, A. A. (2020). Brown girls dreaming: Adolescent Black girls' futuremaking through multimodal representations of race, gender, and career aspirations. *Research in the Teaching of English, 55*(2), 109–133. https://library-ncte-org.ezproxy.lib.uconn.edu/journals/RTE/issues/v55-2/31020

Woods, J. (2016). *Heavn* [Album]. Jagjaguwar.

CHAPTER 5

MULTIMODALITY AS ACCESSIBILITY

A Critical Perspective of Universal Design in Theory, Research, and Practice

Kyesha M. Isadore
University of Wisconsin-Madison

Angélica Galván
California State University, Northridge

ABSTRACT

Disability studies provide us with a framework to understand accessibility within educational contexts and the role of multimodal accommodations in creating equitable spaces (Evans et al., 2017). Accessibility often centers individual accommodations to support students with different ability statuses; namely, students with disabilities. However, the onus to be adaptable and acquire accommodations regularly falls on individual students and fails to critique the environment which creates the conditions that require accommodations. The capaciousness of multimodality diverts the responsibility to the educational system to provide multiple modalities including text, visual, audio, and sensory within learning environments and in the development of physical and online spaces. The presence of multiple modalities, despite differing needs by ability status, would create a structure that leads to increased student agency and the opportunity of different perspectives and interpretations within educational spaces.

Universal design is "the design of products and environments to be usable by all people, to the greatest extent possible, without the need for adaptation or specialized design" (Connell et al., 1997, para. 7). The seven principles of design include equitable use, flexibility in use, simple and intuitive use, perceptible information, tolerance for error, low physical effort, and size and space for approach and use. A critical approach requires recognition of both environmental conditions that create inaccessible educational spaces and internal beliefs and attitudes that exclude and demean marginalized students. Evans et al. (2017) provide three principles for universal design grounded in social justice:

1. understanding the role that power and privilege have played in excluding nondominant groups, including students with disabilities;
2. affirmation that individuals are unique and worthy of respect from those around them, and that their voices should be included in any discussion of issues that affect them; and
3. recognition that disability is largely an environmental condition—although aspects of individual impairments can play a role in disability—and that the environment needs to be changed to provide equitable educational opportunities for all students.

Building off Evans et al. (2017) principles, we hope to expand the understanding of universal design to benefit all students despite ability status through a critical lens. Through expanding on the seven principles of universal design, we will provide a critical multimodal view of each principle that expands the capacity for universal design to be applied in theory, research, and practice.

The goals of this chapter are to (a) describe current research on accessibility and universal design in educational spaces; (b) describe of role of multimodality as accessibility; (c) provide a critical lens of universal design and apply the seven principles of universal design to theory, research, and practice; and (d) outline examples of modalities that can be applied in theory, research, and practice through an accessible lens.

Critical disability studies provide us with a framework to understand accessibility within educational contexts and the role of multimodality in creating equitable spaces (Evans et al., 2017). Accessibility often centers on individual accommodations to support students with different ability statuses, namely students with disabilities. However, the onus to be adaptable and inquire about accommodations regularly falls on individual students and fails to critique the environment, which creates the conditions that require accommodations through the social model of disability (Shakespeare,

2017). The capaciousness of multimodality diverts the responsibility to the educational system to provide multiple modalities including text, visual, audio, and sensory input within learning environments and in the development of physical and online spaces. The presence of various modalities, despite differing needs by ability status, would create a structure that leads to increased student agency and the opportunity for different perspectives and interpretations within educational spaces.

Multimodality is central to critical disability studies as multimodality holds the basic assumption that meanings are made through many representational and communicational resources (Jewitt, 2008); while critical disability studies question how systems of power interact to decide which representational and communication resources are provided, which largely excludes people with disabilities. Universal design (UD) contrasts this exclusion as its principles aim to create products and structures that are usable by all people without the need for accommodation or changes (Connell et al., 1997). The principles of UD include equitable use, flexibility in use, simple and intuitive use, perceptible information, tolerance for error, low physical effort, and size and space for approach and use. These principles have been applied to education, however, a critical approach to UD requires recognition of both environmental conditions that create inaccessible educational spaces and the importance of providing individual accommodations required by students with disabilities.

These concepts are important to us, authors, as educators and clinicians specializing in the needs of students with disabilities and other marginalized students due to race, ethnicity, sexual orientation, and other minoritized identities. We see first-hand how ableist perspectives in education cause additional barriers for students with disabilities, and we know the importance of a critical perspective to incite impactful change. We believe in the dismantling of barriers because of our own experiences benefiting from multimodal resources and the engagement of our own literacies in these modes as we have varying abilities and cultural backgrounds. In addition, as educators, we have seen the benefits firsthand as students engage differently when they have options that increase accessibility.

By discussing critical approaches to UD with critical disability studies as our theoretical framework, we hope to expand the understanding of UD to center students with disabilities through a critical lens. We theorize the ways that accessibility can be expanded as multimodality to provide a more critical foundation of UD and universal design for learning (UDL) that emphasize social and cultural contexts for students with disabilities. This chapter will describe the role of multimodality as accessibility, provide a brief history of UD/UDL, and discuss critical perspectives on UD/UDL. As we expand on accessibility, multimodality, and UD/UDL, implications for theory, research, and practice will be discussed throughout the chapter.

MULTIMODALITY AS ACCESSIBILITY

Kress and colleagues (2005) define a mode as the name given to the culturally shaped resources for making meaning and and using the prefix, *multi*, referring to how modes never appear in isolation, but always in relation to others. A multimodal approach is "one where attention is given to all the culturally shaped resources that are available for making meaning" (Kress et al., 2005, p. 2). Multimodality, therefore, is described by the "presence and use of a multiplicity of modes" (Kress et al., 2005, p. 2). Educational spaces that are not accessible often lack a multimodal approach where the culturally shaped resources provided for meaning making are not available or accessible for students with disabilities. This oversight burdens students with disabilities to adapt to a limiting educational environment. The presence of multiple modalities, despite differing needs by ability status, would create a structure that leads to increased student agency and the opportunity for different perspectives and interpretations within educational spaces, while also increasing accessibility specifically for students with disabilities.

With the creation of multiple modes comes "modal preferences" (Kress, 2010, p. 83) which dictate the use of specific modes for certain purposes. Kress (2010) expands on the concept of modal preferences as influenced by community:

> *Socially*, what counts as mode is a matter for a community and its social-representational needs. What a community decides to regard and use as mode *is* mode. If the community of designers have a need to develop the potentials of *font* or of *color* into full means for representation, then *font* and *color* will be mode in that community. Of course, their decision to do this will not be confined to that community alone: anyone who comes into contact with their work will become affected by that decision. (p. 87, emphasis in original)

The presence of power is central to multimodality because the "community of designers," described by Kress (2010), decides what and how modes are created which impact an entire community and those who enter that community. The influence of community within the inception of multimodal preferences yields multimodal interpretations which are socially constructed and dependent on cultural experiences within that community. The utility of modes continuously transforms along the lines of "the social requirements of those who make meanings" (Kress, 2010 p. 82) in which modes are aligned with social practices and social change insofar as whatever is not a social need is not materialized into a mode. This is significant to the concept of accessibility because modes can be created, shifted, and transformed to create or limit access. Individuals with this power to create or limit access are parallel to those with power to create, shift, and transform educational spaces through multimodality.

Historically, accessibility has been centered on physical access into buildings, but has broadened to include access in multiple forms. In an effort to expand the notion of accessibility away from solely wheelchair access and towards sensory and cognitive levels of accessibility, Ford (2013) coined the term *deep accessibility* to explore the difference between places or events that are accessible to various people and those individuals being able to make meaning from that experience, versus a place or event that is difficult to enter, confusing, or unavailable. Dolmage (2017, p. 118) summarized Ford's five levels of deep accessibility:

1. Movement—getting there—how we get to an event or class.
2. Sense—being there—how we access the material, the conversation.
3. Architecture—orienting—how the space and layout structure our belonging and understanding.
4. Communication—how we join the conversation, engage, understand and are understood.
5. Agency—autonomy—how we can come to have a shaping role in the event or class, as well as the right to define our own identity and involvement.

Each level of deep accessibility represents specific modes that require a shift from rigid, stagnant modes, to modes that can be transformed and adaptable for people with disabilities. Each level contains modal preferences which relate to the utilization of modes for a specific purpose. At the movement level, accessibility is related to physically accessing a space—getting everywhere, being able to move around, reach, and navigate the space. The Americans With Disabilities Act (1990) outlines design standards regarding the appropriate width, height, and size of ramps, doorways, handles, bookshelves, hallways, elevators, and so forth. Within this level, we can understand the modal preferences in which architectural designers can design physical spaces using dominant modes such as signage, lighting, and physical layout.

At the sense level, accessibility is related to when a person can be present in a space and distinguish multiple relevant modes while avoiding a sensory overload. Modal preferences that should be interrogated at the sense level include sound, lighting, smell, and modes of communication. This can directly benefit students with sensory disorders, cognitive or developmental disabilities, psychiatric disabilities, and processing disorders. By understanding the sensory level of accessibility, educators can provide access to multimodal stimuli and resources to meet students' specific needs in educational spaces.

Accessibility at the architectural level is linked to "the emotional state of the person in relation to the function of the space, or the question of how the space leads people into its function" (Ford, 2013, "Architecture

– orienting," para. 1). Within this level, function itself can be seen as a mode that is predicated upon not just the function of the physical building or space, but as a way for individuals to organize the space into its functions. The function, therefore, is made up of multiple modes such as the size of spaces, colors, windows, the flow of people, signage, and heights (Ford, 2013). The space would be considered accessible if students are able to organize it into its functions just by looking and/or feeling the space, without reading or language.

At the communication level, accessibility is related to whether an individual can make themselves understood and understand others in the space. Language is the primary modal preference in this level, which is composed of other modes including images, speech, and writing. Ford (2013) described organizational schemes that allow individuals to understand a space in its own terms and structures. Ford provides a stark example:

> There is a scheme for using a library, that most people know only because they have been taught it explicitly: you browse for as long as you want; you are allowed to read books in the library without checking them out; you are not supposed to re-shelve them yourself; and so on. An accessible library might prominently explain that scheme and not just expect people to know. People who are autistic can often miss the scheme for spaces such as entertainment venues, hospitals, or other places with a fairly complex set of expectations. The act of ordering an item in an unfamiliar eating establishment, for example, can be impossible for someone who doesn't know the terminology; they may not understand what the staff is saying to them. So, being able to know the scheme for a place is an essential part of accessibility. ("Communication," para. 2)

The concept of organizational schemes is related to the mode of language in that individuals must be aware of and understand the scheme to understand and make themselves understood in the space. For this to occur, there must be sufficient time and space for individuals to understand the scheme which may involve talking, typing, or signing (Ford, 2013). The social and cultural characteristics of multimodality are imperative when considering the communicational level of accessibility which is dependent on how students interpret the modes available to them. Since multimodal interpretations are socially constructed, educators must understand who their students are and create a space that is inclusive of all their identities in order to understand themselves and others in the space.

Accessibility at the agency level relates to individuals having autonomy over their own experience and control over their ability to "participate and achieve the results they want equally to others...it's about the program and power dynamics" (Ford, 2013, "Agency – autonomy," para. 1). Modal preferences in this level can include personal physical space, time, power, and representation. Ford discusses that an inaccessible space at this level may have commonalities with an abusive relationship, for example, due to the similar loss of perspective as those who are denied access may lose their sense of self-worth. Continuing with this logic, autonomy within accessible spaces is predicated upon power dynamics and privileges of those within the space, which is not determined solely by ability status, but the multiplicity of identities students hold, and the amount of power shared by educators.

Critical Disability Studies

Critical disability studies posit a method for questioning how systems of power operate and critiques social norms and social structures that stigmatize certain populations (Minich, 2016). Critical disability studies offer a framework to shift how accessibility and UD/UDL are conceptualized and practiced within educational contexts and allows us to consider the role of multimodal accommodations by centering students with disabilities. Central to critical disability studies is the acknowledgement of how ableism, or systemic oppression against people with disabilities, is embedded throughout the educational system and the ways in which the role of the environment shapes how disability itself is socially constructed. Multimodality is fundamental to critical disability studies in which critical disability studies are predicated upon the addition, subtraction, shifting, and adjustment of modes.

As multimodality and critical disability studies both emphasize the role of power and cultural contexts, a multimodal approach that does not center students with disabilities may perpetuate ableism and exclude students with disabilities in educational spaces. Critical disability studies provide a useful framework in which to explore multimodality as accessibility because it

> aims to situate understandings of disability not just in the body or the environment, but in how specific bodies are understood in context, how they move or do not move, how they interface with social structures, the self, and power. (McRae, 2019, p. 221)

This understanding of bodies within their context relates to the levels of deep accessibility and the function of modes as they are used to create meaning and determine what is worth attributing meaning to.

A BRIEF HISTORY OF UNIVERSAL DESIGN

As we begin to consider a critical perspective of UD and UDL, it is important to understand the history of access and how policy changes were made to better understand how far we have come and what changes continue to be necessary. This historical view will shape how our understanding of accessibility has evolved and how it must continue to develop in order to fit the needs of students with disabilities. In educational settings, the importance of multimodality is highlighted within the introduction of UD to physical spaces. Although its implementation is recent, the implications were and will continue to be instrumental in physical accessibility and accessible education for students with disabilities. UD had a tremendous impact on physical access as disability was mostly viewed as a person's individual challenge to overcome rather than an environmental and social issue. To fully appreciate this impact, we will highlight a few historical events.

The onset of the philosophy of UD appears at varying times in history due to specific events such as the return of injured veterans after World War II, advocacy efforts for barrier-free access in the 1950s, recognition of access exclusion in the 1970s, advocacy for aging populations in the 1980s, and the passage of the Americans With Disabilities Act in the 1990s ([ADA]; Catanese, 2012). These different groups (injured veterans, aging populations, etc.) had to advocate for their rights at different points in time. Although other federal legislation existed, the ADA was widely recognized as a push for the civil rights of people with disabilities (Simmons, 2020). With these historical shifts and the introduction of the ADA, physical spaces began to adapt to the needs of people with disabilities. Public buildings and spaces then included ramps, elevators, building markings, and wider doorways to increase access (Pisha & Coyne, 2001). Here is where we begin to see multimodality enacted within physical spaces.

Robert Mace, an architect, coined the term *universal design* as he envisioned accessibility as a concept in architecture to be implemented throughout the design process, which would increase accessibility for everyone (Dalton et al., 2019; Pisha & Coyne, 2001). However, this view was still limited to only those with physical disabilities and lacked consideration of how social and cultural factors affect how individuals interact with their environment.

Before using the term universal design, other designers were instrumental in developing the philosophy of UD. One such visionary was Marc Harrison, who began rethinking design after his own experiences with rehabilitation and recovery, and having had the experience of limited access. At age 11, Harrison had to relearn how to walk and talk due to a traumatic brain injury after a sledding accident (Catanese, 2012). These experiences increased his awareness of design needs, which led him to pioneer changes in design aimed to help people with disabilities that would also be useful for others without disabilities in the 1960s and 70s. In the 1970s and 80s, Richard Hollerith, another designer, took this perspective a step further by approaching the needs of people with disabilities from an inclusive perspective. Hollerith emphasized the ableist view of design that prevents accessibility in product development. He proposed that product design "should be designed for those with disabilities while keeping the able-bodied in mind" (Catanese, 2012, p. 214). This ground-breaking perspective led UD to become the desired approach to enhance access to people with disabilities and a step closer to inclusive design for all.

Establishing Universal Design as a Design Approach

UD refers to product and environmental designs that make items and structures functional for as many people without additional changes. Its implementation reduces physical and attitudinal barriers for all people, as it is a human-centered design that considers how individuals change over time and may need adjustments to access their environment due to injury, aging, or physical and health changes. UD is an approach with a social consciousness that blurs the environmental differences for individuals with special access needs (Catanese, 2012). With these aims in mind, Robert Mace helped establish the Center for Universal Design at North Carolina State University (Simmons, 2020). The Center for Universal Design identifies seven principles of UD in the environment, and in 1997 released its second iteration. These principles marked a shift in focus on accessibility and include:

1. equitable use as design was aimed for its usability and marketability to people with disabilities;
2. flexibility in use to accommodate fluctuating preferences and abilities;
3. simple and intuitive use that is easy to understand by users regardless of their previous experiences, language proficiency, or concentration at time of use;
4. perceptible information to have effective communication regardless of ambient challenges or user's sensory ability;
5. tolerance for error to minimize hazards and accidents;
6. low physical effort to promote efficiency and minimum fatigue; and
7. appropriate size and space for approach and use regardless of body size or mobility.

The introduction of the seven principles of UD requires a multimodal shift for the "community of designers" (Kress, 2010, p. 87) to consider how modal preferences and the five levels of deep accessibility must now transform to create spaces to be accessible for as many people. Since establishing the concept of UD, more features that increase access are seen in architecture. Many of these modal shifts are now widely used, such as curb cuts (depressed curb), ramps, automatic doors, rocker light switches (flat switches), and lever door handles, to name a few (Pisha & Coyne, 2001). These designs are not exclusive to people with disabilities, but they have the added benefit of destigmatizing specific disability types.

The Foundation of Universal Design for Learning

After the rise of UD in the architectural field, educational environments began to adopt similar principles. Like the consideration of universality in the design of products and buildings, universality and the inclusion of multimodality are considered in the instructional design of courses. The aim was then to design courses to fit the varying needs of students whether or not they had disabilities. UDL originated from research in neuroscience and questions around how the brain learns (the why, what, and how of learning). UDL applies concepts of inclusion and accessibility into education for people with different needs and addresses a broad range of barriers to learning and discriminatory practices (Dalton et al., 2019). Like the long history of ableist practices and the inclusion of declarations and legislation in physical spaces, access to education has a similar journey as UDL aspires to be a cornerstone for change of accessibility in education.

Since the Universal Declaration of Human Rights in 1948, education has been considered a right for all individuals (United Nations, 1948). Meanwhile, additional declarations and statements from the United Nations Educational, Scientific, and Cultural Organizations (UNESCO) have fortified the goals of adequate education. The World Declaration on Education for All (UNESCO, 1990) focused on inadequate education and the importance of literacy and basic education for social progress. The Salamanca Statement (UNESCO, 1994) attended to policy changes needed to promote inclusive education, particularly for those with special needs. The Dakar Framework for Action (UNESCO, 2000) underlined the specific requirements for each country to meet the goal of education for all and pledged to support those countries that needed resources. The Policy Guidelines on Inclusion in Education (UNESCO, 2009) reinforced the rights for individuals to have access to education, regardless of their ability. With these declarations, access to education, equity and opportunities, and rights to adequate and appropriate accommodations and support were at the forefront of the United Nations and their cause of ensuring the fundamental right to an education.

In the United States, similar gains were made with the addition of three laws that have been established to protect the rights of students with disabilities. These laws are Section 504 of the Rehabilitation Act of 1973, the

Individuals With Disabilities Education Act (IDEA) of 1975, the ADA of 1990, and their corresponding amendments.

Section 504 and the ADA are anti-discrimination laws that protect students against discrimination in education and public institutions due to disability, while IDEA mandates free appropriate education in the least restrictive environment for students with disabilities. To qualify for the IDEA, students must have a disability from 13 categories identified under this law and have a need for special education to make progress in school. These laws further encourage the inclusion of students with disabilities in education and the need for accommodations to support their success. However, the onus of requesting accommodations and supporting the requests with documentation still lies with the students or parents. Additionally, diverse learning needs are not always accommodated if they do not fall into one of the designated categories. This leaves students out of the conversation of inclusion if they do not fit into the status quo or have a documented disability in one of the preselected categories. These policies do not address social, cultural, and experiential components of how students learn.

Universal Design for Learning as a Framework

When considering the positive effects of UD to the environment for increased access, UDL is no different. Building education with accessibility in mind for students with disabilities can lead to a better equipped educational system that will support all students and teachers. UDL is a scientifically supported framework of educational instruction that is flexible and reduces barriers while maintaining expectations of developmentally appropriate achievement from students (King-Sears, 2014). It is considered universal when all students benefit from its application (Edyburn, 2021). UDL aims to support students and provide a scaffold education as they continue to build on what they have learned, including language learners (King-Sears, 2014; Ok et al., 2017). A leading source in the application of UDL is the Center for Applied Special Technology (CAST). Since the 1990s, CAST has developed and conducted research on UDL and has focused on the importance of flexibility that engages different learning networks and different learners (Ok et al., 2017). The CAST framework for UDL consists of three principles: multiple means of engagement (how students practice new content), multiple means of representation (how students take in new information), and multiple means of action and expression (how students show what they have learned). In addition, the CAST framework also contains nine guidelines and 31 checkpoints that are used to examine inclusive design (full guidelines can be found at https://udlguidelines.cast.org/). The framework has been previously updated to reflect societal and research-based changes. It is currently under review for a new edition that will consider systemic barriers and inequities in learning opportunities and outcomes (CAST, 2018).

UDL highlights three levels of deep accessibility including the sensory, communication, and autonomy levels which are reflected within the CAST framework. It considers how students access the course material through multiple means of engagement, how students engage in classroom conversations through multiple means of representation, and how students develop their position and autonomy within the course through multiple means of action and expression. The multiple means of engagement, representation, and action and expression represent a multimodal approach that considers the multiplicity of ways that students engage, interact, and are understood in educational spaces. UDL is imperative to consider as we expand our conceptualization of accessibility and consider the ways we can center students with disabilities in future systemic decisions.

CRITICAL PERSPECTIVES ON UD AND UDL

UD and UDL have been positioned as "the design of products and environments to be usable by all people, to the greatest extent possible, without the need for adaptation or specialized design" (Connell et al., 1997, n.p.). Expanding accessibility as a multimodal approach aligns with Connell and colleagues' (1997) intention of creating products and environments to be usable by all people. However, the qualifier of "without the need for adaptation or specialized design" inadvertently excludes students with disabilities who will need specific accommodations not covered through the implementation of UD and UDL. By viewing accessibility as multimodality, a critical approach to UDL requires educators to consider how we can expand our multimodal approach through the inclusion of students with disabilities throughout the design process. There have been many other critiques on the utility of UD and UDL and what they aim to accomplish. To understand the necessary trajectory of UD and UDL, we must view UD and UDL through a critical lens to understand why they need to evolve based on social and cultural contexts.

The universality of UD and UDL has been connected to a sense of normativity in which spaces are impossible to be rendered "usable by all people...without the need for adaptation" (Connell et al., 1997, para. 7). This impossibility erases students with disabilities because it aims to accommodate most students rather than to accommodate disability. Dolmage (2017) describes this as being mapped onto the three-part UDL approach in which "students are seen as specific types of receivers of representation, or they become specific types of expressers, or they are engagers" (p. 146). This erasure presents a major problem for those advocating for UD and UDL which can be addressed by explicitly linking learning strategies to disability needs and centering students in the design process (Dolmage, 2017).

The rejection of adaptable accessible design such as assistive technology and design features that are specifically created for people with disabilities is a major critique of the intention of UD and UDL. Erkilic (2012) stated,

> UD asks users with diverse abilities to adapt or modify themselves to the "design-for-all" products, which have been designed in the adaptable form (not in specialized form)... with this approach, it is not the physical environment but individual bodies, able-bodied, or disabled, that are to be 'adaptable' when using UD products. (p. 185)

Furthermore, with its centralization on "design for all," UD does not center adaptable design, which can include remodeling buildings or adjusting products for people with disabilities as a significant goal (Erkilic, 2012). This critique parallels those of other researchers and practitioners who believe that the broad nature of the goals of UD limit the impact to address specific issues faced by people with disabilities, particularly people with multiple marginalized identities (Evans et al., 2017). Dolmage (2005) argued that to address the limitations of UD, people with disabilities must be in

> the role not of consumers but of innovators or co-creators [which] can circumvent medical model thinking, confront paternal attitudes and shift entrenched roles and stereotypes. Usability-testing, when it allows for input from people with disabilities, can affirm human ingenuity and diversity and can confront mass-produced normativity. (para. 13)

As a result, students with various disability types should be included in all stages of the planning and development of designs for new built environments in educational settings and be asked for feedback when considering modifications to existing environments.

Another critique of UD and UDL is the checklist approach. Dolmage (2017) discussed the desire for spaces to conceptualize UD and UDL through a checklist approach which diverts UD and UDL from verbs to nouns and often presents itself as checklists for designing spaces that are accessible and usable. Dolmage argues, rather, "UD should be registered as action—a patterning of engagement and effort" (p. 145). This distinction is an important consideration because if UD and UDL are not intentionally implemented in a flexible and adaptable manner with the needs of students with disabilities at the forefront, then the implementation of UD and UDL can become monotonous and lose its intention of increasing accessibility.

Furthermore, UD does not explicitly require feedback from users of the built environment, and UDL does not incorporate student evaluation or input in the design process or course revisions (Dolmage, 2005). In addition, UDL assumes that educators have the awareness, skills, and expertise to develop designs that will be appropriate for students with diverse access needs (Ostiguy et al., 2016). To address these critiques and to use UD as a socially just pedagogical approach, institutions and individual instructors must build multiple points for feedback into courses for student voices, particularly those with disabilities, to be represented in the construction of the syllabus and pedagogy (Dolmage, 2005). In this process, course creators can connect with not only students with disabilities, but campus organizations that support these students and create a larger community, truly integrating and centering disability in the co-creation of courses.

Dolmage (2017) discusses UD as a product of the neoliberal university in which UD may become a way of promising everything while not being effective at anything. Dolmage continues to describe neoliberalism as taking "the values of free choice, flexibility, and deregulation and translates them into market reforms and policies designed to maximize profits, privatize industry, and exploit all available systems" and as a "system that powerfully masks inequalities and readily co-opts concepts like diversity, tolerance, and democracy" (p. 139). Positioning UD as a product of neoliberalism can allow for an interrogation of its utility and goals for supporting people with disabilities. Through this interrogation, school faculty, staff, and administrators can understand their role in the neoliberal university as neoliberalism has been shown to integrate its logics into the way we are socially conditioned "so that we run our classrooms and cultural institutions like corporations" (p. 139). However, through a critical approach to UD and UDL, we can dismiss the desires of neoliberalism by recognizing both the environmental conditions that create inaccessible educational spaces and take steps to evolve with UD and UDL based on social and cultural contexts and the progressing needs of students.

To evolve UD and UDL based on social and cultural contexts, we can look to understanding UD and UDL as a form of social justice. Evans and colleagues (2017) provided three principles for UD grounded in social justice:

1. understanding the role that power and privilege have played in excluding nondominant groups, including students with disabilities;
2. affirmation that individuals are unique and worthy of respect from those around them, and that their voices should be included in any discussion of issues that affect them; and
3. recognition that disability is largely an environmental condition—although aspects of individual impairments can play a role in disability—and that the environment needs to be changed to provide equitable educational opportunities for all students.

Additionally, as part of a presentation made at the Pacific Rim Conference on Disabilities in 2006, Higbee and colleagues presented seven UD principles for multiculturalism and anti-racism. In this presentation, they encourage the creation of spaces and programs that foster a sense of community for all students, particularly students from underrepresented communities. This is significantly important when multimodal interpretations are socially constructed and dependent on culture and varied experiences (Kress et al., 2005). Higbee and colleagues (2006) also emphasized building barrier-free welcoming environments with attention paid to attributes that include disability, diverse content, access to artwork and graphic design, and geographic location relative to function. They further encouraged designing accessible and appropriate physical environments that provide ease of use for people who use different modes of interacting or communicating and allow for confidential use based on the services, programs, or benefits being delivered. Additionally, it is important to create inclusive and respectful policies and programs that, from the beginning, take into consideration the diverse student populations within educational settings and provide natural and cognitive supports to ensure full utilization of programs by students. They also suggest ensuring that nonelectronic information environments are accessible and appropriate so that information is delivered in formats (e.g., Braille, captioning, different languages) understandable and easily usable by diverse users without requiring unnecessary steps to go through for completion. And finally, Higbee et al. (2006) recommend designing and maintaining internet and other electronic environments to ensure accessibility and appropriate confidentiality or privacy for those who use various adaptive equipment, hardware (that may vary in age and capacity), and software for those that require or need confidentiality or privacy. These considerations represent modal shifts to increase accessibility and have major implications for students with disabilities.

Each UD principle for multiculturalism and social justice is related to multimodality or is required for a cultural shift to increase recognition of the environmental conditions that create inaccessible educational spaces. The recommended actions by Higbee and colleagues (2006) provide multiple accessible and adaptable modes of learning, interacting, and communicating; discuss fostering a sense of inclusivity and hiring personnel who value diversity; and emphasize confidentiality and privacy for students who may need specific accommodations which are imperative for students with disabilities who may need additional support. The three principles for UD grounded in social justice and the UD principles for multiculturalism and anti-racism should be considered in UD and UDL developmental conversations and embedded within the design framework. As faculty, staff, and other educators are considering implementing UD and UDL, these principles and the voices of students with disabilities should be central to the creation of inclusive spaces.

CONCLUSION

As educators, researchers, and practitioners explore UD, UDL, accessibility, and multimodality, it is necessary for students with disabilities to be centered throughout the design and evaluative process. Ford (2013) stated, "The main guideline for knowing if a space is accessible is that people don't feel assaulted there; they feel safe, and their needs are being met. The measure is by what the users of the space say themselves, not what observers say" ("Accessible space," para. 3). As researchers continue to examine UD and UDL, the experiences and voices of students with disabilities should be at the forefront of conversations and decision-making. Educators designing UD and UDL should continue to design spaces that support most students while also accounting for individual needs and accommodations that students may have due to the impossibility of designing for all. A multimodal approach should take up issues of disability in substantively critical ways as critical disability studies provide us with a direction to consider the role of power in the shifting and transformation of modes. By understanding accessibility as multimodality in educational spaces, we begin to dismantle barriers for students with disabilities and encourage equitable spaces and equitable access to education.

REFERENCES

Catanese, L. (2012). Thomas Lamb, Marc Harrison, Richard Hollerith and the origins of universal design. *Journal of Design History, 25*(2), 206–217. https://doi.org/10.1093/jdh/eps013

Center for Applied Special Technology. (2018). *Universal design for learning guidelines version 2.2.* http://udlguidelines.cast.org

Connell, B., Jones, M., Mace, R., Mueller, J., Mullick, A., Ostroff, E., Sanford, J., Steinfeld, E., Story, M., & Vanderheiden, G. (1997). *The principles of universal design: Version 2.0.* Center for Universal Design, North Carolina State University. https://design.ncsu.edu/research/center-for-universal-design

Dalton, E. M., Lyner-Cleophas, M., Ferguson, B.T., & McKenzie, J. (2019). Inclusion, universal design and universal design for learning in higher education: South Africa and the United States. *African Journal of Disability, 8*(0), a519. https://doi.org/10.4102/ajod.v8i0.519

Dolmage, J. T. (2005). Disability studies pedagogy, usability and universal design. *Disability Studies Quarterly, 25*(4). https://dsq-sds.org/article/view/627/804

Dolmage, J. T. (2017). *Academic ableism: Disability and higher education.* University of Michigan Press.

Edyburn, D. L. (2021). Universal usability and universal design for learning. *Intervention in School and Clinic, 56*(5), 310–315. https://doi.org/10.1177/1053 451220963082

Erkilic, M. (2012). Conceptual challenges between universal design and disability in relation to the body, impairment, and the environment: Where does the issues of disability stand in the philosophy of UD? *Middle East Technical University Journal of the Faculty of Architecture, 28*(2), 181–203. https://doi.org/10.4305/METU.JFA.2011.2.9

Evans, N. J., Broido, E. M., Brown, K. R., & Wilke, A. K. (2017). *Disability in higher education: A social justice approach.* John Wiley & Sons.

Ford, S. (2013, September 6). *Deep accessibility.* Ianology. https://ianology.wordpress.com/2013/09/06/deep-accessibility/#comment-296

Higbee, J. L., Lundell, D. B., Barajas, H. L., Cordano, R. J., & Copeland, R. (2006, March). *Implementing universal instructional design: Resources for faculty* [Conference session]. 22nd Annual Pacific Rim Conference on Disabilities, Honolulu, HI.

Jewitt, C. (2008). Multimodality and literacy in school classrooms. *Review of Research in Education, 32*, 241–267. https://doi.org/10.3102/0091732X07310586

King-Sears, P. (2014). Introduction to learning disability quarterly special series on universal design for learning: Part one of two. *Learning Disability Quarterly, 37*(2), 68–70. https://doi.org/10.1177/0731948714528337

Kress, G. (2010). *Multimodality: A social semiotic approach to contemporary communication.* Routledge.

Kress, G., Jewitt, C., Bourne, J., Franks, A., Hardcastle, J., Jones, K., & Reid, E. (2005). *English in urban classrooms: A multimodal perspective on teaching and learning.* RoutledgeFalmer.

McRae, L. (2019). Disciplining disability: Intersections between critical disability studies and cultural studies. In K. Ellis, R. Garland-Thomson, M. Kent, & R. Robertson (Eds.), *Manifestos for the future of critical disability studies* (pp. 217–229). Routledge.

Minich, J. (2016). Enabling whom? Critical disability studies now. *Journal of the Cultural Studies Association Lateral, 5*(1). https://doi.org/10.25158/L5.1.9

Ok, M. W., Rao, K., Bryant, B. R., & McDougall, D. (2017). Universal design for learning in pre-k to grade 12 classrooms: A systemic review of research. *Exceptionality, 25*(2), 116–138. https://doi.org/10.1080/09362835.2016.1196450

Ostiguy, B. J., Peters, M. L., & Shlasko, D. (2016). Ableism. In M. Adams & L. A. Bell (Eds), *Teaching for diversity and social justice* (pp. 299–337). Routledge.

Pisha, B., & Coyne, P. (2001). Smart from the start: The promise of universal design for learning. *Remedial and Special Education, 22*(4), 197–203. https://doi.org/10.1177/074193250102200402

Shakespeare, T. (2017). The social model of disability. In L. J. Davis (Ed.), *The disability studies reader* (pp. 190–199). Routledge.

Simmons, P. (2020). *The evolution of universal design: A win–win concept for all.* Rocky Mountain ADA Center. https://rockymountainada.org/news/blog/evolution-universal-design-win-win-concept-all

United Nations. (1948). *Universal declaration of human rights.* https://www.un.org/en/about-us/universal-declaration-of-human-rights

United Nations Educational, Scientific and Cultural Organization. (1990). *World declaration on education for all and framework for action to meet basic learning needs* [Program and meeting document]. https://unesdoc.unesco.org/ark:/48223/pf0000127583

United Nations Educational, Scientific and Cultural Organization. (1994). *The Salamanca statement and framework for action on special education needs* [Programme and meeting document]. https://unesdoc.unesco.org/ark:/48223/pf0000098427

United Nations Educational, Scientific and Cultural Organization. (2000). *The Dakar framework for action: Education for All: Meeting our collective commitments (including sic regional frameworks for action)* [Program and meeting document]. https://unesdoc.unesco.org/ark:/48223/pf0000121147

United Nations Educational, Scientific and Cultural Organization. (2009) *Policy guidelines on inclusion in education* [Program and meeting document]. https://unesdoc.unesco.org/ark:/48223/pf0000177849

SECTION II

CRITICAL MULTIMODALITY AND STORYTELLING
FOR AGENCY AND REVISIONING

CHAPTER 6

ALL THE STARS ARE CLOSER

Black Girl Multimodal Practices for Time Traveling in a Dystopian World

ThedaMarie Gibbs Grey
Ohio University

Jennifer D. Turner
University of Maryland

Alexis Morgan Young
University of Maryland

ABSTRACT

The purpose of our chapter is to disrupt and resist the ways that Black girls' multimodal practices are silenced in traditional research and in the broader U.S. social context. Specifically, we center Black girls' multimodal, self-expressive practices to dismantle oppressive, eurocentric constructions of Black girls' ways of being and temporality. We ask: (a) "How do Black girls use multimodal practices to time travel between their pasts, presents, and futures in a dystopian world?" and (b) "Why is it significant for us as Black Women scholars to advocate for spaces that allow Black girls to time travel through multimodal practices?"

Black girls are living in a dystopian reality that needs to be interrupted now. For them, the future is now and it is causing them harm. Traditionally, the notion of dystopia refers to a future filled with immense suffering; however, this is the current condition for Black girls due to gendered anti-Blackness (Collins, 1991). Black girls are failed by linear timelines that set the future as a rigid destination, ultimately restricting the range of possibilities by through hyper-analysis of the present. Thus, Black girls must be provided opportunities to time travel through multimodal practices which will amplify and honor their past histories and present realities to author their own futures.

Building on this premise, we conceptualize Black girls' time travel in a Black feminist futurities framework (Barnard Center for Research on Women, 2014) layered with Black girlhood theories (Brown, 2009, 2013) to elucidate how Black girls critically leverage their own multimodal practices (e.g., making images, videos, material objects) for personal communication and meaning making (New London Group, 1996). Through these conceptual lenses, we theorize how Black girls use multimodal practices to enter temporalities that are matriarchal, communal, and nonlinear, allowing them to engage in self-expression, social critique, collective healing and future making. We first discuss popular multimedia (e.g., films) as a multimodal practice that pushes back against dominant constructions of Black girls by centering them as technocultural creators, scientists, purveyors of knowledge and time travelers, such as *Black Panther* (Coogler et al., 2018) and *See You Yesterday* (Bristol et al., 2019), a Netflix sci-fi film which focuses on C. J., a Black girl scientist who develops a time-traveling machine to save her older brother. We then turn to academic scholarship to examine how Black girls open possibilities to the past, present, and future through visual art practices (e.g., drawing/sketching, photography, digital collage) and embodied practices (e.g., hair). We conclude with a call to action for literacy researchers and educators to create spaces where Black girls' critical multimodal practices facilitate their ability to travel beyond the oppressive logics, temporalities, and realities of a White patriarchal capitalist dystopia, as they reclaim their power and histories, re-center their lived experiences, and envision their futures on their own terms.

> *This may be the night that my dreams might let me know*
> *All the stars are closer, all the stars are closer*
>
> —Kendrick Lamar and SZA, *All the Stars* (Duckworth et al., 2018)

We open our chapter with lyrics from "All the Stars" (Duckworth et al., 2018), the first song on the *Black Panther* soundtrack, because they serve as a call to Black girls everywhere. To freedom dream. To build. To shine. To grow. And, to time travel. To see themselves in the past, present, and the future. To see themselves both within and beyond the boundaries of time. To make their own Black girl time a reality. To know that although the world is broken, they possess the brilliance, beauty, and boldness to bring the stars closer. Those stars are Black girls' hopes, dreams, aspirations, and magic, and Black girls have their own practices necessary to guide those stars into their own orbits.

The purpose of our chapter is to center Black girls' critical multimodal practices and privilege the ways Black girls use these practices to define and manifest their own ways of being and temporalities. In so doing, we dismantle oppressive eurocentric constructions of Black girls and their temporalities, and resist the ways their critical multimodal practices are silenced in traditional research and in the broader U.S. social context. Thus, we ask: (a) "How do Black girls use critical multimodal practices to time travel between their pasts, presents, and futures in a dystopian world?" and (b) "Why is it significant for us as Black women scholars to advocate for spaces that allow Black girls to time travel through critical multimodal practices?"

We raise these questions with a sense of urgency since the very lives of Black girls are in grave peril. At the conceptualization of this piece in one of our early meetings, we began by holding space to process the untimely and tragic death of Ma'Khia Bryant. Ma'Khia was a beautiful 16-year-old Black girl who was fatally shot by police in Columbus, Ohio. As Black women, we mourned her life and the lives of Black girls in similar situations seeking refuge as they are forced to navigate or fight for their lives in the foster care system, in interactions with police, and in all aspects of their lives. It was through this conversation in our sadness and anger that we named the type of realities that disrupt the lives of Black girls as dystopias. Traditionally, the notion of dystopia refers to a future filled with immense suffering; however, the term dystopia is sadly and hauntingly befitting of the current conditions for many Black girls. These realities can manifest in differing ways for Black girls including anti-Black girl violence that claims their lives (Smith-Purviance, 2021) and harmful school-based disciplinary practices (Morris, 2016). These dystopias are rooted in what Collins (1991) refers to as gendered anti-Blackness (Collins, 1991).

Throughout our work, we rely on the future and Black futurity to "see hope in a dystopian reality" (Phillips, 2015, p. 7). Such realities include the space for healing, protection, and the ability to not just envision, but to also actualize realities and futures. These healing places and paradises are necessary given that Black girls are living in a harmful dystopian reality that must be interrupted now. In *Sisters of the Yam*, bell hooks (1993) recounts a conversation with sage Ntozake Shange about care for Black women where they ask: "Where is the healing place?" (p. 164). In asking this question, hooks then reminds Black women of the importance of communal spaces for well-being and care, inclusive of opportunities to develop healthy understandings of their power, worth, and capabilities. We envision these communal, healing spaces for Black girls as non-fixed and nonlinear, since linear timelines fail Black girls by assigning the future as a fixed point which "imposes limits on what *could* be by imposing a hyper analysis of what is" (Young, 2021, p. 422). Simultaneously, society does not position Black girls in ways that allow them to remain in and safely enjoy their girlhoods (Brown, 2013). Instead, they experience multiple forms of adultification, disrupting linear time movement for them as they are seen as grown women in tandem with their realities as girls (Evans-Winters & Esposito, 2010; Morris, 2016). In response, we reclaim the timelines imposed on Black girls by society and see their time traveling, or their movement across time and space, as healing. Our understanding of healing times is expansive and allows us to not think of actual time periods in Black girls' lives, but to also think on a time–space continuum where their healing is connected to their pasts, presents, and futures. Through this time–space continuum, Black girls' memories and knowledge of the past shapes how they see themselves in the present, and how they dream about their future. These spaces can be sites for restoration and healing, as Black Girls interact with different healing technologies, and enact critical multimodal practices which amplify and honor their past histories and present realities to author their own futures.

Our chapter begins with our researcher positionalities and situatedness as Black girl time travelers. Next, we conceptualize Black girls' time travel in a Black feminist futurities framework (Barnard Center for Research on Women, 2014) layered with Black girlhood theories (Brown, 2009, 2013) to elucidate how Black girls leverage their own critical multimodal practices for personal communication and meaning making (New London Group, 1996). Through these framings, we articulate how Black girls enact critical multimodal practices, developed from the legacy of our Black foremothers, for their own communication, personal meaning-making, and survival in an anti-Black patriarchal society (Price-Dennis et al., 2017). For us, Black girls' critical multimodal practices are everyday Black girl literacies (Muhammad & Haddix, 2016) that serve as time machines and time-traveling portals. Based on findings from a thematic synthesis (Thomas & Harden, 2008), we then highlight three key time-traveling, multimodal practices Black girls take up/enact to open possibilities to the past, present, and future: (a) popular media practices, including films centering Black girls as technocultural creators, scientists, purveyors of knowledge and time travelers; (b) visual art practices, including Black girls' drawings/sketchings, photography, and digital collaging; and (c) embodied practices such as Black girls' hairstyling and bodies as sites for affirmation and resistance. We demonstrate how Black girls use these critical multimodal practices to enter into temporalities that are matriarchal, communal and nonlinear, allowing them to engage in self-expression, social critique, collective healing and future making. We conclude with implications for practice and final thoughts.

OUR POSITIONALITY

We come to this piece as three Black women scholars committed to honoring and supporting the lives of Black girls and women. This space is divine for us and has offered support and community. Through our writing, we honored our multiple connections with each other; all of us graduates from Michigan State University; we are all urban Black girls (Alexis and Theda are from Detroit; Jen is from Philadelphia), and we all are scholars and educators in colleges of education at predominantly White institutions (PWIs). Our connections and shared identities as Black women reinforce that our liberation is tied to each other's and the Black girls we advocate for. At the beginning of each time we gather to write, we authentically hold space to check in with each other. Although we are conscious of the time, we constantly ask "Are you good?" first. We celebrate personal and professional milestones and offer encouragement and love when needed. In this way, our communal writing space serves as an example of a Black woman healing space, where our individual and collective pasts, presents, and futures converge.

Through these multiple connections, we acknowledge how we are also Black girl time travelers—moving through time and space to evoke family and community memories that sustain us; to theorize in the present from the past writing and experiences of bell hooks, Patricia Hill Collins, and other Black women scholars; and to envision futures that are humanizing and liberating for us and for all other Black girls. We have come to our work with Black girls through multiple entry points and timeframes, including our lived experiences, mentorship of Black girls in our families and communities. Throughout Theda's life, she has understood the beauty and necessity of being cared for, loved and mentored by Black women in her family, school, and community. In understanding the value of relationships between Black girls and women, especially to affirm and protect against society's devaluing of Black girls, she has continued to hold space for Black girls in her family and community. Through her research, Theda focuses on school-based mentorship programs as sites of love for Black girls and also dismantling inequitable disciplinary practices that harm Black girls. Alexis' scholarship focuses on the imaginative practices and liberatory fantasies of preadolescent Black girls. She has always held true that Black girls are knowledge-makers and world-shakers as evidenced by the Black girls and women she has had the honor of knowing and loving. Alexis' time as an elementary school teacher made it clear that Black girls are deserving of access to what they choose for themselves. Her commitment to working in tandem with Black girls is bolstered through her mothering as she seeks to help usher in a new world for her daughters and other Black girls. Finally, Jennifer's relationships with the Black women in her family (e.g., mom, sisters, niece) and her experiences as a college access counselor have inspired her interests in and commitments to centering and elevating Black Girl Futures. In her research, Jennifer seeks to create imaginative spaces where Black girls engage print and/or digital multimodal practices to manifest their freedom dreams. In so doing, Jennifer seeks to help Black girls to (re)member (Dillard & Neal, 2021) their full Black Girlness and to assert the futures and otherworlds that they desire through joy, creativity, spirit, and love.

THEORIZING BLACK GIRLS AS TIME TRAVELERS

In situating Black girls as time travelers, we invoke the wisdom of Ruth Nicole Brown's (2009, 2013) theorization of Black girlhood in concert with Tina Campt's articulation of Black feminist futurity (Barnard Center for Research on Women, 2014). We lean on Brown's (2013) conceptualizing of the "creative potential of Black girlhood" (p. 3) to identify Black girls' creative modes of knowing and being as our compass through naming Black girls' as experts of their individual freedoms and liberation writ large. Our premise is that Black girls are critical and imaginative beings and can use their imaginations to construct otherwise worlds even in the most abysmal circumstances. In constructing new worlds, or spaces, Black girls also define new temporalities. This is essential, because conceptualizations of Western time are rooted in whiteness and capitalism and therefore are considered White property (Barnard Center for Research on Women, 2014; Cooper, 2016; Phillips, 2015, 2021).

Consequently, Black girls are living in dystopia because the future is already here (Phillips, 2015). Campt's Black feminist futurity helps us manipulate how we conceive time (Barnard Center for Research on Women, 2014). She assists us in understanding Black girls' multimodal time traveling by reminding us of language to conceptualize an interruption of linear time. Of Black feminist futurity, Campt (2017) writes,

> It is a performance of a future that hasn't yet happened but must. It is an attachment to a belief in what should be true, which impels us to realize that aspiration. It is the power to imagine beyond current fact and to envision that which is not but must be. (p. 34)

Calling back to Hortense J. Spillers (1987) *Mama's Baby, Papa's Maybe: An American Grammar Book*, Campt employs grammar to describe the urgency of not waiting for an aspirational future to arrive, but rather, doing work in the present to realize desired conditions. This is done by utilization of the future conditional tense "or that which will have had to happen" (p. 114; Barnard Center for Research on Women, 2014). The future conditional tense is typically operationalized by the word "if," for example, "Black Girls can be safe in the future *if* we, those who love Black Girls, are present and tend to their demands for a liberated world" (Young, 2021, p. 428). In this context, the future conditional tense helps demonstrate that to create the future Black girls desire, action must occur. That is, Black feminist futurity dismantles the reliance on the past to set the realities of the future by requiring action now. For us, this action is trusting the expertise of Black girls' multimodal renderings of the future. To be clear, we are not encouraging Black girls to disregard their individual or collective pasts. Phillips (2015) teaches us that pattern-based analysis of the past helps us contend with and envision "possible, probable, and preferable future(s)" (p. 14). As future makers and time travelers, Black girls need researchers and practitioners to assist them in combating dystopia now in order to co-create new demands and conditions for the world(s) in which they wish to live that attend to the specificity and humanity of Black girlhood. Before turning to these three practices, we first articulate why critical multimodal practices are restorative for Black girls who desire to (re)make and (re)shape their own dreams, aspirations, and temporalities.

RESTORING REPRESENTATIONS OF BLACK GIRLS IN MEDIA, VISUAL ARTS & EMBODIED SPACES

Black Women scholars committed to increasing healing spaces for Black girls critically unpack the power in media, visual, and embodied representations of Black girls. McArthur (2016) asserts "media representations of Black girlhood, both as entertainment and in the news, are largely subtractive and dehumanizing" (p. 468), and often do not hold space for Black girls as intellectuals, worthy and beautiful. In the visual arts, Black girls are also made to feel invisible.

Both historical and contemporary paintings, photographs, films, and other visual images frequently hypersexualize Black girls' and women's bodies. For example, Saartjie Baartman, a South African Khoisan woman, was objectified by White men who publicly displayed her in the nude in England and Paris during the 1810s, and by caricatures which render her body as grotesque and abnormally developed (Jackson, 2013). This unfortunately serves as one of myriad marginalizing images of Black girls and women, erasing their existence or relegating them to the shadows, because they are taken through the gaze of dominant society (Brown, 2013; hooks, 1995). Feminist writer bell hooks (1995) contends these images proliferate in a White patriarchal capitalist society as a way to "reinforce and perpetuate the accepted, desired subjugation and subordination of black bodies by white bodies" (p. 96).

Thus, educators and activists committed to disrupting the negative impact that such images can have on Black girls' healthy identity development, continue to create counter spaces where their identities and agencies are centered in humanizing ways. In an effort to transform the type of curricular spaces held for Black girls, researchers and educators have increasingly highlighted curricula that allow Black girls to both critique and create Black Girl media narratives. Jacobs (2016) advocates for spaces where Black girls can develop an "oppositional gaze," pushing back against dominant stereotypes that render them invisible or in negative ways in the media, visual arts, and through their bodies. Dahlia in Muhammad and McArthur's (2015) study wrote about the importance of countering media images that overwhelmingly depict Black girls as violent. Her proposed solution focused on Black girls creating their own representations in order to positively influence how Black girls see themselves (p. 137). These practices allow Black girls to engage in what Stornaiuolo and Thomas (2018) poignantly refer to as re-storying, where young people who are marginalized in school and society including Black girls, utilize a range of tools to author their own humanizing stories instead of those told from a White gaze. These stories and images created by Black girls in their own likeness, remind them of what is possible in their own lives and allow them to dream in ways that surpass the confines of society.

In the context of this chapter, we importantly advocate for expansive stories and imagery depicting Black girls' excellence—including as scientists and time travelers. Although images of Black girls as such have increased over the past several decades, albeit slowly, the vast majority of scientific innovators and time travelers in the media are White men and boys (Holbert et al., 2020; Turner & Griffin, 2022). This invisibility in such roles for Black girls sends implicit messages that they are neither worthy, nor capable of such roles in their own lives and in media fiction. Yet, the truth is that Black girls have and will continue to make scientific contributions that improve society. Thus, Black girls deserve media, visual arts, and embodied representations to match their authentic brilliance and re-imaginings of their power and beauty. To that end, Figure 6.1 presents a visual collage of multiple images of Black girls curated from social media and from our own work. More specifically, Figure 6.1 is a visual representation of the three sets of Black girl critical multimodal practices (i.e., popular multimedia practices, visual art practices, and embodied practices) that we discuss in the remainder of the chapter.

Figure 6.1 Black girl critical multimodal practices. *Sources*: Antonia, 2021; Children's Hair Care, 2020, 2021; Guzman, 2021; Hall, 2021; Inclusive Innovation Incubator, 2018; Richardson, 2020; She's My Twin Sister, 2021; Smithsonian Magazine, 2021; Watkins, 2019.

BLACK GIRLS' POPULAR MULTIMEDIA PRACTICES

The first set of critical multimodal practices, popular multimedia practices, focus on media representations of Black girls highlighting their creation or involvement in time-traveling practices. We do so by exploring representations of three Black girls across three movies including: *LoveCraft Country* (Green, 2021), a horror drama based on a novel that centers Black characters; *See You Yesterday* (Bristol et al., 2019), a science fiction film that centers Black teenage scientists; and *Black Panther* (Coogler et al., 2018), a superhero film based on a Marvel comic that centers Black superheroes and a thriving African nation, Wakanda. In the context of this chapter, we focus more specifically on Black girls' agency in the films based on their positioning as scientists, innovators, and time travelers. While we highlight Black girl characters in these films, we also acknowledge the writers and directors of each of these films who include both Black men and women. Their imaginations brought to life depictions of Black girl characters that stand in stark contrast to the vast majority of media images of Black girls.

Black Girls Media Narratives as Scientists, Innovators, and Time Travelers

Black Girls as Superheroines

We begin by first detailing representations of Black girls in the media as creative illustrators of Black girls and women superheroes. Dee in *Lovecraft Country* (Green, 2021), a middle school Black girl, creates a powerful comic, "The Interplanetary Adventures of Orithyia Blue." Orithyia Blue is a Black woman superheroine and time traveler who Dee powerfully sketches with blue hair. Dee's parents, Hippolyta and George are explorers who travel to develop a Greenbook, a travel guide that identifies businesses that welcome Black travelers amidst segregation. She creates new adventures as gifts for her parents' enjoyment during their travels. During one of their quests, Dee's mother is transported on a self-realization trip where she begins to remember her own dreams of being an explorer. As a result of this experience, her hair turns blue, signaling that she channeled the powerful capabilities of Orithyia Blue. Dee's Black girl comic creations were so powerful that her mother eventually evolved into Orithyia Blue.

Black Girls as Scientists and Creators of Time-Traveling Innovations

In *See You Yesterday* (Bristol et al., 2019), C. J. (Claudette) and her best friend Sebastian are high school science prodigies who utilize their genius to create a time-traveling machine. The movie begins with C. J. explaining protons, molecular structures, and quantum leaping as she and Sebastian initiate their first attempt to travel. They initially see their machine as a means to obtain scholarships to colleges including MIT, Spelman, and Morehouse, two historically Black colleges and universities that are not often centered in dominant media. After the tragic wrongful death of her brother at the hands of police, she and Sebastian work tirelessly to repurpose the machine to undo his death. As the movie progresses, viewers watch C. J.'s scientific prowess as she spends her time in Sebastian's garage refining the machine to serve as a justice-seeking, time-traveling machine.

The third representation of Black Girls as scientists includes Shuri in *Black Panther* (Coogler et al., 2018). In Wakanda, a thriving African country, Shuri, an eighteen-year-old Black Girl is the country's lead scientist, a role not commonly assigned to Black Girls in popular culture. Her creations include Black Panther's superhero suit and devices that allow leaders to fight for justice, saving lives in various ways by teleporting to distant locations.

While the plots differ, a constant is the powerful representation of Black girls as brilliant, scientists, and innovators. They are also each deeply committed to their families and communities in ways that allow them to innovate as a means for racial justice. These representations are groundbreaking since as previously noted in our chapter, they exist in relatively small numbers. They also have the power to influence how Black girls tap into the power of science and technology to engage in their own identity work. Holbert et al.'s (2020) study illustrates this as they focus on the power in creating spaces for Black girls to utilize films such as *Black Panther* to engage in their own Afrofuturist envisioning. In Bateman and Gibbs Grey's scholarship (2021), Bateman, Black girl advocate and middle school educator, details how Black middle school girls respond to reading Black woman author Nic Stone's (2020) book, *Shuri*. Through watching Shuri and reading about her character, the girls in Bateman's book club noted how Shuri was constructed as powerful, and beautiful, in contrast to dominant images where they noted Black girls are rendered invisible. The exposure to Shuri's character and the space to discuss her, became an opportunity to acknowledge difficult personal experiences related to the lack of honoring they felt regarding their skin tones, names, and hair. Shuri's character served as a source of affirmation, through which they saw physical reflections of themselves. This deep sense of seeing, then strengthened their ability to see the beauty and possibilities in themselves.

As the Black girls in Bateman's book club noted, the aforementioned depictions of Black girls and women can spark their imaginations and career desires. Seeing Black girls like themselves can be inspiring and open portals to their own futures. While characters including Dee, Orithyia Blue, C. J., and Shuri are fictional and often inspire Black girls' costumes (Figure 6.1, far right and bottom left), many of the practices they engage in, outside of physical time traveling to the past, are those that Black girls can enact in their own lives and are already doing so. These examples include Black girl teenagers India Skinner, Mikayla Sharrieff, and Bria Snell (Figure 6.1, bottom right) who, in 2018, utilized aerospace technology to create a system for eliminating lead from water in their school's drinking fountains. In the midst of their accomplishments, they faced racist online bullying and hackers who erased their votes in the competition. In spite of the racism meant to deny their excellence, they won second place in a NASA scholarship competition. Dasia Taylor (Figure 6.1, bottom center), another contemporary Black girl teenage scientist, invented color-changing sutures in 2021 to detect infections at the site of surgical incisions. Collectively, they represent what is possible when Black girls are affirmed in the midst of threats to their identity and are provided pathways to become scientists. In addition to finding inspiration in fictional characters, Black girls can be motivated to pursue science by Black women scientists like Valerie Thomas (Figure 6.1, top center) who created the illusion transmitter, advancing scientific capabilities to project 3D images, or Jessica Watkins (Figure 6.1, bottom far left) who in April 2022 became the first Black woman to participate in a long-term space travel mission, aboard the International Space Station.

Black girls' future pathways can also include becoming artists who craft powerful images of Black girls and women including Afua Richardson (Figure 6.1, right) who utilizes her design skills to place Black women heroines and time travelers in films and books including Orithyia Blue (Figure 6.1, left). In calling just a few names of Black girls and women who are artists, scientists, and time travelers, we also recognize the importance of honoring the real-life multimodal practices of Black girls. Thus, in the section that follows, we secondarily delve into the ways researchers have highlighted Black girls' authentic multimodal creations for time traveling.

BLACK GIRLS' VISUAL ART PRACTICES

The second set of critical multimodal practices honors Black girls' production of visual practices and artistic compositions that combine words and images to communicate sociohistorical meanings and represent racialized and gendered identities (Greene, 2021; Griffin & Turner, 2021, in press; Muhammad & Womack, 2015; Player et al., 2023). More specifically, through their visual arts practices, Black girls produce drawings/sketches, photography, and digital collage that serve as time-travel portals, allowing them to (re)claim a past, present, and future that is rightfully theirs.

Drawings/Sketches

Black girls have journeyed to the future through their drawings and sketches. Young Black girls ages 8–10 in Turner's (2022) study utilized drawings and sketches to manifest their STEM career dreams and life aspirations (Figure 6.1, top left). Thematically, these drawings showcased (a) the professional work that they wanted to do in science and math, (b) their racialized and gendered motivations for doing that work (e.g., racial uplift), and (c) their bodies as sites of STEM knowledge and expertise which disrupted and dismantled dominant narratives of STEM as White male property (Turner, 2022). Along similar lines, Sonia, a Black 12th grader in Coles' (2019) study, envisioned a bright future through her body map. By centering her own self-perceptions on the inside of her body image (e.g., strong, intelligent, hardworking) and decentering others' negative perceptions of Black girls on the outside of her body image, Sonia created a sustaining space which promoted the self-love, self-care, and self-determination necessary for liberating futures.

Black girls in their adolescent years have also engaged drawings to critique the past and envision alternate futures. Rochelle, a Black 12th grader, sketched a burning cross on the left and the Black Lives Matter mantra "Hands up, don't shoot" on the right to represent her conception of anti-Black racism (Coles, 2019). Rochelle's sketch demonstrates how violence against Black people in America has continued throughout history, with new iterations emerging all the time (Coles, 2019). Yet, we also see hope for the future in Rochelle's sketch, as she invokes the Black Lives Matter movement and the spirit of other civil rights projects that fight for justice for Black people and for all. Similarly, following the murder of Mike Brown by police officer Darren Wilson, Black girls (and boys) in a middle school social studies class created posters that critiqued the anti-Black racism in society and radiated hope for the future. Through their creative renderings, the girls and the other young people resisted historic and contemporary racial injustice through reflective questions (e.g., "Why?") and commentary (e.g., "history keeps repeating itself") and called for an imagining of a Black world free of violence against Black bodies (Griffin & Turner, 2021).

Photography

While we often presume that photographs capture present life conditions, Black girls may also use photography to travel to times beyond the image. The combination of historical and contemporary photographic images in Figure 6.1 demonstrate how photography serves as a lens for manifesting time scapes where Black girls are fully recognized "as social beings with historical legacies, emergent identities, and [future] social commitments" (Wissman, 2008, p. 14). In Wiseman et al.'s (2016) study, Ella, a 9-year-old African American girl, used photography to evoke memories of going to the hair salon with her mother. In traveling back in time and recalling past trips with her mother, Ella recreated a scene from the hair salon with two friends in her classroom, and used this photograph to compose a story. Refuting her teacher's claim that she was a struggling writer, Ella used the photograph to more clearly visualize the setting and action in her story, as well as include more details in her story. Ella's time traveling through her photography was highly beneficial to her writing process, as she explained, "My picture helps me and my story because it talks about in my story it talks about my hair and the hairdresser and my mom being there and she got her hair done" (pp. 541–542).

Clearly, the ways Black girls see themselves, their communities, and their lives through photography is vital to the humanity, liberation, and survival of Black women (Price-Dennis et al., 2017). Moreover, through photography, Black girls privilege their own Black girl gaze which enables them to reclaim their voices, tell their own truths, and determine their own futures (Brown, 2013; Taaffe, 2016; Manning et al., 2015; Player et al., 2023; Wissman, 2008). Echoing the tradition of Carrie Mae Weems, Jeanne Moutoussamy-Ashe, Lorna Simpson, Michelle Agins, and other Black women photographers (Alemany, 2017), Black girls' photographic images are powerful because they "talk back to the authorizing voices that refuse to see them" (Brown, 2013, p. 23) and they rupture the restrictive and tragic futures prescribed by an anti-Black patriarchal society. As such, Black girls "see" future possibilities and present conditions that are liberatory through photographic images, disrupting stereotypes that demonize them (e.g., they are too loud and aggressive); illuminate their joyful living and friendships; and represent the complexities of Black Girl/Womanhood. For example, Black teen girls (the "Sistahs") in Wissman's (2008) study integrated photography and poetry to compose rich visual autobiographies illuminating their cultural lifeworlds (e.g., friends, families, schools, neighborhoods) and asserted their identities in those spaces. Relatedly, Black teen girls create photographic selfies to center aspects of their identities that are important to them, and to travel to otherworlds where Black girls are free to define their themselves and their lives as they desire (Player et al., 2023). Collectively, these studies demonstrate how the photography of Black girls is situated "within the legacy of Black girls and Women determining for themselves what is important about their lives, what needs to be changed and how to incite that change in ways that work in the interest of Black Girls and the communities of which they are a part" (Taaffe, 2016, p. 24).

Digital Collage

As exemplified by Figure 6.1, Black girls' digital collage entangles visual imagery of the past, present, and future. Black teen girls compose digital collage to challenge and disrupt negative (mis)representations of Black girls that seek to pathologize their temporalities and life possibilities (Griffin & Turner, in press). Scholars like Griffin (2021), Muhammad and

Womack (2015), and Turner and Griffin (2020) have found that Black girls create collages in digital spaces to authentically and creatively represent salient aspects of their past and present lives, including sexuality, physical beauty (e.g., hair, body image, skin color), educational goals/aspirations, and self-love. Through collaging in the public digi-sphere, Black girls create conditions for a more liberatory future by centering "the joy, brilliance, and dynamism of Black girlhood... [and] (re)positioning themselves as the expert authority on their own lives" (Griffin, 2021, p. 7).

Moreover, Black girls use a variety of digital platforms, including Prezi, Pinterest, and Padlet, to (re)present themselves, their lived experiences, and their futures (Muhammad & Womack, 2015; Griffin & Turner, in press; Turner & Griffin, 2020, 2022). Nikayla ruptured the time–space continuum, through images, words, and music videos that enabled her to restore her future by learning from (and letting go) of the hurt and trauma from her past (Muhammad & Womack, 2015). Relatedly, Black girls play with temporal registers in their digital collages, evoking past memories and integrating present interests and experiences to compose new career futures and life trajectories. For example, Shani, a 15-year-old girl in Turner and Griffin's study (2022), created a digital collage resembling a blueprint because she aspired to be an architect. In her blueprint collage, Shani integrated 12 online images with personal photographs to map the personal and professional success that she planned for her life. Recognizing that there were not many Black women in architecture, Shani used photographs of herself working at a drafting table at a summer camp (past), and snapshots of her supportive family and friends (present), to (re)claim a scientific future. Moving across these temporalities, Shani was a future maker, using multimodal images to honor past and present life forces (e.g., family, friends, Christian spirituality) and to name the sacred work (e.g., using architecture to "build things and make people's dreams come to life") that she felt called to do in her future.

BLACK GIRLS' EMBODIED PRACTICES

The third set of critical multimodal practices, embodied practices, reaffirms that Black girls' themselves are sites of future making and resistance. Austin (2018) offers the theorization of Black girl genius to articulate Black girls' distinct ways of knowing the world. She defines Black girl genius as "gender, race, age and class specific language, art, performative arts and musical sensibilities used to enact freedom at a time of national Black antigirlness" (Austin, 2018, p. 10). We suggest that Black girls' embodied multimodal practices are an articulation of Black girl genius that allows them to reimagine freer, safer worlds "in the meantime, in-between time" (ross, 2020, p. 20).

Black girls across time have deployed embodied multimodality as a means of self-definition and future making. Embodied multimodal practices assist Black girls in "clapping back" (Kaler-Jones et al., 2020; McPherson, 2019) against a dystopian world full of anti-Black girl violence (Smith-Purviance, 2021, p. 182) and White supremacist norms and ideologies. We have identified evidence of Black girls' embodied multimodality to reject harmful tropes by using mediums such as hair and textiles to rename and set new terms for their current conditions and as sites of healing and resistance.

Hair

In her chapter "Curls, Coils, and Codes" in *Strong Black Girls: Reclaiming Schools in Their Own Image* (Apugo et al., 2020), Kaler-Jones (2020) time travels through history to demonstrate how Black girls' hair has long been a contested terrain (Phelps-Ward & Laura, 2016) that simultaneously serves as a site of resistance and as a site of hyper-surveillance. She argues that hair is an "arts-based practice" (p. 61), and as such, Black girls' hair serves as a creative expression. Through the rendering of hair as a creative practice, we come to understand that Black girls can, and do, use their hair to construct otherwise ways of being (Figure 6.1, center). For example, before her state-sanctioned murder, Ma'Khia Bryant often used the social media platform TikTok to showcase her creativeness. In addition to showcasing her mastery of styling her hair into unique styles, the videos created by Ma'Khia included her expressing herself through music selection, dance, and facial expressions.

Black girls use their hair and hair spaces (including TikTok and YouTube) as sites of healing and responding to psycho-emotional needs (Mbilishaka, 2018). Black hair and virtual hair spaces can serve as "symbolic homeplace" (Phelps-Ward & Laura, 2016, p. 818) where Black girls are able to engage in self-love. Griffin's (2021) study further extends what we know about the ways Black girls use hair and digital hair spaces as multimodal expressions of the future. The Blacks girls centered in her study used hair to foster inclusivity in the multimodal expressions of their online spaces.

In addition to using their hair as a form of creative expression and as a healing site, Black girls use hair as a site of resistance to White normative standards and stereotypes. Many Black girls are aware of the politics surrounding their hair, meaning that their decisions around styling their hair demonstrate their agency over how they choose to respond to eurocentric standards and norms. For example, one of the Black girl hair vloggers in Phelps-Ward and Laura's (2016) study described her decision to wear her hair in its natural state as "revolutionary" (p. 817). Another striking example of Black girls using hair as resistance against anti-Black norms is located in Jacobs' (2016) study amplifying the ways Black girls develop and deploy their critical lenses to analyze and understand race, class, and gender. One participant, Cheryl, created a poster of a "Black girl with natural hair and hoop earrings and in the figure's hair are the affirming words "foundation," "versatile," "brilliant," "empowered," and "stunning"—all serving as a counternarrative to the words and phrases often used to describe Black Girls and women" (p. 233). Through this multimodal rendering of hair, Cheryl pushed back against harmful tropes of Black girls by instead asserting positive attributes and thus re-authoring the ways Black girls exist in this and otherwise worlds.

Black Girl Bodies

Black girls also utilize their creativity and self-expression through the clothing and jewelry they adorn their bodies with. In Gibbs Grey and Stanbrough's (2019) research which affirms Black girls' magic through their multiple literacies, Stanbrough highlights what she refers to as Black girls "self-advocating creations" (p. 12). Crane, a brilliant high school debater, created a sweatshirt for the debate team centering a picture of three beautiful Black girls with different hairstyles accompanied by the logo "Debate Like a Girl" (Figure 6.1, top). Crane utilized multimodal forms of expression including drawing, literacy, and clothing making to push back against mainstream images that do not center Black girls as the norm for debating excellence. Similarly, Griffin (2021) and her Black girl co-researchers wore matching t-shirts created by one of the girls in the group. Printed with the words "Beautiful in Every Shade" in yellow lettering, the black t-shirts embodied the girls' perceptions of themselves and their beauty, evoking the self-love, creativity, multimodality, and dignity of the Black parade (Griffin, 2021). Relatedly, Black adolescent girls in the Remixing Wakanda program (Holbert et al., 2020), apprenticed with artists and educators, utilizing STEM technologies to artistically design materials that expressed their own futures on their own terms. Aida, a 10th-grade student created a medallion infused with African symbols allowing her to touch on several important topics including her strong belief in the power of self-reflection, the need to reposition the African continent as worthy, and the challenges she experiences where her Blackness is objectified in public spaces.

CO-CREATING CURRICULUM WITH BLACK GIRL TIME TRAVELERS: PRACTICAL IMPLICATIONS FOR SCHOOL AND COMMUNITY EDUCATORS

Black girls are time travelers who use their multimodal brilliance and creativity to critique unjust societal systems, suspend disbelief, and open new worlds full of infinite possibilities. In one of the earlier scenes in the film *See You Yesterday*, C. J.'s science teacher questions her ability to extend scientific capabilities to allow actual time traveling. He then compels C. J. to dig deeply and engage in scientific inquiry to essentially change the world by asking her: "If you had that kind of power, what would you do, what would you change?" We remixed and reframed this question rooted in knowing not questioning that Black girls indeed do possess this kind of power. Thus, we ask: If schools and society truly believed in, honored, and cultivated the power that Black girls possess, how would this belief be reflected in school structures and curricula?

As an essential starting point, we must attend to the beliefs that educators possess about Black girls. When educators possess deficit beliefs about Black girls and their educational and career capabilities, their curriculum development and engagement, engagement with Black girls, and advocacy for their lives is impacted (Evans-Winter & Esposito, 2010). We also call for educators to engage in critical media analysis of how their media consumption has impacted their constructions of Black girls given the potential to perpetuate Black girls' invisibility in their own curriculum. This requires critical reflection of the beliefs they possess about Black girls and their capabilities, with the intention of developing new and more humanizing narratives (Nyachae, 2016). These new narratives must expand to assume, acknowledge, and affirm Black girls' power and capabilities as opposed to questioning it, rendering it invisible and stunting its development.

Moreover, educators must purposefully create spaces within school and community programs where they can work with Black girls to co-create curricula (Griffin, 2021; Turner & Griffin, 2020, 2022) that promotes time traveling through multimodal projects. Providing space to co-create curriculum and pedagogy with Black girls is crucial since traditional curriculum dehumanizes Black girls with its discursive terror and torture (Ohito, 2016). Those trapped within its walls often feel as if they must conform to the tragic timelines determined by society and placed upon them. Conversely, classrooms designed for White students allow them to time travel through building their imagination for future possibilities. Without interruptions, they are situated in spaces where the scientific norms, and most examples of excellence are projected through people who look like them. However, dominant school spaces do not work this way for Black girls as their likenesses are not perceived as scientific norms, nor does curricula nurture their ability to pursue STEM careers (Collins et al., 2020; Lane & Id-Deen, 2020; Turner & Griffin, 2022). Thus, when these spaces are interrupted to make room for Black girl greatness across all fields including STEM and English classrooms, it also builds and expands their future-oriented imaginations. Black girls may elect to watch films like *See You Yesterday*, *Black Panther*, and episodes of *LoveCraft Country* to discuss and analyze media representations of Black girls and women based on themes related to time travel, power, family and romantic relationships, and technology. They may also create their own media representations (e.g., videos, short films) as multimodal projects which enable them to create storylines and timelines that nourish their past, present, and future (McArthur, 2016). Black girls may also build upon and extend their STEM literacies and knowledge as they develop scientific innovations reflected by the characters in these films.

In these school and community educational spaces where curricula are co-created with Black girls, they have the freedom to (re)imagine futures and (re)make their worlds in humanizing and restorative ways. "Black women and girls desire visions of themselves in the future even though they are often subjected to futuristic violence in the mainstream imaginary" (Toliver, 2020, p. 331). This future-making work Black girls engage in may include reading Afrofuturistic novels that center Black girl characters, and even writing their own speculative fiction, where they are not constructed as the "dark other" whose future is nonexistent or filled with darkness (Thomas, 2018). Instead, Black girls can write themselves as the superheroines, scientists, and creators of time-traveling machines as depicted in the focal films. In addition, Black girls may also engage in critical multimodal projects that illuminate their career futures, life goals, and societal visions through visual practices (Griffin & Turner, 2021). When Black girls in Griffin's (2021) study engaged curricular topics they desired to discuss, including career aspirations, financial literacies, health and wellness, embodied practices (e.g., hair, colorism), and self-love practices, they critiqued historic patterns of oppression against Black girls and women, recognized present-day traumas, and imagined more liberatory futures for themselves and other Black girls. By enabling Black girls to play with temporal registers through technologies, media, books, and the visual arts, these multimodal projects nurture their capacity to imagine, to dream, and to heal. (Re)constructing curriculum with Black girls is also imperative because it enables Black girls to bring the fullness of their minds, bodies, and souls to educational spaces (Nyachae, 2016). Through their constructions of hair practices, Black girls have demonstrated that engaging with multimodality is not merely something they do, it is an embodied experience. As such, educators must recognize and acknowledge Black girls' experiential knowledge and ways of being in classroom spaces.

In closing, our chapter serves as a call to action for school and community educators to cocreate spaces with Black girls, where they can engage critical multimodal practices to facilitate their ability to travel beyond the oppressive logics, temporalities, and realities of a White patriarchal, capitalist dystopia, in order to reclaim their power and histories, re-center their lived experiences, and envision their futures on their own terms. Our chapter also serves as an affirmation for all Black girls, and thus we connect back to our opening sentiments. We wish to remind Black girls of their brilliance and ability to time travel through pasts, presents, and futures that allow them to reach for their own stars and dream boldly, turning their dreams into beautiful realities.

REFERENCES

Alemany, J. (2017, October 16). A new book gives us the world as seen by Black female photographers. *Vogue.* https://www.vogue.com/article/black-female-photographers-mfon

Antonia, T. [@tori.antonia]. (2021, April 28). Did someone say "#nationalsuperheroday "? Throwing back to my favorite superhero cosplays [Instagram photograph]. https://www.instagram.com/p/COONV5ilQ7Q/

Apugo, D., Mawhinney, L., & Mbilishaka, A. (Eds.). (2020). *Strong Black girls: Reclaiming schools in their own image.* Teachers College Press.

Austin, S. J. (2018). *Black girl genius: Theorizing girlhood, identity and knowledge production* [Unpublished doctoral dissertation]. The Ohio State University. https://etd.ohiolink.edu/apexprod/rws_olink/r/1501/10?clear=10&p10_accession_num=osu1532077146785451

Barnard Center for Research on Women. (2014, October 21). *Tina Campt: Black feminist futurities and the practice of fugitivity* [YouTube video]. YouTube. https://www.youtube.com/watch?v=2ozhqw840PU

Bateman, R., & Gibbs Grey, T. (2021, March 14). *Acknowledging the power and necessity in centering Black Girls' stories* [Conference presentation]. Michigan Reading Association 2021 Annual Conference, Virtual.

Bristol, S., Bailey, F. (Screenwriters), & Lee, S. (Director). (2019). *See you yesterday* [Motion picture]. 40 Acres and a Mule Filmworks.

Brown, R. N. (2009). *Black girlhood celebration: Toward a hip-hop feminist pedagogy* (Vol. 5). Peter Lang.

Brown, R. N. (2013). *Hear our truths: The creative potential of Black girlhood.* University of Illinois Press.

Campt, T. M. (2017). *Listening to images.* Duke University Press.

Children's Hair Care [@toddlersandtangles]. (2020, July 19). I spy with my little eyes a #star...this star-studded #braid design features a top #ponytail with hanging braids in the back [Photograph]. Instagram. https://www.instagram.com/p/CC2IWH8Drca/

Children's Hair Care [@toddlersandtangles]. (2021, May 3). #WhoseReadyForSummer This #protectivestyles features #cornrows and #twist with white and yellow #hairbead at the ends [Photograph]. https://www.instagram.com/p/COarW9hr3I1/

Coles, J. (2019). The Black literacies of urban high school youth countering Antiblackness in the context of neoliberal multiculturalism. *Journal of Language and Literacy Education, 15*(2), 1–35. https://eric.ed.gov/?id=EJ1235199

Collins, K. H., Joseph, N. M., & Ford, D. Y. (2020). Missing in action: Gifted Black girls in science, technology, engineering, and mathematics. *Gifted Child Today, 43*(1), 55–63. https://doi.org/10.1177/1076217519880

Collins, P. H. (1991). *Black feminist thought: Knowledge, consciousness, and the politics of empowerment.* Routledge.

Coogler, R., Cole, J. R., Lee, S., Kirby, J. (Screenwriters), & Coogler, R. (Director). (2018). *Black Panther* [Motion picture]. Marvel Studios.

Cooper, B. (2016). *The racial politics of time* [Video]. TED Conferences. https://www.ted.com/talks/brittney_cooper_the_racial_politics_of_time?language=en#t-735729

Dillard, C. B., & Neal, A. M. (2021). Still following our North Star: The necessity of Black women's spiritual (re)membering in qualitative (re)search. *Qualitative Inquiry, 27*(10) 1182–1190. https://doi.org/10.1177/1077800421102180

Duckworth, K., Shuckburgh, A. W., Spears, M., & Rowe, S. (2018). All the stars [Song recorded by Kendrick Lamar and SZA]. On *Black Panther.* Hollywood Marvel Music.

Evans-Winters, V., & Esposito, J. (2010). Other people's daughters: Critical race feminism and Black Girls' education. *Educational Foundations,* 11–24. https://files.eric.ed.gov/fulltext/EJ885912.pdf

Gibbs Grey, T., & Stanbrough, R. J. (2019). We are "#BlackGirlMagic": Exploring the multiple literacies that Black Girls utilize for storytelling. *Michigan Reading Journal, 52*(1), 6–15. https://scholarworks.gvsu.edu/mrj/vol52/iss1/5

Green, M. (2021). *Lovecraft country* [TV series]. Monkeypaw productions, Bad Robot Productions, Warner Bros. Television Studios.

Greene, D. (2021). Black adolescent girls' multimodalities in out-of-school literacy spaces. In D. Price-Dennis & G. E. Muhammad (Eds.), *Black girls' literacies: Transforming lives and literacy practices* (pp. 200–217). Routledge.

Griffin, A. A. (2021). Black parade: Conceptualizing Black adolescent girls' multimodal renderings as parades. *Urban Education,* 1–31. https://doi.org/10.1177/00420859211003944.

Griffin, A. A., & Turner, J. D. (2021). Towards a pedagogy of Black livingness: Black students' creative multimodal renderings of resistance to anti-Blackness. *English Teaching: Practice and Critique, 20*(4), 440–453. https://doi.org/10.1108/ETPC-09-2020-0123

Griffin, A. A., & Turner, J. D. (in press). Imagining possible Black girl futures: Critical self-reflection as praxis for theorizing with Black girls. In E. Tuck & K. W. Yang (Eds.), *Theorizations of Blackness in education.* Routledge.

Guzman, W. (2021, April 20). *Valerie Thomas (1943–).* Black Past [Photograph courtesy of NASA, Public Domain]. https://www.blackpast.org/african-american-history/valerie-thomas-1943/

Hall, R. (2018, May 3). *Afua Richardson talks about her music, her art, and her mermaids at ACE Comic Con AZ* [Photograph]. https://www.nerdteam30.com/creator-conversations/afua-richardson-talks-about-her-music-her-art-and-her-mermaids-at-ace-comic-con-az

Holbert, N., Dando, M. B., & Correa, I. (2020). Afrofuturism as critical constructionist design: Building futures from the past and present. *Learning, Media and Technology, 45*(4), 328–344. https://doi.org/10.1080/17439884.2020.17 54237

hooks, b. (1993). *Sisters of the yam: Black women and self-recovery*. South End Press.

hooks, b. (1995). *Art on my mind: Visual politics*. The New Press.

Inclusive Innovation Incubator [@in3dc]. (2018, April 23). *These 3 High School young ladies India, Bria, & Mikayla are 1 of the Top 10 finalists for @nasa OPSPARC, GLOG CHALLENGE!* [Photograph]. Instagram. https://www.instagram.com/p/Bh6reVYAnjn/

Jackson, T. (2013). Metelling: Recovering the Black female body. *Visual Culture & Gender, 8*, 70–81. http://vcg.emitto.net/index.php/vcg/article/view/76

Jacobs, C. E. (2016). Developing the" oppositional gaze": Using critical media pedagogy and Black feminist thought to promote Black girls' identity development. *Journal of Negro Education, 85*(3), 225–238. https://doi.org/10.7709/jnegroeducation.85.3.0225

Kaler-Jones, C. (2020). Curls, coils, and codes: An examination of Black girls' hair as a form of expression and resistance. In D. Apugo, L. Mawhinney, & A. Mbilishaka (Eds.), *Strong Black girls: Reclaiming schools in their own image* (pp. 61–78). Teachers College Press.

Kaler-Jones, C., Griffin, A., & Lindo, S. (2020). The CLAPBACK: Black girls responding to injustice through national civic engagement. In G. Logan, & J. Mackey (Eds.), *Black Girl civics: Expanding and navigating the boundaries of civic engagement* (pp. 159–174). Information Age Publishing.

Lane, T. B., & Id-Deen, L. (2020). Nurturing the capital within: A qualitative investigation of Black women and girls in STEM summer programs. *Urban Education, online*. https://doi-org.proxy.library.ohio.edu/10.1177/0042085920926225

Machemer, R. (2021, March 25). *This high schooler invented color-changing sutures to detect infection*. Smithsonian Magazine. https://www.smithsonianmag.com/innovation/high-schooler-invented-color-changing-sutures-detect-infection-180977345/

Manning, K., Duke, A., & Bostic, P. (2015). Me, myself, and I: Exploring African American girlhood through an endarkened (photographic) lens. In V. E. Evans-Winters & B. L. Love (Eds.), *Black feminism in education* (pp. 143–152). Peter Lang.

Mbilishaka, A. (2018). PsychoHairapy: Using hair as an entry point into Black women's spiritual and mental health. *Meridians, 16*(2), 382–392. https://doi.org/10.2979/meridians.16.2.19

McArthur, S. A. (2016). Black girls and critical media literacy for social activism. *English Education, 48*(4), 362–379. https://www.jstor.org/stable/26492574

McPherson, K. (2019). 'We need a seat at the table': Black Girls using new media to construct Black identity. In A. S. Halliday (Ed.), *The Black girlhood studies collection* (pp. 235–256). Women's Press.

Morris, M. W. (2016). *Pushout: The criminalization of Black girls in schools*. The New Press.

Muhammad, G. E., & Haddix, M. (2016). Centering Black girls' literacies: A review of literature on the multiple ways of knowing of Black girls. *English Education, 48*(4), 229–336. https://www.jstor.org/stable/26492572

Muhammad, G. E., & McArthur, S. A. (2015). "Styled by their perceptions": Black adolescent girls interpret representations of Black females in popular culture. *Multicultural Perspectives, 17*(3), 133–140. https://doi.org/10.1080/15210960.2015.1048340

Muhammad, G. E., & Womack, E. (2015). From pen to pin: The multimodality of Black girls (re)writing their lives. *Ubiquity: The Journal of Literature, Literacy, and the Arts, Research Strand, 2*(2), 6–45. https://ed-ubiquity.gsu.edu/wordpress/wp-content/uploads/2016/01/Muhammad_Womack_Abstract_2-2_v2.pdf

New London Group. (1996). A pedagogy of multiliteracies: Designing social futures. *Harvard Educational Review, 66*, 60–92. https://doi.org/10.17763/haer.66.1.17370n67v22j160u

Nyachae, T. M. (2016). Complicated contradictions amid Black feminism and millennial Black women teachers creating curriculum for Black girls. *Gender and Education, 28*(6), 786–806. https://doi.org/10.1080/09540253.2016.1221896

Ohito, E. (2016). Refusing curriculum as a space of death for Black female subjects: A Black feminist reparative reading of Jamaica Kincaid's "Girl." *Curriculum Inquiry, 46*(5), 436–454. https://doi.org/10.1080/03626784.2016.1236658

Phelps-Ward, R. J., & Laura, C. T. (2016). Talking back in cyberspace: Self-love, hair care, and counter narratives in Black adolescent girls' YouTube vlogs. *Gender and Education, 28*(6), 807–820. https://doi.org/10.1080/09540253.2016.1221888

Phillips, R. (Ed.). (2015). *Black quantum futurism theory & practice (Vol. 1)*. AfroFuturist Affair.

Phillips, R. (Ed.). (2021). *Black quantum futurism theory & practice (Vol. II)*. AfroFuturist Affair.

Player, G., Animashaun, O., & Thornton, T. (2023). "Getting lost in stars and glitter": Black girls' multimodal literacies as portals to new suns. *International Journal of Qualitative Studies in Education, 36*(3), 411–429. https://doi.org/10.1080/09518398.2022.2025490

Price-Dennis, D., Muhammad, G. E., Womack, E., McArthur, S. A., & Haddix, M. (2017). The multiple identities and literacies of Black girlhood: A conversation about creating spaces for Black girl voices. *Journal of Language and Literacy Education, 13*(2), 1–18. http://jolle.coe.uga.edu/wp-content/uploads/2017/11/Price-Dennis_JoLLE2017.pdf

Richardson, A. (2020). [Sketches of the Interplanetary Adventures of OrithyiaBlue]. Retrieved on February 1, 2022 from https://bleedingcool.com/comics/afua-richardson-is-the-artist-for-lovecraft-country/

ross, k. m. (2020). On Black education: Antiblackness, refusal, and resistance. In C. A. Grant, M. J. Dumas, & A. N. Woodson (Eds.), *The future is Black: Afro pessimism, fugitivity and radical hope in education* (pp. 65–71). Routledge.

She's My Twin Sister. (2021, February 11). It's International Day of Women and Girls in Science. We're taking back to when Amel & Amira wanted to be Rocket from @dapsdraws @nathanbryon book Look Up! And Ada Twist from @andreabeatyauthor and @dr.illustration book Ada Twist Scientist [Facebook photograph]. Retrieved from https://www.facebook.com/Shes-My-Twin-Sister-1585533961494225

Smith-Purviance, A. L. (2021). Masked violence against Black women and Girls. *Feminist Studies, 47*(1), 175–200. https://doi.org/10.1353/fem.2021.0000

Spillers, H. J. (1987). Mama's baby, papa's maybe: An American grammar book. In S. Stryker & D. M. Blackston (Eds.), *The transgender studies reader remix* (pp. 93–104). Routledge.

Stone, N. (2020). *Shuri: A Black Panther novel #1*. Scholastic, Inc.

Stornaiuolo, A., & Thomas, E. E. (2018). Restorying as political action: Authoring resistance through youth media arts. *Learning, Media and Technology, 43*, 345–358. https://doi.org/10.1080/17439884.2018.1498354

Taaffe, C. O. (2016). *Black girl gaze: A visual (re)membering of Black girlhood as an act of resistance* [Unpublished doctoral dissertation]. University of Illinois at Urbana-Champaign. https://www.ideals.illinois.edu/items/93297

Thomas, E. E. (2018). Toward a theory of the Dark Fantastic: The role of racial difference in young adult speculative fiction and media. *Journal of Language and Literacy Education, 14*(1), 1–10. https://files.eric.ed.gov/fulltext/EJ1175839.pdf

Thomas, J., & Harden, A. (2008). Methods for the thematic synthesis of qualitative research in systematic reviews. *BMC Medical Research Methodology, 8*(45). https://doi.org/10.1186/1471-2288-8-45

Toliver, S. (2020). "I desperately need visions of Black people thriving": Emancipating the fantastic with Black Women's words. *Journal of Adolescent and Adult Literacy, 64*(3), 323–332.

Turner, J. D. (2022). We see the stars: Young Black girls' creative imaginings of intersectional STEM futures through art. *The Educational Forum, 86*(2), 396–407. https://doi.org/10.1080/00131725.2022.2101827

Turner, J. D., & Griffin, A. A. (2020). Brown girls dreaming: Adolescent Black girls' futuremaking through multimodal representations of race, gender, and career aspirations. *Research in the Teaching of English, 55*(2), 109–133. https://library.ncte.org/journals/rte/issues/v55-2/31020

Turner, J. D., & Griffin, A. A. (2022). Dream a little [STEAM] of me: Exploring Black adolescent girls' STEAM career futures through digital multimodal compositions. In B. Guzzetti (Ed.), *Genders, literacies, and cultures: Understanding intersecting identities* (pp. 49–61). Routledge.

Watkins, J. [@astro_watkins]. (2019, November 14). #tbt to my first suited run in the @nasa Neutral Buoyancy Laboratory last year. There is nothing (on Earth) quite like spacewalk training in the largest indoor pool in the world [Photograph]. Instagram. https://www.instagram.com/p/B4223GGhdYc/

Wiseman, A. M., Mäkinen, M., & Kupiainen, R. (2016). Literacy through photography: Multimodal and visual literacy in a third grade classroom. *Early Childhood Education Journal, 44*(5), 537–544. https://eric.ed.gov/?id=EJ1106038

Wissman, K. (2008). "This is what I see": (Re)envisioning photography as a social practice. In M. L. Hill & L. Vasudevan (Eds.), *Media, learning, and sites of possibility* (pp. 13–45). Peter Lang.

Young, A. M. (2021). Witnessing wonderland: Research with Black girls imagining freer futures. *English Teaching: Practice & Critique, 20*(4), 420–439. https://eric.ed.gov/?id=EJ1320354

CHAPTER 7

BLACK JOY, LOVE, AND RESISTANCE

Using Digital Storytelling to Center Black Students' Full Humanity

Davena Jackson
Boston University

ABSTRACT

In recent years, critical multimodal research suggests that students can explore issues around social justice, race, racism, and Whiteness (Aguilera & Lopez, 2020; Love, 2014; Matias & Grosland, 2016; Rolón-Dow, 2011; Turner & Griffen, 2020). Digital storytelling, a multimodal tool, can be used as a critical approach for students to work in solidarity to question, interrogate, and dismantle anti-Blackness and anti-racist ideology, which benefits all students (Kress & van Leeuwen, 2001).

This chapter explores how a Black teacher and I, a Black teacher-researcher, used justice-oriented solidarity (JOS) to carve out Black space (Paris, 2017) in an 11th grade English classroom. Thus, Black students created digital stories. I highlight how students critically reflected on and interrogated each other about love, joy, pain, and trauma that affect Black bodies to center

Blackness. I also discuss how the students engaged in critical consciousness-raising where they "challenged the underlying assumptions that work in the internal and external worlds to privilege some while disprivileging others" (Willis et al., 2008, p. 5). Building on having a critically conscious perspective, I show how a Black teacher and I fostered a Black space where students engaged in what I termed *critically conscious talk* ([CCT], Baker-Bell, 2020; Jackson, 2019). CCT served as catalysis in students' storytelling in which they "interrogat[ed] the everyday social realities of power, representation, and identity" (Aguilera & Lopez, 2020, p. 583), and their narrative served as the basis of the written script for their digital story (Robin, 2008).

I show how students' digital stories depict visual anti-Blackness and Blackness, representing their critically conscious conceptions of living a full Black life. I use *visual discourse analysis* to analyze and interpret the students' visual representations and their narrative because it "offers a way of thinking about meaning in which language and visual texts work in concert, and which language is not the primary source through which meaning is mediated and represented" (Albers, 2014, p. 87). I also employ counterstorytelling as a lens because "counterstories challenge dominant narratives of race, equal opportunity, and responsibility, and thereby advance movements toward justice" (Kinloch et al., 2020, p. 387). By employing both visual discourse analysis and counterstorytelling of the students' digital stories, I show the importance of teachers incorporating critical multimodal practices that help students understand the interconnectedness of race, racism, and anti-Blackness to ultimately center Blackness (Dumas & ross, 2016; Baker-Bell, 2019; Johnson, 2018; Jackson, 2020).

This chapter shows a Black teacher and a Black teacher-researcher's anti-racist approach to teaching, learning, and a commitment to work in solidarity to support Black students' critical consciousness- raising to center Blackness. By providing a Black space where Black joy, love, and resistance are at the nexus of Black students' critical consciousness-raising, Black students' lived experiences can be supported and affirmed. Finally, critical digital storytelling is "digital hope used to combat" (Matias & Grosland, 2016, p. 162) anti-Blackness and anti-Black racism.

"I AM MY BLACK SELF"

The Production: Centering Blackness

Moving quietly around the classroom, I observed some students hesitantly whispering during their conversation. At the same time, another group loudly voiced their perspectives about structural and systemic racism, racial violence, and how anti-Blackness has affected their families, community, and the world. This group of students titled their story "I Am My Black Self," which served as the script for the groups' visual depiction of anti-Blackness and Blackness. The classroom teacher asked students to construct a story to accompany their critical digital story. This particular group's overarching message was Black joy, love, and resistance, conveying their understanding of the effects of anti-Black racism on Black humanity, including themselves.

Despite having witnessed or experienced trauma, pain, and injustice, the students' oral and visual representation of their Black life demonstrated that they remained resolute in their opposition to anti-Blackness.

The data (part of a larger study) in this chapter focuses on a critical digital story that a Black teacher (Ms. Thomas)[1] and I, a Black teacher-researcher, assigned 11th graders to co-construct in an English classroom. A critical digital story includes text production and text design that provides the opportunity for a range of exploration, analysis, and interrogation of literature and the world (Freire, 1970; Janks, 2014; Vasquez et al., 2019). We constructed this assignment from a shared commitment to supporting and affirming students' full Black humanity in a Black space (Jackson, 2020). Paris (2017) defined a Black space as a space where one could share stories of their present and past lived experiences that they might associate with trauma, resistance, and healing. Extending Paris's conception of a Black space, I argue that it is also a place where Black students participate in collective storying, thus offering them a space to heal from the traumas, pain, and injustices they might have experienced or witnessed.

In this chapter, I illuminate what is possible when Black students work in a community to reflect on and critically interrogate each other for a shared understanding of issues relative to anti-Black racism while centering Blackness. Tatum (2017) described anti-Black racism as the institutional policies, structures, and cultural messages that created and contributed to the marginalization of Black people. Ultimately, anti-Black racism fuels the pervasiveness of anti-Blackness. Anti-Blackness represents the omnipresence of disdainfulness and violence toward Black people (Dumas & ross, 2016). However, Blackness is the centering and the acceptance of the multiple identities and lived experiences of Black lives (Johnson et al., 2017). hooks (1994) argued that "our solidarity must be affirmed by a shared belief in a spirit of intellectual openness that celebrates diversity, welcomes dissent, and rejoices in collective dedication to truth" (p. 33). In accord with hooks' stance, I contend that focusing on students working in solidarity while designing a multimodal artifact to center Blackness contributes to Black students becoming agents in their learning and transformation.

It is important to note that I draw on the inspiration of critical educators (e.g., Paulo Freire, Toni Morrison, and bell hooks.) In doing so, I call attention to a group of six students (Davonté, MJJ, James, Simone, Shayla, and Casey) to illuminate how they worked in solidarity to examine the histories, languages, knowledges, and experiences of Black people historically omitted or demonized in the "traditional" English curriculum. This study is critical because too few educational spaces center Blackness because "racist educational policies meant to standardize and minimize teaching and learning in indeterminable ways" persist (Thomas, 2020, p. 112). As such, few learning environments support and affirm Black students, "mak[ing] visible the cultural knowledge that contributes to the formation of racial consciousness and positive cultural identity constructions" (Thomas, 2020, p. 112).

Thus, this chapter speaks to a creative, critical literacy engagement—the critical digital story. The multimodal production described in this study highlights a group of students' visual perceptions, multiple consciousnesses, and multivoiced depictions of race, racism, anti-Blackness, and Blackness. More specifically, to support Black students' intellectual and critical consciousness development, I explored the following research questions:

RQ1: *How did a group of Black students work in solidarity to make sense of race, racism, anti-Blackness, and Blackness?*

RQ2: *How did one group of Black students depict visual anti-Blackness and Blackness, representing their multiple consciousnesses of living a full Black life in a critical digital story?*

THEORIZING JUSTICE ORIENTED SOLIDARITY WITH BLACK STUDENTS

Working in Solidarity

Although critical multimodality is central to this chapter, the first research question on how students worked together to make sense of race, racism, anti-Blackness, and Blackness needs to be addressed. Thus, I draw on justice-oriented theories (Ladson-Billings, 1994, 1995; Alim & Paris, 2017; Johnson, 2018; Love, 2019; Kinloch et al., 2020). Specifically, I foreground the theoretical framework, justice-oriented solidarity ([JOS]; Jackson, 2020), to consider how one group of six students collaborated to co-create a compelling critical digital story about race, racism, anti-Blackness, and Blackness. JOS entails a willingness to examine, interrogate, and dismantle anti-Black racism, anti-Blackness, and White supremacy.

Also, understanding the social, political, and economic systems and structures and their impact is vital to actualizing more just systems. Agreeing with Razfar and Rumenapp (2013), I contend that "working in solidarity [represents] strategic conscious synergy with those we share identity affiliations with and those we do not" (Jackson, 2020, pp. 435–436). Furthermore, I assert that the students worked in solidarity because they shared a commitment to centering Blackness (Jackson, 2020).

JOS is essential for relationship building among teachers, teacher-researchers, and students. A key component of students working with and learning from each other is mutual learning, ultimately holding one another responsible. During this representation of JOS, students demonstrated their commitment to building on each other's cultural assets (e.g., identities, histories, and languages; Jackson, 2020). Thus, this chapter illuminates how students collaborated during a multimodal project in a Black space where Blackness took precedence over anti-Blackness (Jackson, 2020).

CRITICAL DIGITAL STORYTELLING: A MULTIMODAL EXPERIENCE CENTERING BLACKNESS

This study examined students' multimodal learning during a particular experience in an English classroom. In this instance, it was a critical digital story. Multimodal research emerged from social semiotics (Kress, 2010). What is compelling about multimodal work is that it attends to meaning making and how images, gestures, writing, music, and so forth, function together to convey meaning (Jewitt, 2008). Lam et al. (2021) argued that multimodal work, specifically multimodal storytelling, expands our understanding of the "types of semiotic tools, artifacts, knowledge, and experiences from students' communities that are included and represented in the educational context" (p. 341). Lam et al. 's project shows the need for continued work to support students' learning, reflect marginalized students' voices, and center their lived experiences, which are not always valued in English classrooms.

Researchers (e.g., Aguilera et al., 2020; Hill, 2009) who explore transforming schooling experiences to reinforce meaningful, democratic learning argue that educational spaces should support critical approaches to engagement. For example, these approaches recognize the benefits of students' critical multimodal opportunities. Critical digital stories, a multimodal tool, can be a valuable resource. For example, Aguilera et al. (2020) suggested that critical digital storytelling could be used to "reframe academic marginalization and celebrate students' stories of resilience" (p. 583). Similarly, Love (2014) used critical digital storytelling to forefront counterstories. Counterstorytelling is one way to engage in resistance and challenge dominant narratives that demonize Blackness and characterize Black students and other racialized groups as inferior. In the study, Love (2014) offered students the opportunity to develop a critical voice through counter- narratives in an English classroom of a hip-hop-based education (HHBE) course titled Real Talk: Hip Hop Education for Social Justice (Real Talk).

Finally, this project examined how students used their understanding and learning to visually depict the intersections of race, racism, Blackness, and anti-Blackness. In addition, the critical digital story was multidimensional (e.g., crafting the multivoiced story, gathering pictures and music, and putting it all together for the presentation). Using various composing modes opened many opportunities to interrogate print, digital, and visual texts. What was most compelling about the possibility of using critical digital stories was that the project focused on students' lived experiences, explicitly centering Blackness and dismantling anti-Black racism.

Moreover, Davonté, MJJ, James, Simone, Shayla, and Casey's critical digital story illuminated how they worked in solidarity to name, question, and dismantle anti-Black racism and anti-Blackness. By working collectively, they focused on what to write in their counternarrative and how to visually represent their understandings of living a full Black life.

METHOD

Situating the Site as Exploration: Collaborating in Solidarity With a Black Woman Teacher

School Context and Teacher Partnership

I partnered with Ms. Thomas, a Black woman teacher at Sutton Academy, a predominantly Black high school in the Midwestern United States, Grades 9–12 (Jackson, 2020). We explored the possibilities of how to center Blackness with 11th-grade students. We exchanged ideas and made joint decisions about the curriculum and pedagogy. The partnership was reciprocal. We fostered a classroom environment that supported and sustained the students culturally, linguistically, and racially (Jackson, 2020). Our inspiration, practitioner inquiry (Cochran-Smith & Lytle, 2009), supported our learning and growth. Our commitment to engaging in mutual learning motivated us to provide the same opportunity for the students in this study. Moreover, our approach to teaching and learning was justice-oriented, leading toward centering Blackness.

The Students

In response to the growing need to carve out educational spaces for Black students (Thomas, 2020), I invite readers to learn from the following students: Davonté, MJJ, James, Simone, Shayla, and Casey. Five of the students self-identified as either Black or African American. James, the only non-Black student in the class, self-identified as White. The students ranged in age from 16 to 17. In an 11th-grade English classroom, the students' experiences of working in solidarity demonstrate how centering Blackness fostered a Black space where Black love, joy, and resistance existed.

Critical Synergy: Davonté, MJJ, James, Simone, Shayla, and Casey

I define critical synergy in an educational context as two or more groups working alongside each other towards the greater good to name, question, disrupt, and dismantle anti-Black racism, White supremacy, and dominant hegemonic ideologies that dehumanize Black people. To achieve solidarity, a groups' efforts focus not on one individual but on the strength of their collective humanity (e.g., their identities, knowledges, backgrounds, languages). For instance, in carving out a Black space in an English classroom where students worked collaboratively, I observed the students' critical synergy facilitate the production of a compelling critical digital story.

During an interview about working as a group to create their critical digital story, Shayla expressed,

> I think [working collectively] allowed for me to hear and to mentally process a bunch of different ideas that were similar and different from my own, and because we all have so many different experiences so many different interpretations of what it means to be Black, it was nice to come together all these different stories, and then to find something that works that accommodates all our different interpretations of what it means to be Black.

Equally joyful about the opportunity to work collectively, MJJ shared,

> I would say that having the opportunity of working with a group of people and putting together the digital story, for me, I would say it was a good experience. Mostly because, we all contributed to different aspects. Like Simone, wrote the poem... and I was able to offer, like, some photos and music. And when I offered the music, I offered a song "Bittersweet." And I would say that—it encapsulated the whole idea of being and having a Black identity.

What is most revealing about the students' collaboration and their statements was that they had a space to explore the possibilities of representing Blackness to disrupt anti-Blackness. The students had a critical orientation to the work and could build on and interrogate each other's perspectives about the classroom texts and their lived experiences. While expressing their sentiments and making discoveries about each other's conceptions of Blackness and dealings with anti-Black racism, the students produced a critical synergy, which fostered their solidarity towards valuing and building on each other's critical consciousness without judgment.

Educating for Critical Consciousness: Centering Critically Conscious Talk

Freire (1970) stressed that conscientization, critical consciousness, is an approach involving critical reflection, inviting learners to engage critically about oppressive systems and structures that may lead to transformation. Also, McDonough (2009) illuminated that a critical consciousness engagement can involve analyzing power dynamics and employing reflection and inquiry to question assumptions. Similarly, Willis et al. (2008) argued that critical consciousness refers to how a person can "challenge the underlying assumptions that work in the internal and external worlds to privilege some while depriviliging others" (p. 5). I share how developing students' critical consciousness engagement involved working in solidarity to produce one critical digital story. Finally, the students' evolving critical consciousness correlated with their ability to decenter anti-Blackness to highlight Blackness.

I offer that this multimodal engagement occurred from students participating in what I have termed *critically conscious talk* ([CCT]; Baker-Bell, 2020; Jackson, 2019). The operating tenets of CCT are the following:

1. As part of working in solidarity, share in the responsibility of and commitment towards collaborating with and learning from each other.
2. Name, question, disrupt, and dismantle anti-Black racism, anti-Blackness, White supremacy, White supremacist narratives, and address other factors such as power, racism, inequity, sexism, classism, ableism, homophobia, transphobia, xenophobia.
3. Build on the critical consciousness of others' multiple consciousnesses.

I define White supremacist narratives as "anti-Black positioning that contribute to the harm, shame, and violence and 'spirit murdering' (Johnson, 2018; Love, 2019) of Black lives" (Jackson, 2022). CCT is where students build on each other's multiple consciousnesses. At the heart of CCT is criticality. I draw on Muhammad's definition of criticality. Muhammad (2020) posited that

> criticality is also related to seeing, naming, and interrogating the world to not only make sense of injustice, but also work toward social transformation. Thus, students need spaces to name and critique injustice to help them ultimately develop the agency to build a better world. (p. 12)

CCT helps to facilitate spaces that center students' critical consciousness. Moreover, in this space, students can offer alternative ways of thinking and

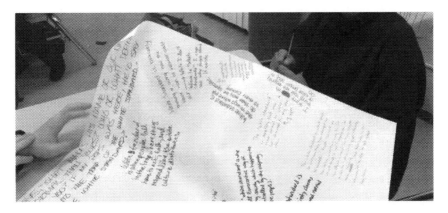

Figure 7.1 Photo of CCT in action. I videorecorded, took pictures, and wrote field notes about the students in action.

being that do not dehumanize each other's existence, leading to learning from one another and offering liberating ideas (hooks, 2003). In amplifying students' multiple consciousnesses in this project, CCT allowed the students to question, interrogate, and dismantle White supremacist narratives that operationalized Black suffering (Dumas, 2014). Furthermore, engaging students in CCT constructed knowledge. As a result of their participation, they shared their thinking without having to experience shame and judgment about their language use (e.g., if they used Black language) and their understanding of anti-Black racism, White supremacy, and Blackness.

After carefully planning the curriculum, Ms. Thomas and I created an opportunity for the students to participate in a *chalk talk*, a discussion tool that we used to support CCT. We intentionally created our questions for this activity. They reflect several chapters from *The Hate You Give* ([T.H.U.G.]; Thomas, 2017). Moreover, we wanted to guarantee a greater likelihood that the students' responses would be in connection with their having to think critically about issues surrounding anti-Black racism, White supremacy, and Blackness. For instance, I zoomed in on one group participating in CCT after they had used chalk talk to respond to some questions about the novel and direct quotes taken from T.H.U.G. Ms. Thomas and I constructed questions and extracted quotes from the novel so that the students could think about and respond to them as a group:

1. Why add the character Fo'ty Ounce?
2. Why do you think Thomas decided to make Uncle Carlos a police officer and Chris (Starr's boyfriend) White?
3. How can we become more community-minded to engage in community action to disrupt anti-Blackness?

4. "Way too many people are watching. I cannot go angry black girl on her" (p. 340).
5. "Khalil and I have been on trial since he died" (p. 333).
6. Seven says, "What makes his name or our names any less normal than yours? Who or what defines 'normal' to you? If my pops were here, he'd say you've fallen in the trap of the White standard" (p. 401). What is the White standard?

Walking around the classroom with the video recorder in hand, I documented (Figures 7.1 & 7.2) how the students talked back and forth while building on or interrogating each other's multiple consciousnesses. I heard bits and pieces of the students' CCT. Encountering one particular group, who entered a discussion about the importance of names, I stopped to listen to their enactment of CCT. I heard Shayla read a passage from the text in which the character, Seven, asked the following questions: "What makes his name or our names any less normal than yours? Who or what defines 'normal' to you? If my pops were here, he'd say you've fallen in the trap of the white standard" (Thomas, 2017, p. 401). Ms. Thomas and I added to Seven's question by posing: "What is the White standard?" To her group members, Shayla shared, "By saying that the White culture is the standard is telling people to change from their own culture and assimilate to White culture is basically anti-Blackness." I observed the entire group nod their heads in agreement with Shayla's analysis. Shayla's remark revealed her acknowledgment and understanding of Black people being expected to "blend into the dominant culture as much as possible, distancing oneself from one's ethnic group" (Tatum, 2017, pp. 244–245). Also, Thomas's (2017) portrayal of some characters highlights how we think and operate within a world impacted by what Morrison (1992) called the White gaze. The embodiment of Morrison's (1992) White gaze is the centering of Whiteness and its impact. Thus, the characters in the novel cope with how the effect of the White gaze operates through racism, anti-Black racism, poverty, inequity, the White standard of beauty, and so forth. Moreover, by engaging in CCT, students addressed the complexities of the White gaze in T.H.U.G. and their lives while dismantling anti-Black racism.

Later, Davonté remarked on how "the White standard did not just kinda happen because since the beginning of time...even the framers of the Constitution were White so [they] kinda set up a White standard from the beginning of time." Shayla followed up with a seemingly unapologetic response stating, "America is known as the melting pot, where all kinds of people with different cultures, races, and religious backgrounds can come together and co-exist but like still be different but by having this White standard you're basically saying that everyone has to be the same way or act a certain way..." Throughout the students' engagement in CCT, they

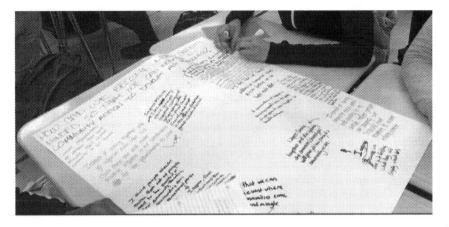

Figure 7.2 Photo of CCT in action.

acknowledged their understanding of how Black people experience anti-Black racism and its effects.

To continue participating in CCT, another group grappled with the question: "How can we become more community-minded to engage in community action to disrupt anti-Blackness?" This question was more challenging than the prior questions for the students. One group member called attention to a student's response and voiced, "I think that in addition to coming together and building each other up, we need to address what's wrong in our communities. Start building our youth up and exposing them to possible opportunities for their future. Lead, guide, and nurture them." For the next moment or so, they looked at the other responses and occasionally nodded in agreement or disagreement with a particular answer. Although the group wrestled with which proposed solution they should share, they came to a consensus about the significance of civic activism. Making room for CCT opened opportunities for students to engage in criticality. More specifically, it served as the foundation for the groups' critical consciousness-raising, which led to working in solidarity to produce their critical digital stories.

Visual Discourse Analysis: Visual and Textual Conceptions of Anti-Blackness and Blackness

Rose (2016) acknowledged that a critical approach to examining images is needed, especially one that considers the image, the social practices, and the effects on those viewing the images. Although some researchers do not explicitly articulate that they used visual discourse analysis (VDA) in their research, their work represents a critical approach to understanding the visual, multimodal production of students' work. For example, Turner and Griffin (2020) examined the visual images of two Black adolescent girls' career dreaming and multimodal futuremaking. Relatedly, Vasudevan (2006) bridged counterstorytelling and multimodality to explore one boy's conceptualization of his multiple selves through visual and textual production. Also, Love (2014) fostered a learning environment where students could use urban storytelling to engage in moviemaking to challenge anti-Black narratives about Black youth. Finally, similar to my work in this chapter, these examples represent the multifaceted approaches to critical multimodal representation, analysis, and the possibilities of "creativity, imagination, and exploration" (Vasudevan, 2006, p. 2007).

Alternatively, Albers (2014) called attention to VDA. *Visual discourse analysis* is a theoretical approach grounded in semiotics. More explicitly, it is an approach that examines the signs and systems relative to the significance of expression, representation, and communication. For instance, Albers (2014) studied "student-generated visual texts, the discourses that emerged within the text, the text itself, the macro conversations surrounding the making and viewing of texts, and the visual text as a communicative event" (p. 87). Building on Alber's (2014) study, I employed VDA as an analytical tool. Thus, I examined the visuals in the students' critical digital story, the text that emerged in their written counterstory, the conversations about their texts, and the critical digital story as an opportunity to disrupt anti-Blackness.

To analyze the groups' multiple consciousnesses and the visual and textual representations, I coded (Figure 7.3) the group's critical digital story into three categories: the students' images representing each stanza, their multiple consciousness representations, and the text from the poem, "I Am My Black Self." While the group employed many visual images, I chose to sample the images that centered Blackness while simultaneously decentering anti-Blackness due to space.

Equally helpful was how the group shared their thoughts about their text and images during one-on-one interviews. For example, during an interview with MJJ, I learned that the group chose to focus on the theme of identity. Also, MJJ shared that they determined they could more easily focus on the constructs of race, racism, anti-Blackness, and Blackness by looking for patterns across their collected images, shared experiences, and perceptions of anti-Black racism and Blackness. Finally, I ascertained that although Simone had composed the poem's first draft, she and the group members collectively made revisions and edits to reflect everyone's multiple consciousnesses. The final version is represented in Figure 7.3.

A Sampling of Images	Multiple Consciousness Representations	Text (Poem)
Stanza 1 	Blackness	1 **I am my Black Self**
Stanza 2 	Blackness	2 I am my Black Self 3 But not just from the outside, but on the inside 4 I have this culture that follows me around 5 like a vulture that stalks its prey 6 However, in a good way
Stanza 3  	Blackness	7 I know from this that I am what has made me 8 From the beautiful colors, songs, dances, and faces 9 That have collided into one to make the person that I am today 10 But for some reason, my blackness has been viewed as a way to insult
Stanza 4  	Anti-Blackness/ Race/Racism	12 I cannot wear my hair out in its natural state 13 Without it being labeled as "dirty" or "unruly" 14 That I should straighten it to conform to these standards that have 15 somehow 16 Been the "correct" way of doing things

Figure 7.3 The Poem—I am my Black Self

Stanza 5		Anti-Blackness/ Race/Racism	17 I cannot be seen without the color of my skin
			18 Being the first thing that people notice about me and now there is
			19 This curiosity within me that has to wonder why I have to ponder
			20 Over these insecurities that I have
Stanza 6		Blackness	21 "I cannot speak to someone without thinking about which language
			22 I shall speak in *their* presence
			23 But who controls articulation? The English language is a
			24 multifaceted oration subject to indefinite transformation"
			25 Therefore, how I say what I say, it still maintains its essence"—Jamila Lyiscott
Stanza 7		Blackness moves to Anti-Blackness/ Race/Racism	26 **I am my Black Self**
			27 Not just from outside looking, but from outside looking out
			28 I see all these black men being killed over the color that they were born with
			29 And it makes me think of *why* they are killed over the color that they were born with
Stanza 8		Anti-Blackness/ Race/Racism	30 And by the police?
			31 The ones who are supposed to "protect"
			32 But who are they "protecting" when they are the ones who are "assuming"
			33 That Black men are the abominations to this nation that we call "America"?

Figure 7.3 The Poem—I am my Black Self

Black Joy, Love, and Resistance • **161**

Stanza 9	Anti-Blackness/Race/Racism	34 And that brings me to another topic which is *the* Black Man
		35 The Black Man, also referred to as the "Negro"
		36 And the bottom of the American societal chain
Stanza 10	Anti-Blackness/Race/Racism	37 One cannot fathom how much has been thrown at them
		38 Without losing their own minds and spirits
Stanza 11	Anti-Blackness/Race/Racism	39 The false charges, stop and searches and situations
		40 Where a hairbrush or phone are "mistaken" for a gun
		41 And these "mistakes" that have been going on for a while now
		42 Have made someone lose a husband, father, or son
Stanza 12	Blackness	43 No, I am not apologetic for my Blackness and my pride
		44 No, I am not apathetic to what is happening and happened my people
Stanza 13	Blackness	45 **I am** just my **Black** self
		46 Blackness is defined through multiple characteristics, some of which are:
		47 Strength, courage, family, unity, culture, identity.
		48 Who I am and who I always will be.

Figure 7.3 The Poem—I am my Black Self

Stanza 14	Blackness	49 A network of similarities with its own unique language.
		50 Yes, Black Language. The way I talk.
		51 And it ain't wrong either.
Stanza 15	Blackness	52 It's my race, and my ethnicity.
		53 My physical characteristics and my nationality.
		54 What society made me and what I am made of.
		55 Yes, at times it's a struggle
		56 Fighting all these labels and boundaries
		57 Trying not to be what the system wants me to be,
		58 Simply because what they see
		59 When they look at me.
Stanza 16 	Blackness	62 **I am my Black Self**

Figure 7.3 The Poem—I am my Black Self

FINDINGS

Justice-Oriented Solidarity: Centering the Critical Digital Story

The following findings represent what can happen when students are invited to work collectively during a multimodal literacy engagement. As discussed in the theoretical framing for JOS, JOS fosters students working in solidarity and having a shared commitment to center Blackness and de-center anti-Blackness. While working alongside each other to co-create the critical digital story, the students shared their thoughts about witnessing or first-hand experiences with trauma, acts of resistance, or moments of healing. Thus, this groups' critical digital story, "I Am My Black Self," powerfully depicts students dismantling of anti-Blackness to ultimately center Blackness. I organized the findings around three themes: (a) critical synergy, (b) Blackness, (c) anti-Blackness and racism. The following discussion illuminates the importance of and need for transformative critical multimodal practices that support the critical consciousness building of all students.

Critical Synergy

Working collaboratively and showing a strong sense of Black pride, joy, and love for oneself which foreground Blackness, the group wrote the poignant first line of Stanza 1, "I am my Black Self." What is most compelling about the opening is that the group depicts their solidarity—the unity of their multiple consciousnesses as one. For example, the pronoun "I" is used rather than "we." In addition, the group's multiple consciousnesses reflect how the students worked together to reflect on their lived experiences both in and out of school, examined systemic and structural racism, and interrogated each other towards dismantling systems that contribute to anti-Black racism through their poem and images.

Blackness

To center Blackness in Stanza 2, the group acknowledges that their Black beauty is inside and outside. First, they highlight the image of a Black woman, a Black meal, and a vulture looking overhead. the poem's first draft in Lines 2–6 and represent Blackness despite Black peoples' marginalization. Their shared consciousness suggests their acknowledgment of Black pride. Next, in Stanza 3, they chose the images of a basketball, Black food, a Black girl, and a Black boy dancing, pictured over the rainbow flag, representing LGBTQ+ identities. The objects within this stanza are consistent with their depiction of Black pride and multiple intersecting identities representing Blackness. Finally, there is a shift in Line 10, where they wrote: "But for some reason, my Blackness has been viewed as a way to insult." In symbolizing Blackness and attending to the dichotomy of Blackness and anti-Blackness, the students acknowledge the tension between the two. For example, in showing the body of a Black boy and juxtaposing the words, "My Blackness has been viewed as a way to insult," the students illuminate how Black bodies experience Black suffering (Dumas, 2014).

In reference to Blackness, in Stanza 13, they return to the refrain, "I am just my Black Self" in Line 45. In Stanza 12, they write in Lines 44–46: "No, I am not apologetic for my Blackness and my pride/No I am not apathetic to what is happening to and happened to my people." The group provides the image of President Barack Obama, the United States' first Black president. The image and the text reveal how the group remains resolute. Specifically, they accept their Black humanity despite the ongoing oppression that Black people have endured. They depict a sense of hope and resiliency. Moving back to Stanza 13, the students continue to center Blackness. The image from the "Blackish" television show and the figure representing the words "culture, unity, family, and strength" and a Black baby call attention to the force of Blackness.

Being Black is not only about Black suffering but also Black solidarity, hope, and courage.

Next, in Stanza 14, the group celebrates Black language by representing the image of the word "ain't" and juxtaposing it with a picture of a Black fist denoting Black pride and power.

Baker-Bell (2020) noted that "Black students navigate and negotiate their linguistic, racial, and sociopolitical identities within multiple, hostile contexts" (p. ix). The students' text and images counter the anti-Black narrative around Black language. Later, in the poem, the students expose how Black language is weaponized and used to malign Black language speakers.

Anti-Blackness and Racism

Focusing on anti-Blackness and racism, the shared visual images in Stanza 4 highlight the shame and violence that Black people withstood. The image of the local news station reporting that the mother is battling the school about her daughter's hair juxtaposed with a picture of a young Black girl bombarded with questions and statements: "Why don't you do something with your hair?; "Do you speak African?"; or "Black girls are loud." These remarks index the reality and ongoing relationship between the inhumanity of Blackness because of slavery (ross, 2021).

As represented in Lines 13–14, they recognize that "I cannot wear my hair out in its natural state/without it being labeled as 'dirty' or 'unruly.'" They implicitly understand how Black peoples' actions remain under surveillance of the White gaze and how anti-Black actions and sentiments can contribute to their experiencing racial shame, trauma, and policing (Dumas & ross, 2016).

Moving on to Stanza 5, in Lines 19–20, the group employs the images of Black faces and dice with question marks. Therefore, they help show how they may question the negative experiences relative to Blackness. Many Black students are in a constant state of ambivalence about their Black humanity based on false perceptions and inhumane portrayals of Blackness. Moreover, they acknowledge their sentiments of having to navigate an anti-Black world. For example, anti-Black racism undergirds anti-Black linguistic racism (Baker-Bell, 2020). Baker-Bell (2019) argued that "Anti-black linguistic racism refers to the linguistic violence, persecution, dehumanization, and marginalization that Black Language (BL) speakers endure when using their language in schools and everyday life" (p. 2). Using CCT on Black language, a student remarked, "I feel like there is a common stereotype in the U.S., especially within urban cities, that Black people speak ghetto." The images of diverse languages and the excerpted Lines 21–26 in Stanza 6 from Jamila Lyiscott's (2014) TED Talk capture a similar sentiment,

(21) I cannot speak to someone without thinking about which language
(22) I shall speak in *their* presence
(23) But who controls articulation? The English language is a
(24) multifaceted oration subject to indefinite transformation.
(26) Therefore, how I say what I say, it still maintains its essence.

The students recognize their agency in using Black language in "their" presence. During the group interview, Casey stated,

A part of me wanted to suppress that Blackness... but I am Black, and I am not White, and I have to take pride in what I am and who I am [has] helped to strengthen my love for myself, and my culture, and language

The students made connections to how deficit thinking plays a role in how White supremacy is inextricably linked to anti-Black linguistic racism. In addition, the students foreground how racial violence and police brutality contribute to the constant Black pain and suffering of Black people in Stanzas 7–11. The images of a handcuffed Black man and man in chains and the image of the civil rights movement represent the exploration of Black suffering and an era of mobilization and activism, respectively. Further, in Lines 31–34 and Lines 40–43, they share the following lines:

(Lines 30–33)

(30) And by the police?
(31) The ones who are supposed to "protect"

(32) But who are they "protecting" when they are the ones who are "assuming"
(33) That Black men are the abominations to this nation that we call "America"?

(Lines 39–42)

(39) The false charges, stop and searches and situations
(40) Where a hairbrush or phone are "mistaken" for a gun
(41) And these "mistakes" that have been going on for a while now
(42) Have made someone lose a husband, father, or son

Lines 30–42 show how racial violence (e.g., unjust harassment, beatings, and killings triggered by false claims and racial stereotypes) represents "an overarching climate of Black suffering" (Coles & Stanley, 2021, p. 2).

Overall, the students illuminate the tension between anti-Blackness and Blackness. They recognize, "Yes, at times it's a struggle/Fighting all these labels and boundaries" in Lines 55–56 of Stanza 15. Grant (2020) argued that "many Black people continue to have hope in their collective effort and resiliency even when beset by dominating forces" (p. 70). The image of a group of happy Black children, fried chicken and watermelon, and a Black man shaking his head appear to capture their feelings of experiencing joy amid racial stigmas. Finally, the group returns to the poignant reminder of "I am my Black Self" as an indication of their solidarity and acceptance of Black humanity in contrast to the ongoing omnipresence of anti-Black racism.

Implications of Critical Multimodal Engagements Centering Blackness

How might using different mediums to understand students' cultural contexts and consciousness about race, racism, anti-Blackness, and Blackness help educators "to encompass diverse perspectives, epistemologies, and ways of being in the world" (Thomas, 2020, p. 128)? This chapter argues broadly for a school curriculum that supports critical multimodal engagements like critical digital stories. Also, I contend that JOS is an approach educators can employ to foster critical multimodal composition. For example, the poem **"I Am My Black Self"** represents the students' effort to engage in JOS. It also represents an engaging multimodal experience that centers students' multiple consciousnesses of critical synergy, which can support and affirm Black students' humanity. This study's findings demonstrate how providing Black students with an opportunity to engage in creative, critical multimodal work is vital.

The very practice of students working in solidarity can be used as an opportunity for them to dismantle anti-Blackness. Given what we can learn from Davonté, MJJ, James, Simone, Shayla, and Casey, educators should be willing to create liberatory spaces and act as change agents by providing multimodal opportunities that are meaningful and consequential to their students (Turner & Griffin, 2020). Moreover, educators should be compelled to make pedagogical and curricular choices that promote criticality and center Blackness.

Finally, "Transforming the curriculum requires that teacher educators, themselves, are committed to such transformation and that they are prepared to teach content in ways that do not perpetuate and reinforce inequity" (Milner & Laughtner, 2015, p. 352). I argue that the multimodal experience represented in this chapter is humanizing and just one of many ways to decenter anti-Blackness. A humanizing approach to students' learning, which centers Blackness, is about "designing and enacting projects that heal wounds and foster love through the process of critical inquiry and praxis" (Baker-Bell et al., 2017, p. 373). Thus, to truly embrace the humanity of Black students, I passionately contend that educators must provide meaningful liberatory experiences that foreground justice and equity.

NOTE

1. The teacher's name, the students' names, and the school's name are all pseudonyms.

REFERENCES

Aguilera, E., & Lopez, G. (2020). Centering first-generation college students' lived experiences through critical digital storytelling. *Journal of Adolescent & Adult Literacy, 63*(5), 583–587. https://doi.org/10.1002/jaal.1037

Albers, P. (2014). Visual discourse analysis. In P. Albers, T. Holbrook, & A. S. Flint (Eds.), *New methods on literacy research*. Routledge.

Alim, H. S., & Paris, D. (2017). What is culturally sustaining pedagogy and why does it matter? In D. Paris & H. S. Alim (Eds.), *Culturally sustaining pedagogies* (pp. 1–21). Teachers College.

Baker-Bell, A. (2019). Dismantling anti-Black linguistic racism in English language arts classrooms: Toward an anti-racist Black language pedagogy. *Theory Into Practice, 59*(1), 8–21. https://doi.org/10.1080/00405841.2019.1665415

Baker-Bell, A. (2020). *Linguistic justice: Black language, literacy, identity, and pedagogy.* Routledge.

Baker-Bell, A., Paris, D., & Jackson, D. (2017). Learning Black language matters: Humanizing research as culturally sustaining pedagogy. *International Review* of *Qualitative Research, 10*(4), 360–377. https://doi.org/10.1525/irqr.2017.10.4.360

Cochran-Smith, M., & Lytle, S. L. (2009). *Inquiry as stance: Practitioner research for the next generation*. Teachers College Press.

Coles, J. A., & Stanley, D. (2021). Black liberation in teacher education: (Re)envisioning educator preparation to defend Black life and possibility. *Northwest Journal of Teacher Education, 16*(2), 1–24. https://doi.org/10.15760/nwjte.2021.16.2.6

Dumas, M. J. (2014). 'Losing an arm': Schooling as a site of black suffering. *Race, Ethnicity and Education, 17*(1), 1–29. https://doi.org/10.1080/13613324.2013.850412

Dumas, M. J., & ross, K. M. (2016). "Be real Black for me": Imagining BlackCrit in education. *Urban Education, 51*(4), 415–442. https://doi.org/10.1177/0042085916628611

Freire, P. (1970). *Pedagogy of the oppressed*. Continuum.

Grant, C. A. (2020). Radical hope, education and humanity. In C. Grant, A. N. Woodson, & M. J. Dumas (Eds.), *The future is Black: Afropessimism, fugitivity, and radical hope in education* (pp. 65–71). Routledge.

Hill, M. L. (2009). *Beats, rhymes, and classroom life: hip-hop pedagogy and the politics of identity*. Teachers College Press.

hooks, b. (1994). *Teaching to transgress: Education as the practice of freedom*. Routledge.

hooks, b. (2003). *Teaching community: A pedagogy of hope*. Routledge.

Jackson, D. (2019). Black symmetry: Carving out a Black space in an eleventh-grade class [Unpublished doctoral dissertation]. Michigan State University. https://d.lib.msu.edu/islandora/search?type=dismax&f%5B0%5D=subject_display%3AAfrican%5C%20Americans%5C-%5C-Study%5C%20and%5C%20teaching

Jackson, D. (2020). Relationship building in a Black space: Partnering in solidarity. *Journal of Literacy Research, 52*(4), 432–455. https://doi.org/10.1177/1086296X20966358

Jackson, D. (2022). Making sense of Black students' figured worlds of race, racism, anti-Blackness, and Blackness. *Research in the Teaching of English, 57*(1), 43–66.

Janks, H. (2014). Critical literacy's ongoing importance for education. *Journal of Adolescent & Adult Literacy, 57*(5), 349–356. https://doi.org/10.1002/jaal.260

Jewitt, C. (2008). Multimodality and literacy in school classrooms. *Review of Research in Education, 32*(1), 241–267. https://doi.org/10.3102/0091732X07310586

Johnson, L. L. (2018). Where do we go from here? Toward a critical race English education. *Research in the Teaching of English, 53*(2), 102–121. https://www.jstor.org/stable/26802728

Johnson, L. L., Jackson, J., Stovall, D. O., & Baszile, D. T. (2017). "Loving Blackness to death": Imagining ELA classrooms in a time of racial chaos. *The English Journal, 106*(4), 60–66. https://www.jstor.org/stable/26359464

Kinloch, V., Burkhard, T., Penn, C., & Sealey-Ruiz, Y. (2020). *Race, justice, and activism in literacy instruction*. Teachers College Press.

Kress, G. (2010). *Multimodality: A social semiotic approach to contemporary communication*. Routledge.

Kress, G., & Van Leeuwen, T. (2001). *Multimodal discourse: The modes and media of contemporary communication*. Arnold Publishers.

Ladson-Billing, G. (1994). *The dreamkeapers: Successful teachers of African American children*. Jossey-Bass.

Ladson-Billings, G. (1995). Toward a theory of culturally relevant pedagogy. *American Education Research Journal, 32*(3), 465–491. https://doi.org/10.3102/00028312032003465

Lam, W. S. A., Chang, A. A., Rosaria-Ramos, E. M., Smirnov, N., Easterday, M. W., & Doppelt, J. C. (2021). Multimodal voicing and scale-making in a youth-produced video documentary on immigration. *Research in the Teaching of English, 55*(4), 344–368. https://bpb-us-e1.wpmucdn.com/sites.northwestern.edu/dist/d/3663/files/2021/07/Lam-et-al.-RTE-2021.pdf

Love, B. L. (2014). Urban storytelling: How storyboarding, moviemaking, and hip-hop-based education can promote students' critical voice. *The English Journal, 103*(5), 53–58. https://www.jstor.org/stable/24484246

Love, B. L. (2019). *We want to do more than survive: Abolitionist teaching and the pursuit of educational freedom*. Beacon Press.

Lyiscott, J. (2014, June). *"3 ways to speak English"* [Video]. TED. https://www.ted.com/talks/jamila_lyiscott_3_ways_to_speak_english?language=en

Matias, C. E., & Grosland, T. J. (2016). Digital storytelling as racial justice. *Journal of Teacher Education, 67*(2), 152–164. https://doi.org 10.1177/0022487115624493

McDonough, K. (2009). Pathways to critical consciousness: A first-year teacher's engagement with issues of race and equity. *Journal of Teacher Education, 60*(5) 528–537. https://doi.org/10.1177/0022487109348594

Milner, H. R., & Laughtner, J. C. (2015). But good intentions are not enough: Preparing teachers to center race and poverty. *The Urban Review, 47*(2), 341–363. https://eric.ed.gov/?id=EJ1061133

Morrison, T. (1992). *Playing in the dark: Whiteness and the literary imagination*. Vintage Books.

Muhammad, G. (2020). *Cultivating genius: An equity framework for culturally and historically responsive literacy*. Scholastic.

Paris, R. (2017). *The forgetting tree: A rememory*. Wayne State University Press.

Razfar, A., & Rumenapp, J. C. (2013). *Applying linguistics in the classroom. A sociocultural perspective*. Routledge.

Robin. (2008). Digital storytelling: A powerful technology tool for the 21st century classroom. *Theory into Practice, 47*(3), 220–228. https://doi.org/10.1080/00405840802153916

Rolón-Dow, R. (2011). Race(ing) stories: Digital storytelling as a tool for critical race scholarship. *Ethnicity and Education, 14*(2), 159–173. https://doi.org/10.1080/13613324.2010.519975

Rose, G. (2016). *Visual methodologies: An introduction to researching with visual materials*. SAGE.

Ross, K. M. (2021). On Black education: Anti-Blackness, refusal, and resistance. In C. Grant, A. N. Woodson, & M. J. Dumas (Eds.), *The future is Black: Afropessimism, fugitivity, and radical hope in education* (pp. 7–15). Routledge.

Tatum, B. D. (2017). *"Why are all the Black kids sitting together in the cafeteria?" and other conversations about race*. Basic Books.

Thomas, A. (2017). *The hate u give*. Balzer and Bray.

Thomas, D. (2020). One love, one heart. In V. Kinloch, T. Burkhard, & C. Penn (Eds.), *Race, justice, and activism in literacy instruction* (pp. 112–129). Teachers College Press.

Turner, J. D., & Griffin. A. A. (2020). Brown girls dreaming: Adolescent Black girls' futuremaking through multimodal representations of race, gender, and career aspirations. *Research in the Teaching of English, 55*(2), 109–133. https://educatorinnovator.org/wp-content/uploads/2021/02/RTE_Volume_55_Issue_2_Brown-Girls-Dreaming_-Adolescent-Black-Girlsrsquo-Futuremaking-through-Multimodal-Representations-of-Race-Gender-and-Career-Aspirations.v1-1.pdf

Vasquez, V. M., Janks, H., Comber, B. (2019). Critical literacy as a way of being and doing. *Language Arts, 96*(5), 300–311.

Vasudevan, L. (2006). Making known differently: Engaging visual modalities as spaces to author new selves. *E-learning and Digital Media, 3*(2), 207–216. https://doi.org/10.2304/elea.2006.3.2.207

Willis, A. I., Montavon, M., Hall, H., Burke, L., & Herrera, A. (2008). *On critically conscious research: Approaches to language and literacy research*. Teachers College Press.

CHAPTER 8

IT STARTS WITH A (DIGITAL) STORY

Agentive Inquiry Through Digital Storytelling

Andrea N. Franyutti-Boyles
Voxy

Sara Cooper
Murray State University

Gregory Ramírez
Madera Community College

ABSTRACT

One teacher-researcher joins a staticky recording of her phone interview with her immigrant father with photographs of his life growing up in Mexico to reveal the origins of her work with English language learners. Another, a writing instructor at a community college, takes viewers on a video tour of his work commute through California's Central Valley to a campus deserted due to COVID-19. His steady voice overlays the landscape, asking us to consider the connection between place, technology, and access for Latinx students. This chapter, written by the composers of these stories and the instructor of their instructional technology course, demonstrates how graduate students and practicing teachers in an English pedagogy program used digital storytelling as a point of entry into academic inquiry, thus practicing embodied collaborative storytelling forwarded by scholars promoting feminist (Calderón et al., 2012; Glenn, 2018; Royster & Kirsch, 2012) and critical race theory (Solórzano & Yosso, 2016) research methodologies.

Jason Palmeri (2012), Jodi Shipka (2011), and others have challenged a preoccupation with multimodal compositions as a course product, arguing for the use of multimodal invention activities at various stages of the research process. Responding to this critique, this chapter positions digital storytelling as a generative story-based research practice allowing teacher researchers beginning an inquiry project to merge personal, scholarly, and teacherly identities toward greater agency and awareness of researcher positionality. Incorporating screenshots of student digital stories, this multimodal chapter demonstrates how digital story, through an emphasis on self-revelation, first-person voice, experimentation (Lambert, 2018), and collaboration, becomes a "democratizing medium" (Trimboli, 2020) with potential to disrupt traditional Western research paradigms grounded in hierarchies and false notions of value neutrality (Calderón et al., 2012; Glenn, 2018).

Sara Cooper draws on student digital stories and statements of goals and choices (Shipka, 2011) to demonstrate how graduate students readying to embark on their final capstone projects identified personal connections to a scholarly question through the genre affordances of an embodied collaborative storytelling practice.

Andrea Boyles describes how her digital story, centered on her immigrant father, served as a means of exploring how her family history and life experiences shaped her values and professional path. She advocates using digital storytelling to encourage agency among English language learners who frequently have unwanted identities imposed on them by others.

Gregory Ramírez describes how his digital story engages with issues of educational equity and access by focusing on the often-ignored challenges faced by his Latinx students.

His story, situated and embodied, exists as a form of "counter-storytelling" that counteracts "monovocal stories about the low educational achievement and attainment of students of color" (Solórzano & Yosso, 2016, p. 130). He situates multimodal composition as a collaborative practice that can promote equity in the face of the digital divide.

Engaging in teacher-research and autoethnography, the authors analyze digital composing practices to illustrate "the role that narratives of self—stories about who we have been in the past and who we want to become in the future—can play in construction of agentive identities" (Hull & Katz, 2006, p. 44).

> *When our lived experience of theorizing is fundamentally linked to processes of self-recovery, of collective liberation, no gap exists between theory and practice.*
> —bell hooks (2004, p. 61)

One teacher-researcher joins a staticky recording of her phone interview with her immigrant father with photographs of his life growing up in Mexico to reveal the origins of her work with English language learners (ELLs). Another, a community college writing instructor, takes viewers on a video tour of his commute through California's Central Valley to a campus deserted due to COVID-19. His steady voice overlays the landscape, asking us to consider the connection among place, technology, and access for Latinx students. These digital stories were created by graduate students in an English pedagogy doctoral program in the Spring of 2020. As the world reeled at the hands of an unprecedented virus, and as many of us turned inward—literally and figuratively retreating from public space—these students, also practicing teachers, went inward to understand the roots of their academic obsessions. They looked to their homes, families, geographies, workplaces, and histories to identify connections between their scholarly and personal stories, connections they explored further through the affordances of multiple modes. This "self-recovery" work, to borrow from the hooks epigraph above, became an entry point into the students' culminating doctoral projects, and a way to blur the line between the academic and the personal, a division that has proved contrary to liberatory teaching practices.

Scholars of feminist (Calderón et al., 2012; Glenn, 2018; Royster & Kirsch, 2012) and critical race theory (CRT) methodologies (Solórzano & Yosso, 2016) extoll the value of research methodologies that center story. In their work on Chicana feminist epistemologies, for example, Calderón et al. (2012) call for "anti-oppressive researched rich frameworks" with potential to "suture the bodymindspirit split common in positivist and so-called 'objective' forms of research" (pp. 514–515). They draw especially on the work of Anzaldúa, who asserts that "for images, words, stories, to have ... transformative power, they must arise from the human body ... and from the earth's body" (as cited in Calderón et al., 2012, p. 521). Place and corporeal experience are centered and intertwined in this conception and, as we will demonstrate here, within the digital story genre.

While scholars have linked CRT and digital storytelling (Lovvorn, 2011; Matias & Grosland, 2016; Rolón-Dow, 2011; Trimboli, 2020), there is limited work on how digital storytelling might be a generative tool for teacher-researchers, especially in the early stages of research, to reflect on the relationship between their academic interests and their own subject positions. Palmeri (2012), Shipka (2011), and others have challenged a preoccupation with multimodal compositions as course products, arguing for the use of multimodal invention activities at various stages of the research process. Further, scholars of multimodality (Dunn, 2001; Kress, 2010; Rule, 2020; The New London Group, 1996) insist on the body's role in all meaning making, attending to modes deeply linked to the body—the kinesthetic, gestural, spatial—and thus affect. Building on this work and research methodologies that refuse the myth of disembodied neutrality, the project we describe here positions digital storytelling as a generative, story-based, context-specific, and embodied research practice. By engaging with the affordances of multiple modes, teacher-researchers at the start of an inquiry project merged personal, scholarly, and teacherly identities toward greater agency and awareness of researcher positionality.

AFFORDANCES OF MULTIMODALITY AND DIGITAL STORYTELLING

Scholars challenging the exclusivity of Western research paradigms have demonstrated the value of story as a form of evidence and means of disrupting master narratives. Solórzano and Yosso (2016) point to the need for *counter-storytelling*, telling stories about experiences rarely shared, as "a tool for exposing, analyzing, and challenging the majoritarian stories of racial privilege" (p. 133). This works, in part, by allowing room in our scholarly work for the (gendered and racialized) body. As hooks (1994) points out, too often stories are told in ways that erase the body, resulting in the illusion of neutrality (p. 140). Ladson-Billings (2015), applying CRT to the field of education, argues that stories about ordinary people resist positivistic universalism toward a recognition that truth is situational. Context—the localities and materiality we experience with our bodies—is foregrounded. By naming their realities, storytellers provide "necessary context for understanding, feeling, and interpreting" (Ladson-Billings, 2015, p. 20).

What, though, makes digital storytelling a particularly valuable tool for counter-storytelling? In other words, what are the unique affordances of digital stories as compared to stories told via alphabetic text? Lovvorn (2011), in his work on the connections between digital storytelling and CRT-informed counterstories, suggests digital stories are uniquely mobile (they can be shared easily online), personal, and connective (merging identity and "larger social structures"; p. 97). The latter feels especially crucial to work responding, via story, to systemic exclusion. While these are, indeed, affordances of the digital story, and while Lambert (2018) and others emphasize the personal and social work of the genre, texts written in solely alphabetic form also have the potential to be shared digitally, and to engage the personal and social in meaningful ways. As many scholars of multimodality argue, all texts are multimodal (Ball & Charlton, 2015; Kress, 2010;

The New London Group, 1996; Prior, 2015; Selfe, 2009). Digital stories, then, differ from primarily alphabetic texts in the visceral experience they evoke within maker and viewer. Multiple modes (aural, visual, alphabetic, kinesthetic, gestural, and spatial) activate and merge multiple felt experiences, presenting a more explicit relationship to embodiment.

Kress (2010), in his seminal work on social semiotics, refuses the false binary of mind and body, cognition and affect. By emphasizing the materiality of mode, he engages with the relationship between communication, the body, and social contexts, attending especially to the relationship between sign-making and agency. This emphasis on agency can be found throughout early work on multimodality. The New London Group (1996), for example, insists on the relationship between meaning making, signs, and power. Their work on multiliteracies arose originally as a response to fast capitalism and pedagogies that devalued diversity of language and culture. Reacting against the appropriation of "private life and community" for "commercial and institutional ends," they assert the value of meaning making practices in which "lifeworlds—spaces for community life where local and specific meanings can be made—can flourish" (p. 70).

Others have taken up the relationship between non-alphabetic modes and the body. Butler (2017), writing about her experiences as a Deaf teacher, emphasizes the communicative work of spatial and kinesthetic modes, the latter of which allows us to "express complex, nonlinear meaning" (p. 76). She describes kinesthetic movement, which she incorporates into her first-year- writing courses, as reliant on an "awareness of both our bodies and our interactions with other bodies and media—including texts, the technologies we use, and the writing process" (p. 75).

Similarly, Arola and Wysocki (2012), in their edited collection on the relationship between media and embodiment, identify the body as our "primary medium," drawing on McLuhan to consider how media both "extend what we can do with our given sensory apparatus" and "modify... our sense of engagement" with others and our environment (p. 4).

Digital stories make room for the body, for the ways in which our bodies interact with the places and people impacting our sense of home and belonging. Horner (2020) asks us to consider modality as a social practice, always materially situated. Digital stories of the kind we describe here bring this situatedness to the forefront. This affordance is particularly significant when the larger project is responding to structural inequities that disenfranchise bodies. There is potential, in this move, to prioritize felt experience, to ultimately move (in both senses of the word) both maker and viewer. In being moved by a story, both are potentially moved toward action.

METHODOLOGY

Our methodology aligns with the epistemology informing the digital storytelling project. We use narrative to theorize our lived experiences and create new knowledge. Applying Ngunjiri et al.'s (2010) autoethnography continuum, our process is more evocative than analytical.

Analysis is "built into the story" so that story becomes a kind of theory (Jensen-Hart et al., 2010, p. 451). In turn, research becomes an "extension of researchers' lives" that foregrounds sociocultural context, a foundation of autoethnographic research (Ngunjiri, 2010, pp. 2–3). We access critical reflection through personal narratives that rely on creative descriptions (Richardson, 2000, as cited in Jensen-Hart et al., 2010), emotion, and introspection (Ellis, 2004, as cited in Jensen-Hart et al., 2010).

Our work is also co/autoethnographic (Taylor et al., 2014). The authors of this chapter, which include the instructor leading the digital storytelling project and two teacher-researchers who completed it, engaged in both individual and collaborative reflective practices at various stages of the process. In addition to formal reflections Andrea and Gregory completed as part of the digital story project, each of us have reflected, through writing and conversations with one another, on the relationship between theory and our individual stories. In this way, our project aligns with the criteria of co/autoethnography outlined by Taylor et al. (2014) since it includes "writing, rewriting, and sharing narratives, talk and discussion..., making sense of theory and research, and collaboratively analyzing the generated texts" (p. 8).

Inevitably our subject positions as researchers, writers, and composers impact the way we shape this story. Sara, the instructor, is a tenure-track professor and teacher educator. While committed to social justice pedagogies, she acknowledges, as Matias and Grosland (2016) suggest we must, this is not enough to counteract the problem of Whiteness in teacher education. As a White middle-class woman, she is among the demographic occupying the majority of teacher preparation positions in the United States (Matias & Grosland, 2016, p. 153). Leading students through processes aimed at destabilizing colonizing research paradigms, then, requires a willingness to

1. engage in culturally responsive self-reflection (Ladson-Billings, 2015),
2. foreground listening (Royster, 1996), and
3. use her privilege to amplify the voices of disenfranchised students.

Andrea is an ESL/EFL instructor and content developer who has taught English online, in the United States, and in Mexico. She is a biracial woman, born to a Mexican father and a White American mother, and was raised in rural West Virginia, a place where poverty is ubiquitous. Her cultural roots and familiarity with poverty and racial discrimination have shaped her research interests, which include social justice pedagogies, learner empowerment, and ELL identity development.

Gregory is a tenured English instructor at Madera Community College and a recent graduate of the doctoral program. As a Chicano and a lifelong resident of California's rural Central Valley, he has experienced and witnessed the challenges common in that region, which include being a first-generation college student, valuing work over pursuing higher education, and combating food insecurity. He is therefore committed to pedagogical practices that counter the achievement gap among students of color, particularly those who are Chicanx or Latinx.

In what follows, we each consider the role of narrative and multimodality in composing agentive teacher-researcher identities. Sara describes the project itself, noting its roots in her own personal and academic trajectory; Andrea emphasizes the early stages of composition, collecting and reflecting on personal stories and artifacts (and her embodied response to these) as a means of accessing her relationship with her father and ultimately her complex identity as a student and scholar; Gregory focuses on choices made on the editing floor, presenting through images of his campus and region, how the COVID-19 lockdown exacerbated inequity in an oft-ignored region of California.

THE PROJECT (SARA'S STORY)

The digital storytelling project was part of a 16-week synchronous online instructional technology course required for doctoral students in an online English pedagogy program based at a small public university. Students met via Zoom each week from towns and cities across the country where they taught a range of English courses in middle schools, high schools, community colleges, language schools, and libraries. Most would begin their capstone projects, a 1-year practitioner inquiry, the following year. Having led two cohorts through this process, I knew the students would bring energy, curiosity, and purpose to their projects, engaging deeply with scholarship and reflective processes. I also knew many simply didn't know where or how to begin. Further, as was often apparent in early conferences, many continued to subscribe to positivistic notions of research as neutral.

The digital story, then, had two primary objectives: (a) to allow students practice with a form of composing they might use in their classrooms and (b) to allow those readying to embark on a major research project an opportunity to link their personal and academic trajectories, laying a foundation for situated inquiry grounded in liberatory pedagogical practices. As

I wrote in the assignment overview: "Most if not all research projects arise from some sort of personal obsession, question, or interest." A departure from the overly used and problematic idea of "best practices," the project was grounded in the idea that the lines of inquiry we take on arise from our specific contexts as educators and human beings, echoing values associated with feminist and CRT-based research paradigms as well social semiotic approaches to meaning making.

My decision to incorporate this project into the course was also personal. Before taking on a PhD in pedagogy, I completed an MFA in poetry and taught creative writing and digital storytelling workshops. I often felt frustrated by attempts to merge what felt like conflicting identities as maker and academic. I was committed to the study of teaching, to the meaningful work of deep and sustained attention to pedagogical practice. But it wasn't clear how my values as a creative writer, as a facilitator of storytelling, fit into the analytic processes required of a PhD student. I felt called to consider, more fully, the relationship between teaching practice, story, and form as conceived of by poets—that inextricable relationship between content and the shape it takes.

Like many digital storytelling projects, ours drew upon the StoryCenter model. Students read excerpts from Lambert's (2018) *Digital Storytelling: Capturing Lives, Creating Community*; were introduced to a range of tools and resources; and participated in small-group workshops. They submitted, with their digital stories, a reflection that included a statement of goals and choices (SOGC) analyzing their composing processes (Shipka, 2011).

The project was designed to draw out the potentially deep connections between the digital story, a genre described by StoryCenter as a process prioritizing self-revelation, first-person voice, and experimentation based in experience (Lambert, 2018) and teacher inquiry, a practice with personal experience, reflection, and storytelling at its heart. As Dana and Yendol-Hoppey (2019) tell us, teacher inquiry starts with a "wondering" that comes from "real world observations and dilemmas or 'felt difficulties'" (p. 30). Both practices privilege what is felt and lived. The assignment challenged traditional ways of positioning research as shown in the guidelines I shared with students:

> For this project, I'm not asking you to consider your potential topic from an academic or scholarly perspective. Not yet. Instead, I'm asking you to prioritize the heart over the head, telling a story, in digital form, that demonstrates your personal connection to your research question. After all, storytelling is meaning making. And good research involves making meaning from experience.

The students composed stories about their childhoods, their identities, and the challenges they've experienced as educators and human beings. Topics included supporting high school seniors through the pandemic, teaching CRT in an AP British literature classroom, countering misconceptions about one's region, understanding refugee college students' experience of place, and the relationship between one's own writerly identity and providing feedback on student writing. Students grappled with Lambert's (2018) call to tell a story about the self even when telling a story about others. This was uncomfortable. And as is so often the case in academic and personal work, this discomfort was productive.

As Vasudevan (2006) argues, when "the call for counterstories intersects with the possibilities of multimodal composing," what emerges are "new kinds of spaces for storytelling and story-listening" (p. 208). I found myself positioned, through the facilitation of this process, as a listener, attending to what students had to teach me about why the work they were pursuing mattered beyond its ability to fill a gap in scholarship or practice. They demonstrated a kind of agency I had lacked in my own graduate program, struggling to reconcile conflicting identities.

They laid a foundation for moving, through the body, more fully into an academic practice that so often rejects living and teaching as contextual.

COMING HOME (ANDREA'S STORY)
[ANDREA'S DIGITAL STORY: HTTPS://YOUTU.BE/WIE24XIL8MA]

I arrived on my father's doorstep on a balmy Saturday night, digital recorder in hand. I had driven to the sleepy town of Philippi, West Virginia to record an interview and collect photos for my digital story. Sitting beside my father on his worn couch, we leafed through his albums. It was one of the most beautiful evenings that I have ever spent with him, but also one of the most painful.

It is difficult to articulate the sharp burning of my eyes and nose and the choking sensation I experienced as I tried to hold myself together while viewing my father's pictures and listening to his stories. There was a story about getting to West Virginia after missing his bus in Chicago and having no way to communicate his need for help, food, or shelter; a story about a make-or-break English exam that determined whether he would continue studying in the United States or be sent home; a story of humiliation and romantic rejection following a glance at his tattered shoes; and the overarching story of a painfully shy yet courageous boy who had been born into poverty but had managed to become a physician specializing in surgery, pathology, and internal medicine, a boy who had come to the United States at the tender age of 21 and who had thrived in a foreign land with virtually no money, family, friends, or knowledge of English. I sat in awe, admiration, and heartbreak as I confronted the fact that the man beside me was

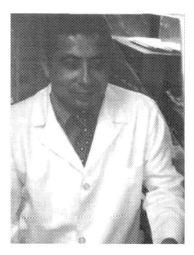

Figure 8.1 Andrea's father as a young man at work in a WV hospital.

Figure 8.2 Recent photo of Andrea and her father that was used to open and conclude her digital story.

no longer seeking professional accolades, nor did he resemble the young, strong, smooth-bodied man in the pictures (Figures 8.1 & 8.2).

It was the Spring of 2020, and I was a second-year doctoral student in Dr. Cooper's instructional technology course. I had spent the last 11 years building a career in TESOL, which included the completion of two very traditional graduate degrees. The class was quite different from my prior courses, and our final project was unlike any other I had completed. Looking back, it was not only the story's 1 to 4 minute-length guideline but also its personal focus that led me to expect it would be easy. This view of the personal as antithetical to the scholarly, of rigorous research as synonymous with objectivity, had been ingrained from my previous graduate programs.

As I contemplated the project, I was pulled in opposing directions; my heart argued for its merit while my scholarly head argued against it. Feeling this tension, I realized that I was drawn to the personal on a deep, visceral level, yet I had been taught to reject it or risk being viewed as a nonacademic, an undesirable Other. Anzaldúa (2000) notes the disempowerment that results from fragmenting an individual and the difficulty involved in attempting to "connect up the body with the soul and the mind with the spirit" (p. 525), a painful and unnatural fragmentation that I connect to academia's devaluing of the personal; this debasing of the subjective has been outlined by various scholars. For instance, Chernouski (2017) discusses western science's obsession with objectivity, an ideal only achievable via an "impersonal tabula rasa" (p. 2) and a goal encouraging the erasure of self, while Barnacle (2005) notes the positioning of doctoral students as individuals with pain-free knowledge acquisition, a frame that dehumanizes emerging scholars by portraying them as struggle and emotion free. These scholars' assertions collectively portray academia as an environment hostile to the personal and, by extension, individual identity.

It is a place with which I am familiar, a world in which many professors did not care about the person I was outside of my studies, the single mother who struggled with bills, her health, and sleep deprivation, who had little time to clean, prepare meals, and do laundry. It is the environment wherein I ultimately became the "used to" lady, the mother who used to dance and giggle with her little girl in the living room, the daughter who used to pop over on late nights "just because," the friend who used to be steadfast and reliable, and the woman who used to have time for herself. These sacrifices were assumed in academia, and so there was no comfort, no support, no complaining, and no commiserating; what mattered was my ability to synthesize research, to locate and fill a gap in the literature, to think and write like a scholar, to seek publication in reputable journals. And so, over time, I learned to focus intensely on these things, which often came at the expense of my relationships, my physical health, and, at times, my sanity. I had entered this world brimming with energy and lofty dreams, only to end up losing touch with myself and my reasons for entering academia in the first place.

This insight vis-à-vis how higher education had contributed to my own personal fragmentation stirred my interest in the final project. It was a piece that I chose to center on my father, a man who had grown up poor in a tiny village in southern Mexico but who ultimately achieved professional success through education and learning English (Figure 8.3). His was the story that had inspired me to become an English as a second/foreign language teacher, a connection I would capture and share through digital storytelling.

Figure 8.3 Andrea's father (circled in red) on the day of his medical school graduation.

Listening to my father's stories that Saturday night while viewing their corresponding artifacts was almost otherworldly; I felt drawn into his narratives in a way that transcended both time and space. As I made this journey alongside my father, I became heart-wrenchingly aware of the gap between the past and present. The pictures, which my father explained in his thick Mexican Spanish accent, collectively illustrated his personal sojourn. Once upon a time there had been a boy who had grown into a handsome, hardworking, and successful man, who had subsequently become a wise, benevolent elderly man. I fought back tears, angry at those who dared to hurt him, praising those who were kind enough to help him, and applauding him for the man that he had become. Encompassing the overall experience was a strange sense of loss; pushing the pain aside, I grabbed my daddy's hand, stroked his cheek while lightly brushing his curly dark hair with my fingers, and told him how much I loved him and how proud of him I was.

From this experience, I took away a critical realization: multimodal compositions offer channels of expression and meaning making that move beyond the affordances of alphabetic text. I had heard many of my father's stories before, but the addition of images made for a fuller, more detailed experience, one supporting Kress' (2010) assertion that the affordances of images differ from those of alphabetical texts (e.g., in their immediacy and spatial arrangement of elements).

Images enhanced my experience by providing me with information not present in my father's words. I could see the people he named, their build, expressions, postures, and manner of dress. I could see the dirt roads and their humble abodes. I felt their friendliness, their love, and their sadness. I saw their poverty and their hardship.

I recall a photograph of a middle-aged woman, a family member who had passed away long before my birth. As my father spoke of her, I gazed at her image. Her clothing and surroundings made her financial hardship evident, yet her facial expression and body language spoke to me most. Her body appeared to draw in on itself while slightly sagging as though weighted down. She appeared to narrow herself as if seeking self-comfort or wishing to disappear. Her facial muscles were slack, her brows knitted, and her eyes, slightly downcast, had a look of exhaustion and desperation. The visual information intermingled with my personal memories as a feeling of recognition bubbled up from within. I too have sat like that, collapsing in on myself while feeling great vulnerability. I too have had that look on my face, feeling helpless, defeated, and hopeless. I experienced a dropping sensation in my gut; deep sadness and pity for this woman washed over me as the lines between us temporarily blurred. Amplifying the pain of the experience was the sadness I detected in my father's voice, which attested to his fondness for her, a person who no longer occupied a place in this world. In these moments, the kinesthetic, linguistic, visual, and spatial modes provided me with a powerful and immersive experience, one that culminated in a feeling of connection to the woman in the photograph. It is an experience which I connect to Rule (2020) who, writing about the multimodal nature of alphabetic text, asserts that "modes are not just sequentially and separately engaged . . . but simultaneously enacted" (p. 78).

That night, my father shared many of his most intimate stories. His voice conveyed strong emotions towards his lived experiences while evoking a kinesthetically affective response in me and influencing my own feelings. His happy stories were marked by fast speech and rising intonation; I felt his excitement. His sad stories were marked by a softening of speech, falling intonation, a quivering and sometimes breaking in his voice, and long pauses between words; I felt his struggle and his pain. His funny stories were accompanied by audible, rapid breathing, the lengthening of words, and an almost squealing pitch that ended in a crescendo of roaring laughter; my ears rang from the volume while I howled and laughed with him because I felt like I was there. The experience was as close as I could get to living these events with him.

I arrived home that night with a multitude of photos but no formal interview, as the experience had become more emotionally intense than I had anticipated. A week later, I finally conducted my father-daughter interview over the phone, the one that would become the voiceover for my digital story. Again, I found myself struggling to stay in control of my emotions as I listened to him detail his journey from poverty to prosperity. By this point, I had come to the realization that this project was anything but simple and easy. It was damn hard emotional labor, a construct that Shuler and Sypher (2000) define as emotional management necessitated by one's work. This project had unexpectedly added to the emotional labor that already came with being a doctoral student and single mother; it was a form of labor that I knew well, a painful fight to handle strong and sometimes overpowering emotions that, if left untempered, could derail my efforts and undermine the project's success.

By this point, I had all the requisite data, but hours passed, and I was getting nowhere. Much frustration led to an insight that I had been using my head instead of my heart. I opened my laptop, turned the recording back on, and forced my mind to quiet. I focused on my senses, allowing my ears to listen carefully to my father's voice, my eyes to scan the photos, and my feelings to weigh in on the data. I quickly noticed that certain photographs and parts of the interview data evoked strong reactions in me; at times, there was a clenching in my gut, a tingling in my scalp, a squeezing sensation behind my eyes, and a tightening in my throat. I focused on these sensations, using my body as an instrument, with the intention of understanding their meanings. Opening myself emotionally, I was hit by overwhelming sadness, love, gratitude, and admiration; I used these emotions to select photos and interview portions with the strongest emotional impact (Figure 8.4). Working within the visual, kinesthetic, and aural modes provided me with nontraditional ways of knowing, avenues long undervalued in the field of composition, yet increasingly supported by scholars of multimodality.

Figure 8.4 Andrea's paternal grandmother against a skyward-looking background of trees and sunlight.

The remainder of the creative process involved merging the head and heart. This was done by examining each element, posing self-questions, and then listening to my body and feelings for answers. It was an experience that stood in stark contrast to the "mindbodyspirit split" (Calderón et al., 2012, p. 514), a view often embraced in the academic world and one in which nonlinguistic modes tend to be viewed as soft and lacking in sophistication (Rule, 2020). It is also an experience that I connect to Johnson et al. (2015) who argue for the body as a means of knowing and who call for research that attends to bodies, noting that we are not merely thinking but also feeling beings. This process, along with the task guidelines, led to critical self-exploration and self-discovery. It allowed me to make previously unnoticed connections between my father's life and my own (e.g., our longstanding pursuits of education, our passion for helping others, our disdain for social hierarchies, and our belief in the power to change one's life, even in the humblest of circumstances). The process also enabled me to realize that I had made subconscious links between my father's story and the possibility others might experience a similar story, finding success through education and learning English (Figures 8.5 & 8.6). Two years after completing my digital story, I would focus my capstone on motivation and ELLs. Driven by my deep gratitude for having had a secure, privileged upbringing, I had entered the TESOL field to give back in a way that carried his story forward.

Immersing myself in the creative process not only allowed me to discover these things, but it also boosted my sense of professional motivation and reified my identity by clarifying who I was, what I wished to accomplish, and who I ultimately wanted to become; in this way, I was able to get in

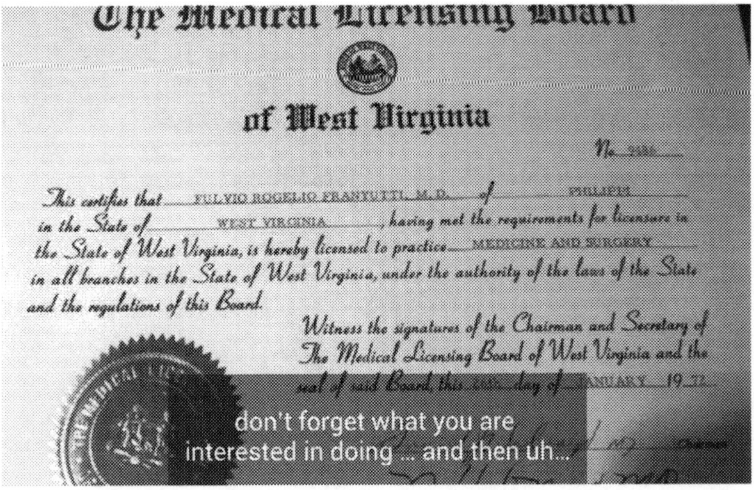

Figure 8.5 One of Andrea's father's medical licenses.

Figure 8.6 Andrea's father as a young boy.

touch with my deepest personal values (beyond the performance of my academic self), from which I could operate in the world more purposefully and with greater drive and satisfaction. As noted by Hull and Katz (2006), digital storytelling has the power to augment motivation, increase agency, and positively alter identity. Adding to these assertions is Crawford (2002) who argues for the harnessing of emotion to increase self-knowledge.

Experiencing the power of digital storytelling has radically shifted my perspective on the value of personal narrative; the stories we hear and tell shape our perspectives, values, expectations, and behaviors, thereby carving out our life path and situating our place in the world. As Fivush (2008) asserts, stories are what enable individuals to mold and comprehend themselves and their environment. Given their power, stories are the stuff of control and consequence, and so it behooves us to create our own narratives and to think critically about those we choose to internalize and embody.

PANDEMIC PONDERINGS OF EQUITY (GREGORY'S STORY) [GREGORY'S DIGITAL STORY: HTTPS://YOUTU.BE/ I53BOZIPEJS]

Although I had committed to focus on equity and first-year composition (FYC) for my capstone project prior to enrolling in Dr. Cooper's technology course, I was in no way prepared for how enlightening the digital story and its composing process would be. I have, in part, the pandemic to thank for this; after all, I had no way to anticipate such a global event nor the spontaneous modifications it would bring. By relying on such a format, I found the freedom to articulate my ideas with images and sound much in the way my Latinx students would relish expressing themselves without the challenges of Standard Edited American English (SEAE). Despite being the final assignment of a core class for my doctoral studies, the digital story required no scholarship nor sophisticated vocabulary but rather liberating myself from alphabetic text so as to engage my senses and in turn appeal to the senses of my viewer.

My process began when I reflected both on my situation as a tenured English instructor and on the condition of my campus early on in the lockdown resulting from the COVID-19 pandemic. The efforts of Madera Community College (MCC)—situated in California's rural Central Valley—to offer laptops and hotspots to its students following the switch to fully online instructional delivery were undoubtedly well-intentioned. But how would students access such information? Vogels (2021) states, "Rural adults remain less likely than suburban adults to have home broadband and less likely than urban adults to own a smartphone, tablet computer or traditional computer" (para. 1). A socioeconomic catch-22 was therefore inevitable.

Gloria Naylor (1986), in her *New York Times* article, "Hers," comments on the limitations of alphabetic text:

> I consider the written word inferior to the spoken, and much of the frustration experienced by novelists is the awareness that whatever we manage to capture in even the most transcendent passages falls far short of the richness of life. (p. C2)

Such a description, while relating to the challenges of novelists, is nonetheless applicable to digital storytelling as I would discover in the course. People outside of California commonly associate the Golden State with beaches, celebrities, Los Angeles, San Francisco, and maybe Yosemite. More often than not, the rural Central Valley is ignored. A pathos occurs when, instead of simply referring to the region via alphabetic text, I open my digital story with footage from my drive on Highway 99 (Figure 8.7) of dried farmland and a dreary sky (a most fortuitous touch).

The voiceover in my digital story, entitled *Pandemic Ponderings of Equity*, starts with these words: "Even though I was born here in California's Central Valley, raised here, and reside here, I cannot help but think I have had it easier than others." In retrospect, what I experienced as a Chicano simply did not occur to me until recently as being significant. My parents often took me to functions where my father would meet up with migrant workers he befriended via his citizens band (CB) radio. The mingling of Spanish speakers, playing in the vineyards with other children, and even some trips to Mexicali and Ensenada felt routine. This is not to say there were

Figure 8.7 Commute on Highway 99 North to Madera Community College.

never incidents that I was among the Other. In seventh grade, one classmate laughed when she learned that I lived in Pinedale, the working-class neighborhood—where many residents are of color—in northwest Fresno. Another male classmate also labeled me as a "Mexican in poverty." Finally, my lack of fluency in spoken Spanish has led to bewilderment from both Whites and Mexicans.

When I was interviewing for a full-time position at a local community college over 15 years ago, one of the two administrators (both men of color) asked after learning about my two college degrees and high grade point average, "What's it like growing up smart in the valley?" I was puzzled by the question. The other administrator said, "Maybe a better way to word the question is, 'What's it like growing up smart in the valley when the expectation is not to?'" My lifelong residence in the valley insulated me to outside assumptions regarding educational shortcomings.

Several years later, while visiting Louisville, Kentucky to serve as a reader for the Advanced Placement (AP) English Language and Composition exam, I sat with a group of men one evening in a sports bar. One who was from Southern California quipped (in the presence of a couple of readers from New England), "So, do you all have color television in Fresno?" After a forced chuckle, I replied, "Yeah, the Central Valley serves no purpose. We only feed the world." (It is worth noting that I was the only person of color at that table.) Even though I had attained an admirable level academically by becoming a full-time community college instructor, I nevertheless encountered the low expectations that nonresidents generally have towards those from the

Central Valley. By presenting commonplace concerns towards remote learning and humanizing the students, my digital story allowed me to disrupt both the ignorance and stereotypes that exist towards my region.

Following the filming of my commute (Figure 8.7), I arrived at MCC and chose to film the campus without leaving the sidewalk at the front. (Doing otherwise would have required permission from an administrator because of concern over the transmissibility of COVID-19.) This did not deter me during the editing stage. The artistic choice offers a subtext of the Other; the viewer is forced to observe rather than participate in whatever action—however limited—may be occurring on campus. We therefore see how "'distance can be manipulated in a shot in film...to indicate *deference* or *amelioration*" (Kress, 2010, p. 74). In this case, I deferred to the proverbial powers that be and in turn required viewers to do the same.

The footage also alludes to a fringe relationship that those identifying as Latinx have with higher education. United States Census Bureau (2021) reveals only 21% of Latinx adults (25 years or older) possess at least a bachelor's degree as opposed to 38% of White adults. While this statistic would galvanize anyone committed to equity, the coerced distance—an example of the spatial mode, which includes "arrangement, organization, and proximity between people or objects" (Ball et al., 2018, p. 18)—yields empathy with the marginalized.

This footage along with the narration and music undoubtedly allowed me to dismiss a reliance on SEAE. Oftentimes, my students arrive in my classroom either as ELLs or with no prior generation in their household fluent in English. Nevertheless, opportunities to articulate thoughts and emotions present themselves, reminiscent of the villagers of Macondo in Gabriel García Márquez's (1967/2006) novel, *One Hundred Years of Solitude*, for whom "the world was so recent that many things lacked names, and in order to indicate them it was necessary to point" (p. 1). Students who engage in digital composition may point the device of their choice to capture what they wish without a hypervigilance towards diction, syntax, or verb tense. Those accustomed to marginalization, whose accents may complicate verbal delivery, may find some freedom from linguistic translation by relying on images.

Following footage of Highway 99 and the campus at a distance (Figure 8.8), a 22-second close-up (Figure 8.9) occurs of me staring blankly and delivering the following questions via voiceover:

> But have we really solved every problem that this pandemic has produced? How can we anticipate the mental well-being of our students through quarantine? Are we providing the proper accommodations for students with disabilities? Is loaning out laptops enough? Even if I am gracious towards my students, what about any other instructors they have?

Figure 8.8 The college sign and the empty parking lot.

Figure 8.9 Dutch angle close-up of digital composer.

Such questions align with Brewer et al. (2014), who declare "access is a moving target, a concept that sounds promising on its surface yet frequently offers little more than empty gestures" (p. 151). Despite the investment of school districts, efforts to equip students digitally cannot eradicate variable personal challenges such as familial commitments, living situations, and employment, among others.

The questions from the voiceover therefore imply no easy answers and suggest that variables exist that cannot allow for an equitable panacea. Even though none of the students appear in the digital story, my appearance becomes a representation for them. I share more—thanks to my last name, olive complexion, Chicanx upbringing, and racial experiences—with the

70% of MCC students who identify as Latinx—according to the Research and Institutional Effectiveness page for the State Center Community College District website (2021)—than with my fellow full-time English instructors (among whom I am the only person of color).

After the close-up segment, footage of the campus returns (Figure 8.10). However, it is noticeably more distant, as I moved to the southwest part of the campus when filming. Delivered with this footage are the two adages, "Only time will tell" and "Time heals all wounds"—both of which are incompatible with the COVID-19 pandemic and inapplicable to a populace relatively new to higher learning. A challenge to traditional pedagogy therefore occurs, suggesting that the Other can no longer be ignored and that doing so would be to the detriment of higher education overall. This is reinforced as the narration declares, "I am not naïve to think that every student will benefit from what we determined we must do, nor do I think we can just go back to the way things were."

During the clause, "Without a doubt," the screen cuts to black as I deliver these final words: "This is a game-changer." Such a choice implies uncertainty about what those specific changes will be, yet declares that change is inevitable. Will it come from educators, from activists, or from politicians? (Perhaps all three, even?) Whatever form it takes, the digital story—not even two full minutes in length—can be viewed and understood by anyone possessing some English fluency, casting a wider proverbial net than an article that is dismissed as erudite and that merely "preaches to the choir." Also, with it being uploaded on YouTube, one doesn't have to be a college student using a library database or an academic at an out-of-town

Figure 8.10 Long shot of Academic Village 1 building.

conference; instead, this digital story—even if it never becomes viral—is accessible to any interested viewer.

Following the technology course, the digital story would serve as a catalyst for my capstone project, the final requirement for attaining my doctorate. I chose to focus on equity and first-year composition courses. Joe Feldman's (2019) book, *Grading for Equity*, resonated with me:

> Late work penalties can disproportionately hurt the most vulnerable students. They may not have been able to entirely control all the circumstances that caused the assignment to be late, and our implicit biases influence the assumption we make about whether they had. (p. 115)

With remote learning still in effect during the Fall 2020 semester, it was virtually impossible for the digital story not to serve as a reference. Four specific moments from the narration steered me toward focusing on late-submission policies for out-of-class essays.

The opening sentence of my narration—which ends with the independent clause, "I cannot help but think I have had it easier than others"—is a reminder to myself that I was a student who had 25 units upon graduating high school thanks to Advanced Placement (AP) courses and the Step-to-College Program at California State University, Fresno (CSUF). Many students are recent high school graduates or are returning after years of being out of school, adding to their obligations of work and family. But remembering my journey allows me to have compassion towards my students. In my first year as a full-time student, I had to adjust to many of my high school friends leaving town (or even the state) for college. (This, along with other circumstances, led me to call a suicide prevention hotline on one occasion and visiting the university's psychological services.) If I experienced such a difficult transition, despite opportunities to excel, it is certainly possible that community college students' transitions would be as or more challenging.

The close-up segment includes five questions essentially raising concerns over the effects of the COVID-19 pandemic on students' academic performance. Visually, having a 22-second titled shot of myself from the chest up while staring blankly emphasizes the collective confusion and sadness that educators felt during the lockdown. Maintaining a voiceover—instead of switching to a shot in which I speak to the camera—further emphasizes the inquisitive tone of the questions and the somber feeling towards the shortcomings of the adjustments that the pandemic incurred. By having the five questions spoken and presented with a static image, the viewer must focus on the uncertainties raised. Wysocki et al. (2019) suggest "multimodal work... asks us to acknowledge the fact that our departments, institutions, and field at large are changing in response to the increasingly networked systems of composing and consuming in global economies" (p. 25). This shift in perspective creates an opportunity for a shift toward more equitable practices for community college students.

Echoing Feldman, being gracious towards students given circumstances unseen in recent memory transcends generational coddling: It becomes the right thing to do. Instead of applying traditional academic policies—rife with implicit bias—that perpetuate failure among (most notably) students of color, the necessity for empathy emerges so as to keep students on track. If one among the student's instructors can make a difference, imagine the impact if more instructors are on board.

Later in the narration, I assert: "It is safe to say that students are only one bad experience away from giving up." Embedded in traditional academic policies—along with the failure of students of color—is the delivery of discouragement. The temptation among some community college instructors may be to question why students cannot simply channel the innate resilience that they themselves summoned, which ignores systemic barriers and perpetuates inequity.

The final words—"This is a game-changer"—also influenced the capstone project. Anyone can point out problems; not everyone can offer solutions. Countless hours of research and of interviewing community college instructors throughout the state of California could not but lead me to much-needed change. Essentially, deciding to offer incentives for timely submission in lieu of punitive measures was the most sensible contribution to advance equity. Students of color have grown up with recurring punishment from teachers, law enforcement, and employers who have made it their collective mission to preserve subordination. Advocating for equity among students is a belief that resides for me at the gut level, and I would not have realized my personal connection to the capstone project had it not been for the digital story assignment.

CONTINUING THE STORY

Gregory and Andrea's stories highlight the affordances not just of the digital story as product, but of the process itself, one defined by engagement with embodied modalities. Andrea makes clear that finding her way through the project required a willingness to experience her relationship to her father's stories through the senses, activated by the interaction of multiple modes; Gregory describes his physical movements—and the ability to communicate spatial arrangement through video editing—as crucial to the composing process. We see the embodied nature of multimodal composing in the stories themselves as these composers engage with the gestural, the kinesthetic, the spatial, the affective. When Andrea shares, through her digital story, not a retelling of her father's story or a description of his countenance, but his recorded voice, the vibration of his vocal cords, the evidence, in his accent, of the multiple geographies he has inhabited, she creates an intimacy between her father, herself, and the viewer. Juxtaposed with her voice, the story of a set of relationships emerges (between Andrea and her father, between geographies, between the personal and the academic). Similarly, Gregory's story does not ask us to imagine California's Central Valley: He takes us there. We are passengers on his commute and visitors to his workplace. When he pauses at the perimeter of his campus, we pause there with him. We engage with not only the affordances and limitations of the genre, but of this geography and spatiality. We are asked to consider, through the senses, what it means to occupy, to belong in, a space. This is apt given his subject: the challenge his students faced gaining access to the proverbial classroom when COVID-19 forced them to attend remotely. What better way to speak to issues of in-person vs. online teaching, to the realities of a particular region—in this case rural and economically strained—than by showing us these places in relation to the maker/viewer? As Kress (2010) reminds us, social and semiotic power are intimately connected (p. 73). By attending to their personal and professional contexts, both composers made evident what scholars of social semiotics also teach us—that we cannot disconnect inequity from the material and situated experiences of it. They thus moved toward their final practitioner research projects with a greater awareness of—and embodiment of—their own relationships to subjectivity and to grand narratives about education and research.

As Dominguez (2017) reminds us, "Teacher education has largely failed to be liberatory" (p. 229). While digital storytelling projects like the one described here carry potential for encouraging teacher-researchers to center the stories of traditionally marginalized groups, it is important to remember digital storytelling is not a neutral practice and "in and of itself does not lead to critical reflections of race" (Trimboli, 2020, p. 51) or "change inequalities in how voices are valued" (Dhher, 2009, as cited in Trimboli, 2020, p. 49). Crucial to this work is encouraging productive forms of storytelling that result in "knowledge construction" (Ladson-Billings, 2015, p. 20), thus avoiding stories that reify stereotypes of existing power imbalances.

An important part of our reflective work here, then, is considering how we might revise our digital storytelling projects so they are centered "intentionally and intensely—on the humanity and possibility of students of color" (Dominguez, 2017, p. 232). This means making connections to frameworks like CRT and feminism explicit. Further, beyond incorporating digital storytelling into the research process, teacher-researchers might unite this kind of multimodal composing with reflection activities like those proposed by Hammond (2014) in her work on culturally responsive pedagogy. She suggests educators can widen their "interpretation apertures" by considering how their shallow, surface, and deep cultural values and beliefs impact marginalized students. How might approaching this work, which already relies upon thick description, multimodally—composing through photographs or interviews with loved ones—influence the kinds of projects teachers take on both as educators and researchers?

Teacher education has too long been a White space, privileging White research paradigms and cultural experiences. As Dominguez (2017) notes, "If our discussions around diversifying content are not equally concerned with repositioning what valued knowledge and cultural patterns are, we continue to perpetuate coloniality" (p. 230). Placing digital storytelling at the intersection of research and education, as our digital storytelling project did, allowed teacher-researchers a means to resist, through multimodal stories about and arising from place and the body, the myth of value neutrality problematic within both spheres. We thus forward digital storytelling as a preliminary step in the inquiry process that might move us toward a revaluing of what counts, who counts, in teacher education.

REFERENCES

Anzaldúa, G. (2000). Doing gigs. In A. Keating (Ed.), *Gloria Anzaldúa: Interviews/entrevistas* (pp. 211–234). Routledge.

Arola, K., & Wysocki, A.F. (2012). *Composing (media) = composing (embodiment)*. University Press of Colorado.

Ball, C. E., & Charlton, C. (2015). All writing is multimodal. In Adler-Kassner, L., & Wardle, & E. (Eds.), *Naming what we know: Threshold concepts in writing studies* (pp. 42–43). Utah State University Press.

Ball, C., Sheppard, J., & Arola K. (2018) *Writer/designer: A guide to making multimodal projects* (2nd ed.). Bedford/St. Martin's.

Barnacle, R. (2005). Research education ontologies: Exploring doctoral becoming. *Higher Education Research & Development*, 24(2), 179–188. https://doi.org/10.1080/07294360500062995

Butler, J. (2017). Bodies in composition. *Composition Studies*, 45(2), 73–90. https://www.jstor.org/stable/26402784

Brewer, E., Selfe, C. L., & Yergeau, M. (2014). Creating a culture of access in composition studies. *Composition Studies*, 42(2), 151–154. https://eric.ed.gov/?id=EJ1044059

Calderón, D., Bernal, D. D., Huber, L. P., Malagón, M. C., & Vélez, V. N. (2012). A Chicana feminist epistemology revisited: Cultivating ideas a generation later. *Harvard Educational Review*, 82(4), 513–539. https://doi.org/10.17763/haer.82.4.l518621577461p68

Chernouski, L. C. (2017, March 4). *Society, scientific authority, and linguistics: The need for epistemic justification* [Paper presentation]. Purdue Languages and Cultures Conference, West Lafayette, IN. https://docs.lib.purdue.edu/cgi/viewcontent.cgi?article=1048&context=plcc

Crawford, I. (2002). Building a theory of affect in cultural studies composition pedagogy. *JAC, 22*(3), 678–684. http://www.jstor.org/stable/20866519

Dana, N. F., & Yendol-Hoppey, D. (2019). *The reflective educator's guide to classroom research: Learning to teach and teaching to learn through practitioner inquiry* (4th ed.). Corwin.

Dominguez, M. (2017). "Se hace puentes al andar": Decolonial teacher education as a needed bridge to culturally sustaining and revitalizing pedagogies. In D. Paris & A. Alim (Eds.), *Culturally sustaining pedagogies: Teaching and learning for social justice in a changing world* (pp. 225–246). Teachers College Press.

Dunn, P. A. (2001). *Talking, sketching, moving: Multiple literacies in the teaching of writing.* Boynton/Cook.

Feldman, J. (2019). *Grading for equity: What it is, why it matters, and how it can transform schools and classrooms.* Corwin.

Fivush, R. (2008). Remembering and reminiscing: How individual lives are constructed in family narratives. *Memory Studies, 1*(1), 49–58. https://doi.org/10.1177/1750698007083888

García Márquez, G. (2006). *One hundred years of solitude* (G. Rabbasa, Trans.). Harper Perennial Modern Classics. (Original work published 1967)

Glenn, C. (2018). *Rhetorical feminism and this thing called hope.* Southern Illinois University Press.

Hammond, Z. (2014). *Culturally responsive teaching and the brain: Promoting authentic engagement and rigor among culturally and linguistically diverse students.* Corwin.

hooks, b. (1994). *Teaching to transgress: Education as the practice of freedom.* Routledge.

Horner, B. (2020). Modality as social practice in written language. In P. R. Powell (Ed.), *Writing changes: Alphabetic text and multimodal composition* (pp. 21–40). The Modern Language Association of America.

Hull, G., & Katz, M. (2006). Crafting an agentive self: Case studies of digital storytelling. *Research in the Teaching of English, 41*(1), 43–81. http://www.jstor.org/stable/40171717

Jensen-Hart, S., & Williams, D. J. (2010). Blending voices: Autoethnography as a vehicle for critical reflection in social work. *Journal of Teaching in Social Work, 30*(4), 450–467. https://doi.org/10.1080/08841233.2010.515911

Johnson, M., Levy, D., Manthey, K., & Novotney, M. (2015). Embodiment: Embodying feminist rhetorics. *Peitho Journal, 18*(1), 39–44. https://cfshrc.org/article/embodiment-embodying-feminist-rhetorics/

Kress, G. (2010). *A social semiotic approach to contemporary communication.* Routledge.

Ladson-Billings, G. (2015). Just what is critical race theory and what's it doing in a *nice* field like education? In E. Taylor, D. Gillborn, & G. Ladson-Billings (Eds.), *Foundations of critical race theory in education* (2nd ed., pp. 15–30). Routledge.

Lambert, J. (2018). *Digital storytelling: Capturing lives, creating community* (5th ed.). Routledge.

Lovvorn, J. (2011). Theorizing digital storytelling: From narrative practice to racial counterstory. In D. Journet, B. Boehm, & C. Britt (Eds.), *Narrative acts: Rhetoric, race and identity, knowledge* (pp. 97–112). Hampton Press Inc.

Matias, C., & Grosland, T. J. (2016). Digital storytelling as racial justice: Digital hopes for deconstructing Whiteness in teacher education. *Journal of Teacher Education, 67*(2), 152–164. https://doi.org/10.1177/0022487115624493

Naylor, G. (1986, February 6). Hers. *The New York Times*, C2. https://www.nytimes.com/1986/02/06/garden/hers.html

Ngunjiri, F. W., Hernandex, K. C., & Chang, H. (2010). Living autoethnography: Connecting life and research. *Journal of Research Practice, 6*(1), 1–17. http://jrp.icaap.org/index.php/jrp/article/view/241/186

Palmeri, J. (2012). *Remixing composition: A history of multimodal writing pedagogy.* Southern Illinois University Press.

Prior, P. (2015). Writing, literate activity, semiotic remediation: A sociocultural approach. In G. Cislaru (Ed.), *Writing(s) at the crossroads: The Process-product interface* (pp. 185–202). John Benjamins Publishing Company.

Rolón-Dow, R. (2011). Race(ing) stories: Digital storytelling as a tool for critical race scholarship. *Race Ethnicity and Education, 14*(2), 159–173. https://doi.org/10.1080/13613324.2010.519975

Royster, J. J. (1996). When the first voice you hear is not your own. *College Composition and Communication, 47*(1), 29–40. https://doi.org/10.2307/358272

Royster, J. J., & Kirsch, G. (2012). *Feminist rhetorical practices: New horizons for rhetoric, composition, and literacy studies.* Southern Illinois University Press.

Rule, H. J. (2020). Beyond page design: Writing as a multimodal embodied meaning. In P. R. Powell (Ed.), *Writing changes: Alphabetic text and multimodal composition* (pp. 62–82). Modern Language Association of America.

Selfe, C. (2009). The movement of air, the breath of meaning: Aurality and multimodal composing. *College Composition and Communication, 60*(4), 616–663.

Shipka, J. (2011). *Toward a composition made whole.* University of Pittsburgh Press.

Shuler, S., & Sypher, B. D. (2000). Seeking emotional labor: When managing the heart enhances the work experience. *Management Communication Quarterly, 14*(1), 50–89. https://doi.org/10.1177/0893318900141003

Solórzano, D., & Yosso, T. (2016). Critical race methodology: Counter-Storytelling as an analytical framework for educational research. In E. Taylor, D. Gillborn, & G. Ladson-Billings (Eds.), *Foundations of critical race theory in education* (2nd ed., pp. 127–142). Routledge.

State Center Community College District. (2021, March 12). *Research & institutional effectiveness.* https://www.sccd.edu/departments/educational-services-and-institutional-effectiveness/research-and-institutional-effectiveness/index.html

Taylor, M., Klein, E. J., & Abrams, L. (2014). Tensions of reimagining our roles as teacher educators in a third space: Revisiting a co-autoethnography through a faculty lens. *Studying Teacher Education, 10*(1), 3–19. http://dx.doi.org/10.1080/17425964.2013.866549

The New London Group. (1996). A pedagogy of multiliteracies: Designing social futures. *Harvard Education Review, 66*(1), 60–93. https://doi.org/10.17763/haer.66.1.17370n67v22j160u

Trimboli, D. (2020). *Mediating multiculturalism: Digital storytelling and the everyday ethnic.* Anthem Press.

United States Census Bureau. (2021, April 21). *Educational attainment in the United States: 2020.* Census.gov. https://www.census.gov/data/tables/2020/demo/educational-attainment/cps-detailed-tables.html

Vasudevan, L. (2006). Making known differently: Engaging visual modalities as spaces to author new selves. *E-Learning and Digital Media, 3*(1), 207–216. https://doi.org/10.2304/elea.2006.3.2.207

Vogels, E. A. (2021, August 19). *Some digital divides persist between rural, urban and suburban America*. Pew Research Center. https://www.pewresearch.org/fact-tank/2021/08/19/some-digital-divides-persist-between-rural-urban-and-suburban-america/

Wysocki, R., Udelson, J., Ray, C. E., Newman, J. S. B., Matravers, L. S., Kumari, A., Gordon, L. M. P., Scott, K. L., Day, M., Baumann, M., Alvarez, S. P., & DeVoss, D. N. (2019). On multimodality: A manifesto. In S. Khadka & J. C. Lee (Eds.), *Bridging the multimodal gap: From theory to practice* (pp. 17–30). University Press of Colorado. https://www.jstor.org/stable/j.ctvg5bsxf.4

SECTION III

CRITICAL MULTIMODALITY
FOR REIMAGINING CURRICULUM

CHAPTER 9

"DON'T TELL ME IT'S NOT RESEARCH"

Using Multimodal Critical Inquiry Projects to Disrupt the Deficits in the Traditional ELA Paper

Sarah M. Fleming
State University of New York, Oswego

ABSTRACT

If we are to reframe social semiotics and multimodality as decentering dominant ideas of power and what "counts" as purposeful meaning making, then it is imperative that we acknowledge our students as intentional, skillful, and knowledgeable creators of multimodal text. Students who practice research positioned as critical inquirists are invited to question and challenge the very instructional design and purpose of their schooling, are self-empowered to question the status quo, recognize inequities where they are present, and use their learning to speak out, share their experience and advocate for change they see as necessary. The purpose of this chapter is to explore what happens when teachers and students abandon the traditional paradigm of research-based writing (or in other words, "the paper") for the study and construction of multimodal, critical, inquiry-based texts meant for community consumption via a digital platform. The Digital Museum Project represents the shift to implementing research-based writing assignments using a critical inquiry framework as one that privileges youth perspectives, experiences, and calls for action.

The chapter will begin with an overview of this teacher's curricular aims and the resulting driving questions that guide student learning. In the case of this particular instructional practice, students are being asked to consider the question, "How do we use inquiry and activism to tell our truths?" This will include a discussion of the learning unit's connection to the theoretical frameworks of social semiotics and criticality as focused upon in this volume. In other words, this chapter will explain how students, along with their teachers, can be invited to become critical multimodal authors through the construction of digital museum exhibits that "advanc[e] criticality and [push] youths to cultivate the tools to dismantle deficit ways of the world, protect themselves against wrongdoing, and ultimately transform the world for the better" (Muhammad, 2018, p. 139).

Next, the chapter will provide a review of instructional moves made to assist students in the critical reading of multimodal texts, focusing specifically on physical and virtual museum exhibit designs. Focus is placed on which modes of design and expression, voices, and lived experiences are privileged, and which are missing. Students are then tasked to construct their own virtual museum exhibit for the culminating assessment of their critical inquiry as evidence of their work toward answering the driving question noted above. The construction of their digital museum exhibit requires them to consider the multiple modes they will be communicating their intention to their given audience. Both the content of their inquiries as well as their methods of and purposes for the work relates to Muhammad's call for criticality, in that they speak to critical issues important to them as young people and as understood from their traditionally marginalized positions. The chapter will conclude with samples of instructional materials and student work, as well as a discussion of implications and next steps for this work in the following school year.

The New York State Next Generation ELA Standards (New York State Education Department, n.d.) tasks 10th grade English students to do the following:

- 9-10W6 Conduct research to answer questions, including self-generated questions, or solve a problem; narrow or broaden the inquiry when appropriate. Synthesize multiple sources, demonstrating understanding of the subject under investigation.
- 9-10W7 Gather relevant information from multiple sources, using advanced searches effectively; assess the usefulness of each source in answering the research question; integrate information into the text selectively to maintain the flow of ideas; avoid plagiarism and follow a standard format for citation.

In other words, upon graduating high school, students are expected to know how to both conduct and then write in response to research. Typically students demonstrate their ability to meet these standards by writing a research-based essay, complete with introduction, thesis statement, body paragraphs, cited evidence, conclusion, and works cited.

But there are many problems with the research paper as a traditional means of communication. First of all, the paper's audience is quite limited; after all, the paper is only written for an audience of one person, the teacher. It is highly unlikely that the paper will be read by anyone else, unless the teacher has worked peer review time into the instructional design, and even then such reading tends to be overly perfunctory and done in the name of proofreading rather than to make substantial editing changes. Another issue with the research paper in its traditional model is that it often lacks voice from the author; students assume a distanced, academic position that removes any evidence of their own identity or positionality from the material or purpose.

That is often the case even in papers demanding the student writer take an argumentative stance; because of the form itself, research papers still tend to report about an issue rather than advocating for a particular response or action to an issue. And even if the paper does lean toward a greater stance of advocacy, the problem still lies with the audience of one; the student has no real chance to advocate for the issue to their peers or a larger targeted audience.

While the research paper may still be the primary and most accepted mode of academic discourse found in college settings, the reality is that most of our students are more likely to encounter multimodal discourse in their daily lives and in their adult lives after high school and/or college (Hinchman et al., 2003; Jewitt, 2005; Kress, 2003). Lim (2018) tells us that "to be considered literate in this day and age is to be able to effectively communicate multimodally" (p. 1).

As such, students need to spend as much time preparing for the consumption and production of multimodal texts so that they are better equipped to critically read and wisely respond to them (Doerr-Stevens, 2016). However, doing this kind of work disrupts the traditional paradigm of both the research paper itself as well as its purpose, in that it places greater control and ownership of meaning making in the hands of the students.

If we are to reframe social semiotics and multimodality (Kress, 2010) as decentering dominant ideas of power and what "counts" as purposeful meaning making, then it is imperative that we acknowledge our students as intentional, skillful, and knowledgeable creators of multimodal text. Students who practice research positioned as critical inquirists are invited to question and challenge the very instructional design and purpose of their schooling; are self- empowered to question the status quo; recognize inequities where they are present; and use their learning to speak out, share their experience, and advocate for change they see as necessary (Vasquez et al., 2019). The purpose of this chapter is to explore what happens when teachers and students abandon the traditional paradigm of research-based writing (or in other words, "the research paper") for the study and construction of multimodal, critical, inquiry-based texts meant for community consumption via a digital platform. The Digital Museum Project represents the shift to implementing research-based writing assignments using a critical inquiry framework as one that privileges youth perspectives, experiences, and calls for action.

CONTEXTUALIZING THE DIGITAL MUSEUM PROJECT

This project took place in my two 10th grade English honors courses during the 2020–2021 school year in a small suburban school in upstate New York with a K–12 population of less than 2,000 students. The student population was predominantly White (approximately 90%)—fewer than 10% of students identified as Black or African-American, as Hispanic or Latinx, as Asian or native Hawaiian, as multiracial, or as American Indian. Fewer than 15% of students were identified as having learning disabilities, coming from lower socioeconomic status, or as being limited English proficient. Students in this particular class reflected the overall school's demographics. These classes were labeled with an honors distinction, indicating that students had previously taken an advanced-designation course or had been recommended by their ninth grade ELA teacher. This particular unit took place at the end of the school year as a culminating assessment, asking students to draw upon the experiences and skills they had developed throughout the year, such as the critical reading of literary texts and both the reading and writing of research-based texts. This also occurred simultaneously with other independent choice-based work, in which students read novels in literature circles, so students were challenged in the pursuit of multiple objectives at this time.

As both the practicing teacher and researcher for this project, my work was informed by practitioner inquiry (Cochran-Smith & Lytle, 2009) which suggests that such research empowers teachers by privileging their voices and valuing their contributions to existing scholarship. As such, I position myself as both a teacher and as a researcher who inquires into her own teaching practice, as it is informed by educational theory. Adopting Cochran-Smith and Lytle's (2009) "inquiry as stance" allowed me to both model for my students and share in their own experiences of what it meant to do research, or to approach learning from an inquisitive mindset. I continuously saw myself as engaged in my own investigations, just as I was guiding students to see themselves as researchers and inquirers of greater knowledge. While I had to account for my subjectivity and manage my own biases throughout the project, considering my observations in relationship to my position of power as the classroom teacher (Zeni, 1998), I also maintain that such a position allowed me to help establish what I believe was a community of researchers: my students and I working alongside one another to explore and share new knowledge. Consequently, I use the term "we" throughout this chapter to refer to the work my students and I did collectively, honoring that my role as guide was intended to support them in their development of their own stance as researchers.

Curricular Aims

In the case of this particular instructional practice, students were being asked to consider the question, "How do we use inquiry and activism to tell our truths?" Students were invited to become critical multimodal authors through the construction of digital museum exhibits that "advanc[ed] criticality and [pushed] youths to cultivate the tools to dismantle deficit ways of the world, protect themselves against wrongdoing, and ultimately transform the world for the better" (Muhammad, 2018, p. 139).

Students must be composers of the types of texts they are more likely to consume. From the websites they visit to the social media platforms they navigate, teens are bombarded with multimodal texts and must learn how to navigate the interplay between text, image, symbol, and meaning (Alvermann et al., 2012). They almost never have to consume text that isn't accompanied by some photo or graphic, so why are they routinely being asked to produce text in this manner? Or at least, why do we privilege print- or linguistic-based writing over the opportunity for students to create and communicate meaning through multimodal means? Perhaps it has more to do with the other aspect of assessment through traditional paper mode, in which a student works to convince the teacher that she or he has the right answer, by proving that they have sufficiently learned or mastered the material. But when the audience of a student text changes and is more broadly defined, the student author must contend with a larger and possibly more complicated and demanding audience, one who may need more attention. The audience's purpose for consuming the text is not necessarily done with the intention of evaluating the author for a grade, but for a more authentic desire to engage with the information, provided they feel so compelled (Hackney, 2020; Maniotes & Kuhlthau, 2014).

Instructional Moves

After a year of reading and thinking critically about texts, who produced them and who they were meant for, the students and I began our final unit. This would be a chance for students to engage in a passion project, to focus their learning on something they were interested in, that they felt strongly about and wanted to be able to share with other people. The hope was that their work would serve as a call to action for their audience, that they would inspire the readers of their multimodal research text to feel called to do something or learn something more. Students as authors of these provocative texts would then be engaging in their critical digital literacies (Stornaiuolo et al., 2019) and activist literacies (Humphrey, 2013; Muhammad, 2018, 2019; Simon & Campano, 2013), where they had a purpose for their work that was much larger than the completion of an instructional unit or the earning of a single grade. Students could see the work they completed for an assignment as part of a much larger, collective culture of activism, thereby giving themselves a sense of purpose and agency in sharing their own voices and perspectives about critical issues.

In order to do this work, students had to complete multiple steps of the research process, informed by my understanding of the guided inquiry design (GID) framework (Kuhlthau et al., 2012; Maniotes & Kuhlthau, 2014). This instructional model is a specific approach that seeks to equip students with the tools to engage in deep, sustained learning experiences driven by their own questions, interests, and pursuits for greater knowledge. In this framework (Table 9.1), students are given much more time at the beginning of the process in the first three phases of "Open," "Immerse," and "Explore" to have their curiosity stimulated, to explore their interests, and to read deeply about the subject, in response to a question for inquiry typically determined by the teacher. In this particular case, students were asked to try their hand at designing a question of their own choosing, so that they could see their research as answering a question they had about a particular social issue.

Database Scavenger Hunt

If students were going to be able to complete their final research-based experience from this activist perspective, then they would need to spend time thinking carefully and deliberately about the topics they would pursue. That meant we had to spend time sifting through critical issues that were important to them in order to Explore (GID Phase 3) and eventually Identify (GID Phase 4) their focus. We were fortunate to have access to an incredible resource in our library; we subscribed to a database that was organized in multiple ways meant to stimulate students' curiosity, such as listing topics for potential inquiry on the main database page. For example,

TABLE 9.1 Guided Inquiry Design (GID) in the Digital Museum Project

GID Phase	Description (adapted from Kuhlthau et al., 2007, 2012)	Digital Museum Project
1. Open	Invite to inquiry, open minds, stimulate curiosity.	• Instructional units leading up to culminating inquiry; young adult novel topics & themes (2+ months prior) • The unit driving question (1–2 class sessions)
2. Immerse	Build background knowledge, connect to content, discover interesting ideas.	• Database scavenger hunt (3+ class sessions)
3. Explore	Explore interesting ideas, look around, dip in.	• Scavenger hunt continued; local museum analysis (3–4 class sessions)
4. Identify	Pause and ponder, identify inquiry question, decide direction.	• Proposals: Establish research questions. Write research proposal (2+ class sessions).
5. Gather	Gather important information, go broad, go deep.	• Examine local museum exhibits as mentor texts (3+ class sessions). • Individual research continues, peer/teacher conferencing, add to existing bibliography (4–5 class sessions).
6. Create	Reflect on learning, go beyond facts to make meaning, create to communicate.	• Constructing the digital museum project, individual creation of exhibit slides (3–5 class sessions)
7. Share	Learn from each other, share learning, tell your story.	• Publish student exhibits using linked slide decks; share out sites in class (1–2 class sessions). • Host showcase event for family and community members to attend and interact with exhibits.
8. Evaluate	Evaluate achievement of learning goals, reflect on content, reflect on process.	• Student self-assessment and written reflections (1+ class sessions)

this page contained an alphabetical list of hundreds of possible social issue topics meant to inspire teens to want to do more reading and research—from gun control to marriage equality to climate change. Each selection would then take the user to a specific page in the database that provided an initial overview of that topic, followed by links to resources organized by type: reference, audio, critical essays, biographies, magazines, websites, images, news, videos, academic journals, and related topics.

Students were tasked with completing a database scavenger hunt. When confronted with this long list of potential topics in the database, they were given extensive time over several class sessions to sift through all the topics and spend time clicking on them to get to the home pages for each. I modeled how to do this by first selecting a few topics that would be popular with the class, such as "mental health" and "social media." I demonstrated how to walk through the homepage for an individual topic, explaining to students how the information was organized by resource type and how they could make the most out of their open inquiry time to explore more about the topic. We spent time slowly and deliberately investigating each section of the specific page so that students could see beyond what is typical in student research—that phenomenon when a student (or adult, for that matter) does a quick Google search, clicks on the top three hits, and then feels as if she's exhausted her resources.

Students were given the time to do this kind of curiosity-based hunting and pecking. Too often students are pushed into the library, told to "do their research," rushed to fill out a quick graphic organizer, and then a day later they're expected to start writing (Maniotes & Kuhlthau, 2014). The intention here was to slow down that process and give students time to click, peruse, read, go back, and click into a new topic. Students kept track of their moves by engaging in some form of listing, note-taking, or concept mapping in their class notes so that they could be more aware of ways they jumped from link to link. The task was, after having spent several full class sessions hunting through the long list of potential topics, to identify five possible inquiries.

Students had to submit a list of these five topics, with an explanation for each as to why they found the topic interesting or important, and how it could relate to the current driving question: "How do we use inquiry and activism to tell our truths?"; or in response to a previous driving question from earlier in the year: "Whose stories get included and whose stories get excluded?"

Students' initial scavenger hunt yielded a variety of interests. While a few individuals indicated interest in unique topics, such as genetic engineering, organ donation, vaccines, and school violence, other topics of a more socially critical nature were more popular, such as climate change, immigration, human trafficking, disability rights, Islamophobia, gun control, poverty, gentrification, Palestinian statehood, gender, LGBTQ+ rights, and toxic masculinity. By far the most popular categories for student inquiry during this phase of the research process were police and criminal justice reform, Black Lives Matter, as well as mental health issues, including body image and the effects of online education. In their rationales, students spoke of their personal connection to the topic or their curiosity about what was going on in the world around them. Ben (all student names are pseudonyms) suggested that

> Criminal justice has been at the forefront of the news lately, especially in America, with the BLM protests. But the issue of unfair criminal justice is worldwide, and when poor criminal justice systems exist, it creates many prob-

lems." Ben further defended the connection between his interest in criminal justice reform and work from earlier this year by explaining that "many times inequality leads to injustice, and these people often have their voices excluded."

In expressing her interest in researching about the #MeToo movement, Kimberly demonstrated some previous knowledge, identifying that the movement began in 2006 and that she wanted to "learn about the differences the movement has made in the past 15 years. I want to learn about how I can help and understand people's stories. I would also like to learn more about their goals moving forward." Kimberly continued, "People who have been sexually assaulted are having their stories heard and informing society that there is something wrong with the stigma of being afraid to tell their stories." Kelly identified one of her possible topics as being "LGBTQ+ community equality," listed subtopics such as marriage equality, religious beliefs, sexual orientation, bullying, and human rights, and then explained that "members of the LGBTQ+ community's voices have been excluded all throughout history compared to straight people's. It is important that we hear their stories from the past and present to make a difference for the future with the help of activism."

Local Museums and the Rhetorical Triangle

The next step in this Explore phase of the process was to help students envision the product they would be creating as a result of their inquiry. Knowing they wouldn't be writing a traditional paper that only I would get to read, we had to reconsider the ways in which students could communicate their learning and the audience for whom they're doing so. The purpose of the driving question was to help students understand that effectively communicating their research to others was a form of activist literacies (Humphrey, 2013). Students would need to create a product that could be consumed by a larger public audience. This is when we began to study the purpose and design behind museum exhibits as a mode of discourse. Unfortunately, this is also the point of the learning unit in which trying to teach and learn in a COVID-19 world affected how we moved from our curricular intention to the lived reality. My intention was to organize a field-trip to visit three local museums so that students would have the opportunity to engage with specific exhibits and engage in focused activities asking them to carefully consider the rhetorical purpose and visual design behind the exhibits they saw. I imagined them being able to stand in front of an exhibit's full wall display and have to question the elements of multimodal design (Kress, 2003, 2010) as they observed them, such as: "Why are the words placed here and not there?"; "Which image does my eye travel to first?"; "How likely am I to read this bulleted list of information, rather than that paragraph in the photo caption?"; "Why is the panel that color?"; and so on.

To be able to do this, students needed to have a greater understanding of the rhetorical design of a multimodal text, like they would see when visiting a museum. A museum exhibit could involve the combination of different images, words, colors, lights, moving objects, and so on, and students would be tasked with having to think about why an exhibit would be designed in such a way in the first place. When needing to convey information to a live audience, how would a museum exhibit designer make decisions about what type of content to display, how to do so, and why? To do this, we consulted websites for museum exhibition design (Colorcraft, n.d.) and studied the Smithsonian Exhibits' Guide to Exhibit Development (Smithsonian Exhibits, n.d.). We discussed the role and responsibilities of the exhibit designer and compared it to the role of an author of a written text, making note of the different tools being used, and we consulted lists of suggested steps for curating museum displays to inform our thinking.

Because we could not travel to the museums themselves, we instead engaged in a critical analysis of the museum's websites. Students had to select three local museums' websites to explore, looking for information on specific exhibits. For each exhibit, I asked them to report out in a GoogleDoc what they determined were the speaker, intended audience, message, and purpose of the exhibit based upon the information they could find on the website. The purpose of this was for them to perform a rhetorical analysis on the exhibit as a text in and of itself. More specifically, one that went beyond simply identifying the topic of an exhibit and that resisted the temptation of naming the intended audience as "anyone who wanted to know about the topic," a typical answer for students not used to carefully considering a more targeted audience. In her description of a local historical association, Jennifer was able to speak more precisely about the potential audience for a photography exhibit about the downtown area by imaging more specifically that the exhibit "would also be appealing to families who have lived here to show younger generations what it looked like when they were their age." Brittney's description of an energy exhibit at the local science museum at first indicated that the exhibit was for "anyone interested in energy production," but then she specified more clearly that it would be for those interested in "finding ways to make the world a better place." This suggests that she has a sense that the exhibit was meant to provoke an explicit response from the reader, even if she struggled with explaining what that response should be.

Inquiry Proposal

Once students had spent sufficient time examining real museum exhibits and exploring their own interests for pursuing lines of inquiry and prompting action, it was time for the "Identify" phase: They were asked to submit a formal proposal for the focus of their project. Their one-page proposal needed to include the following: the general topic; three or more potential subtopics to be investigated within the larger topic; a brief acknowledgement of the speaker (ethos), audience (pathos), and message (logos); a discussion of the exhibit's intention (purpose); a list of potential multimodal elements to include in the exhibit (photos, video, audio, technology interactives; first-hand interviews, quotes, captions, primary/secondary text panels, etc.); citations (hyperlinked docs are acceptable) for three sources reviewed so far; and, a working driving question the inquiry would answer.

While students had very little trouble meeting some requirements of the proposal, in terms of listing their topic and subtopics and including citations for sources already consulted in the open inquiry phase of investigation, they often struggled when it came to identifying potential multimodal elements to include in their imagined exhibit, as well as trying to draft a working driving question that would lend purpose to their exhibit in the first place.

Students' self-designed driving questions spanned a range of topics and levels of criticality. For example Josie, who was researching topics related to health care disparities, income inequality and the Black Lives Matter movement, wanted to answer the question: "How does inequality help those in power?" Kelly, who was also interested in researching more about the Black Lives Matter movement, wanted to know, "Would this movement be as effective if it were not for the use of social media?" Sometimes students' first attempts at their driving questions indicated a need to be more precise with their language or specific in identifying their audience. Sandra initially asked, "How can we best educate and bring awareness to rape culture?" But by the time she completed her project she had revised her question to be more precise: "How can we best explain rape culture and consent to impede the number of sexual assault cases from going up?" Her second iteration of the driving question suggests a greater awareness of an audience who is expected to be able to answer the question once having consumed her exhibit.

Constructing the Digital Museum Project

The "Gather" and "Create" phases of GID set forth time for students to synthesize their research and work toward the construction of their museum exhibits. Again, in a non-COVID-19 world, students would have worked together in groups to create a real display for their exhibit, one that involved them being engaged in deliberate decision-making about the layout of text and images. The librarian and I envisioned setting up wall-sized panels or easels akin to a research poster-session format for the "Share" phase of the project, so that a real live audience could walk through their exhibits and consume the information and messages these exhibits conveyed. We imagined displays that made use of Chromebooks or iPads so that the audience could engage in interactive displays connecting to the larger panels (and we hope that a future iteration of this project, post COVID-19, will still allow for that). We would have invited other classes in to read the students' exhibits, and we would have held a community event in the evening so that other teachers and family members could do so as well. Because of COVID-19 restrictions for social distancing, we had to leave out this presentation aspect of their inquiry; instead, students shared their work with each other in their class. Despite this limitation, students were still engaged in the same process of having to consider who their audience was and how that audience would interact with the multimodal text they produced in order to clearly and effectively communicate their message and call their reader to some form of action.

To create a digital museum exhibit, we had to create a digital tool that would virtually simulate the feel of walking through a physical museum and visiting multiple exhibits, one at a time. A quick Google search for "digital museum templates" revealed many useful websites and sample Powerpoint and Google Slide backgrounds for use in such interactive displays, as well as suggestions as for how to set them up. We would create a museum homepage that acted as the entry point of the museum, with links to students' individual exhibits. We used a Google slidedeck to simulate the various sections of a wall-sized exhibit. I created a template (Figure 9.1) for students to see that began with a homepage that included a title framed as the driving inquiry question, as well as up to four interactive textboxes, or buttons, that were the subtopics for their inquiry and would link directly to other slides in the deck. Each of these individual slides served as the space for students

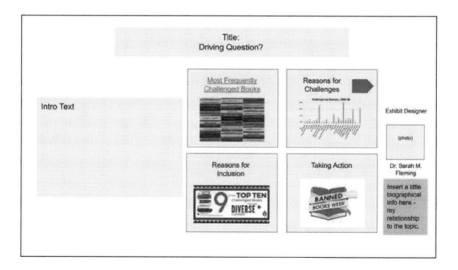

Figure 9.1 Template for designing the digital museum exhibits.

to create their multimodal display, including text boxes, photos, videos, captions, and hyperlinks to outside sources. Each of these slides also had to include a "return to the main exhibit" button that would lead the viewer back to their first slide, which would then include a "return to the main gallery" button leading back to the museum homepage with all the exhibit links. This would allow the digital museum-goer to navigate back and forth through the pages as they would move through a real museum, dipping in and out of exhibits.

Having to envision a real person as their audience for their specific section of the museum site made for much more purposeful decision-making when it came to selecting and arranging information on the few slides they had available to them. This also forced students to think carefully about their use of words and space, specifically the number of words used to convey a certain idea. We discussed the significance of presenting information in brief chunks, in bulleted lists, rather than in strung-together paragraphs like one would find in a paper format. Students acknowledged, thinking about their own perusal of websites and in-person exhibits, that readers are unlikely to read through prose presented as if it were an essay; that readers relied upon the use of physical space in a multimodal text to break up the monotony of a paragraph and to focus reader's attention to follow a deliberate sequence of words, images, and graphics.

Student Self-Assessment and Reflection

One of the most significant aspects of the students' work related to what they did when the project was completed during the final "Evaluate" phase; students were asked to assess their own work using an evaluative rubric and submit a written reflection. For the reflection, I asked students to talk about three moves they made as the author of their multimodal text, and then respond (i.e., "What did you deliberately choose to do in your text, and why did you do it?"). This gave students one final opportunity to consider the relationship between their rhetorical intentions for the text as the author and its effect on the audience. This also gave students a chance to address something they attempted to do that might not have worked as well as they wanted because of technical limitations.

In their responses, students often focused their attention on the inclusion of specific content or elements in their multimodal texts; for example, they explain their reasoning behind the inclusion of certain photos, graphs, or interactive materials. In her project on the climate change crisis, Amy explained that she chose to link a timelapse video of changing global temperature spanning 140 years, explaining that "this shows my audience that our planet is gradually getting warmer, mainly because of humans, and I hope people will feel to indeed to try to do something about it." Amy's explanation addressed what she chose to include, but not necessarily how she chose to include it. It lacked an explanation as to the deliberate design moves she had to make, and I would have asked her to explain further: "Why did you place the video in that specific location?"; "How did you direct your reader's attention to the video using other graphic cues?"

Delia's explanations addressed more details related to her reasoning for making decisions in the construction of her multimodal text. In her project about mental health, she explained that she included the photo and a real story of someone who struggled with depression because she found that "projects that contain personal stories are much more powerful and memorable. I think that pathos is so important because it makes information less about facts and statistics and makes it more human." Delia did include some aspects of design in her reflection, explaining that "to highlight some of my key points, I used a red color so the most important words and phrases were bolder and caught the reader's eye." She also addressed her inclusion of artistic images she described as "artwork that represented the feelings of those mental illnesses. I thought the artwork I chose beautifully showcased the many emotions behind these illnesses." In this case, Delia is attempting to speak to her decision-making that she intended to convey a tone through her collage of images and text that was suited to the topic under discussion.

In her written reflection about her project on criminal justice reform (Figure 9.2), Lily clearly explained her design decisions as relating to her project's call to action:

> On Slide 5, which was my last informational slide, I added 3 hyperlinks. I did this on this particular slide because it was a way to wrap up and leave my read-

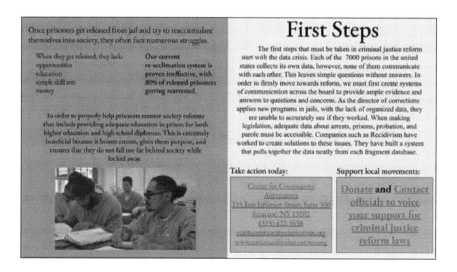

Figure 9.2 Lily's project.

ers with some form of action they could take. Therefore, the links I included, took readers to resources where they could donate, contact political officials, and communicate with a local office. After reading my slides, I hope that everyone feels passionate for criminal justice reform enough to take direct action. I specifically included the contact information of a local center for criminal justice reform, as most of my viewers are from here, they might feel more inclined to help if they can make an impact on a more local level.

Lily's understanding of her own work here demonstrates that she saw her audience as real and able to be influenced by the text she designed. Her desire to connect her reader with information for local organizations should they wish to take action after having read her text represents the very best we could wish for in this project—that a student felt motivated by the purpose of their work to inspire others to take up that call to action.

Jennifer's description of her deliberate decision-making spoke more to the design aspects of her project about "fast fashion" and her critique of the fashion industry's unethical practices (Figure 9.3). She explained:

> As the exhibit is about fashion, which can be a very expressive and deliberate tool on many people's lives, I wanted the exhibit to reflect that. Large fashion consumers will likely be drawn to aesthetics and visual elements as they express those ideals on themselves daily. Those consumers might be wearers of fast fashion. So this could help them think about their purchases and consumerism in their daily lives.

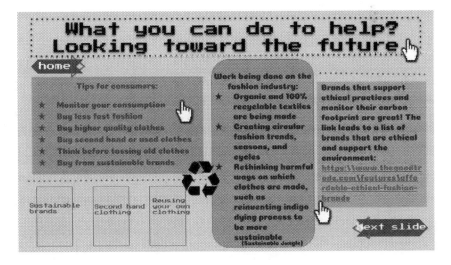

Figure 9.3 Jennifer's project.

Jennifer's reflection spoke more to her use of bright colors, a striking modern font, and her placement of elements on each particular slide, what she notes as being the "aesthetics" of her project. Her work suggests that she knew there should be a match between the design elements of her text, the content about the problems with fast fashion, and the audience's interests.

Teacher Reflection

As this was the first iteration of this instructional unit, there are many next steps to take with this particular project now that I can anticipate the areas where students will struggle. The greatest impediment to this work was our inability to go visit museums in person so that students could have the full experience of reading individual exhibits as multimodal texts, and could then better envision themselves as authors of similar multimodal texts. Students adapted to this challenge as best they could, engaging in class conversations that asked them to envision their slidedeck spanning the breadth of an entire wall-sized panel, but the reality is that they missed out on what could have been the most impressionable part of an in-person learning experience.

Indeed, since students were tasked with making individual digital exhibits as opposed to collaborating to make tangible wall-sized displays, some dimension of the social interaction of the project was lost here, too. Perhaps, if we could have instead had students see their work projected onto larger screens rather than stay captured on their chromebook screens, they would have felt more impressed with the magnitude of their own work and it could have felt more real to them.

In a second iteration of this work, I would slow down and spend even more deliberate time walking students through a close analysis of the modes and semiotic resources (Jewitt, 2005) in the exhibits we first examined. Doing so would provide students with a better working knowledge of an author's choices and the relationship between design elements such as color, size, font selections, planned white space, and so on. This would have drawn a closer connection between the rhetorical purposes of the museum exhibits they analyzed and the ones they critically produced. While I thought I was addressing these concepts as we worked through the research steps and considering the content of students' texts, the reality is that there was certainly room for more of this conversation to take place. I took for granted that students would be able to speak to these deliberate decisions given the amount of time they are engaged as consumers of multimodal text, but their reflections demonstrated that there is certainly room for improvement in this area.

One final change I would make is giving students more time to reflect throughout the process, as opposed to waiting until after they had completed the whole task. Had we done more periodic reflection, I might have realized sooner that students did in fact need greater support when it came to making decisions about balancing text, image, and blank space, or in choosing colors and fonts more meaningfully and not arbitrarily.

CONCLUSION

In their list of key aspects of critical literacy, Vasquez et al. (2019) remind us that "text design and production, which are essential to critical literacy work, can provide opportunities for transformation" (p. 307). When students are positioned as agents and makers of meaning in their own multimodal texts, they are both transformed and transform others. Students who practice research as critical inquirists and produce multimodal texts to communicate their learning are indeed meeting the standards as laid out at the beginning of this chapter, and they are doing so much more; their work has real meaning and impact for an authentic audience, thereby giving them the chance to engage their critical (Vasquez et al., 2019) and activist literacies (Humphrey, 2013; Muhammad, 2018, 2019; Simon & Campano, 2013) beyond the extent they could have by writing the traditional paper. The Digital Museum Project is one I encourage other practicing teachers to replicate and improve upon, so that other teachers and students may have the same rewarding experiences we did.

REFERENCES

Alvermann, D. E., Marshall, J. D., McLean, C. A., Huddleston, A. P., Joaquin, J., & Bishop, J. (2012). Adolescents' web-based literacies, identity construction, and skill development. *Literacy Research and Instruction, 51*(3), 179–195. https://doi.org/10.1080/19388071.2010.523135

Cochran-Smith, M., & Lytle, S. L. (2009). *Inquiry as stance: Practitioner research for the next generation.* Teachers College Press.

ColorCraft. (n.d.). *10 tips for museum exhibit design success.* https://colorcraft3d.com/blog-post/10-tips-for-museum-exhibit-design-success/

Doerr-Stevens, C. (2016). Multimodal exploration of civic stance in the English language arts classroom. *English Teaching: Practice & Critique, 16*(1), 6–28. https://doi.org/10.1108/ETPC-11-2016-0142

Hackney, S. (2020). "I like the freedom": Digital literacy and authentic audience. *English Journal, 109*(6), 59–65. https://www.proquest.com/openview/0d44eb5867266889123c187003fa77d4/1?pq-origsite=gscholar&cbl=42045

Hinchman, K. A., Alvermann, D. E., Boyd, F. B., Brozo, W. G., & Vacca, R. T. (2003–2004). Supporting older students' in- and out-of-school literacies. *Journal of Adolescent and Adult Literacy, 47*(4), 304–310. https://www.jstor.org/stable/40014776

Humphrey, S. (2013). Empowering adolescents for activist literacies. *Journal of Language & Literacy Education, 9*(1), 114–135. http://jolle.coe.uga.edu/wp-content/uploads/2013/05/Empowering-Adolescents.pdf

Jewitt, C. (2005). Multimodality, "reading" and "writing" for the 21st century. *Discourse: Studies in the cultural politics of education, 26*(3), 315–331. https://doi.org/10.1080/01596300500200011

Kress, G. (2003). *Literacy in the new media age.* Routledge.

Kress, G. R. (2010). *Multimodality: A social semiotic approach to contemporary communication.* Taylor & Francis.

Kuhlthau, C. C., Maniotes, L. K., & Caspari, A. K. (2007). *Guided inquiry: Learning in the 21st century.* ABC-CLIO.

Kuhlthau, C. C., Maniotes, L. K., & Caspari, A. K. (2012). *Guided inquiry design: A framework for inquiry in your school.* Libraries Unlimited.

Lim, F. V. (2018). Developing a systemic functional approach to teach multimodal literacy. *Functional Linguistics, 5*(1), 1–17. https://doi.org/10.1186/s40554-018-0066-8

Maniotes, L. K., & Kuhlthau, C. C. (2014). Making the shift: From traditional research assignments to guided inquiry learning. *Knowledge Quest, 43*(2), 8–17. https://eric.ed.gov/?id=EJ1045936

Muhammad, G. E. (2018). A plea for identity and criticality: reframing literacy learning standards through a four-layered equity model. *Journal of Adolescent and Adult Literacy, 62*(2), 137–142. https://www.jstor.org/stable/26632909

Muhammad, G. E. (2019). Protest, power and possibilities: The need for agitation literacies. *Journal of Adolescent & Adult Literacy, 63*(3), 351–355. https://doi.org/10.1002/jaal.1014

New York State Department of Education. (n.d.). *New York State next generation English language arts learning standards.* http://www.nysed.gov/curriculum-instruction/new-york-state-next-generation-english-language-arts-learning-standards

Simon, R., & Campano, G. (2013). Activist literacies: Teacher research as resistance to the "normal curve." *Journal of Language & Literacy Education, 9*(1), 21–39. https://files.eric.ed.gov/fulltext/EJ1008171.pdf

Smithsonian Exhibits. (n.d.). *A guide to exhibit development.* http://exhibits.si.edu/wp-content/uploads/2018/04/Guide-to-Exhibit-Development.pdf

Stornaiuolo, A., Thomas, E. E., Campano, G., & Plummer, E. C. (2019). Critical digital and media literacies in challenging times: Reimagining the role of English language arts. *Research in the Teaching of English, 54*(2), 105–108. https://www.proquest.com/scholarly-journals/critical-digital-media-literacies-challenging/docview/2329715987/se-2?accountid=13025

Vasquez, V. M., Janks, H., & Comber, B. (2019). Critical literacy as a way of being and doing. *Language Arts, 96*(5), 300–311. https://hilaryjanks.files.wordpress.com/2020/09/vasquezjankscomber-cl_as_a_way_of_being_and-copy-3-1.pdf

Zeni, J. (1998). A guide to ethical issues and action research. *Educational Action Research, 6*(10), 9–19. https://doi.org/10.1080/09650799800200053

CHAPTER 10

THE PLAT AND THE GAVEL

Multimodal Critical Family History in Rural Teacher Education

William S. Davis
University of Oklahoma

Vicki Mokuria
Stephen F. Austin State University

ABSTRACT

This chapter explores the design, implementation, and future of an educational foundations course in a university teacher education program in rural East Texas. The fully online introductory course takes a critical perspective toward the social and historical roots of education in the United States. It is also the entry point for most undergraduate preservice teachers into their elementary and secondary level teacher education program at the institution.

We write from the perspective of two White, middle-class secondary level teacher educators. Students enrolled in the courses are typically, though not exclusively, White monolingual English speakers who do not reflect the growing diversity of U.S. schools. Because of this, we sought to provide a more stimulating and transformative experience for our developing preservice teachers. At the end of 2020, we collaborated to reconceptualize the course as an immersive, multimodal space with a strong focus on disrupting dominant narratives and colorblind beliefs towards diverse children. We sought to encourage the requisite "irritation" arising from challenging deeply ingrained perspectives, specifically around issues of racism and ways we, along with our students, have been socialized to understand our positionality in a racialized society.

Central to this objective were our and our students' personal journeys through *critical family history* (CFH). Conceived and researched by Christine Sleeter (2015), CFH is a framework for analysis that requires one to reach "back historically, usually multiple generations, in order to understand the interplay between past and present" (Sleeter, 2020, p. 3). The process involves deep critical self-reflection and an historical investigation of the power relationships between our ancestors and other groups at the time, as well as how that impacts our own identity formation and current lives.

In our adaptation of CFH, students led and presented multimodal research projects examining how their family (and ancestral) histories intersected with White supremacist ideologies and policies. Students interviewed family members, collected artifacts (e.g., photos, documents), and researched historical trends and policies as part of their analyses which they presented through a narrative video format. The exploratory and vulnerable nature of the project incited highly personal meaning making within the diverse realities of each individual student. The process of CFH was transformative for many of them. Of particular importance was that these transformations were often actualized through the discovery and presentation of tangible family artifacts documenting how their family or ancestors benefitted—or were harmed—from White supremacist ideologies and policies.

In this chapter we analyze the multimodal nature of this course through collaborative autoethnography (Chang et al., 2013). In the spirit of multimodality, we re- present the findings in the form of a kaleidoscopic bricolage and dialogue between us that includes embedded photos and historical documents which support our collaborative autoethnographic analysis (Bhattacharya, 2008). We also highlight our own sensations of "irritation" arising from facilitating such a jarring, vulnerable, and transformative experience for new teachers.

Teacher education programs in the United States face various hurdles in preparing primarily white pre-service teachers (PSTs) to enact equitable school experiences for a growing majority of public school students who are Black, Indigenous, or children of color (Taie & Goldring, 2020). Without the requisite beliefs and pedagogical skill, White teachers are inclined to forward actions which erase their students' identities while sustaining Whiteness in schools and the curriculum. Research has shown how White teachers, in contrast to teachers of color, are likely to hold deficit or "colorblind" belief systems toward children of color (Baldwin et al., 2007), such as believing they are less capable (Gershenson et al., 2016) and more culpable

(Gilliam et al., 2016), leading to substandard teaching and disproportionate disciplinary action (Riddle & Sinclair, 2019).

Teacher education programs, however, have the agency to disrupt and dismantle these cycles. White PSTs can begin to develop structural and individual understandings of Whiteness and learn to make race visible given the right curricular and pedagogical supports (Matias & Mackey, 2016; Sleeter, 2015). One salient barrier is the tendency of White PSTs to have difficulty moving from external understandings of White supremacy (i.e., that it exists exclusively out in the world) to identifying it internally (i.e., that it is maintained through one's own beliefs and actions). Hambacher and Ginn (2021) recommend that instead of simply highlighting painful narratives of marginalized people to evoke PSTs' feelings of urgency, further alienating students from recognizing their own contribution, teacher educators should center their curricula around their own critical self-interrogation of beliefs. In this way, teacher educators can model for PSTs how to identify one's ways of knowing and being as playing a role in maintaining inequity in schools and society.

To this end, Berchini (2017) advocates for the creation of spaces in teacher education where White PSTs can turn their gaze inward and which promote "learning about, and engaging with, the ways by which Whites are collectively implicated in structural injustice" (p. 472).

Further, Sleeter (2015) expands on this work through her contribution of a pedagogical approach titled *critical family history* (CFH). CFH seeks not only to support students in identifying themselves as part of a collective group, but also connecting their own collective past to individual and collective present through multimodal genealogical research. Sleeter (2015) writes, "Ultimately, the process of learning to situate family within wider historical, social, and cultural patterns helps students see connections between their lives today and the complex past we share" (p. 10). Through this highly personal and often discomforting work, PSTs can begin to identify themselves as advocates in the fight for equity and justice.

In this chapter we examine how we and our rural teacher education students leveraged *critical multimodality and social semiotics* (CMSS) to participate in CFH (Sleeter, 2020) in a social foundations in education course. Through the use of critical collaborative autoethnography, we present narratives of our own critical family histories and how those narratives overlapped with and were influenced by those of our students. We center our research on the artifacts (Pahl & Rowsell, 2010)—the signs—representing the codification of White supremacy by powerful signmakers in various contexts. We position teacher education and the integration of CFH as a means of enacting CMSS to identify, denaturalize, and repurpose such signs while simultaneously guiding PSTs in the development of a critical and structural consciousness.

We begin this exploration of CMSS in teacher education by identifying ourselves. Author 1 is a White teacher educator and assistant professor specializing in world languages pedagogy. Prior to entering higher education he was a German teacher at an urban high school in Arkansas. Before recently beginning a tenure-track position at his current institution, he taught as a visiting professor in a teacher education program at a rural public university in Texas. Author 2 is a cisgender woman of Ashkenazi Jewish descent who has benefited from White privilege her entire life, while also appearing ethnically ambiguous. After teaching high school in a large urban public school for over 20 years, she pursued higher education and earned her PhD in curriculum and instruction. She currently teaches at a rural public university in Texas.

CRITICAL FAMILY HISTORY

Named and explored by Christine Sleeter (2008, 2020), CFH is genealogy which "interrogates the interaction between family and context" (Sleeter, 2016, p. 11). CFH challenges family and ancestral historians of all formalities (i.e, ourselves, our families, students, and teacher educators) to critically examine the power relationships among groups in the past, how one's family and ancestry were impacted by or impacted (positively and negatively) these relationships, and how these findings influence one's present life. Informed by and in support of frameworks such as critical race theory (Lynn & Dixson, 2013), critical feminist theories (hooks, 1994), critical land-based family history (French et al., 2020), and others, CFH situates "families within larger contexts that draw attention to unequal relations" (Sleeter, 2015, p. 3) along intersecting lines of race, gender, sexual orientation, and class. CFH encourages historians to engage in multimodal family research and examine their ancestral pasts via paths of inquiry such as:

- What other groups were around?
- What policies and ideologies provided or barred autonomy for some groups over others, and which groups forwarded them?
- In which ways are these forces present or missing in family narratives? Whose families' narratives, and why?
- Which groups' memories and histories were kept, and whose were not?
- How has this influenced whose perspectives are dominant in U.S. discourse and school curricula?

With the growth of interest in one's lineage and family past, it is no surprise that online family history and genealogy services have become more mainstream and accessible. Yet with this growth has come a harmful impact:

the romanticization and amplification of stories which reaffirm what Ronald Takaki (2008) called the "master narrative of American history" (p. 4), in which the history and perspectives of European Americans have been planted at the center of American discourse, thought, and policy. This has come at the expense of the marginalized and erased histories, ways of knowing, and perspectives which shed light on the colonizing and dehumanizing past (and present) of the United States. CFH, however, directs historians (in our case, students and teacher educators) in multiple ways to engage critically with ancestral experiences and to begin to uncover characteristics of one's self and history that have been normalized as "American."

Like genealogy, CFH relies on searching for, identifying, and collecting artifacts which bring to light family connections between people, perspectives, actions, policies, and land.

Artifacts can be anything that brings meaning to these connections, such as family sources—photographs, oral history, videos, diaries, keepsakes, letters, heirlooms, stories, and memories—but also public records—census records, land and policy documents, government acts, maps, books, and articles (Sleeter, 2015). These can naturally be combined, or some used to elicit others, such as in the case of Trinh (2020) who presented family photographs to his father and uncles to begin conversations with them about his grandparents.

CRITICAL FAMILY HISTORY AND CRITICAL MULTIMODALITY AND SOCIAL SEMIOTICS

Given the diverse modes involved in CFH, CMSS is well suited to explain its powerful influence on students' developing capacities as new teachers to question dominant narratives in the classroom. In this study, we examine CMSS from the complementary understandings of social semiotics and sign formation offered by Kress (2010), Sandoval (2000), and Barthes (2013). Each approach recognizes how *meaning* (signified) and its attachment to *form* (signifier) are always socially shaped. *Signs*, comprising meaning and form, are arbitrary formations which are forged by influential social forces. Further, social semiotics is inherently critical; it recognizes that the forces behind the creation of signs (meaning and form) are motivated, and, therefore, signs reflect the interests, motivations, and power of the sign makers. In this way, the relationship of meaning and form—or the aptness of a sign—is a historically produced link, often manifesting the urges and agency of sign makers endorsing dominant social ideologies. Even those who do not intend to create dominant signs may unintentionally do so, as "inevitably, what has been and what is 'around' and available, has shaped and does shape the interest and the attention of the maker of the sign" (Kress, 2010, p. 74).

Sandoval (2000), in discussing Barthes (2013), conceptualizes critical social semiotics as an emancipatory semiotics involved in the deconstruction of signs, or "ideologies." Those engaged in emancipatory semiotics, or "mythologists," employ "a de-ideologizing and emancipatory form of perception" which "shatters any dominant ideology into these constituent parts" (p. 101). Referring to Kress (2010), such powerful ideologies carried within the aptness of signs (the relationship between meaning and form) can be identified and disrupted. In an application of his semiotic approach, Barthes (2013) refers to the cover photo of a 1956 issue of the magazine *Paris Match* depicting a young Black soldier in full dress uniform and beret looking up and forward in salute. Sandoval (2000) writes how "the image and its (historically and materially situated) meanings are appropriated—to signify (unashamedly) something else" (p. 97); namely, an ideology of the greatness of the French empire. Via critical semiology, Barthes unravels the sign and, instead, repositions the photo of the youth as an alibi of French colonialism.

CFH provides an opportunity for teacher education to integrate CMSS into their teacher development courses in order to enact an emancipatory semiology. To promote equal power, teacher educators should consider engaging in CFH work alongside their students. Paulette Cross' work in teacher education embodies this approach in action. In her multicultural education course, Cross (2020) approached uncomfortable course themes, such as those centered around intersectionality and history, by engaging students in writing a family history book, or "life stories." The project involved students interviewing family members, collecting family photographs, letters, documents, and researching the historical context, looks, and signs of the time in which their families or ancestors were situated. Students then critically examined these artifacts regarding how they intersected with "power, social class, race, capitalism, as well as individual and collective experience" (p. 3).

Adding to her course, Cross used excerpts and photos from her own family history book (Cross, 1997) as examples and guides for her students. In one instance in her book, she critically examines a photograph of her family's homestead in combination with family interviews and analysis of historical books and articles. For Cross (2020), the photograph signifies the self liberation of Black families in the U.S. South which, joined with family dialogue, "continues to transmit the stories for posterity" (p. 6). In this way, Cross positions images as powerful vehicles for meaning and recognizes how interrogating family artifacts through CFH can forge new signs (or deconstruct dominant ones). In the case of the family homestead, Cross, her family, and her students acted as agentic sign makers to fuse form—the homestead photograph—with meaning—the significance of ancestors and Black self liberation.

Not only can teacher educators model CMSS as a pedagogical approach for use by PSTs in schools, they can also reconceptualize their teacher education curricula to embed opportunities for PSTs to take part in CMSS themselves. Thus, CFH acts as a compelling pedagogical representation of integrating CMSS in teacher education. In CFH, however, the analyzed and "de-ideologized" signs are the teacher education students' own personal and ancestral artifacts.

OUR SOCIAL FOUNDATIONS IN EDUCATION COURSE

This context of the CFH work took place in a teacher education program at a rural university in Texas. Over a few semesters in 2020 and 2021, we regularly taught sections of a social foundations in education course at both the elementary and secondary levels. Over the span of 8 weeks, the course guided students to examine the social and historical foundations of American education from a critical perspective, with a particular emphasis on race, class, power, culture, and identity. Course themes and resources often required students to engage for the first time with the perspectives and narratives of historically marginalized student groups in the United States.

Of importance to note is the historical moment in which the courses were taught; namely, during the spread and early 2021 peak of the COVID-19 pandemic, the effects of which forced all courses in the department to an online distance format. While some courses remained synchronous through livestream, the social foundation in education courses were transitioned to be fully online and asynchronous (i.e., module based with no livestreams). Because of this we had little to no live/interpersonal contact with our students.

At the time, the course was an entry point for students into the teacher education program at the university. Enrolled students were predominately White, monolingual residents of Texas who did not reflect the student makeup of Texas public schools (27% White; 21% emergent bilingual; Du et al., 2021). Given these realities and the potential for White teachers to enact inequitable teaching without training (Iruka et al., 2020), we felt a responsibility and urgency to make the online course as impactful for the students as possible as they progressed deeper into their teacher education coursework and as they began their field experiences. Thus, in the Fall of 2020, we collaborated to re-envision the course as a space where critical consciousness could thrive despite the new limitations as a shortened, asynchronous, module-based learning experience.

Our "Critical Family History Project" is based on the ideas of Christine Sleeter's scholarship. Students are asked to engage in multiple paths of inquiry, such as (a) interviewing elders and family members, (b) conducting genealogical research on ancestors to trace their families back as far as they can, and (c) searching for any primary documents or photos that can contribute to developing a greater understanding of their family's history.

Students are expected to create genograms of at least three generations. While students are given latitude about what side of their family to study and what kinds of stories to gather, they are expected to inquire about the social and historical factors that may have benefited their ancestors or oppressed them. They are also asked to inquire about how their families feel or felt about people from backgrounds, religions, ethnic/racial groups or sexual orientations other than their own. Students are given a link so they can identify and name the Indigenous people who lived on the land where their family now resides. The final product is either a three to five page paper, a 20-slide presentation, or a 3 to 5 minute video in which students share their findings from conducting CFH.

CRITICAL COLLABORATIVE AUTOETHNOGRAPHY

Due to the shared and critical nature of our and our students' engagement with CFH, our research was guided by critical collaborative autoethnography. Critical collaborative autoethnography (Ashlee et al., 2017; Bhattacharya, 2008; Chang et al., 2013) grew from the qualitative research genre of autoethnography and is built upon foundational work of anthropologist Clifford Geertz and others, who introduced novel ways to express how people make meaning of their lives (Ellis, 2003). The dramatic shift from ethnographic work to autoethnographic work turns the gaze of the researcher inward. According to Ellis and Bochner (2000), autoethnography is "an autobiographical genre of writing and research that displays multiple layers of consciousness" (p. 739), but as a research methodology, "autoethnography, native ethnography, self-ethnography, memoir, autobiography, even fiction have become blurred genres" (p. 742) within qualitative research.

Critical autoethnographies include a deeper analysis on systemic "asymmetries of power, unequal opportunities to render judgements, and maldistributions of responsibilities and rewards" (Banks & Banks, 2000, p. 236) and are intended to be both personal and evocative. Pennington and Brock (2012) use the term "critical autoethnographic self-studies" and link critical autoethnographies with critical White studies, which applies to our current research. Further, Adams (2017) suggests that critical autoethnographies "ascertain vital and often unforeseen connections between personal experiences and cultural experiences; identify manifestations of power and privilege in everyday practices; discern social injustices and inequities; and describe beliefs and practices that should—and should not—exist" (p. 79).

We also acknowledge the roots of autoethnography in the work of Freire (1970/2012), who writes that "human beings are not built in silence, but in word, in work, in action-reflection" (p. 88). We see in Freire's writing that "false words" and "silence" will not nourish human existence, pushing us to engage in "action-reflection" as protagonists for deeper societal change, beginning with "true words." This kind of action-reflection is the heart of critical autoethnography, with the starting point being reflection from which action emerges.

The work in which we engage links our reflections of our experiences to larger issues of social U.S. inequities that lie at the root of our stories and those of our students. Too often stories are kept secret and hidden away with the notion that they will be forgotten. However, it is through this kind of evocative and communal critical autoethnographic work that a "true" history emerges from within our lives and those of our students so we can begin the collective work of healing. As part of our collaborative analysis of stories, artifacts, and conversations, we approach the findings through two separate narratives illustrating how CMSS was embedded in our CFHs. Each narrative will center on our and our students' deconstruction of powerful semiotic signs—the plat and the gavel—through the use of emancipatory semiology (Sandoval, 2000).

THE PLAT

With the revised version of the course starting in a few days, I (William) felt apprehensive and on edge. This was the time I had assigned a CFH project in one of my teacher education courses—and in the first week, no less. Suddenly, it felt unfair to require students to engage with such vulnerable and uncomfortable work without also being vulnerable myself. And as a White teacher educator of primarily White students, I recognized my responsibility to model for the students what it means to be critical, focused, and reflective. Yet, until now, I had never been that vulnerable with students before, especially when it came to addressing how race, class, and power intersect with my own family history and who I am today. I felt unsure about sharing with students I had never met, nor would probably ever meet. Was it truly necessary to do? That is how White supremacy functions: It works at all costs, by eliciting feelings of anxiety and fear and irritation, to obfuscate our histories and resist any critical examination of our ancestors. It seeks to maintain silence.

The narrative of my CFH, shared with my students, centers on the land currently owned by my family. The land is situated in a small area of this continent that, since about 150 years ago, has been referred to as Faulkner County, Arkansas. The area lies about 40 miles (64 km) north of Little Rock and the Arkansas River. Following one of our project's paths of inquiry examining the relationships between property ownership, inheritance, and colonization, the CFH research I shared with my students sought to identify the forces which removed the Osage people from their lands and denatured the area for White colonization. For the colonization of my ancestors, whose benefits I still feel today.

I recount this narrative here through the contrasting Indigenous and Western epistemologies of space offered by Linda Tuhiwai Smith. Smith (2012) writes how Western, colonial conceptions of space, dominated by mathematics, "attempts to define with absolute exactness the parameters, dimensions, qualities and possibilities of space" (p. 53). Space, from this view, is something to be altered, consumed, renamed, and controlled. Smith presents three spatial concepts characterizing this colonial epistemology: the line, the center, and the outside. Lines were used "to map territory, to survey land, and to establish boundaries and to mark the limits of colonial power" (p. 53). Invaders used lines to suggest they had (falsely) discovered and cataloged space for the first time. Anything outside of these lined boundaries was simply "empty space" (p. 53) yet to be colonized, and any people there did not exist. Informed by critical social semiotics, I draw the reader's attention to an artifact from my CFH research—an image—representing a violent sign which, designed by a powerful and motivated sign maker, employed a colonial conception of space to assume control of Indigenous lands in Arkansas.

Three stages represented the transmogrification of Indigenous conceptions of space into Western dominance: claiming, taming, and demarcating. First, the United States enacted policies over time which sought to delegitimize tribal sovereignty and facilitate American invasion. In the hundreds of years leading up to European colonization, three major groups of Native peoples recognized the Arkansas area as part of their home or lands: the Caddo, Ugahxpa (Quapaw), and Osage. Our family land rests within Osage ancestral territory (recognized as hunting grounds), which encompasses the majority of Arkansas (Burns, 2004; The Osage Nation, n.d.). The purchase of the Louisiana territory in 1803, including the area now known as Arkansas, signaled a broad American claim to a substantial portion of the continent. The boundary was drawn around the perimeter of Indigenous space, thus laying claim to it.

Next, the U.S. colonizers sought to tame, alter, and rename the land. In Arkansas, a series of treaties forced Osage land cessions in 1808 (Treaty of Fort Clark) and 1818 (Treaty of St. Louis) and Quapaw cessions in 1818, 1824, and 1834. White Americans used violence to destroy Native property and drive them from their homes. With Indigenous refugees now facing lethal conditions on the way to Native land now renamed "Indian Territories," the U.S. government actively withheld vital material and financial support, leading to the deaths of thousands. By the mid-1830s, the U.S. government barred all Caddo, Osage, Quapaw, Cherokee, and Choctaw sovereignty over their historic lands and hunting grounds in Arkansas. In concert with removal, the United States forwarded policies designed to convert, survey, and reappropriate stolen land for the invasion of Whites.

Policies such as the Military Tract of 1812, Land Act of 1820, Preemption Act of 1841, and the Homestead Act of 1862 made Indigenous lands highly affordable, or even free, for settlement by European American men.

But before the land could be conveyed into White ownership, Indigenous space underwent a final form of transmogrification: mathematical demarcation. After their claim to the Louisiana territory in 1803, the U.S. government began to order land surveys a few years later. Over time the surveys produced land plats and, further, marked boundaries for parcels for distribution to settlers. The survey of what is now known as Faulkner County, Arkansas was completed in August 1819 by Deputy Surveyor Jenifer T. Sprigg and approved by Surveyor General William Rector. The final product of this process can be seen in Figure 10.1: a 12 by 12 grid of cells

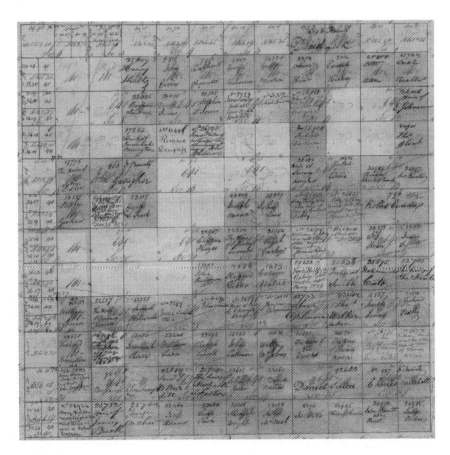

Figure 10.1 Initial land survey (1819) of township 7N 11W in Faulkner County, Arkansas. Each square represents 160 acres. *Source:* Pubic domain image. Bureau of Land Management, Land Catalog.

with varying colors (unknown significance), numbers, and names. Numbers correspond to plat sections and acreage estimates, and the names represent landowners or their heirs.

If I were to have seen this image a few years ago, I would have found it rather interesting, or even something to print and save for family records. But looking at it now is jarring and mournful. The image represents the first time this area of Osage land was scarred with lines, objectified with arbitrary dimensions and boundaries, and designated to White families. The survey, its lines, and its significance comprise a sign which promotes Western conceptualizations of space.

Now, just over 200 years later, the sign remains the same. Formed digitally rather than by hand on paper, Arkansas township 7N 11W is still marked by the same lines and plat section numbers. The 36 sections still comprise 23,040 of the same acres. It is also not surprising to share that, even 203 years later, many of the landowners' surnames have remained the same.

This stringing together of past and present illuminates the lasting impact of White supremacist policies in the United States. While the sign was formed originally to signify White ownership, dominance, and the product of hard work, a CMSS approach deconstructs it instead into an ancestral windfall at the expense of Indigenous peoples. In this way, CFH research has pushed me to recognize the access, resilience, and "tailwind" (Kimmel, 2017) I have been afforded by the intergenerational transfer of land ownership. Bell (2020) writes:

> Sleeter (2014) identifies the specific transfer of family wealth, in the forms of inheritance and/or financial aid from living relatives, as operating as "footholds" that "enable opportunity" and "cushions" that "protect from misfortune." Even small transfers of such wealth can make a crucial difference, boosting the efforts of individuals to get onto and to scale the career and property ladders that secure their financial and status positions. (p. 5)

This is where CMSS intersects with teacher education, specifically CFH; we, together with our students, have the opportunity to analyze our family artifacts to recognize the power they signify and to identify who and for what reason it was signified. Sandoval (2000) refers to this process generally as an emancipatory pedagogy or semiology, where, through a critical examination of the sign maker's motivations and the semiotic relationship between the signifier (form) and signified (meaning), the sign may be released from its hegemonic roots and reclaimed. Sandoval (2000) writes that the recognition of a sign as arbitrary, or artificially and socially produced, rather than naturally occurring, is at the heart of emancipatory semiology. While Kress, Barthes, and Sandoval's perceptions of semiotics vary in many ways, each share the need for a critical gaze toward the power and interests of the sign maker. In the artifact from this CFH, the sign makers (White

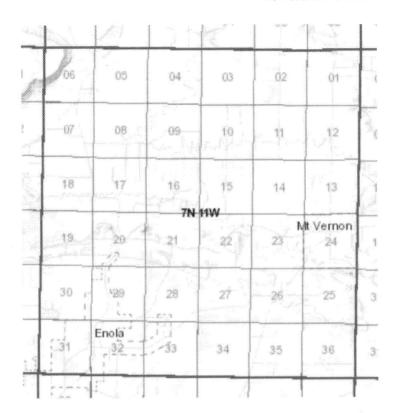

Figure 10.2 Screenshot of how township 7N 11W and its 36 sections are digitally represented in 2022 by the Bureau of Land Management's Land Catalog system. Each square represents 640 acres.

American men) leveraged an official U.S. land survey (the sign) formed of lines (signifier) to proclaim the false founding of "new" land (signified). CMSS, in teacher education, encourages PSTs to identify the unnatural origins of this colonial epistemology and recognize how they may unintentionally sustain it as individuals and educators. Through this work, PSTs can begin to internalize their role in maintaining Whiteness rather than stopping at the notion that it only exists elsewhere.

In recent months I have found that the principles of CFH and CMSS have deeply informed my meaning making process as both a researcher and a teacher educator. In a recent class session, I challenged my students to consider how the experiences they had growing up, as well as the beliefs their families hold, may have influenced their beliefs about the capacities of emergent bilingual children, and how those beliefs may impact how they teach. In the spirit of collaborative CFH, I facilitated these discussions by responding to the questions alongside my students. We, as teacher educators, have a responsibility to model criticality and vulnerability for our PSTs if we want to move them to develop critical, structural, and temporal understandings of themselves as racialized individuals.

THE GAVEL

I (Vicki) first learned of Christine Sleeter's work when I attended a session at AERA in New York, where college professors shared their experiences using CFHs in their classes. I was hooked from the moment I heard the idea, since I already had developed the notion that each of us must do very deep inner work if we were ever going to truly face and eliminate racism, regardless of our upbringing and backgrounds. In previous research, I saw how each of us is socialized from a very early age and part of our socialization process includes how our families explicitly or implicitly teach us to view those groups of people our families "other," based on racial, ethnic, economic, or religious distinctions.

Recognizing that this type of research needed to begin within me, I reflected on my upbringing and childhood. In the course of my ruminations, I dramatically shifted how I saw my second grade teacher, who was someone I adored and respected until I deconstructed my unexamined childhood experiences. In the course of deep inner digging, I came to realize my second grade teacher had encouraged me to become a young minstrel who imitated and made fun of African Americans through retelling a children's story called *Epaminondas and His Auntie* in the vernacular in which it was written. This childhood story, that was central to my life as a young child, was much like the original versions of *Little Black Sambo* and *Uncle Remus' Tar Baby* and *Brer Rabbit* stories that were written in the ways rural African Americans in the South spoke—something a young Jewish child should never have been imitating. As a young Jewish child, I was simultaneously othered by the White Anglo Saxon Protestant (WASP) community in the deep South where I lived, while also completely benefiting from White privilege. If I had not worked so hard to question and challenge my socialization, my childhood minstrel show of *Epaminondas* could have unwittingly instilled in me a notion about White superiority, in the process of making fun of the simpleton African-American boy, the main character. Oh, how I made everyone laugh in my retelling of the story. I was both a victim and a perpetrator of a sick ideology, and it took me well over 50 years to recognize that painful truth. I saw my second grade teacher, my childhood, and my family in a different light, and I had to embark on a never-ending journey to navigate the inner work of reconciling some painfully conflicting feelings in this ongoing process.

It was when I recognized how my second grade teacher served to perpetuate White supremacist ideology in her role as a teacher that I came to see how every single teacher either reproduces White supremacist ideology—knowingly or unknowingly—or consciously seeks to challenge and interrupt that way of thinking that continues to pervade our society and schools. This is precisely where I see the value and importance of using CFHs with students.

I recently encountered a student's story that haunts me, and I asked her if I could share it because I just cannot "shake" it. She said, "Yes, because I think others may have similar stories in their families, and they need to know about this" (personal communication, September 5, 2021). Due to the nature of the familial revelation, the student's name will remain anonymous, and I will refer to her as Abigail.

Abigail is from a very small rural town in Texas. The week before the CFH project was due, she frantically reached out to me because she said she was having trouble finding anything out and no one in her family wanted to share any stories with her. I asked if there was anyone at all that she could visit with again—especially to uncover her family's thoughts or views about people from other races. I believe her dad decided to open up.

What she discovered shocked her and me. The "heirlooms" her family passed down from her great-grandfather were photographs of lynchings in her small town. Her great grandfather and his friends photographed the lynchings-hangings and these photos were passed down in the family. Abigail was able to acknowledge and recognize the extent to which her great grandfather and his friends were racists and how this way of thinking and being was normalized in the 1920s and 1930s in the rural South amongst White people. She could see how this impacted her grandfather, her father, and her family, though she shared how she had seen shifts in her father since she and her sister began to openly discuss issues about racism and since her sister had a baby whose father was of Mexican descent. Abigail shared that she felt that with the birth of her niece of mixed heritage, her father's views and heart shifted dramatically.

When I clicked on the link at the end of Abigail's presentation, I went to an official Texas A&M Forestry website that provided further information about the lynchings in her hometown. On that website, it states that the victim of the 1920 lynching was 18, but further research I conducted indicates that the young man, Lige Daniels, was 16 years old at the time of his alleged crime. "A mob of more than 1,000 people" broke down the doors in the jail where he was held, as the jailers looked on, and hung Lige from the tree in front of the courthouse on August 2, 1920 ("Texas Mob Lynches Negro in Jail Yard," 1920; Figure 10.3). In 2018, the Montgomery, Alabama-based Equal Justice Initiative (EJI) erected a marker in Abigail's hometown, to honor young Lige's memory, with nine of his family members present. EJI

Figure 10.3 Historical photograph of the tree before it died and was removed. *Source:* Texas A&M Forest Service.

documented that Texas had over 330 lynchings between 1877 and 1950, with more than 4000 lynchings of people of African descent in all of the United States (Equal Justice Initiative, 2018).

Eight years after the small town mob lynched Lige, another young man of African descent was hung from the same tree branch on May 21, 1928. In some accounts, he is referred to as "Eolis 'Buddy' Evans" (Lynching in Texas, 2018); in the *Miami* [Oklahoma] *Daily News-Record*, he is listed as "Ceodep 'Buddy' Evans" (Strange Fruit and Spanish Moss, 2016); and in another accounting of this event, he is called "Buddy" Evins (Texas Archive of the Moving Image, 1976). The texasarchive.org website includes a student-made documentary of residents who had heard of and witnessed these lynchings, and on this website, we learn that "the Shelby County sheriff and constable surrendered Evins to a mob of 200 to 300 men, who took Evins to the courthouse in Center and lynched him" (Texas Archive of the

Moving Image, n.d., para. 1). In this case, we have evidence that law enforcement, representing the hegemony of the state, was actively complicit with lynchings.

Abigail mentioned in her project report that the tree in her town that had been used in the lynchings had died and was no longer in the town's square. She struggled believing that all this happened in her beloved small town and her great grandfather had photographed the lynchings. She was shocked and in disbelief about this discovery and her family's connection to it.

When I further explored the link at the end of Abigail's project, I read that after the tree died, a local craftsman took branches of the tree and made gavels from them. Further research indicated that the local craftsman was Eugene Latimer (1894–1977), who had developed a project that included "the carving of gavels from historic trees" (Chamberlain, 1966, p. 51). To fully grasp this situation, we need to explore the socially-constructed meaning of a gavel as a sign, along with its history.

Initially, gavels were linked to payments to landlords and go back to 725 CE in England, but as used today in the United States and the world, gavels have come to be the crystallization of the rule of law, and the person who has the authority to strike the gavel can command orderly discourse (Parker, 2018). The carpenter, Latimer, who chose to take the branches of a dead tree where two African American men were lynched by racist mobs outside of the rule of law, knew exactly what he was doing when he crafted gavels from that tree. With uncertain certainty, it cannot be a coincidence that he transformed the vestiges of a tool for upholding White supremacy in Texas into a symbol and apparatus of law and justice.

Sandoval (2000) helps us recognize that "language...aims at 'eternalizing' the hierarchies of the dominant order" (p. 107). A gavel serves as the "language" of law and order, which seeks to reproduce itself through the maintenance of dominance. Remaking wood from the dead branch of a tree from which men died at the hands of racist mobs outside the rules of law served to "eternalize" the rule of the mob and transmogrify the horror of a lynching into a carefully crafted gavel, later to be used in a court of law in the same town where the mob once ruled and possibly still does today, though in subtler forms.

Once I read the story of the local craftsman using the tree branch to make gavels, I realized I could never look at a gavel again, without wondering—who had made it, using what kind of wood, and what had happened to the tree from which the gavel had been made? The local carpenter, Latimer, sought to transform the branch of a tree that itself could no longer live—having in some way been part of (most likely an innocent African American young man) being hung from one of its branches by a mob of Southern White racists. The tree itself could no longer sustain life. And so, a local carpenter, Eugene Latimer, who was a citizen of Abigail's community used the dead wood to create a gavel—one of the most sacred symbols of law, order, and justice in our society, used by judges and in democratically elected boards at every level of U.S. government.

It is important to consider how Latimer used his agency to change the form and meaning of the wood from a tree that died after two men were hanged. We know Latimer was intentional in his interest to imbue gavels with the energy of the racist mob in that he presented the gavels to a judge and local leaders to use these gavels in official community functions, based on information in a formal letter sent from the Agricultural Extension Service of Texas A&M University on August 23, 1971 to the Texas Forestry Service (Figure 10.4).

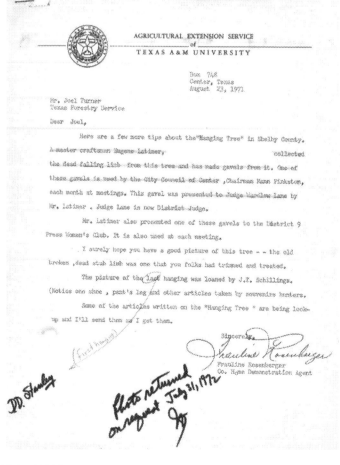

Figure 10.4 1971 letter to the Texas Forestry Service regarding the origin of the gavels. *Source:* Collection of Texas A&M Forest Service.

When I realized what Latimer had done, I felt a deep pit in my stomach, commingled with outrage and deep sadness. Whose justice? Whose laws? The gavel is a socially constructed sign that purportedly represents blind justice, law, and order, though we know that laws are written and enacted by those in power and to benefit them. In our perspective, gavels are metaphors for putative order and justice. He intentionally sought to imbue the gavels he created from the wood of the dead tree by embedding a White supremacist ideology within the gavels he created and gifting them to a judge and other local leaders.

DISCUSSION

CFH and CMSS are inextricable frameworks that make identity and power visible for PSTs in teacher education. Throughout this critical collaborative autoethnographic research, it became clear that the captivating and highly effective nature of CFH as a pedagogical tool in teacher education could be explained by its embodiment of the sharp, disruptive analytical framework of CMSS. Not only did we and the PSTs engage in an emancipatory semiology toward dominant signs, the signs we and our students examined were deeply personal, emotional, and pronounced in our lives. The signs were strung—often invisibly so—between our presents and pasts, and to and from each other. When comparing the 1819 land survey with current land plats and property owners in Arkansas, little has changed in over 200 years, speaking to the dominance and pervasiveness of the sign. In addition, when Abigail discovered uncomfortable aspects of her family's history, she could no longer claim to be ignorant of the racism so prevalent in her community and family.

Anzaldúa (1987/2012) writes,

> The whites in power want us people of color to barricade ourselves behind our separate tribal walls so they can pick us off one at a time with their hidden weapons, so they can whitewash and distort history. Ignorance splits people, creates prejudices. A misinformed people is a subjugated people. (p. 108)

It is precisely for this reason that resistance and the deconstruction of taken-for-granted signs are the pathways to challenge the ways White supremacist ideology has tainted us all. Not a single person in these United States is immune from the ways racism has affected us. As teacher educators, we will continue encouraging PSTs to examine their families' histories with a critical eye on issues of race, ethnicity, power, class, religion, and sexual orientation. Through an emancipatory semiology, PSTs will face, untangle, and dismantle deeply rooted internalized racism that takes deceptive and highly normalized forms, such as gavels in judges' hands—possibly embedded with the bigotry and hate of racist White mobs—along with innocent looking familial plots of land, neatly hiding any trace of Indigenous presence. Through this communal breaking down of ideology, we and our students take steps to resignify schools as spaces for justice.

REFERENCES

Adams, T. E. (2017). Critical autoethnography, education, and a call for forgiveness. *International Journal of Multicultural Education, 19*(1), 79–88. https://doi.org/10.18251/ijme.v19i1.1387

Anzaldúa, G. (2012). *Borderlands/La frontera: The new mestiza* (4th ed.). Aunt Lute Books. (Original work published 1987)

Ashlee, A. A., Zamora, B., & Karikari, S. N. (2017). We are woke: A collaborative critical autoethnography of three "Womxn" of color graduate students in higher education. *International Journal of Multicultural Education, 19*(1), 89–104. https://doi.org/10.18251/ijme.v19i1.1259

Baldwin, S. C., Buchanan, A. M., & Rudisill, M. E. (2007). What teacher candidates learned about diversity, social justice, and themselves from service-learning experiences. *Journal of Teacher Education, 58*(4), 315–327. https://doi.org/10.1177/0022487107305259

Banks, S. P., & Banks, A. (2000). Reading "the critical life": Autoethnography as pedagogy. *Communication Education, 49*(3), 233–238.

Barthes, R. (2013). *Mythologies: The complete edition, in a new translation* (2nd ed.). Hill and Wang.

Bell, A. (2020). Reverberating historical privilege of a "middling" sort of settler family. *Genealogy, 4*(2), 46. https://doi.org/10.3390/genealogy4020046

Berchini, C. N. (2017). Critiquing un/critical pedagogies to move toward a pedagogy of responsibility in teacher education. *Journal of Teacher Education, 68*(5), 463–475. https://doi.org/10.1177/0022487117702572

Bhattacharya, H. (2008). New critical collaborative autoethnography. In S. N. Hesse-Biber & P. Leavy (Eds.), *Handbook of emergent methods* (pp. 303–322). The Guilford Press.

Bureau of Land Management. (n.d.). *Land catalog.* https://glorecords.blm.gov/LandCatalog/Catalog

Burns, L. F. (2004). *A history of the Osage people.* The University of Alabama Press.

Chamberlain, C. K. (1966). East Texas. *East Texas Historical Journal, 4*(1), Article 10. https://scholarworks.sfasu.edu/ethj/vol4/iss1/10

Chang, H., Ngunjiri, F., & Hernandez, K. C. (2013). *Collaborative autoethnography.* Routledge.

Cross, P. T. (1997). *WARSAW: The Newton-Patrick-Smith family history book.* [Unpublished manuscript]. University of California at Irvine.

Cross, P. T. (2020). Writing lifestories: A methodology introducing students to multicultural education utilizing creative writing and genealogy. *Genealogy, 4*(1), 27. https://doi.org/10.3390/genealogy4010027

Du, J., Gaertner, F., Wright, B., Nagy, S., Whalen, C., & Kallus, R. (2021). *Enrollment in Texas public schools 2020–21.* Texas Education Agency. https://tea.texas.gov/sites/default/files/enroll-2020-21.pdf

Ellis, C. (2003). *The ethnographic I: A methodological novel about autoethnography.* AltaMira Press.

Ellis, C., & Bochner, A. P. (2000). Autoethnography, personal narrative, reflexivity: Researcher as subject. In N. K. Denzin & Y. S. Lincoln (Eds.), *Handbook of qualitative research* (2nd ed.; pp. 733–768). SAGE Publications.

Equal Justice Initiative. (2018, December 28). "*Lynching in America.*" https://eji.org/news/eji-partners-shelby-county-texas-community-install-historical-marker/?fbclid=IwAR2QCphAQVUFJN3Ad2JN1b76ZPCbYwip_ru18jifeuuoSY2rDtpShO6rdcI

Freire, P. (2012). *Pedagogy of the oppressed.* Continuum. (Original work published 1970)

French, K. B., Sanchez, A., & Ullom, E. (2020). Composting settler colonial distortions: Cultivating critical land-based family history. *Genealogy, 4*(3), 84. https://doi.org/10.3390/genealogy4030084

Gershenson, S., Holt, S. B., & Papageorge, N. W. (2016). Who believes in me? The effect of student-teacher demographic match on teacher expectation. *Economics of Education Review, 52,* 209–224. https://doi.org/10.1016/j.econedurev.2016.03.002

Gilliam, W. S., Maupin, A. N., Reyes, C. R., Accavitti, M., & Shic, F. (2016). *Do early educators' implicit biases regarding sex and race related to behavior expectations and recommendations of preschool expulsions and suspensions?* (Policy brief from Yale University Child Care Center). https://beatrix.yale.edu/api/media/documents/75afe6d2-e556-4794-bf8c-3cf105113b7c/blob

Hambacher, E., & Ginn, K. (2021). Race-visible teacher education: A review of the literature from 2002–2018. *Journal of Teacher Education, 72*(3), 329–421. https://doi.org/10.1177%2F0022487120948045

hooks, b. (1994). *Teaching to transgress: Education as the practice of freedom.* Routledge.

Iruka, I., Curenton, S., Escayg, K-A., & Durden, T. (2020). *Don't look away: Embracing anti-bias classrooms.* Gryphon House.

Kimmell, M. S. (2017). Introduction: Toward a sociology of the superordinate. In M. S. Kimmell & A. L. Ferber (Eds.), *Privilege: A reader* (4th ed.; pp. 1–12). Taylor & Francis.

Kress, G. (2010). *Multimodality: A social semiotic approach to contemporary communication.* Routledge.

Lynching in Texas. (2018). *Lynching of Buddy Evins: May 21, 1928.* http://www.lynchingintexas.org/items/show/34

Lynn, M., & Dixson, A. D. (2013). *Handbook of critical race theory in education.* Routledge.

Matias, C. E., & Mackey, J. (2016). Breakin' down Whiteness in antiracist teaching: Introducing critical Whiteness pedagogy. *Urban Review, 48*(1), 32–50. https://doi.org/10.1007/s11256-015-0344-7

Pahl, K., & Rowsell, J. (2010). *Artifactual literacies: Every object tells a story.* Teachers College Press.

Parker, J. E. (2018). Gavel. In J. Hohmann & D. Joyce (Eds.), *International law's objects* (pp. 214–224). Oxford University Press.

Pennington, J. L., & Brock, C. H. (2012). Constructing critical autoethnographic self- studies with White educators. *International Journal of Qualitative Studies in Education, 25*(3), 225–250. https://doi.org/10.1080/09518398.2010.529843

Riddle, T., & Sinclair, S. (2019). Racial disparities in school-based disciplinary actions are associated with county-level rates of racial bias. *Proceedings of the National Academy of Sciences of the United States of America, 116*(7), 8255–8260. https://doi.org/10.1073/pnas.1808307116

Sandoval, C. (2000). *Methodology of the oppressed*. University of Minnesota Press.

Sleeter, C. (2008). Critical family history, identity, and historical memory. *Educational Studies: A Journal of the American Educational Studies Association, 43*(2), 114–124. https://doi.org/10.1080/00131940801944587

Sleeter, C. (2015). Multicultural curriculum and critical family history. *Multicultural Education Review, 7*, 1–11. https://doi.org/10.1080/2005615X.2015.1048607

Sleeter, C. (2016). Critical family history: Situating family within contexts of power relationships. *Journal of Multidisciplinary Research, 8*(1), 11–23. https://www.proquest.com/docview/1804901902

Sleeter, C. (2020). Critical family history: An introduction. *Genealogy 4*(2), 64. https://doi.org/10.3390/genealogy4020064

Smith, L. T. (2012). *Decolonizing methodologies* (2nd ed.). Zed Books.

Strange Fruit and Spanish Moss. (2016, January 30). *May 21, 1928: Ceodep "Buddy" Evans*. https://strangefruitandspanishmoss.blogspot.com/2016/01/may-21-1928-ceodep-buddy-evans.html

Taie, S., & Goldring, R. (2020). *Characteristics of public and private elementary and secondary schools in the United States: Results from the 2017–18 National Teacher and Principal Survey. First Look* (NCES 2019-140). National Center for Education Statistics. https://nces.ed.gov/pubs2019/2019140.pdf

Takaki, R. (2008). *A different mirror: A history of multicultural America*. Little, Brown and Company.

Texas Archive of the Moving Image. (1976). *The Ouida Whitaker Dean collection, no. 25–Hanging in Shelby County (1976)*. https://texasarchive.org/2014_00438

Texas Mob Lynches Negro in Jail Yard. (1920, August 3). *New York Times*. https://www.nytimes.com/1920/08/03/archives/texas-mob-lynches-negro-in-jail-yard-batter-steel-doors-and-wreck.html

The Osage Nation. (n.d.). *Ancestral map*. https://www.osageculture.com/culture/geography/ancestral-map

Trinh, E. T. (2020). Photovoice in a Vietnamese immigrant family: Untold partial stories behind the picture. *Genealogy, 4*(3), 67. https://doi.org/10.3390/genealogy4030067

CHAPTER 11

CRITICAL MULTIMODALITY AT THE MUSEUM

How a Community–University Partnership Supports Transformative Praxis

Matthew R. Deroo
University of Miami

ABSTRACT

Whether engaged in speaking, listening, reading, or writing, speakers communicate across multiple modes, a term used to refer to the material resources used to make and convey meaning, such as visuals, gestures, bodily movement, inflection, and tone (Kress, 2011; Serafini, 2014; Van Leeuwen, 2008). This proposed chapter draws upon preservice teacher learning in a disciplinary literacy for secondary education (pseudonym) undergraduate course for students minoring in education and majoring in content areas such as English, psychology, science, or social studies.

Specifically, I highlight how a 3-year, ongoing community–university partnership between a local art museum and a department of teaching and learning supports critical multimodal learning for preservice teachers. In this chapter, I would begin with an overview for how course readings about Photo-Voice (Gubrium & Torres, 2013) and critical multilingual language awareness Christensen, 2017; Prasad, 2018) cultivate preservice teacher awareness about critical multimodal approaches to teaching and learning. Next, I will highlight how multiple visits to a local art museum provided space and opportunity for preservice teachers to engage critically with art objects (as multimodal texts) through object-based discussions and visual thinking strategies (Yenawine, 2013). To operationalize critical multimodality as informed by museum-based learning, I will center preservice teacher learning on a task where they remixed and/or hacked (Jocson, 2013; Knobel & Lankshear, 2008) an art object from the museum to address issues of marginalization in their content areas. Across the chapter, I will examine moments where my instruction and students' criticality fell short of the liberatory aims to disrupt power dynamics across texts, institutions, and society. To support my claims, this chapter will draw upon multiple sources of data collected from 2019–2021 including: field notes, recordings of museum-based interactions, preservice teachers reflective dialog journals, their coursework including lesson plans and text sets, and preservice teacher interviews. The chapter will conclude with implications for how teacher educators might call upon museums as sites of learning to cultivate and develop preservice teachers' critical multimodal awareness.

Teacher educators committed to issues of equity and justice seek to center teacher learning from a critical lens (Price-Dennis & Sealey-Ruiz, 2021). However, many of the preservice teachers (PSTs), minoring in education and majoring in other content areas like English, science, music, or mathematics, enter my Disciplinary Literacy for Secondary Education (pseudonym) course reporting that they have limited exposure to critical views of teaching and learning. Since these future teachers will be responsible for supporting their students to use multiple literacies or modes related to their content areas (Hillman, 2014), such as reading and interpreting charts, graphs, and tables in the context of science or mathematics, criticality is needed, especially in response to increasing disinformation in the media landscape (Segall et al., 2019).

In my class, I center critical approaches for engaging with curricula. Early in the semester, PSTs read Paris and Alim's (2014) article on culturally sustaining pedagogies. I want them to understand how students of color's literacies, histories, languages, and cultural ways of being have predominantly been marginalized in schools, in favor of White and Westernized ways of knowing. To reinforce learning, I have PSTs journal as a reflective writing practice. They share their thinking in response to course readings that speak back to marginalization based on race, gender, sexuality, and other identifications (Baker-Bell et al., 2017; Storm & Rainey, 2018) further understood through Crenshaw's (2017) lens of intersectionality. Additionally, I infuse the class with opportunities to extend university-based classroom learning through partnership with an art museum. As PSTs interact with art objects at the museum, they take part in critical multimodal, meaning-making activities, like visual thinking strategies (Yenawine, 2013). While one course, let alone a few assignments, do not necessarily lead to lasting changes in pedagogy and practice (Deroo & Ponzio, 2021), I believe multiple visits to a museum extend classroom learning and support students to critique dominant forms or visual "language used to convey power and status in contemporary social interaction" (Kress & van Leeuwen, 1996, p. 13). In this chapter, I highlight how an art museum supported PSTs critical, multimodal learning, while also recounting my own shortcomings as a teacher educator in helping PSTs to grow in their criticality. Specifically, I asked: "How might an art museum and its art objects support PSTs remixes and hacks to address issues of marginalization in their disciplines?"; "How, if at all, might they apply this critical, multimodal approach as they plan for future instruction?"

THEORETICAL FRAMEWORK

To support my analysis, I draw together interrelated theoretical understandings of multiliteracies and multimodality, placing them in conversation with remix and hacking as critical approaches to address issues of marginalization. I situate this work within hybrid spaces of learning in teacher education.

Critical Multimodal Literacies

My work in this chapter is primarily concerned with the transformation of texts, broadly understood, and draws upon interrelated fields of multiliteracies (The New London Group, 1996) and by extension multimodal literacies (Bezemer & Kress, 2016). Moreover, this study is situated within the field of disciplinary literacies (Shanahan & Shanahan, 2008), or the types of literate practices found within content area classes like mathematics, social studies, and/or science. Given that literacy pedagogy and curricula have responded to shifts in the last 25 years toward an increasingly digital and global society, scholars have rightfully come to highlight how textual forms are enhanced through multimodal resources (Ajayi, 2015). According to Jewitt (2009), the perspective of multimodality takes into account how language is yet one of the communicative resources in which meaning is interpreted, made, and remade. In this chapter, multimodality centers the interrelationship among modes of representation (Bezemer & Kress, 2016) as taken up in PSTs remixes and hacks of art objects. A focus on these relationships reveals the affordances and constraints of modes in supporting the interpretation of texts (Bezemer & Kress, 2016).

Multimodal approaches presuppose that students call upon many literate practices to interact with cultural, social, and domain related contexts (Cope & Kalantzis, 2005) as part of their meaning making processes. However, given that students represent a plurality of identifications and come from different cultural backgrounds that shape their meaning making, critical lenses are important. To this end, I also draw on critical multimodal literacy (Ajayi, 2015; Huang, 2019) to highlight how PSTs multimodal compositions, and their written reflections, allowed them to address issues of marginalization in response to dominant discourses within their respective disciplines.

Critical multimodal literacy represents the "sophisticated, interconnected skills learners need to receive and process multiple media, navigate cultural codes and interpersonal interactions, and re/act accordingly" (Rhoades et al., 2015, p. 309). Specifically, Rhoades (2020) has noted how critical multimodal literacies help students to reflect on the ways modes shape reality in response to considerations of power and identity. By extension, Cappello et al. (2019) argued critical multimodal literacies should examine shifts in power relationships in order to critique and ultimately transform pressing sociopolitical realities. This chapter also contributes to Price-Dennis and Sealey-Ruiz's (2021) call for teacher educators to engage in critical multimodal curation that supports the selection, organization, and presentation "of multimodal artifacts that probe the intersection of race, equity, and power" (p. 82). In the context of this study, PSTs multimodal remixes and hacks of art objects became a collected body of work that sought to reframe understandings of "complex ideas about education, access, humanity, and equity" (Price-Dennis & Sealey-Ruiz, 2021, p. 82).

Remix and Hacking to Address Marginalization

To support critical multimodal literacies, students in my course read about remixing and hacking as a form of multimodal composition. Remixing and hacking differ in approach, but can similarly be applied critically to address issues of power. The practice of remixing involves taking cultural artifacts and manipulating or combining them into new creative forms (Jocson, 2013; Knobel & Lankshear, 2008). While the practice of remixing has historically been grounded in the field of audio production, it has been "expanded to include music and sound as well as moving and static images taken from films, television, the Internet, personal archives, and elsewhere" (Knobel & Lankshear, 2008, p. 22). An art museum, therefore, is a productive space to engage in remixing. Importantly, remixing is helpful for gaining insights into insider or outsider points of view.

In a similar way, a hacking ethos (Baker-Doyle, 2017) may be taken up to support social change in alignment with critical perspectives. As Baker-Doyle

(2017) argued, hacking is about seeking systemic changes and to "hack a social system one must have a critical understanding of how power operates in that system and between people and groups" (p. 112). Specifically, Baker-Doyle draws upon the work of Gee (1996) and discourse to advance the idea that "certain discourses and narratives or stories circulating within them tend to be privileged in society as more legitimate or valuable than other stories" (p. 113). In order to hack a discourse, individuals need to hold critical understandings for the linguistic and cultural codes shaping a discourse, and then draw upon cultural tools that provide opportunity to rewrite these narratives (Baker-Doyle, 2017). Since PSTs held understandings of dominant discourses in their fields and the linguistic and cultural understandings behind these beliefs, they were able to use this knowledge in support of their critical multimodal compositions. Specifically, in alignment with Baker-Doyle (2017), I asked PSTs to contend with marginalization, or how individuals, groups, or concepts in their reactive disciplines were treated as peripheral or insignificant. I used an art museum and works of art to support these considerations.

Spaces of Hybridity in Teacher Education

Museum-based learning in the context of teacher education is growing as a field of inquiry (Barry, 2012; Cuenca & Gilbert, 2019; Hamilton & Van Duinen, 2021). In partnering with the art museum as a site of learning for students to engage in remixing and hacking, I draw upon the work of Falk and Dierking (2016) who encourage museums as a meaningful alternative to the types of learning that may take place in traditional, classroom-based settings. This approach draws on hybrid spaces in support of teacher education (Beck 2020; Gutiérrez, 2008; Zeichner, 2010).

For example, Hamilton and Van Duinen (2021) highlighted the ways a teacher educator and her PSTs spent time with small groups of sixth-grade students in support of their literacy and learning at the Museum School, which was located within a public museum. They found working with youth in a hybrid space supported PSTs to articulate and recognize multimodal definitions of literacy. Additionally, museums as sites of learning can support PSTs to recognize ways they might draw upon community and civic locals in support of future teaching that promotes shared learning across contexts (Guillen & Zeichner, 2018).

LITERATURE REVIEW

While teacher education programs have historically needed to prepare teachers to take up broader understandings of literacy from print-based orientations towards digital multiliteracies practices (Rowsell et al., 2008), the field of teacher education across disciplinary contexts continues to grow in its understanding of how to support teacher learning about multimodality (Ciciottoli & Campoy-Cubillo, 2018; Jones et al., 2020; Lewkowich, 2019; Tour & Barnes, 2021). These approaches respond to calls by researchers to examine multimodal literacy instruction in the contexts of higher education (Loerts & Belcher, 2019). Language and literacy educators have increasingly examined how integrating critical, multimodal assignments into teacher learning can help beginning teachers to implement different modes in their pedagogy and practice (Cappello et al., 2019; Li, 2020; Yi & Angay-Crowder, 2016). However, even though PSTs draw upon their already-enacted multimodal composition practices across social media and their cell phones, research continually suggests these PSTs are often less well equipped to leverage these practices pedagogically (Farias & Veliz 2019; Kędra, 2018; Yi & Angay-Crowder, 2016).

Preservice Teachers, Multimodal Composition, and Critical Approaches

Recent scholarship has traced teacher learning about multimodality by having PSTs create multimodal compositions as part of their coursework. For example, Lewkowich (2019) detailed his multimodal work with preservice teachers through an approach he calls "thought chronicle," where students responded to course readings multimodally. In their responses, some students engaged in transmediation, or the composition of a response in a medium differing from the original text (Zoss, 2009), to show their understandings across modes. In the context of two graduate level Teaching English to Speakers of Other Languages (TESOL) courses, Li (2020) examined how different learning tasks allowed students to draw upon multiple modes to make sense of course material. She found a multimodal learning approach was motivating to students, allowed them to retain and deepen their knowledge of course concepts, and increased their motivation for implementing multimodal pedagogy to their future practice. In a different context, Capello (2019) drew on a partnership between her institution and the Center for Pacific Studies. Her research supported expanded perspectives on literacies within a standards-based curricular framework through a digital storytelling project in a graduate level course for American Samoan teachers. Specifically, students' digital stories and analysis of multimodal conversations "among the maker, viewer, and content revealed several ways students asserted and built upon their social and cultural identities while using images to target curricular understandings" (Capello, 2019, pp. 17–18). Importantly, teacher education students confronted well-established cultural norms and the multimodal approach led to deeper understandings for connections between the local community and broader culture formerly absent in students' school experiences (Capello, 2019).

Collectively, these studies highlight the value of multimodal compositions for supporting critical perspectives, which I have tried to advance in my own work. For example, my colleague and I demonstrated how PSTs across two universities created multimodal compositions to show the nexus between K–12 students' languages and identities within broader sociocultural settings in relationship to power (Deroo & Ponzio, 2021). This included responses to raciolinguistic ideologies and the ways in which the White listening subject perceived the minoritized language speaker (Rosa, 2019). In a different study, Ponzio and Deroo (2021) examined how preservice and inservice teachers in a graduate TESOL level course offered at the undergraduate and graduate level engaged in multimodal learning tasks, including the viewing of a video centered on critical approaches to language revitalization. These tasks were accomplished in order to support teacher's understandings of translanguaging, a dynamic view of language use in which individuals draw on their full linguistic repertoires in support of meaning making (García & Li Wei, 2014). These combined studies highlighted the critical aspects of languaging theory through multimodal lenses.

While recent research in disciplinary literacy has examined PSTs' approaches to multimodality through art, such as photography (Cappello & Lafferty, 2015) graphic novels (Kwon, 2020), picturebooks (Youngs & Kyser, 2021), and primary sources (Lawrence et al. 2019), use of art museums in support of critical, multimodal composition and meaning making in the field of disciplinary literacy in higher education is still developing. The work of this chapter can therefore make a contribution to the extant research base. In support of drawing together theoretical understandings of multimodal composition within and across the realm of teacher education, this study asks: "How might an art museum and its art objects support PSTs remixes and hacks to address issues of marginalization in their disciplines?" and "How, if at all, might they apply this critical, multimodal approach as they plan for future instruction?"

METHODS

The goal of this chapter is to highlight how an art museum served as a resource for PST learning about remixing and hacking toward the development of critical, multimodal pedagogy. The qualitative research highlighted in this chapter is part of an ongoing community–university-based partnership with Jodi Sypher, the curator of education at the Lowe Art Museum, which is located on my university's campus. Additional scholarship from this ongoing project has examined teacher learning about multimodality connected to content area literacies and how the museum might be leveraged to support the teaching of emergent bi/multilingual students (Deroo, 2022). In alignment with a critical perspective, I offer the following information about my positionality. I am a White, bilingual male communicating across features of English and Chinese, a former high school English teacher, and language teacher educator. The work shared here is based on my first time teaching the course under investigation, as I too was developing deeper understandings for how to guide PSTs learning about multimodality and social semiotics.

Participants and Data Sources

PSTs in my Disciplinary Literacy for Secondary Education class gave permission to use their coursework for research purposes, and I receive the names of students who agree to participate in research after their final grades are posted. For this chapter, the participants included 17 students: 10 White females, one Black female, one Asian-American female, one Indian-American female, three White males, and one Black male (all student names are pseudonyms).

Two students identified as bilingual. The overall demographics of PSTs aligns with those of other teacher education programs in that PSTs are predominantly monolingual, female, and White. I highlight these identifications because I am preparing these teachers to work with an increasingly racially, ethnically, and linguistically diverse group of PreK–12 students. Here, I draw upon 17 students' art object hacks/remixes and reflections from PSTs' thoughts shared in interviews, and PSTs' reflective writing about museum learning in dialog journals and assignments across the ongoing community–university partnership.

Disciplinary Literacy for Secondary Education, composed of PSTs minoring in education, is divided into four units of study. In Spring 2019, I instructed the class for the first time. I significantly revised the former professor's syllabus. I added both a critical lens through course text selection and instituted the museum partnership as a means of extending classroom learning. This chapter draws primarily on theoretical learning in Unit 2 that is later applied in Unit 4 (Table 11.1).

During Unit 2, PSTs engage with readings and activities that support learning about multimodality. *Reading the Visual: An Introduction to Teaching Multimodal Literacy* by Frank Serafini (2014) informs this unit of study. PSTs also read the work of critical scholars (i.e., Haddix & Sealey-Ruiz, 2012; Mirra et al., 2018), published in practitioner-based journals to demonstrate how teachers might take up critical pedagogies in schools. After a

TABLE 11.1 Units in Disciplinary Literacies for Secondary Education Course

Sequence	Unit Title	Duration
Unit 1	Content Area Literacy	3 weeks
Unit 2	Teaching Students to Read and Respond to Multimodal Texts	4 weeks
Unit 3	Applying Content Area Literacies to Lesson Planning	4 weeks
Unit 4	Developing Text Sets for Reading and Responding to Multimodal Texts	4 weeks

foundational understanding of the theories about multimodality and critical literacies is established, PSTs apply theory to praxis. One approach is through a remix/hacking assignment and reflection on this learning task.

The Lowe Art Museum. PSTs visit the Lowe Art Museum four times across the course, one time for each of the major units in the course. The Lowe has served the local community since the 1950s. Its collection of close to 20,000 art objects represent a variety of pieces with strengths in American, Asian, Baroque, and Renaissance art. The museum hosts visits by students in local schools and offers professional development opportunities for teachers.

PSTs were given an assignment sheet with the following learning task (Table 11.2). My design for this task was informed by curricular resources for a different remix and hacking assignment shared by Dr. Emery Petchauer. Ahead of class, PSTs read Baker-Doyle's (2017) chapter "Organizing with a Hacker Ethos" and the Knobel and Lankshear (2008) article about remix and hacking as central to youths' literate practices. In an educational space at the Lowe, I began class with a read aloud of two picture books: *The Paper*

TABLE 11.2 Remix and Hacking Assignment Sheet Outlining Learning Task

Assignment Overview	Description
Part 1: Selection of Art Object	Choose a work or works of art from the Lowe Art Museum to remix or hack using a medium of your choice.
Part 2: Discussion of Remix or Hack	You will write a brief narrative that discusses your remix/hacking process, including: the choices you made in selecting the work of art; how your remix addresses marginalizing discourses within your discipline; references to course readings
Part 3: Reflection	Share your reflections about completing this learning task. Possible questions to consider: • How did the assignment shape your understanding of what it means to remix/hack? • How might you apply remixing and hacking to future classroom teaching and learning? • How did this assignment disrupt or extend previous assumptions you held about remix and hacking?

Bag Princess (Munsch et al., 1980) and *Battle Bunny* (Scieszka & Barnett, 2013) based on Dr. Petchauer's advice. These books extend ideas raised in the Knobel and Lankshear (2008) article. I also referenced, but did not read, Mansbach's (2011) *Go the F**k to Sleep*. Next, I asked PSTs to verbalize connections between my reading of the picture books and the Knobel and Lankshear (2008) article. We co-constructed our understandings about remix and hacking building on my commitment to criticality, ahead of PSTs visit to the gallery spaces.

Data Collection

Data were collected in Spring 2019. This included student produced work in the course from late January to May (PSTs reflective writing in dialog journals and products they created for four museum-based learning tasks) and retrospective interviews, audio recorded and transcribed verbatim. I also took audio and video recordings of each museum visit, however the video camera was focused solely on Jodi and the museum's works of art to protect PST anonymity. Field notes and researcher memos from multiple museum interactions are used for data crystallization (Ellingson, 2009).

For initial data analysis, I created a table (see Table 11.3) in Google Drive to inventory (Jewitt, 2009) the multimodal hacks or remixes that PSTs created. This allowed me to (a) inventory the original art objects PSTs sought to remix or hack (e.g., paintings, glassworks, tapestries, cultural, artifactual objects such as a paddle), (b) denote the digital tools or approaches they used in support of their hacking (Photoshop, Snapchat, MP4 for podcasting, Adobe Illustrator), and (c) to code for the marginalizing discourses they sought to address with their remix or hack (e.g., ecology and preservation, gender differences stemming from the objectification of women, gun violence, racial and socioeconomic differences in STEM).

I told PSTs ahead of time I was more interested in their ideas, than the quality of their remixes or hacks. Therefore, I center analysis on PSTs' written reflections. My assessment of PSTs work was based on their final compositions, not their in-process multimodal composing. However, PSTs written reflections included their design decisions (i.e., "I hacked the painting to put conservative clothing on the woman"). Following an initial organization and analysis of the data, I memoed for trends I was noticing.

During a second round of coding, I reorganized the original table to group PSTs multimodal compositions, that is, their remixes and hacks by the issue(s) of marginalization they sought to address. This re-rendering of the original table allowed me to compare within and across PSTs and their remixes/hacks. With the data organized in this way, I found seven students, mostly music majors, who critiqued the role of gender as related to music.

Critical Multimodality at the Museum • 251

TABLE 11.3 Selected Examples of First Round Coding

PST	Art Object	Digital Tools or Resources PSTs Used to Remix or Hack (PST language)	Issue Addressed (PST language)
Renee	*Madeleine With Birds* by Janusz Walentynowicz (Painting)	Snapchat: the student drew a shirt, tie, and pants onto the woman in the artwork. This draws the viewer away from being distracted by the sexual nature of the woman, and rather, it poses her as a strong individual.	Gender (women) and opera: • Often, women in opera are sexualized and viewed as the "muse" of male desire. Further, being viewed as such often puts the woman in a position of compromised power, or of power mainly gained through being sexually desired.
Sean	Sand painting rug (YEI Navajo, ca. 1947)	I went to find a piece where there were multiple versions of the same thing [to add drums], I did this because this is how music has been represented for hundreds of years, and with my hack, I can teach my students about breaking the norms of society. [overlaid drums]	Gender stereotypes in music: • I went in with the intention of exploring gender and music. There are so many stereotypical assumptions made about music, especially in terms of White men dominating the community
Seleste	*The Judgment of Paris* by Jacob Jordaens (painting)	I chose to remix *The Judgment of Paris* by PhotoShopping three prominent female rappers onto the faces of Aphrodite, Athena, and Hera.	Gender and race in music: • I made a connection to popular rap culture. Especially among Black female rap artists there is drama, usually caused by social media, beauty standards, and misogynoir based on who is the best. Now these women seek approval in mere men and "fans" to see who is the fairest of them all.
Jason	*The Tyger* by James Prosek (painting)	Going along with the idea of humans and animals switching places, I started brainstorming different scenarios in which this would be interesting. Instantly a few came to mind: zoos, pets, habitat pollution, and potentially even hunting. I decided to make a podcast series focused on these events, with the first episode being about zoos.	Captivity: • In today's society nature is such a marginalized voice. Plants and animals can't speak up for themselves and so few people do that they become more in danger every single day.
Anna	Glass sculptures *Yellow Baby*, paired with *Little Friends* by Christina Bothwell	"Photoshopping' remixes"—I remixed these sculptures by juxtaposing the more traditional childlike things (braiding hair, the baby's pacifier) with the children holding guns.	My remix may not relate to my specific content area of music, but it applies to education as a whole—gun violence.

This approach gave insights into how PSTs own identifications (i.e., White, female) might relate to the issues of marginalization they sought to address in their discipline. Furthermore, by analyzing the subject(s) of the art objects PSTs selected (i.e., a painting of clothed men at a picnic being served by naked women), I was able to make connections for how the museum supported PSTs criticality (i.e., objectification of women in art as related to marginalization of women in music). During this round of coding, I was also able to access PSTs language regarding the ways they grappled with issues of marginalization through remix and hacking: "It forced me to dig deeper... to justify what I was analyzing"; "... doing so in a way that really says something subversive or speaks for marginalizing narratives is not something I had considered."

To analyze PSTs' reflections of their multimodal compositions regarding how they may apply learning to their future teaching, I created a separate document with their answers to Part 3 of the assignment sheet (Table 11.2). This revealed how the learning task either created tensions or fell short of my desired outcomes: "This assignment added another teaching tool"; "I can use such skills and ideas to hack... school/district [resources]"; "I don't think that using this... will be of much use to me"). Collectively, the iterative rounds of data analysis led to three overarching themes regarding PSTs multimodal compositions and visions for their future teaching.

FINDINGS

Using A Museum's Art Objects to Address Marginalization in Disciplinary Contexts Through Multimodal Remixing and Hacking

By having PSTs select art objects from the museum to remix or hack in order to address issues of marginalization within their disciplines, PSTs were able to draw on a wide variety of material resources. However, even though PSTs used painting, tapestries, and glassworks, the artistic medium was less important in their remixes and hacks. That is, most PSTs centered their remixes or hacks based on the subject matter depicted by the art objects rather than the artistic medium and/or modality.

PSTs who wanted to address issues of marginalization related to gender sought out art objects that represented women in objectified ways. This often meant they selected pieces where women were nude and hacked the art to provide clothing. Renee did this for painting of a nude woman surrounded by birds, while Ingrid provided dress for nude women serving men attired in suits at an outdoor picnic luncheon. Alyssa, a White female music major, used a different painting featuring nude women to a similar end. She reflected,

> When I saw the classic painting with naked women, I thought about how ironic it was that classic paintings depict nudity so often and these paintings are respected, but women are often told in this day and age that if they are not "covered up" enough in the clothing that they wear that they will not be respected.

Across examples, PSTs remixed or hacked artwork served a springboard for conversations about: gendered notions for the instruments women are expected to play (i.e., flute, clarinet, or oboe instead of percussion); what gender is viewed as being a conductor or composer, and who is viewed seriously as an artist (i.e., men and not women). In contrast to her peers, Seleste, a Black female music major selected "The Judgment of Paris," which also featured three naked females, but left the deities in her remix unclothed (see Figure 11.1). She Photoshopped "three prominent female rappers onto the faces of Aphrodite, Athena, and Hera."

Figure 11.1 Seleste's remix.

Seleste recounted, "Especially among Black female rap artists there is drama, usually caused by social media, beauty standards, and misogynoir-based on who is the best." She addressed this marginalization further, "Now these women seek approval in mere men and 'fans' to see who is the fairest of them all." Therefore, Seleste's stance complicated what it may mean to be objectified in response to gender and race, and how colorism factors into social views of beauty and/or objectification. Importantly, Seleste's work here, and in other assignments for the course (Deroo & Ponzio, 2021) was born out of her lived experiences and seems to have resonated differently than that of her peers. In short, her work appeared to be more nuanced and layered in terms of the intersecting identities (Crenshaw, 2017), she was critiquing in her remix and hack.

The museum's art objects provided subject matter for those addressing different issues of marginalization too. In her desire to address loss of innocence due to gun violence among youth in schools, Anna gravitated towards two sculptures featuring young children. Using Photoshop, Anna remixed these sculptures "by juxtaposing the more traditional child-like things (braiding hair, the baby's pacifier) with the children holding guns." She recounted how the experience "solidified" her understanding of hacking and remixing to contend with the lack of power marginalized individuals may face in bringing about cultural change, here in the context of gun reform.

However, not all PSTs' use of the museum's art objects led to the critical perspectives advanced in course readings and classroom conversations. Lana, a White female music major, took a cultural artifact, an ceremonial Indigenous canoe paddle, and turned it into a sorority paddle. While Lana positioned her hack as addressing issues of belonging, I found her work uncritical and overall inappropriate. Specifically in feedback to Lana, I noted use of the paddle might reify the very thing her hack sought to address which was acceptance and belonging in a community. I recounted for many people, Greek life is not a space of belonging or acceptance. I stated for me the paddle evoked imagery of hazing for which fraternities and sororities are often critiqued. In retrospect, I fell short in not also critiquing Lana's cultural appropriation of an Indigineous ceremonial object. In future iterations of the course, I have worked to be more explicit with PSTs in my instruction to make sure the marginalizing discourses they seek to address do not end up reifying discrepancies in power or individual's intersecting identifications.

Across their work to remix and hack art objects, PSTs overwhelmingly stayed within the medium or mode of the art they selected. Just two PSTs transmediated (Zoss, 2009) their art objects, but not necessarily to address marginalization in their discipline. Jason, a White male music major, used an ecological tryptic by James Prosek as inspiration to generate a seven episode podcast series focused on a second grader named Ben who highlights

Critical Multimodality at the Museum ▪ 255

Figure 11.2 QR code link to Jason's podcast.

TABLE 11.4 Jason's Podcast Playlist	
Episode	Topic
Episode 1	Unfair Zoos/Bears
Episode 2	Unfair practices with pets, e.g., kennels, shock collars, etc.
Episode 3	Swamp animals polluting human's cities
Episode 4	Forest animals destroying our cities (parallel to deforestation)
Episode 5	Basic everyday ways to combat pollution
Episode 6	Mr. Guy discusses conservationists' work.
Episode 7	How do we spread awareness of these issues?
Next Season	Ben starts teaching his classmates about the environmental issues that he's trying to combat.

humanity's marginalization of nature in its plundering of natural resources (Figure 11.2, Table 11.4).

While Ryan, another White male music major, used the painting "A Lady With a Dog" by Giuseppe Maria Crespi to create a two-page treatment of a children's story book that would use animals to address issues of dehumanization. While transmediation was not directly named in class, PSTs read about text reformulation, a possible impetus for their approach.

Using Art Objects to Challenge PSTs Prior Assumptions About Remix and Hacking

PSTs use of the art museum as a foundation for finding pieces to remix or hack went against their prior assumptions. Michelle, a White female science major reflected, "I originally thought it would be very difficult to find artwork that needed to be remixed because modern art and art museums typically criticize or disrupt current viewpoints," however, she selected a painting

"Atlantic Great White Shark" by Prosek and remixed it to address the preservation of ecology. Samantha, another White female science major, like Jason, used Prosek's tryptic "A Tyger for William Blake" to rework. In her remix, Samantha affixed crowns onto silhouettes of birds in a taxonomy-type tableau to address hierarchies as represented by the food chain. She recounted upending the social order of the food chain to make "the bird the king of jungle."

PSTs written reflections about their multimodal compositions allowed me to recognize the tensions they experienced engaging in the learning task. For example, several PSTs recounted the process as interactive, fun, and humorous, yet noted the challenges that came with being critical. Jason recounted, " I often do a lot of remixes through Photoshop and many other mediums... typically, I just make things that are fun and lighthearted, but this time I had to address marginalization which required a significant amount of thought." In thinking about his future K–8 teaching, he added, "I have to be careful when doing this with music not to cross the line of appropriation." Jason's statement was borne from an earlier class conversation on the topic of cultural appropriation.

In contrasting Jason's response with Lana's work, I recognize that even though PSTs are engaging with the same course readings and class conversations across Unit 2, one course cannot undo prior years of socialization that may lead some students to have less than critical dispositions. Renee, similar to Jason, addressed tensions she felt between engagement and responsibility:

> It is so easy to lean on comedic ideas or ideas that would be merely amusing when remixing artwork, since doing so is a huge part of pop culture. However, merely trying to be funny with this assignment would have likely put the marginalized narrative concentration off to the wayside, when in fact, that is a big part of remixing meaningfully.

Ryan further advanced the need for care and criticality. He shared, "Hacking can be used similarly to a political comic. By reversing the norm, and possibly using satire, remixing a comic or a photo may be used to address the inequalities of racial and gendered representation in the arts." Collectively, the museum's art objects supported PSTs' critical multimodal practices by allowing them to hack or remix works of art to address historically dominant cultural orientations regarding race, gender, and other identifications, extending prior learning from selected course readings and classroom conversations.

Using Remix and Hacking to Address Issues of Marginalization in Their Future Teaching

The results of PSTs to critically apply remix and hacking to their future practice based on museum experiences were mixed. Some PSTs, like

Solomon, a Black male music major noted his general desire to use remixing and hacking, "In the future, with my future students and different pieces of art," but was not very specific regarding how he would do so in a music classroom.

Many female PSTs designed planning to address gender differences in their disciplines. Lana offered some details about how she might take up the approach in her future teaching, albeit in ways that might already be happening pedagogically at her school. She recounted a desire to have students "remix a scene from a Shakespeare play where they will challenge the roles of men and women in the play by changing the lines." Absent from Lana's consideration was how this approach would directly address issues of power or marginalization. Anna, a White female music major, noted she might use hacking or remix in her future classroom to remix a song students were preparing to perform and "blend it with a genre of music that comes from a culture that is not in power."

Alyssa, a White female music major shared, "To hack this systematic inequality, I want to expose my students specifically to female conductors and composers, in order to reshape what they imagine a composer, or conductor, or a musician to be." Yet missing in Alyssa's reflection was what multimodal resources she would use. While I encouraged students to consider, "How can hacking be used to address systemic inequalities and issues of power in your discipline?" I should have asked them to explicitly note ways to do this through a multimodal approach. Renee, a fellow White female music major, noted she "could definitely see remixing incorporated into my teaching. For instance, giving women power in places that they may not have originally been given power would be possible by re-voicing parts of music and designating powerful parts to women." However, neither PST noted the racial, ethnic, or other marginalized identifications of female composers they might call upon. Sean, a White male music major's response was similar in its lack of identifications regarding female composers, but might be taken up differently by students given that he was a male. He envisioned hacking and remixing "old time pieces by men and remix them to include the influences of female composers." Sean concluded such stance taking would "help students see that all genders are equal and deserve the same kind of recognition in and out of the classroom." While I pressed PSTs to be more specific about their potential approaches in my feedback, I missed an important opportunity to re-establish the goals of critical work in re-storying marginalized discourses (see: https://yr.media), especially the power of music as a form of protest and subversion to ruling authorities or governing structures.

Building on the broader gender critique across PSTs, Samantha envisioned how she might address the issue as it related to the field of STEM.

258 ▪ M. R. DEROO

> I will provide students with a case study, possibly depicting the journey of a woman or minority breaking the odds in the science field. I would align the article with the unit we would be covering at the time and would ask students how they feel about this and how this is different than past ideas of individuals in STEM.

However, Samantha's reflection did not name multimodal approaches for enacting a critical case study. Moreover, although PSTs read articles that addressed multiple marginalized identifications, it was not until Summer 2019 and learning from a senior colleague in my department that I began to teach more explicitly about intersectionality (Annamma & Winn, 2019).

Despite the above shortcomings, several PSTs demonstrated criticality in their planning for future teaching. Kori, an Asian-American PST and mathematics major, wanted her future students to contend with climate change and sea level rise, a social issue aligning with Kori's own advocacy work. She remixed a glass object depicting a woman at the seaside with an overlay of a polluted sea (Figure 11.3) to "address systemic inequality and issues of power versus powerlessness because we must attend to the marginalized populations, like nature and animals."

Kori envisioned a future classroom where "we can discuss the ways human actions destructively contribute to deforestation, climate change, and animal deterioration. Students can investigate possibilities to re-balance

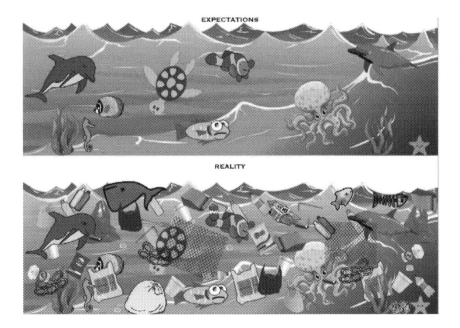

Figure 11.3 Kori's multimodal remix.

systemic inequalities for a variety of discourses, such as gender or race." Similar to Seleste, Kori's work flowed from her lived experiences as a civic agent for social change. Likewise, Genie, an Indian-American female PST science major, provided a detailed example for how she would apply remix and hacking to specific contexts and content. She shared, "I think I am overestimating the amount of people that know about Henrietta Lacks or Rosalind Franklin or Marie Curie or other notable women that have made critical contributions to the field of science." She went on to note, "This shouldn't be the case and a hacking assignment could be a good way for students to explore the basis for this underrepresentation." Specifically, Genie imagined a hacking lesson centering on Henrietta Lacks and the medical community's use of her "essentially stolen" cancer cells. Through her intended plan, informed by the novel and movie based on Lack's life, Genie wished to draw future students to Henrietta Lacks family's lack of rightful compensation for her contributions to science resulting in her family living in conditions of poverty while, she noted, "the 'big shots' that had her cells reaped the rewards."

Based on their reading of Baker-Doyle (2017), PSTs also noted the efficacy of hacking to address broader curricular frameworks that might delimit their future teaching practice. Amelia, a White female music major stated, "In my future teaching experience, I know I can use such skills and ideas to 'hack' some pre-made assignments, texts, images, etc. given to me by my school or district." Recognizing certain voices or perspectives might be marginalized in the mandated curricula, Amelia concluded, "I believe hacking can allow me to give students what would be best for their learning... while still technically following curriculum I could possibly have little control over." Likewise, Alyssa shared that remixing and hacking was purposeful in classrooms because "teachers so often have to teach to pacing guides or biased history books." Finally, Seleste noted that co-construction of relevant curricula through remixing and hacking might allow students to remix texts "to relate more to characters and take a critical stance." She believed teachers could use remix to "find a common ground that students are interested in to create engaging material and learning opportunities for students from different walks of life." Overall, use of the art museum as a hybrid space of learning supported PSTs to engage in critical multimodal composing through remix and hacking, and to envision how they might apply this to their future teaching practice.

When coupled with critical stances through course readings, this approach supported broader awareness for the role of leveraging multimodal resources to critically respond to texts, curricula, and the project of schooling.

Limitations

While the design of the learning task highlighted in this chapter was multimodal, the majority of the learning task depended on the written mode of students' reflective work instead of other nonprint-based modes. Also, the assignment rubric did not include a specific indicator for assessing the quality of students' multimodal compositions (see Tan et al., 2020) which impacted their overall products. While PSTs discussed how they might use remix or hacking with future students, the question remains whether raised awareness will lead to action in actual practice. A key aspect overlooked in my initial teaching of this course and my partnership with the museum was that I did not do enough to trouble the history of museums and their own role in colonization. Therefore, asking PSTs to engage in museums as sites of learning requires teacher educators to draw PSTs attention to how narratives of cultural dominance have shaped museum curation and have historically marginalized underrepresented, intersectional identities (Robert, 2014).

DISCUSSION AND IMPLICATIONS

This chapter highlighted how an art museum created space for PSTs to engage in critical multimodal composition through remixing and hacking, while also denoting some of my imperfections as a teacher educator supporting PSTs to take up critical stances.

Considering the findings shared above, teacher educators who wish to support understandings of critical multimodality (Price-Dennis & Sealey-Ruiz, 2021) might consider using local community resources, such as an art museum, in support of hybrid learning spaces (Zeichner, 2010) towards social change. In the context of this study, university, classroom-based learning, conversations, and course readings were reinforced at the museum, demonstrating the importance of museum learning as an extension of PST learning (Cuenca & Gilbert, 2019; Hamilton & Van Duinen, 2021). Additionally, the museum's works of art contained subject matter worthy of critique, such as the way many PSTs drew upon naked female subjects in art objects to remix or hack in order to address objectification or marginalization of women in their disciplines. That being said, PSTs might have been predisposed to address this topic, since *The Paper Bag Princess* (Munsch et al., 1980; a picture book that challenges stereotypical gender norms) was read shortly before PSTs entered the gallery spaces to select works of art for the assignment.

While PSTs actual multimodal assemblages could be viewed as lacking a sense of sophistication as far as graphic design is concerned, they were able to use resources at their disposal such as Photoshop and Adobe Illustrator

(Knobel & Lankshear, 2008) to rework the art objects they selected towards critical ends. Additionally, PSTs may have had less time overall to spend on the assignment since final exams were quickly approaching. Therefore, reflection was an important part of the equation. PSTs remixes and hacks, on their own, might not have fully communicated their stances, but by writing about their design processes, PSTs choices were made more explicit. Consequently, while a museum visit might provide a solid foundation or springboard for remixing and hacking, other considerations in support of critical multimodality should include reflection, perhaps even calling on digital modes (e.g,, recording a voice memo), to share about design choices factoring into critical, multimodal composition. PSTs could also be explicitly encouraged to transmediate their work like Jason did. By extension, we could have done a gallery walk showcasing students' compositions as a means of mutual sharing in a follow-up class.

PSTs came to understand the role of remixing and hacking to address marginalizing discourse in their disciplines because it was part of course readings. The learning task was required, and completed for points towards PSTs final course grade. However, not all PSTs were equally critical. Even though a number of PSTs mentioned power in their reflections, application of this lens to designing instruction for future teaching did not mean all PSTs contended with this component. Seleste's, Genie's, and Kori's approaches—based on their lived experience—showed deeper criticality with respect to highlighting racialized and gendered figures in science and music, compared to the White male PSTs who mentioned remixing and hacking could be a productive way "to celebrate differences," and who did not always address marginalization within their disciplines. PSTs recounted the tensions they felt taking critical approaches. Jason, Renee, Ingrid, and Ryan, all White, had formerly been drawn to the fun and enjoyable aspects of remixing, but became aware of the deeper work needed for critical remix when engaging with the construct. Others, like Ingrid, found value in learning about remix and hacking, but did not plan to use the approach in her future teaching. Finally, PSTs had difficulty explicitly naming multimodal resources they would use in future teaching to support remix and hacking (Yi & Angay-Crowder, 2016). Teacher educators might glean from my shortcomings. To move critical multimodality forward, our field should continue to infuse additional critical, multimodal activities such as those afforded by remix and hacking across coursework and give explicit reminders of the aims of criticality in addressing systems of power. In doing so, PSTs might better confront marginalizing discourses through multimodal tools and compositions in their disciplines so they might teach and educate towards social change.

REFERENCES

Ajayi, L. (2015). Critical multimodal literacy: How Nigerian female students critique texts and reconstruct unequal social structures. *Journal of Literacy Research, 47*(2), 216–244. https://doi.org/10.1177/1086296X15618478

Annamma, S. A., & Winn, M. (2019). Transforming our mission: Animating teacher education through intersectional justice. *Theory Into Practice, 58*(4), 318–327. https://doi.org/10.1080/00405841.2019.1626618

Baker-Bell, A., Stanbrough, R. J., & Everett, S. (2017). The stories they tell: Mainstream media, pedagogies of healing, and critical media literacy. *English Education, 49*(2), 130–152. https://www.proquest.com/docview/1858879370

Baker-Doyle, K. J. (2017). *Transformative teachers: Teacher leadership and learning in a connected world.* Harvard Education Press.

Barry, A. L. (2012). "I was skeptical at first": Content literacy in the art museum. *Journal of Adolescent & Adult Literacy, 55*(7), 597–607. https://doi.org/10.1002/JAAL.00071

Beck, J. S. (2020). Investigating the third space: A new agenda for teacher education research. *Journal of Teacher Education, 71*(4), 379–391. https://doi.org/10.1177/0022487118787497

Bezemer, J., & Kress, G. (2016). *Multimodality, learning and communication: A social semiotic frame.* Routledge.

Cappello, M. (2019). Reflections of identity in multimodal projects teacher education in the Pacific. *Issues in Teacher Education.* https://files.eric.ed.gov/fulltext/EJ1213187.pdf

Cappello, M., & Lafferty, K. E. (2015). The roles of photography for developing literacy across the disciplines. *The Reading Teacher, 69*(3), 287–295. https://doi.org/10.1002/trtr.1418

Cappello, M., Wiseman, A. M., & Turner, J. D. (2019). Framing equitable classroom practices: Potentials of critical multimodal literacy research. *Literacy Research: Theory, Method, and Practice, 68*(1), 205–225. https://doi.org/10.1177/2381336919870274

Christiansen, L. (2017). Uncovering the legacy of language and power. In E. Barbian, G. Gonzales, & P. Mejia (Eds.), *Rethinking bilingual education: Welcoming home languages in our classrooms* (pp. 97–107). Rethinking Schools.

Ciciottoli, C., & Campoy-Cubillo, M. C. (2018). Introduction: The nexus of multimodality, multimodal literacy, and English language teaching in research and practice in higher education settings. *System, 77,* 1–9. https://doi.org/10.1016/j.system.2018.03.005

Cope, B., & Kalantzis, M. (2005). A multiliteracies pedagogy: A pedagogical supplement. In *Multiliteracies: Literacy Learning and the Design of Social Futures* (pp. 211–242). Routledge.

Crenshaw, K. W. (2017). *On intersectionality: Essential writings.* The New Press.

Cuenca, A., & Gilbert, L., (2019). The museum internship as an analogous learning space for preservice teacher education. *Teaching and Teacher Education, 82*(1), 86–95. https://doi.org/10.1016/j.tate.2019.03.010

Deroo, M. R. (2022). Museums in support of language teacher learning: Expanding understandings of multiliteracies and translanguaging in content area teaching *International Multilingual Research Journal, 16*(3), 227–336. https://doi.org/10.1080/19313152.2022.2079470

Deroo, M. R., & Ponzio, C. M. (2021). Fostering pre-service teachers' critical multilingual language awareness: Use of multimodal compositions to confront hegemonic language ideologies. *Journal of Language, Identity & Education,* 1–17. https://doi.org/10.1080/15348458.2020.1863153

Ellingson, L. L. (2009). *Engaging crystallization in qualitative research: An introduction.* SAGE.

Falk, J. H., & Dierking, L. D. (2016). *The museum experience revisited.* Routledge.

Farias, M., & Veliz, L. (2019). Multimodal texts in Chilean English teaching education: Experiences from educators and pre-service teachers. *Profile: Issues in Teachers' Professional Development, 21*(2), 13–27. https://doi.org/10.15446/profile.v21n2.75172

García, O., & Wei, L. (2014). *Translanguaging: Language, bilingualism and education.* Palgrave Macmillan.

Gee, J. P. (1996). *Social linguistics and literacies: Ideologies in discourses* (2nd ed.). Falmer.

Gubrium, A. C., & Torres, M. I. (2013). The message is in the bottle: Latino youth communicating double standard ideologies through photovoice. *American Journal of Health Education, 44*(3), 146–155.

Guillen, L., & Zeichner, K. (2018). A university–community partnership in teacher education from the perspectives of community-based teacher educators. *Journal of Teacher Education, 69*(2), 140–153. https://doi.org/10.1177/0022487117751133

Gutiérrez, K. D. (2008). Developing a sociocritical literacy in the third space. *Reading Research Quarterly, 43*(2), 148–164. https://doi.org/10.1598/RRQ.43.2.3

Haddix, M., & Sealey-Ruiz, Y. (2012). Cultivating digital and popular literacies as empowering and emancipatory acts among urban youth. *Journal of Adolescent & Adult Literacy, 56*(3), 189–192. https://doi.org/10.1002/JAAL.00126

Hamilton, E. R., & Van Duinen, D. V. (2021). Hybrid spaces: Adolescent literacy and learning in a museum. *Journal of Adolescent & Adult Literacy, 64*(5), 511–520.

Hillman, A. M. (2014). A literature review on disciplinary literacy: How do secondary teachers apprentice students into mathematical literacy? *Journal of Adolescent & Adult Literacy, 57*(5), 397–406. https://doi.org/10.1002/jaal.256

Huang, S. Y. (2019). A critical multimodal framework for reading and analyzing pedagogical materials. *English Teaching: Practice & Critique, 18*(1), 52–69. https://eric.ed.gov/?id=EJ1335839

Jocson, K. M. (2013). Remix revisited: Critical solidarity in youth media arts. *E-learning and Digital Media, 10*(1), 68–82. https://doi.org/10.2304/elea.2013.10.1.68

Jones, P., Turney, A., Georgiou, H., & Nielsen, W. (2020). Assessing multimodal literacies in science: semiotic and practical insights from pre-service teacher education. *Language and Education, 34*(2), 153–172. https://doi.org/10.1080/09500782.2020.1720227

Jewitt, C. (2009). An introduction to multimodality. In C. Jewitt (Ed.), *The Routledge handbook of multimodal analysis* (pp. 14–27). Routledge.

Kędra, J. (2018). What does it mean to be visually literate? Examination of visual literacy definitions in a context of higher education. *Journal of Visual Literacy, 37*(2), 67–84. https://doi.org/10.1080/1051144X.2018.1492234

Knobel, M., & Lankshear, C. (2008). Remix: The art and craft of endless hybridization. *Journal of Adolescent & Adult Literacy, 52*(1), 22–33. https://www.jstor.org/stable/30139647

Kress, G. (2011). Discourse analysis and education: A multimodal social semiotic approach. In R. Rogers (Ed.), *An introduction to critical discourse analysis in education* (pp. 205–226). Routledge.

Kress, G., & Van Leeuwen, T. (1996) *Reading Images—The grammar of visual design*. Routledge.

Kwon, H. (2020). Graphic novels: Exploring visual culture and multimodal literacy in preservice art teacher education. *Art Education, 73*(2), 33–42. https://doi.org/10.1080/00043125.2019.1695479

Lawrence, S. A., Langan, E., & Maurer, J. (2019). Using primary sources in content areas to increase disciplinary literacy instruction. *The Language and Literacy Spectrum, 29*(1), 1. https://digitalcommons.buffalostate.edu/lls/vol29/iss1/1

Lewkowich, D. (2019). The thought chronicle: Developing a multimodal repertoire of response in teacher education. *English in Education, 53*(2), 129–144. https://doi.org/10.1080/04250494.2018.1534531

Li, M. (2020). Multimodal pedagogy in TESOL teacher education: students' perspectives. *System, 94*, 102337. https://doi.org/10.1016/j.system.2020.102337

Loerts, T., & Belcher, C. (2019). Developing visual literacy competencies while learning course content through visual journaling: Teacher candidate perspectives. *Journal of Visual Literacy, 38*(1–2), 46–65. https://eric.ed.gov/?id=EJ1218004

Mansbach, A. (2011). *Go the f** k to sleep*. Open Road Media.

Mirra, N., Morrell, E., & Filipiak, D. (2018). From digital consumption to digital invention: Toward a new critical theory and practice of multiliteracies. *Theory Into Practice, 57*(1), 12–19. https://doi.org/10.1080/00405841.2017.1390336

Munsch, R. N., Martchenko, M., Dann, S., & Berneis, S. (1980). *The paper bag princess*. Annick Press.

Paris, D., & Alim, H. S. (2014). What are we seeking to sustain through culturally sustaining pedagogy? A loving critique forward. *Harvard Educational Review, 84*(1), 85–100. https://doi.org/10.17763/haer.84.1.982l873k2ht16m77

Ponzio, C., & Deroo, M. (2021). Harnessing multimodality in language teacher education: Expanding English-dominant teachers translanguaging capacities through multimodalities entextualization cycle. *International Journal of Bilingual Education and Bilingualism*, 1–17. https://doi.org/10.1080/13670050.2021.1933893

Prasad, G. L. (2018). "But do monolingual people really exist?" Analysing elementary students' contrasting representations of plurilingualism through sequential reflexive drawing. *Language and Intercultural Communication, 18*(3), 315–334.

Price-Dennis, D., & Sealey-Ruiz, Y. (2021). *Advancing racial literacies in teacher education: Activism for equity in digital spaces*. Teachers College Press.

Rhoades, M. (2020). Language arts lessons: A contemporary arts-based approach to critical multimodal literacy. *Language Arts, 97*(3), 178–185. https://library.ncte.org/journals/la/issues/v97-3/30417

Rhoades, M., Dallacqua, A., Kersten, S., Merryfield, J., & Miller, M. C. (2015). The pen(cil) is mightier than the (s)word? Telling sophisticated silent stories using Shaun Tan's wordless graphic novel, "The Arrival." *Studies in Art Education, 56*(4), 307–326. https://resolver.scholarsportal.info/resolve/00393541/v56i0004/307_tpimttstwgna.xml

Robert, N. (2014). Getting intersectional in museums. *Museums & Social Issues, 9*(1), 24–33. https://doi.org/10.1179/1559689314Z.00000000017

Rosa, J. (2019). *Looking like a language, sounding like a race: Raciolinguistic ideologies and the learning of Latinidad*. Oxford University Press.

Rowsell, J., Kosnik, C., & Beck, C. (2008). Fostering multiliteracies pedagogy through preservice teacher education. *Teaching Education, 19*(2), 109–122. https://doi.org/10.1080/10476210802040799

Scieszka, J., & Barnett, M. (2013). *Battle bunny*. Simon and Schuster.

Segall, A., Smith Crocco, M., Halvorson, A., & Jacobsen, R (2019). Teaching in the twilight zone of misinformation, disinformation, alternative facts, and fake news. In W. Journell (Ed.), *Unpacking fake news: An educator's guide to navigating the media with students* (pp. 74–91). Teachers College Press.

Serafini, F. (2014). *Reading the visual: An introduction to teaching multimodal literacy*. Teachers College Press.

Shanahan, T., & Shanahan, C., (2008). Teaching disciplinary literacy to adolescents: Rethinking content-area literacy. *Harvard Educational Review, 78*(1), 40–59. https://doi.org/10.17763/haer.78.1.v62444321p602101

Storm, S., & Rainey, E. C. (2018). Striving toward woke English teaching and learning. *The English Journal, 107*(6), 95–101. https://www.academia.edu/37103856/Striving_toward_Woke_English_Teaching_and_Learning

Tan, L., Zammit, K., D'warte, J., & Gearside, A. (2020). Assessing multimodal literacies in practice: A critical review of its implementations in educational settings. *Language and Education, 34*(2), 97–114. https://doi.org/10.1080/09500782.2019.1708926

The New London Group. (1996). A pedagogy of multiliteracies: Designing social futures. *Harvard Educational Review, 66*(1), 60–92. https://doi.org/10.17763/haer.66.1.17370n67v22j160u

Tour, E., & Barnes, M. (2021). Engaging English language learners in digital multimodal composing: Pre-service teachers' perspectives and experiences. *Language and Education, 36*(3), 243–258. https://doi.org/10.1080/09500782.2021.1912083

Van Leeuwen, T. (2008). *Discourse and practice: New tools for critical discourse analysis*. Oxford University Press.

Yenawine, P. (2013). *Visual thinking strategies: Using art to deepen learning across school disciplines*. Harvard Education Press.

Youngs, S., & Kyser, C. (2021). Bringing form, content and aesthetics together: Preservice teachers reading contemporary picturebooks and designing multimodal responses. *Literacy Research and Instruction, 60*(3), 264–300. https://doi.org/10.1080/19388071.2020.1822472

Yi, Y., & Angay-Crowder, T. (2016). Multimodal pedagogies for teacher education in TESOL. *TESOL Quarterly, 50*(4), 988–998. https://doi.org/10.1002/tesq.326

Zeichner, K. (2010). Rethinking the connections between campus courses and field experiences in college-and university-based teacher education. *Journal of Teacher Education, 61*(1–2), 89–99. https://eric.ed.gov/?id=EJ879286

Zoss, M. 2009. Visual arts and literacy. In L. Christenbury, R. Bomer, & P. Smagorinsky (Eds.), *Handbook of adolescent literacy research* (pp. 183–196). Guilford Press.

SECTION IV
CRITICAL MULTIMODALITY IN PROTESTS
AND SOCIAL MOVEMENTS

CHAPTER 12

BORDADOS

A Feminist Collective Practice of Resistance and Solidarity in the Chilean Estallido

Romina S. Peña-Pincheira
Gustavus Adolphus College

M. Isidora Bilbao-Nieva
Universidad Alberto Hurtado, Universidad del Desarrollo

Lau Romero-Quintana
Northern Michigan University

ABSTRACT

The embroidery is a form of text that goes beyond the linguistic realm. It may include words, but also images, colors, textures, and mixed materials. As a traditional activity practiced mostly by women, embroidery has often been considered a leisure practice, resulting in an ornament, a private and individual activity related to a particular view of the feminine (Pérez-Bustos, 2019). However, in the Latin American context, the textile practices are also connected to precolonial times, with storytelling textile artifacts such as quipus (Ascher & Ascher, 1975). In its etymological origins, the idea of knitting (*tejido*) comes from the Latin textus, which implied the knitting of a story, a tejido (Pérez-Bustos et al., 2016). This form of storytelling and meaning making entails practices that have always existed, although they are often not reappropriated in spaces outside of pure leisure. In the Chilean context, embroidery of burlaps is an example of embroidery outside the private, leisure-only sphere. This practice gained political relevance as a testimony of human rights violations during Augusto Pinochet's dictatorship (Shayne, 2009). These previous forms of embroidery with political ends influence the most current practice, which has become an emblem of the social revolution in Chile, started in 2019. We state that embroidery, as a practice and as an object itself is, therefore, a recontextualization inserted in the previous history of embroidery and a multimodal way of meaning making (Van Leeuwen, 2008).

In this book chapter, and drawing on multimodal semiotic discourse analysis and feminist theories, we will explore how embroidery has become a collective feminist practice of resistance. We will examine embroidery as a process of multimodal semiotic action of recontextualization, collectivization, transformative imaginary, active sociopolitical participation, and social critique. Focusing on the Chilean case, we will describe how contemporary *bordadoras* have used embroidery as a resource for meaning making to mobilize a specific resistance agenda. More specifically, we argue that by using embroidery for exposing social injustice and violence, a tradition of meaning making is being resignified through a social network platform. In this case, we present and analyze the embroideries of an Instagram account (@bordasusojos) that is explicitly political, feminist, and collective. The Instagram post adds a new layer of meaning, as it is accompanied by a written post, and a new level of visibility produced by the exposition on a massive platform. Through its posting on Instagram, the embroidery, often a private and individual object, becomes public and collective, offering new opportunities for advancing a Chilean and Latin American feminist agenda.

FIRST STITCHES: INTRODUCTION

In its occidental etymological origins, the idea of knitting (*tejido*) comes from the Latin *textus*, which implied the knitting of a story (Pérez-Bustos et al., 2016). This form of storytelling and meaning making entails practices that have always existed, although they have been rarely interpreted as practices outside of pure leisure. Traditionally, the act of embroidering has often been portrayed as a female dominated practice, with the main purpose of providing a form of harmless leisure, as well as adornment and decor (Pérez-Bustos, 2019). However, in spaces of resistance and oppression, embroidery takes a new purpose.

Separated from the dominant portrayal of embroidery, several communities of Chilean women used to embroider burlaps for political purposes during the 1970s. This practice gained political relevance as a testimony of human rights violations during Augusto Pinochet's dictatorship between 1973 and 1990 (Shayne, 2009). These previous forms of embroidery with political ends influence the most current practice, which has become an emblem of the social revolution in Chile, in 2019. In this chapter we argue that embroidery—as a practice and as an object itself—is, therefore, a recontextualization inserted in the previous history of embroidery and a multimodal way of meaning making (Van Leeuwen, 2008). More specifically, we argue that the use of embroidery through social network platforms presents nuanced social recontextualization of socioeconomic injustice, police violence, and political legitimation of social protest in Chile. In this case, we present and analyze the embroideries of a Chilean Instagram account (@bordasusojos), an online space that is explicitly political, feminist, and collective. The Instagram post itself adds a new layer of meaning as it is accompanied by written text, and a new level of visibility produced by the exposition on a mass media platform. Through its posting, the embroidery, often a private and individual object, becomes public and collective, offering new opportunities for advancing a Chilean and Latin American political feminist agenda.

In what follows we describe the sociopolitical and historical background of *el estallido* in October of 2019 in Chile. We then present our positionalities and how we situate ourselves as Chilean scholars in the United States. After describing our epistemological approach, textile feminist activism, and methods of inquiry, we present the analysis of three embroidery images we individually and collectively examined. Finally, in our conclusions we provide some implications of our work, as the outcome of a process of mutual and dialogic conscientization, for educational spaces and academic spaces.

HISTORICAL BACKGROUND

In order to fully engage with the meaning of the embroidered pieces, the public must be aware of their sociohistorical and socioeconomic contexts and paradigms. Specifically, the two main events that gave birth to Chile's current situation are Augusto Pinochet's 1973 military coup and the transitional governments that followed. The year 1989 marks the beginning of Chile's democratic period, under a political movement that did little to change Pinochet's biggest legacy: a constitution that carved in stone the neoliberal socioeconomic model. These past 30 years deepened policies such as the privatization of social services, and the shrinkage of the State role and its attributions, as it happened in many other Latin American countries during the 1990s and 2000s (Cecchini & Martínez, 2011). These policies—pushed by the International Monetary Fund and the World

Bank—showed a positive impact on the Chilean national gross income but increased the economic gap between the rich and the poor (Osorio, 2014). Based on the theory of the trickle-down effect, these guidelines became abusive for most Chileans. Even though Chile was governed by politicians of different political tendencies after 1989, including members of socialists and left-wing parties, the economic system remained untouched despite the evidence against it, its detrimental effects, and the political tendencies of the presidents in power. Once again, Chile's socioeconomic model was boiled down to "profit over people" (Chomsky 1999; Harvey, 2007). As expected, the economic impact was directly related to social rights such as education, health, retirement funds, and natural resources, all which became regulated and administered by the private market instead of the State. In the eyes of the middle and lower class, after 30 years of "democracy" and neoliberal reforms, Chile was still a country founded on the basis of structural abuse, underfunding of public services, and its consequent privatization. As a consequence, and in a very 19th century fashion, the ongoing abuse was met with continuous discontent from the working classes and the student sector. Both of these social groups had little to no support from the establishment's political parties, but had grassroots organizations that mobilized tirelessly to uncover and create public awareness about Chile's precarious state due to these extreme neoliberal reforms and its colonial past and legacy (Bellei et al., 2014; Fraser, 2019).

One example of these capitalistic practices of competitiveness, individualization, and privatization was solidified in the LOCE, *Ley Orgánica Constitucional de Enseñanza* (The Organic Constitutional Law of Education, 1990–2009). LOCE introduced standards, high-stakes standardized testing, municipalization (decentralization of education), and choice strategies such as "parental choice" and the voucher system, which allows small businessmen to profit from state vouchers through subsidized private schools (Stromquist & Sayal, 2013). LOCE legitimized the abandonment of state responsibility in securing equal access to quality education (Grugel & Singh, 2015). In 2009, after strong social pressure by different actors (students, teachers, parents; Bellei & Cabalin, 2013), the LGE (General Law of Education) replaced LOCE but did nothing to change the structure of the Chilean education, nor did it eliminate the voucher system (Cabalin, 2012; Oliva, 2010), and increased competition, privatization, and standardization (Inzunza et al., 2019). Students and social agents in education continued to challenge and demonstrate against a segregated, underfunded, and discriminatory educational system and curriculum. Students' social active role has been described as a form of public pedagogy and critical awareness (Williams, 2015). Historically, they have shown effective political organization and strategies, pushing public dialogue through reappropriating public spaces via marches, artwork, performances, poetry, among others. Such active public role of social denunciation and resignification has led to social awakening in various moments of Chilean history.

These events lead us to 2019 when Chile was under the presidency of Sebastián Piñera. Santiago, the overpopulated capital city, was undergoing a series of protests after a public announcement of transportation fare increase. Santiago is a city that visually communicates a strong economic performance, but this is partly based on the striking exclusion and segregation of the rest of the country (Dockemdorff et al., 2000). Therefore, despite the apparent homogeneity in wealth distribution, the announcement of the transportation fare increase of 30 CLP (approximately 0.039 USD) only enhanced the underlying inequalities. A way to confront said unevenness was through massive fare dodging, led primarily by high school students in the underground (Metro) stations. The most significant riot took place on October 10th, 2019, where a mass of high schoolers broke into a closed subway station and evaded paying subway fares.

Chaos broke loose and it wasn't long before police forces (*Carabineros*) were involved, leaving people wounded and/or detained. This was the fuse that set fire to *el estallido* (as in *estallar*, "to burst"). As the discontent spread throughout the following weeks, the social outburst was met with a heavy hand by Piñera's government and the Chilean population took to the streets. In an attempt to control angered citizens, police shot rubber bullets at civilians, targeting their eyes and face. To this date, the National Institute of Human Rights in Chile reports a total of 172 cases of eye trauma (Instituto Nacional de Derechos Humanos, 2021), where 16 are categorized as severe, and 4 resulted in complete loss of vision. A symbol of resistance was born; to cover one's eye with a hand signaled solidarity with those fallen, but also a different way of manifesting one's political discontent and anger towards the government's failed actions.

Overall, president Piñera's decisions continued to fan the flames, and for the protesting public, people's struggles over the years became clearer and more meaningful. A new sense of solidarity and togetherness was born right there, in the epicenter of Santiago, where the well-known Plaza Italia changed its name to *Plaza Dignidad* (Dignity Square). Chileans use several words to talk about this historical moment. We have chosen the use of the word *estallido*, which signals an outburst, explosion, blast, or blow up. We believe that this word synthesizes a history of patience and silence embedded in a fake sense of peace, a rage and despair that was growing in the background, quietly, until it exploded. When el estallido happened, there was a moment of truth, a clear sight of what was hidden in the daily lives of Chileans. When something explodes, it can't return to its original shape, it is forever changed. We believe that the social protest was an estallido because it happened violently, illuminating everything with its brutal truth, inscribing an indelible mark in Chilean history.

AUTHORS' POSITIONALITIES

When the social protests started in Chile in October 2019, we, the three authors of this chapter, were PhD students, researchers, teaching assistants, and instructors living in the Midwest of the United States and attending a predominantly White institution on indigenous land. As Chileans, the social protest was a historical event that we experienced collectively. We observed from the outside how the protesters transformed the geographical, political, and social landscape we grew up in, and we were thrilled and eager to be there and see these transformations with our own eyes. But the fact that it happened when we were not physically in our country gave us mixed feelings. We were only able to see this dramatic moment through social media platforms such as Instagram where, on many occasions, we closely watched unfiltered police violence and brutality against protesters. We were simultaneously frustrated for not being there, proud of our people, hopeful for the transformations, excited for the future, and scared for our family and friends that were facing horrible levels of police violence. We found ourselves searching for spaces (both physical and symbolic) to grieve and connect with others experiencing similar things. Despite the demanding nature of graduate school work in the United States, we felt the need to put aside our regular academic work in order to humanize our grief and connect in any way we could with our people. We found ourselves creating spaces of resistance and healing, in isolation from our academic institutions, and supported by communities from Latin America through our university's Center of Latin American and Caribbean Studies, a space that allowed people with similar experiences of marginalization and exploitation—rooted in colonization and neoliberal reforms—to express themselves and processed what had occurred. We see this chapter as an outlet for our collective reflection, and as a way of contributing to the knowledge production regarding the most important historical event of our time as Chileans. To prepare this chapter we engaged in continuous dialogue and creation of knowledge, each one of us based on our disciplinary fields (education, community psychology, cultural studies). We learned from each other whilst legitimizing our individual and collective experiences as Chileans studying and working away from our homes and people. While our shared experience made us closer, first as friends and then as scholars, it also allowed us to develop individual understandings and elaborations of our subjective experiences.

TEXTILE FEMINIST ACTIVISM

In the Chilean context of October 2019, women-led groups and collectives' participation have been an important moving force in the social protests in public and local spaces. From Las Tesis *Un Violador en Tu Camino* (A Rapist in Your Path) to the organization of *ollas comunes* (community open kitchens) at *Plaza Dignidad* and neighborhoods across the nation, women have created spaces of social denunciation against naturalized abuse and exploitation as a systematic issue, particularly with regard to gender and sexual power relationships and hierarchies (*Ni Una Menos*), and created spaces of creative collectivism. In this chapter, we focus on embroidery as a feminist and collective practice of memory, imagery, and political denunciation.

Historically, embroidery has often been considered a women's activity. As such, it has been relegated to private spaces, confined to produce decorative pieces for domestic use. In Latin America, however, embroidery has also been used as a form of textile activism (Sánchez-Aldana et al., 2019). In the 1960s, the Chilean artist Violeta Parra exposed her embroidered burlaps in the Louvre Museum, becoming the first Latin American female artist to have an individual exposition there. With this historical gesture the artist transformed the private activity into a public one, installing Chilean women's traditional practice into a public, global space. Later, in the 1970s, the *arpilleras*—burlaps embroidered by communities of women—used embroidered burlaps as historical and political testimony, exposing and denouncing the human rights violations of Augusto Pinochet's dictatorship. Arpilleras challenged the apolitical nature conferred to embroideries, showing their potential to achieve justice and preserve collective memory. We thus read the contemporary activity of embroidery as a political manifestation and its posts on Instagram as a way of making it public.

We refer to these two elements—the public and the politic—to sustain our feminist approach for this analysis. Through understanding embroidery as a private and apolitical activity not only its potential agency as artifacts of protest and social change is denied, but also the public and political possibilities of the subjects that exercise such activities. In that line, the small literature regarding textile activism has been focused on North American, middle class, White women, and their *knittivism* (Sánchez-Aldana et al., 2019). Today, there is a growing interest on the potential of Latin American textile activism and its historical and current use of embroideries as a form of political expression and resistance (Ossul-Vermehren & Pacheco, in press), to advance feminist agendas (Sánchez-Aldana et al., 2019), and as a way to heal from political trauma and build feminist solidarity (Ochoa Avalos, 2018).

Different from the analysis of North American textile activism, that splits the feminist agendas into community building on the one hand and political denouncing on the other, Latin American approaches have shown a different, hybrid feminist textile activism in which community and political resistance are interwoven (Sánchez-Aldana et al., 2019). Furthermore, Latin American feminist activism pursues different goals and is practiced by a different population. Traditionally, in Latin America embroidery is an activity that is practiced by indigenous women. Today, the practice of embroidery has been recontextualized as a form of resistance against state violence (Ochoa Ávalos, 2018; Ossul-Vermehren & Pacheco, in press) and colonial legacies of exclusion (Rivera Cusicanqui, 2010). These aspects are particular to Latin America and demand their own analytical frameworks and theoretical developments.

The notion of embroidering as a harmless and innocent practice allows us to connect with Argentinian feminist Josefina Ludmer's (1985) proposal of *las tretas del débil* (the tricks of the weak). In her iconic essay, Ludmer proposes that women have been historically capable of holding *saber* (knowledge/knowing), while also *decir que no saben* (performing ignorance). The same underlying notion exists in the publication of embroideries; through a seemingly innocent and harmless practice, women are conveying a political and defiant public message, disrupting a traditionally male-dominated genre. After all, the embroidery pieces are being posted on Instagram, a social media platform that is also linked with leisure and entertainment, but often not seen as a platform for effective sociopolitical activism. Through textile feminist activism, women are centered as the primary agents in the recontextualization of a meaning making practice traditionally associated with a feminine, personal, and private activity, transforming it into production of political discourse, knowledge creation, and the challenge of status quo. In other words, the use of embroidery for political purposes challenges the idea of embroidery as a harmless and innocent practice and also uses a form of expression that carries several layers of meaning, a diversity of symbols, and multiple modalities to communicate a complex message.

From a feminist perspective, we highlight textile feminist embroidery's agentic and political efficiency as a way to question the subordination of certain social practices, as if they were stripped from agency and voice.

METHODS OF INQUIRY

We understand discourse and meaning-making practices as shaping and being shaped by social contexts, relations, and educational spaces. Critical discourse analysis (CDA) as social semiotics (Halliday, 1978) involves the analysis of social practices of meaning making, appropriation of social elements, and their recontextualization (e.g., relocation, semantic shifts) in discourse (e.g., Fairclough, 2012; van Leeuwen, 2008). Meaning making processes incorporate a wealth of multimodal semiotic resources that include symbols, spoken and written language features (intonation, facial expression, font; van Leeuwen, 2015). Diverse semiotic modalities different from written and oral language contribute a different layer of meaning, adding richness, complexity, and a deeper level of insightfulness to CDA (Lazar, 2005). As some Latin American authors have pointed out, embroidery can carry messages that are not suitable to be delivered by other means, and have shown their potential to portray experiences of trauma and state violence (Ochoa Ávalos, 2018). For the purpose of this chapter, we focused on the CDA of embroidery practices in Chile during el estallido as an important multimodal artifact, and as an agentic and collaborative practice of social critique and social reconfiguration. We limited our analysis to the images on @bordasusojos (which translates as "embroidering their eyes"), a Chilean Instagram account that was created to gather embroidery pieces from Chilean authors during el estallido.

This account serves as an archive of embroidered artifacts that showed the historic, economic, and social entanglements behind social discontent from the perspective of Chilean embroiderers from different backgrounds and located in different cities. Simultaneously, it offered a gallery to make public diverse readings and opinions, and invite people to examine social issues related to el estallido, as a form of public pedagogy.

For our analysis, we are guided by van Leeuwen's approach to CDA. Theo van Leeuwen has developed a series of methodological principles and tools particularly useful for the CDA of visual means (Wodak & Meyer, 2001), which serve as strategies to dissect and understand the different layers of meaning that can be grasped from a multimodal artifact in a systematic way. Different from other authors, van Leeuwen's framework of analysis responds to the aim of this chapter, which is to transcend the particularities of the English language in multimodal and multisemiotic settings.

We focus our analysis on van Leeuwen's understanding of *recontextualization*. The process of recontextualization, which are semantic shifts or transformations that "appropriate, relocate, refocus, and relate" to constitute a new ordering of discursive resources grounded in social practice (Berstein, 1990; van Leeuwen, 2008). According to van Leeuwen (2008), the process of recontextualization works like a chain, in which one can recontextualize sequences of nonlinguistic and linguistic actions. In recontextualization, the social practices can be explicit in different degrees and are often invisible to the speaker, as they are embedded in the practices in which they are inserted.

Furthermore, we analyze discursive moves represented in the chosen artifacts by drawing on van Leeuwen's socio-semantic inventory of the transformations that occur in the recontextualization process. This inventory offers guidelines to understand the different effects of discursive representation of social actors (e.g., role allocation, nomination and categorization, representational choices), social actions (specific grammatical and rhetorical realization, such as action vs. reaction, material vs. semantic representation of actions), time (to understand the fundamental role and power of time in social life, such as the presence of authorities who determine and impose timing), and space (the way we use and understand space in social practices).

According to van Leeuwen (2008), the process of recontextualization provokes transformations on social practices. While there are different types of transformations described by van Leeuwen (2008), we realized that embroidery pieces often added elements to the social practices through legitimation. The concept of legitimation is useful to understand the uses and transformations inaugurated by the analyzed artifacts. Legitimation gives the reasons "why" of recontextualizations and representations of social practices. We believe this is the case of embroidery, as it both legitimizes and delegitimizes (or critiques) social practices related to el estallido. In this chapter, the analysis of the embroidery pieces is focused on making explicit what is legitimized through the pieces, how it is legitimized, and why the embroidery was done.

In addition, this study also refers to the representation of social actions, particularly via metonymic reference and objectivation. According to van Leeuwen (2008), metonymical reference occurs through the process of objectivation, when social actors are referenced through a location or object in which they are actively engaged. Objectivation is the use of the image of an object to represent social actors and/or their actions. In other words, the image representing the object is semantically associated with the person or action. In everyday language, this occurs when, for example, people refer to the crown instead of a member of a royal family. Clear examples from the embroidery pieces analyzed are the inclusion of components representative of larger agencies in Chilean society: the coin as a symbol for government, for example, in Figure 12.1, or a rifle as referencing the army and police forces, in Figure 12.2.

In this chapter, we examine three multisemiotic embroidery artifacts: Figure 12.1: *30 años* (30 years), Figure 12.2: *Sus fusiles caerán* (Your rifles will fall), and Figure 12.3: *Vivir en Chile vale un ojo de la cara* (To live in Chile costs an arm and a leg). To select the images, we reviewed all the posts of the account and selected the ones that included the richest levels of context and semiotic resources. Then, we discussed what were the most frequent elements described by the images and chose the posts that depicted three different but overlapping elements that were key to explain el estallido: socioeconomic and historical context, and the impact of state-sponsored violence.

Therefore, these three images present and resignify one particular event drawing on a different set of components, thus unveiling the extent of the sociopolitical and economic context surrounding el estallido in October 2019. After selecting the specific pieces we wanted to examine, we contacted each of the authors asking for permission to analyze and include the photographs that depicted their pieces, all of whom accepted.

ANALYSIS

In this section, we analyze three images that were reposted by the Instagram account @bordasusojos. In our discussion of findings we provide important historical, economic, and cultural background of the multimodal pieces that resignify and recontextualize Chile's social protest. Following van Leeuwen's approach to CDA, we discuss the use of legitimization, collectivization, objectivation (through metonymical reference), location, among others, in the process of recontextualization of the estallido. We find a common symbol across these embroidery pieces—the open eye. The eye at the center, in combination with other semiotic resources, communicates nuanced and diverse messages that invite the viewer to think historically, examine the status quo, and critique police violence.

Figure 12.1 was posted on Instagram on October 7, 2020—about a year since the estallido occurred in Chile—under the caption *Lo que inició todo* (What started it all), and accompanied by several hashtags, among them #chiledespertó (Chile woke up). The image displays an open eye, more an icon than the mimetic representation of the human version, which holds in its center a peso, an everyday economic transactional object. In the middle of the coin, the iris is replaced by the laurel wreath that adorns the number 30 (the pupil), with a legend underneath. Altogether, the brown-copper eye reads "30 years, 2019." Both the image and the hashtag represent the

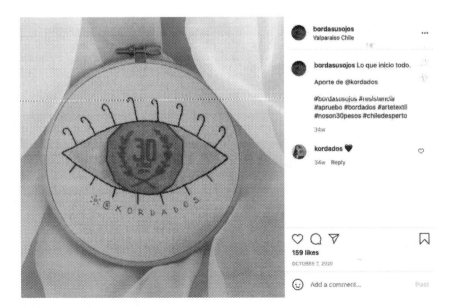

Figure 12.1   *30 años*. Author: @kordados.

social awakening of the people—after their inactivity for 30 years—against the political class and their abusive system. Altogether, they represent a sense of clarity; suddenly people could see (the eye on the picture) in a newly found awakening.

The coin recontextualizes symbolic resources and legitimizes an important event in the present by creating new layers of meaning. For instance, through the use of the establishments' symbolic systems (shape, brown-copper color, the laurel wreath) people's awakening and uprising is legitimized. It becomes a permanent and historical commemoration of a collectivized event (e.g., #chiledespertó), that circulates as a message on every Chilean's pocket. Furthermore, the coin serves also as an official political statement. The message challenges government officials' trivialization of the motives of the protest, treating it as a "30 pesos" problem.

Additionally, the coin recontextualization goes beyond the exchange value that currency carries, it historicizes a collection of events in the past in this new layer of meaning. The embroidery uses the shape of one of the smallest amounts on the Chilean currency—the peso coin—to reinforce that the estallido is not about the transportation fee increase. Through the poetic allusion to the 30 peso rise, the coin recontextualizes the statement *no son 30 pesos, son 30 años* (it is not 30 pesos, it's 30 years)—a phrase at the core of Chilean critique and widely adopted in the protest. Thus, the estallido and the social protest are legitimized through the recontextualization of a single event (30 pesos) into the ongoing systematic oppression in the accumulation of abusive neoliberal social policies experimented by Chilean society in the last 30 years. The fee increase was a catalyst, but not the reason for the social movement. "30 years," on the other hand, refers to the last 30 years of democracy after the Pinochet dictatorship in 1989, that is, the Chilean latest history of implementing a neoliberal capitalist structure and reforms at the core of social and economic reforms that generated deep forms of inequality and discontent among Chilean people.

Lastly, in the image we examined the process of objectivation. Going back to Figure 12.1, objectivation occurs by replacing the pupil with a material and economic object: the coin. Two critiques can be identified. The first is a critique of the neoliberal economic model that privileges economic gain over social well-being. Following this interpretation, the coin represents the embedded motto that normalizes the commodification of humanity represented by the replaced pupil, that is, profit/economic growth over human well-being. The second is a critique of the elected government. In Chile, the government house is called *Palacio de la Moneda* (Coin Palace), and is referred to as *la Moneda* (the Coin) for short. Through objectivation, the embroidery refers to the house of the government and its main inhabitant, President Piñera. This way, the post also legitimates the social movement as a political, economic, and official matter that not only needs to be addressed by public institutions, but it actually places blame and responsibility on said public institution—the house of government—and its main occupant.

The embroidered piece shown in Figure 12.2 echoes the previous image, "30 pesos," as the center of attention remains in the eye. The composition includes, in its center, an open eye that holds a speeding bullet in its pupil. This figure is surrounded by a vibrant outward-oriented red circular design with a black background. Around the red circle, the phrase *Sus fusiles caerán y la calle triunfará* (Their rifles will fall and the streets will triumph) is stitched on. Its rough and unevenly sewn edges resemble a type of path, to transmit a feeling of uneasiness. In a punk fashion, the author of Figure 12.2 mentioned that her creations seek to represent that which is imperfect, dirty, and that is conceived in a public and collective space, the streets.

Figure 12.2 is also created in a way that suggests a reading order. The explosion that is represented with the red thread forces the public to read the image from the inside out, instead of the traditional left to right movement. Following this rhythm we are drawn first and foremost to the kinetic bullet, then the white all-seeing eye, followed by the explosion, and the promise of victory/revenge over the police forces, who are responsible for the attacks of protesters during the months of the social outburst. The bullet seems to be ingrained in the eye of the embroidery and even though it is not actively penetrating it, the idea of the red surrounding the eye is that of a mutilated one. This can be used to communicate that this is not (only) a

Figure 12.2 *Sus fusiles caerán.* Author: @desbordada.

political problem, but a physical experience of human pain too. While the injury is experienced individually, the outward expansive shape reminds us of the collective trauma. Additionally, the black background provides the funerary tone for the image, whereas the words that are stitched around it serve as a premonition that mimics the *y va a caer* ("and it will fall") chant that was popularly sung during Pinochet's dictatorship.

From the words inscribed in this piece, we interpret it as a creation with the purpose of denouncing the Chilean government's violence, through the abusive use of police forces against unarmed civilians who protested during the estallido. Amongst the many atrocities committed against the Chilean people, the most vicious one was the blinding (partial or complete) of protesters with the use of *perdigones* (small lead pellets). Among the 172 eye trauma and severe injuries, one instance of severe police violence was the blinding of Gustavo Gatica, a young man who was shot blind by police forces while he was protesting on November 8, 2019. Yet again, the movement acted as a collective in its calling for public justice, and images of eyes were heavily used as a symbol.

The embroidered phrase *sus fusiles caerán/y la calle triunfará*, can be separated in two parts. The first part, *sus fusiles caerán* (their rifles will fall) refers to the fall of the military/police, particularly, of their ability to shoot citizens, represented by the word fusil and the bullet image.

In this section, by eliding the agent "the police," the phrase removes the social actor, "their," which diminishes their importance and their agency, providing a message that de-centers them and their ability to act. The mention of an object (rifle) instead of an action (shooting), increases the passivity, as objects are considered passive by definition. Thus, instead of saying, "The police will stop shooting," the author constructs a text that acts, removing the social actor's agency. This is another example of objectivation by metonymical reference (van Leeuwen, 2008, 2015), where the word *rifle* is a metonymic representation that signals the police as a whole: *pars pro toto*, a part that encompasses and represents the whole of a violent and deadly institution. There is also an unnamed force, responsible for the falling (*caerán*). In its ambiguity, the message provides a reflection of who would make the police fall, or how it would happen. As an abstract entity, the fall is inevitable. Importantly, the omission of the citizens/people/social movement as responsible from the falling can be a rejection of the claims made by right wing politicians and activists that accused the protesters of being violent. Some of those claims even blamed the protesters for the police brutality, for instance, saying that they were inciting violence. The embroidered message rejects that interpretation suggesting an inescapable outcome or destiny. In addition, the word *triunfará* (will triumph) suggests that a struggle is developing. It is the rifle against the street, referring to the mobilized citizens that have occupied the main avenues of the country.

Bordados ▪ **283**

In the second part of the phrase (*y la calle triunfará*), objectivation (van Leeuwen, 2008, 2015) occurs by the embodiment of the people who inhabit this public space through protests in the word *calle* (street). *La calle* is therefore a mass of people, acting together as a whole, which also means that we can refer to this image as an act of collectivization (van Leeuwen, 2008). In other words, objectivization works as a mechanism to democratically present a heterogeneous collective voice in a way that kneads together subjective realities and positions into a unified will.

In addition, despite Santiago's reputation as the epicenter of the thriving neoliberal economy, la calle remains a contested space where people publicly demonstrate their grievances, and police are the guardians of the symbols of economic prosperity and normality in the streets. The street is then a symbol of the people and its will, in opposition to the political parties. This opposition is an often used figure of speech for Chileans. Politicians that lack the ability to understand the needs of the people are described as *les falta calle* (lacking street smartness). The phrase "the street will triumph," can be interpreted as the will of the people will take precedence, their needs and dreams will dominate and overcome the military in force and power. The whole message communicates resistance and resilience. Despite the pain and the violence, people will persevere and prevail.

Figure 12.3 is a round embroidery that, unlike the other two images, speaks mainly from its geographic placement. The image combines the

Figure 12.3 *Vivir en Chile vale un ojo de la cara.* Author: @mem.ita.

embroidery with a landscape in the background, which is an easily recognizable place in Arica, a city located in the northernmost point of the country. The background of the picture that encompasses the embroidery is an icon of the city, *el Morro*, a rock formation known to be a national symbol after the Pacific war between Chile and the Peruvian–Bolivian alliance, where Arica was ceded to Chilean territory. *El Morro* is known as a patriotic symbol, which creates a juxtaposition with the message contained within the embroidery; the image of an open eye that bleeds a blue tear which, in itself, resembles the geographic shape of the country. Color plays an important symbolic role as well. Blue, red, and white are the national flag colors; however, the national flag, always atop of the Morro as a signal that this is the point of entry to Chile's territory, is left out of the image.

Underneath the image, the words *Vivir en Chile vale un ojo de la cara* are an important part of the message. Roughly translated, this can be understood as the English equivalent of "To live in Chile costs an arm and a leg"; however, the idiom in Spanish is "... it costs an eye." The first portion of the sentence, Vivir en Chile, is written in a font that reminds us of the aesthetics of tourist advertising and souvenirs, as if it was inviting people to visit the country. One of the intentions of the author of this embroidery was precisely that one of an invitation, considering that Arica has historically been a hotspot of cultural and commercial exchange. However, by utilizing CDA as we do so here, we have noticed that an invitation that relates to physical violence can be both an invitation and a warning. Furthermore, the expression "vale un ojo de la cara" is used figuratively to convey a double meaning: to say something is really expensive, while literally alluding to the aftermath of police brutality during el estallido—the eye injuries of the social protest. Thus, the caution is that to live in Chile is both impossible to afford and a physical risk.

The content of Figures 12.1 and 12.2 is present in this image; it is alluding to the socioeconomic policies that provoked el estallido (30 pesos), and the injuries perpetrated by the police against the protesters (eye injury).

Through locating the image in a particular landscape, the post serves as a statement that the system's socioeconomic violence and police brutality expand beyond the capital city, Santiago, affecting all of its people's possibilities to live in a sustainable and dignifying way. This sort of mapping can also be interpreted under van Leeuwen's (2015) idea of association, a way of grouping social actors through an action, in this case "to live in Chile." In other words, considering that those of us who can be grouped by the act of Vivir en Chile are being grouped as a national category: Chileans. With this association movement, this image can also be interpreted as a cautionary message to those who do not live in Chile, as it was suggested above. In that line, the author of this post chooses to show a particular location. Following van Leeuwen (2008), the use of spaces and places also conveys a message.

Known for its value as a border city with Argentina, Peru, and Bolivia, Arica functions as the gateway through which people enter the country and through which the reader is made witness to an undeniable situation, instead of being blindly welcomed.

LAST STITCHES: CONCLUSION

In this chapter, we focused on embroidery as a feminist and collective practice of memory, imagery, and political denunciation through the use of multimodal meaning making and social media networks. We highlighted that the presentation of embroidery pieces through social media communicates nuanced social readings and recontextualization of socioeconomic injustice and police violence, and political legitimation of social protest in Chile. In this sense, we understand embroidery in intimate connection to the word "text" and its connection with textiles. In this imaginary, every thread can be understood as a line of discourse, and the act of combining said threads, the knitting (tejido) that comes out of it is the overall message in all of its complexity and richness. However, unlike an old medieval tapestry that tells a story of a battle, the estallido embroideries made by these Chilean women tell a story from a point of view that does not long for an epic remembrance, but that wishes to leave a mark in the archives in order to prevent oblivion. This is one of the main reasons humans tell stories: to educate, entertain, write counter-narratives of historical events, retell and examine said historical events through an educative lens. In this particular case, embroidery becomes an educative space in two moments. First, artists contextualize abstract concepts through material and shared references. For instance, a relatable protest sign to explain people's shared outrage was "*Son tantas cosas que ya no se qué poner*" (There are so many things I no longer know what to write). As a form of public pedagogy, female artists drew on their own experiences, generational consciousness, and beyond words, politicized and legitimized a shared experience for themselves and the audience. Second, artists created valuable artifacts that were generating public (online and offline) spaces of historical and political dialogue. Embroidery pieces invite educational audiences to elaborate their own interpretations and sensemaking, and examine their own experiences and positionalities in the matrix of naturalized neoliberal and capitalistic abuse and dispossession, as a transnational phenomenon.

Third, as historical multimodal artifacts, the events of October 2019 are portrayed in a wealth of symbols, multisemiotic resources, on social media, and as family's artifacts. These embroidery artifacts support intergenerational consciousness and voices, as generations to come will engage with these contextual pieces that foster and nurture historical, contextual, and sociopolitical knowledge, as we did with our ancestors' stories and memories of violence, torture, and resistance during colonization and dictatorships across the Global South. Lastly, embroidery pieces evidence language and communication nature as socially mediated processes that gather rich semiotic resources afforded by social, historical, and cultural context. Therefore, multimodality is a rich method to display translanguaging practices, knowledge production, students' linguistic autonomy, and culturally sustaining pedagogies across disciplines.

We also aimed to legitimize the activity of embroidery as a political one. While in the northern hemisphere, textile-related activities are considered harmless and domestic, and only recently recognized as useful for political activism (Kelly, 2014), in Latin America, the history, use, techniques and types of textiles, and its current use across the continent for political purposes, questions the suitability of the analytical frameworks developed in the north (Sanchez-Aldana et al., 2019). The lack of systematic studies that describe the use of textiles for activist purposes in Latin America (Sanchez-Aldana et al., 2019) opens the door to the possibility of Latin American embroidery as an activity connected to political purposes. In other words, it completely challenges the idea of embroidery as an a-political, domestic, and private activity, since that conception starts in the practices of the global north, and offers a new perspective that is geographically, historically, and politically located in the Latin American context. This chapter is oriented to contribute to that new perspective, although much more research is still needed to unveil the circumstances, political significance, and explore the material means that have grounded textile activities as political practices in Latin American context.

Throughout this chapter, we show that recontextualization is a practice of resignification, in the sense where meaning making can become a concrete expression for an otherwise silenced or unheard community. In other words, the unspeakable experience of social turmoil lived through the estallido is conveyed and shared with the wider community through embroidering, and this means that embroideries function as living artifacts that are capable of containing (in a sense of "holding" too) a loaded message. This concrete practice of making "the unspeakable speak" is not new. We have mentioned that it dates back to precolonial ways of communication, and how it has been historically linked to a feminine practice; therefore, there is added value in choosing embroidery to tell a message. Of all the ways information circulated denouncing the aftermaths of el estallido, embroideries are a unique combination of visual images and written text because they add to a sense of genealogy. Specifically, by communicating the ineffable, embroideries of el estallido are reconnecting to a different type of collective archive, one that had to be built outside of the borders of government and institutionality in order to survive.

In the historical and sociopolitical background of this chapter, we mention the role of Chilean high school and university students as active social agents. In this pursuit of justice and equity, students have remained loud, public, and organized, while creating massive critical awareness of systemic segregation and exploitation before and after Pinochet's dictatorship. As social actors, they engage in mutual and public *conscientização* (conscientization) in re-imagining and shaping an equitable education and just society. Following this notion of conscientização by the pedagogue Paulo Freire (1970/2000) throughout the work, we engaged in relational and dialogic conscientization and positioned ourselves as knowers and learners. In this sense, as scholars, we brought our individual readings and analysis of the images into group meetings. With surprise, we learned that despite having many similar experiences as Chileans and philosophical stances, we had quite unique artifact analysis. We realized that we were learning from each other and guiding each other by shuttling into untraded analytical paths, while merging our individual embroidery examinations. This collective experience illuminates the multisemiotic wealth and the relational and dialogic nature embedded in historically and sociopolitically grounded embroidery art pieces, as it draws from viewers' socially grounded biographies and lived experiences. In a similar way, we sought to guide readers into the multisemiotic wealth and potential of these three embroidery pieces. We also hope to invite educators across disciplines to integrate multimodal resources such as embroidery pieces into their classroom and delve deeper into historical, cultural, and sociopolitical nuances related to equity and marginalization embedded in activist art creations as a social practice of collective memory, social denunciation, and social resignification at the local and global levels.

Finally, from an analytical standpoint, we understand embroidery as a complex activity and as a multimodal form of discourse. As such, we believe that its analysis supersedes only one disciplinary field. On the contrary, it requires cooperation among different fields that can contribute to a complex understanding. We, the authors of this chapter, had the need to put aside our limited disciplinary backgrounds to develop a wider one, combining our knowledge and expertise to nourish the interpretations and analysis. We adopted a shared vocabulary, developed a collective style of writing, and embraced multivoicedness to create a piece that is not framed in any singular discipline. Our experience writing this chapter makes us believe that analytical practices that advance beyond modern disciplinary distinctions and encourage transdisciplinary approaches are highly fruitful for enriched, humanizing, and novel knowledge production and dissemination.

REFERENCES

Ascher, M., & Ascher, R. (1975). The quipu as a visible language. *Visible Language*, 9(4), 329-356. https://www.proquest.com/openview/38e9069efe810df0be65 5e6fdd2fa21c/1?pq-origsite=gscholar&cbl=1821103

Bellei, C., & Cabalin, C. (2013). Chilean student movements: Sustained struggle to transform a tarket-oriented educational system. *Current Issues in Comparative Education*, 15(2), 108–123. https://www.tc.columbia.edu/cice/pdf/28175_15 _02_Bellei_Cabalin.pdf

Bellei, C., Cabalin, C., & Orellana, V. (2014). The 2011 Chilean student movement against neoliberal educational policies. *Studies in Higher Education*, 39(3), 426–440. https://doi.org/10.1080/03075079.2014.896179

Berstein, B. (1990). *The structuring of pedagogic discourse*. Routledge.

Cabalin, C. (2012). Neoliberal education and student movements in Chile: Inequalities and malaise. *Policy Futures in Education*, 10(2), 219–228. https:// doi.org/10.2304/pfie.2012.10.2.219

Cecchini, S., & Martinez, R. (2011). *Protección social inclusiva en América Latina: Una mirada integral, un enfoque de derechos* [Inclusive social protection in Latin America: A comprehensive look, a rights-based approach]. CEPAL.

Chomsky, N. (1999). *Profit over people: Neoliberalism and global order*. Seven Stories Press.

Dockemdorff, E., Rodríguez, A., & Winchester, L. (2000). Santiago de Chile: Metropolization, globalization and inequity. *Environment and Urbanization*, 12(1), 171–183. https://doi.org/10.1177/095624780001200112

Fairclough, N. (2012). Critical discourse analysis. In J. P. Gee & M. Handford (Eds.), *The Routledge handbook of discourse analysis* (pp. 9–20). Routledge.

Fraser, B. (2019). Violent protests in Chile linked to health-care inequities. *Lancet*, 394(10210), 1697–1698. https://doi.org/10.1016/S0140-6736(19)32720-5

Freire, P. (2000). *Pedagogy of the oppressed* (30th anniversary ed.). Continuum. (Original work published 1970)

Grugel, J., & Nem Singh, J. (2015). Protest, citizenship and democratic renewal: The student movement in Chile. *Citizenship Studies*, 19(3–4), 353–366. https://doi .org/10.1080/13621025.2015.1006172

Halliday, M. A. K. (1978). *Language as social semiotic: The social interpretation of language and meaning*. Edward Arnold.

Harvey, D. (2007). *A brief history of neoliberalism*. Oxford University Press.

Instituto Nacional de Derechos Humanos. (2021, February 2). *Informe de seguimiento recomendaciones: Primer informe de seguimiento de las recomendaciones del INDH en su informe anual 2019*. https://www.indh.cl/bb/wp-content/uploads/2021/02/Primer-Informe-de-Seguimiento-de-Recomendaciones.pdf

Inzunza, J., Assael, J., Cornejo, R., & Redondo, J. (2019). Public education and student movements: The Chilean rebellion under a neoliberal experiment. *British Journal of Sociology of Education*, 40(4), 490–506. https://doi.org/10.1080/ 01425692.2019.1590179

Kelly, M. (2014). Knitting as a feminist project? *Women's Studies International Forum*, 44(1), 133–144. https://doi.org/10.1016/j.wsif.2013.10.011

Lazar, M. M. (Ed.). (2005). *Feminist critical discourse analysis: Gender, power and ideology in discourse*. Palgrave Macmillan US.

Ludmer, J. (1985). Las tretas del débil [The tricks of the weak]. In *La Sartén por el Mango* [The frying pan for the mango]. Ediciones Huracán.

Ochoa Ávalos, M. C. (2018). Mujeres bordando la política: Certidumbres e incertidumbres de una tragedia [Women embroidering politics: Certainties and uncertainties of a tragedy]. In C. I. Castellano González & M. C. Ochoa Ávalos (Eds.), *Feminismos Visuales* [Visual feminisms] (pp. 55–73). Universidad de Guadalajara.

Oliva, M. A. (2010). Política educativa chilena 1965–2009. ¿Qué oculta esta trama? *Revista Brasileira de Educação*, *15*(44), 311–328. https://www.redalyc.org/pdf/275/27518764008.pdf

Osorio, C. (2014). *La difusión de programas de transferencia condicionada en América Latina 1990–2010* (The dissemination of conditioned transfer programs in Latin America 1990–2010) [Unpublished doctoral thesis]. Universidad Pompeu Fabra. https://www.tdx.cat/handle/10803/286738

Ossul-Vermehren, I., & Pacheco, M. I. (Eds.). (in press). *Resistencia Textil: Luchas feministas en Chile contemporáneo* [Textile resistance: Feminist struggles in contemporary Chile]. https://www.resistenciatextil.org

Pérez-Bustos, T. (2019). ¿Puede el bordado (des)tejer la etnografía? [Can embroidery (un)weave ethnography?]. *Disparidades. Revista de Antropología*, *74*(1), 002. https://doi.org/10.3989/dra.2019.01.002.04

Pérez-Bustos, T., Tobar-Roa, V., & Márquez-Gutiérrez, S. (2016). Etnografías de los contactos. Reflexiones feministas sobre el bordado como conocimiento [Ethnographies of contacts. Feminist reflections on embroidery as knowledge]. *Antípoda. Revista de Antropología y Arqueología*, *26*, 47–66. https://doi.org/10.7440/antipoda26.2016.02

Rivera Cusicanqui, S. (2010). *Ch'ixinakax utxiwa. Una reflexión sobre prácticas y discursos descolonizadores* [Ch'ixinakax utxiwa. On decolonising practices and discourses]. Tinta limón.

Sánchez-Aldana, E., Pérez-Bustos, T., & Chocontá-Piraquive, A. (2019). ¿Qué son los activismos textiles? Una mirada desde los estudios feministas a catorce casos bogotanos [What are textile activisms? A look from feminist studies to fourteen Bogota cases]. *Athenea Digital*, *19*(3), 1–24. https://doi.org/10.5565/rev/athenea.2407

Shayne, J. (2009). *They used to call us witches: Chilean exiles, culture, and feminism*. Lexington Books.

Stromquist, N. P., & Sanyal, A. (2013). Student resistance to neoliberalism in Chile. *International Studies in Sociology of Education*, *23*(2), 152–178. https://doi.org/10.1080/09620214.2013.790662

van Leeuwen, T. (2008). *Discourse and practice: New tools for critical discourse analysis*. Oxford University Press.

van Leeuwen, T. (2015). Multimodality. In D. Tannen, H. E. Hamilton, & D. Schiffrin. (Eds.), *The handbook of discourse analysis* (pp. 447–465). John Wiley & Sons.

Williams, J. (2015). Remaking education from below: The Chilean student movement as public pedagogy. *Australian Journal of Adult Learning*, *55*(3), 496. https://files.eric.ed.gov/fulltext/EJ1082528.pdf

Wodak, R., & Meyer, M. (2001). *Methods of critical discourse analysis*. SAGE Publications.

CHAPTER 13

POST-IT, MILK TEA, AND MINI-STONEHENGE

Making Sense of the Multimodality of Protest Artifacts in 2019–2020 Hong Kong Protest Movement

Jason Man-Bo Ho
National Pingtung University

ABSTRACT

This chapter discusses the multimodality of protest artifacts used in the anti-extradition bill movement in Hong Kong in 2019–2020, including Post-it notes, images, graffiti, and other means that filled the streets, shopping malls, and social media. Using social semiotics frameworks, this chapter would argue that these artifacts demonstrate the promising potential of multimodality in drawing popular culture, and linguistic and nonlinguistic resources to create new meanings in sustaining and advocating for social movements. The chapter would end by arguing that it is the responsibility of educators to understand the role multimodality plays in social action that affects everyone on a daily basis.

> *The world of meaning has always been multimodal.*
> —Kress (2010, p. 173).

The Anti-Extradition Law Amendment Bill (Anti-ELAB) protest in Hong Kong since mid-2019 that snowballed into a large-scale pro-democracy social movement has resulted in, among other things, neologisms like "freedom hi" and "popo." In this chapter, I explore how "protest artifacts" manifested in multimodal forms, which include artful expressions and creativity as displayed in slogans, graffiti, miniature road blockades, and street objects, among others, in the protest movement in the territory during 2019–2020.

Studies and reports on the protest literacy practices in Hong Kong in recent years have started to emerge in academic publications. Patsiaouras and his colleagues (Patsiaouras & Veneti, 2017; Patsiaouras et al., 2018) conducted ethnographic studies on the 2014 Umbrella Movement, a 79-day-long Occupy movement demanding more transparent and true universal suffrage in 2014. In their studies, Patsiaouras et al. (Patsiaouras & Veneti, 2017; Patsiaouras et al., 2018) discussed the role political art installments played in occupied protest camps in the territory. Lee and Chan (2018) discussed the use of digital media as a connective action that supported and sustained the 2014 movement. A report by a former Royal Hong Kong police officer, Martin Purbrick (2019), documented how the early development of the protest movement in 2019 was facilitated. Pubrick (2019) also discussed the role digital communication platforms like LIHKG—a forum website equivalent to Reddit—played in becoming channels for protesters mainly composed of young people and students to discuss, gain following, and exchange information. Lee et al. (2021) discusses the role such digital platforms played in social mobilization in the same protest movement.

In this chapter, I argue that the emergence of protest signs, art, slogans, and more from the Hong Kong protest movements have given birth to a new "social language" that involves new literacy and discursive social practices (Gee, 2015). Through applying social semiotics in our analysis of the protest artifacts, I show how this particular type of social language enriches our understanding of the meaning making and our analysis of embedded social, cultural, and political messages. Before discussing relevant social semiotics concepts, multimodal data analysis, and findings, I share my positioning and why these protest artifacts were chosen for semiotic investigation.

My Position as a Pedestrian-Observer and Critical Educator

Born into a generation of Hong Kongers who witnessed the 1989 Tiananmen crackdown, I experienced my first baptism in political awareness when I was a teenager. The 2014 Umbrella Movement has been the second awakening of my sense of national and political identity as a Hong Kong Chinese. My interest in protest artifacts began in the Umbrella Movement when I saw boundless creativity shown by mostly young people in the collective production of artwork like origami, installation arts, Hong Kong Lennon Walls, and chalk paintings on the walls and grounds in occupied camps, as described by Patsiaouras et al. (2018).

My interest in protest texts was more a result of the surprising creativity shown by protesters. In early June, when large-scale marches broke out, widely reported footage of a policeman shouting an offensive "自由閪" (*zi yau hai*) in Cantonese (meaning "freedom cunt")—which is the language of the majority of the local Hong Kong Chinese—went viral on online news platforms and social media. The insult was quickly turned into "自由 hi" (*zi yau hi*), meaning "freedom hi" ("hi" being a pun that sounds close to "cunt") by protesters, which soon appeared in other slogans, banners, and even tee shirts. As an educator hearing the profanity in the local protest, I first felt offended, and as a gay man, I was reluctant to accept the use of the derogatory term describing the female genitalia from the mouth of a public servant. At the same time, I was impressed by the creativity demonstrated in reclaiming a derogatory term and turning it into a positive signifier to refer to fellow demonstrators. These are the reasons I began investigating scholarly work on protest artifacts as a literacy practice.

Protest Artifacts, Protest Literacies, and Critical Pedagogy

Recent years have witnessed growing interest in discourse analysis of artifacts used in or for protest and social activism. Several studies have been published on a variety of protest artifacts, including those using metaphors (Refaie, 2009), swear words (Cook, 2013; Kaye & Sapolsky, 2009), multilingual protest signs used in African countries (Kasanga, 2014), and cartoons (Ndi, 2017; Elnakkouzi, 2019) among other literacy phenomena as social practices associated with war and social movements. Discussion about the multimodality of these protest artifacts was not commonly found in academic journals or publications over the past decade.

Some researchers, however, have more recently turned their attention to the multimodal aspects of protest artifacts. Patsiaouras and Veneti (2017) argue that the artistic creativity and co-creation shown in protest artifacts are successful in simplifying complicated political ideas and emotionally connecting with people about ideas like freedom and democracy. Patsiaouras et al. (2018) point out that the use of multimodal protest artwork was part of the marketing strategies used in the 2014 Umbrella Movement. Hart (2019) published a study on the media representations of multimodal metaphors of the Miners' Strike in the United Kingdom in the mid-1980s. T. V. Reed's (2019) book, *The Art of Protest*, on the variety of art forms used in (mostly) American civil rights movements inspired me in my journey into the protest art that flourished in my local context when the protest broke out in 2019.

In his most recent book, Duncan (2021) considers *protest literacies* as literacy events. He writes that "protest literacies" associated with protest and social movements comprise "campaigning literacies, memorial literacies, media-activist literacies, arts-activist literacies, and demonstration literacies" (p. 228). Duncan is not the first author to take a literacies standpoint to view protest movements. In the past decade, language educators and educational researchers have increasingly explored activist literacies in language and literacy education. Simon and Campano (2013) examine teacher research as resistance, Humphrey (2013) explores empowering adolescents through activist literacies, and Montero et al. (2013) examines activist literacies and aboriginality. Similarly, Kynard (2013) discusses how Black students' literacies and activism influenced tertiary institutions in the United States a century ago. Recently, other writers address movements against racial injustice, including Richardson and Ragland's (2018) examination of the role of language and literacy practices in the recent Black Lives Matter movement. Muhammad (2019), who prefers calling it *agitation literacies* instead of activist literacies, calls for the need for youth to engage with texts as a way to begin to address racial inequality.

Whilst Duncan's (2021) conceptualization of protest literacies is highly original and comprehensive in his consideration of various aspects of protest literacy events, a study on protest artifacts would be interesting if we consider the social semiotic approach to understanding the meaning possibilities involved in such literacy events. Additionally, a study of protest artifacts has pedagogical potential, especially from a critical literacy standpoint, as protest artifacts could be construed as community texts to be studied (Luke et al., 1994). Other studies support this critical pedagogical study of similar, publicly available artifacts as community texts. Reporting on her English language teaching (ELT) classroom study on engaging students in the discussion of gender bias in advertisements and critical analysis of Umbrella Movement signs, Chun (2019) calls for the further exploration of the potential of critical pedagogy creating a class space safe for students to examine "their possibilities and potentialities in working for great social justice goals" (p. 94). As an LGBT-identified person, I deeply understand how it feels for my voice to be silenced, my identity ignored, and my civil rights denied, in an unjust political system. Just like homosexuality was and still can be a banned topic in the educational curricula in many countries, political topics are often ones restricted by governments. For example, at the time of writing, there is an intense debate on the British education authority's "guidance" to restrict critical discussion of political topics like the imperial history of the British empire, political leaders like Winston Churchill, and the Black Lives Matter movement (Adams, 2022).

As American educator and pedagogue Noddings (2005) argues that many teachers only focus on curricula, instruction, and classroom management. However, if educators do not care what issues students are concerned about (in this case, local youths' concern about their civil rights, including their political rights, freedom of expression, freedom of speech, freedom from brutality, etc.), then students may not be prepared to engage in critical discussion of issues like imperialism, racism, gender and sexual injustice, and civil rights issues in the future. By exploring social justice issues through discussing protest artifacts pedagogically, students may both understand how protest artifacts convey ideologies and shared human rights through multimodal meaning making as well as develop and exercise critical thinking and creativity in addressing and working toward solutions involving matters of social justice.

THEORETICAL FRAMEWORK: SOCIAL SEMIOTICS AND MULTIMODALITY

This chapter aims at tackling this question: "How do we make sense of the multimodal protest artifacts from the 2019–2020 Hong Kong protest movement using social semiotics?" It focuses on the use of social semiotics and multimodality, specifically borrowing concepts by Kress, Van Leeuwen, and other theorists to understand the multimodal meanings of protest artifacts. I draw on the concepts of texts, signs, semiotics resources, contexts, framing, and others to determine the meanings of the wide array of promotional literature and artwork that emerged from and for the Hong Kong protests that started in 2019. In addition, Blommaert's (2015, 2019, 2020) idea of chronotype (timespace) will also be employed in my analysis.

Social Semiotics: Key Concepts

Social semiotics arises from the disciplines of semiotics, Halliday's systemic functional linguistics (SFL) and critical discourse analysis; it is a theory that helps us understand meaning making in human communication (Jewitt et al., 2016). I will highlight the role of *text* (composed of semiotic resources including *sign* and *mode*), *meaning*, *user* (signmaker/author, viewer/reader/receiver), and *context* in our understanding of protest artifacts.

The social semiotics approach in my inquiry of protest artifacts provides a framework that aims to achieve three goals:

1. collect, document, and systematically catalog semiotic resources—including their history;
2. investigate how these resources are used in specific historical, cultural, and institutional contexts, and how people talk about them in these contexts—plan them, teach them, justify them, critique them, and so forth;
3. contribute to the discovery and development of new semiotic resources and new uses of existing semiotic resources (van Leeuwen, 2005, p. 3, as cited by Djonov & Zhao [2018]).

Semiotic resources can be understood as things and acts we use to make meanings in particular social contexts. van Leeuwen's (2005) view of semiotic resources is particularly useful in understanding the meaning possibilities of protest artifacts, which are all dependent upon specific social contexts in which the semiotic resources are used. Collecting and investigating the multifarious protest artifacts that were churned out from the protest movement in Hong Kong can contribute to our understanding of the evolving use of semiotic resources, both "existing" and "new," in protest movements amid turbulent social, cultural, political instability in many countries and regions in recent years.

The past 4 decades of literature in social semiotics have built up a rich glossary of concepts in related disciplines. In this chapter, I focus on seven main elements: context, mode, genre, text, sign, audience, and action. Figure 13.1 is a visual diagram demonstrating these elements on three planes, drawing on Blommaert's (2015, 2019, 2020) concept of "chronotopic context" and the three Hallidayan metafunctions of language: the contextual plane (concerning the social, cultural, political, and temporal-spatial contexts), textual-ideational plane (concerning the textual and semantic meanings), and interpersonal plane (concerning the sign makers and audience).

Below are brief descriptions of seven key concepts important to my data analysis of protest artifacts drawing on key social semiotics theorists.

Context

Context, usually described as "social context" and what I will call *context with a big-C*, has often been criticized in social semiotics as being too elusive and failing to provide specificity of a given situation (Blommaert, 2019; Selander, 2017). Context with a big-C refers to the social, cultural, political background against which a semiotic sign is to be understood, whereas *context with a small-c* refers to Blommaert's (2019) notion of "chronotope" or "chronotopic context." The Bakhtinian concept of *chronotope* refers to the specific constellations of timespace in which people with specific identities do specific things (Blommaert, 2015, 2019, 2020).

Chronotope influences the way the audience responds in specific situations when they follow the "moralized behavioral scripts" (Blommaert, 2019, pp. 22–23; see action for elaboration of such behavioral response).

Mode

Modes refers to the social and cultural resources we use to convey meanings (e.g., images, layout, sounds; Kress, 2009).

Genre

A *genre* is defined as a text type with its own particular structure to achieve goals in communication, for instance, to persuade others to do things (van Leeuwen, 2005). Borrowing Matthiessen's fields of communicative activity, Andersen et al. (2015) list seven broad categories of the goals of the communicative events: to expound, to report, to recreate, to share, to do, to enable, to recommend, to explore.

Text

Text is a semiotic entity which is perceived to be complete by the receiver/audience (Kress, 2010). It can be written, audible, or in other forms like drawings, photographs, and games (Selander, 2017). Text is made up of sign(s).

Sign

Signs are units of meaning in which *the signified* is the thing to be meant, signified by *the signifier*, which is something that means it (Kress, 2010). Signs take the center stage in social semiotics. Together with genre, signs help us to recognize the "situations and actions within which the meanings are mobilized" (Bazerman, 2012, p. 227). All signs are metaphorical and encode the ideological positions of the sign maker (Kress, 1993).

Audience

The receiver (i.e., the reader, viewer, consumer, or audience; Kress, 2010) of the text. Some examples of audiences from this research include pedestrians, civilians, protesters, drivers, Netizens, and so on.

Action

The *action* is the behavior, reaction, and response that the audience is motivated to take after interpreting a sign. For example, an audience can act to understand, be informed, accept, share, or to otherwise act upon their interpreted meaning. Note that the action as interpreted by the audience may not be identical to the action intended by the sign maker (even if the latter is identifiable).

CONTEXT OF THE STUDY

Research Design and Questions

The research presented in this chapter was analyzed using a social semiotics analytical approach because of its focus on the representation of multimodal artifacts, as suggested by Jewitt et al. (2016). The empirical focus of my research is on the representation of signs and modes in the meaning making of protest artifacts. With protest artifacts as my research area with a focus on the topic of multimodal meaning making, I have broken down the main research question—"How do we make sense of the multimodal protest artifacts from the 2019–2020 Hong Kong protest movement?"—into three sub-questions:

1. How do the protest artifacts make meanings on the contextual plane?
2. How do protest artifacts make meanings on the textual-ideational plane?
3. How do protest artifacts make meanings on the interpersonal plane?

Data Collection and Criteria for Inclusion

During the period between June 2019 and August 2020, I collected over 500 images of protest artifacts like Post-it notes, posters, and graffiti that I photographed or screenshotted on my personal social media platforms (e.g., Facebook, Instagram, Telegram). I considered these community texts as my objects of study (Luke et al., 1994). These protest artifacts appeared in a variety of locations both (geographical and virtual), as well as forms (modes and media). Additionally, these protest artifacts continued some of the literacy practices prominent in the 2014 Umbrella Movement that were mainly found at the three Occupy camps (i.e., Admiralty, Causeway Bay, and Mongkok; Patsiaouras et al., 2018).

As a researcher who considered myself to be a cultural geographer in this study, I set limitations on the types of artifacts I collected. The selection criteria for the artifacts to be presented in this chapter are that they must be

1. displayed in public spaces like streets, shopping malls, highways, and virtual social media spaces or communication apps such as Facebook, Twitter, and Telegram;
2. accessible by the public for free;
3. displayed and found during the period of June 2019 and August 2020 when major protest activities took place;

4. able to be recorded as still images (e.g., taken by camera; screen-capped by mobile phone, including posters, a picture of a part of wall or shop window, graffiti, road signs, logo plates of public transport, street objects, etc.); and
5. able to allow me to record the data relating to the domains of semiotic practices—discourse and distribution (defined below).

Kress (2010) and Kress and van Leeuwen (2001) indicate there are four semiotic domains: discourse, distribution, design, and production. In this study, I use discourse and distribution analytically. *Discourse* is information about the sign, mode, and medium of the protest artifact.

Distribution is information about the time and location that the protest artifact was distributed and seen. The information about the actual processes of design and production was beyond the scope of my study. The rationale behind using these criteria is that the artifacts being considered for analysis are "community texts" where the general public could gain exposure to them. A temporal and spatial boundary had to be set to consider textual and contextual factors regarding the meaning possibilities of protest artifacts in a manageable manner.

Take Figure 13.2 as an example. I spotted the paint-sprayed graffiti on the MTR Corp, the partially government-owned train company, in mid-October 2019 in a tunnel outside a MTR station. There, pedestrians like me could walk through any time of the day. The picture of the graffiti was taken on my mobile phone, which allows me to see the image and its relevant information such as the date (October 10, 2019) and geographical location when and where the photo was taken (Ngau Tau Kok Station). This information was stored on my phone, and its cloud platform allowed me to retrieve it for data analysis. However, in this study, I do not include artifacts like documentaries, movies, and commercialized comic books because they are neither accessible for free nor necessarily accessible by the public. For instance, *The Fallen City*, a related nonfiction comic work by Liu (2020) which was published and on sale in July 2020, is not considered to be a suitable artifact in this study because it is not accessible by the public for free.

Regarding the selection of the artifacts in my study and in this chapter, it has to be pointed out that since my study does not attempt to present a comprehensive record of all types of protest artifacts; the artifacts shown in the following section only represent those that I believe to be appropriate and relevant to this chapter focusing on meaning making of the multimodality of protest artifacts relating to the three sub questions above. Readers should be reminded that my selection of illustrative examples presented unavoidably reflect my preferences and bias.[1]

Context	**Social context:** 2019 July 21 A large crowd of people in white clothes attack passengers arriving at Yuen Long MTR station from Kowloon or Hong Kong side where massive protests take place earlier that day. Police later claim they did not see anyone possessing offensive weapons, to the contrary of many photos that appear later in the media. MTR Corp, the railway company that owns and operates the railway networks in Hong Kong, delays the release of CCTV (surveillance) security footage from Yuen Long station. 2019 August 31 Anti-riot police enter Prince Edward MTR station after conflicts break out among anti- protesters. Passengers are seen brutally injured. Police ban media from entering the station. MTR Corp refuses to release full footage of CCTV recordings. Rumours about death resulting from the 8/31 incident spread. **Chronotope:** 2019 October 10. Outside Ngau Tau Kok MTR station.
Mode	Image—Spray-painted handwriting bus shelter boxes
Genre	Graffiti (to expound)
Text	
Sign	Material form (signifier): The Chinese radical "尸" spray-painted (in black) above the MTR logo on signpost to form a "shit" (屎) lookalike word. Meaning (signified): The MTR company is "shit" (or, disgusting).
Audience	Pedestrians
Possible Action(s)	To shun, or to boycott, MTR Corp.

Figure 13.2 A defaced MTR logo in Ngau Tau Kok. October 10, 2019. *Credit:* Author.

Data Analysis Procedures

I first used the seven social semiotics elements presented in the theoretical framework section (namely context, mode, genre, text, sign, audience, and action) to interpret the artifacts, broadly divided in three clusters. The first cluster of data related to the contextual plane provides the social context (e.g., events and background related to the artifact) as well as temporal and geographical information where the artifacts were collected and recorded. Mode, genre, text, and sign are grouped under the second cluster related to the textual-ideational plane on each table in the findings section. Audience and action in the third cluster address the interpersonal plane.

Then, I chose 30 out of over 500 collected artifacts for initial coding. Initial labels such as "Post-it," "graffiti," "street object," "road sign," "popular culture," "religion," "swear word," "yellow," "blue," "metaphor," "homophone," and "brick" were created in order to describe various aspects such as the mode, medium, content, and linguistic device used in the artifacts.

Contextual information like time and location was added to each artifact by retrieving such metadata from the cloud platform of my mobile phone. To decide the social context related to the artifacts, I referred to timelines in published works like Kong (2020), Haoqingnian Tudushi [Corrupt The Youth 好青年荼毒室] (2020), and Human Rights in China (https://www.hrichina.org/en) for events and incidents that may be of relevance to the texts and signs used in the artifacts. With the help of the contextual cues, I used the textual-ideational cues of the artifacts to make sense of the possible meaning(s) to the best of my knowledge of relevant semiotic resources. Finally, based on the contextual cues, I identified a probable intended audience and what action(s) the audience is mobilized to take after digesting the entirety of each multimodal protest artifact.

Due to space constraints, only 10 examples are presented in this book chapter. For the sake of clarity, I decided to present the findings using a table for each selected artifact specifying the contextual, textual-ideational, and interpersonal details of my analysis.

FINDINGS

In preparation of the presentation of these findings, it appeared to me that while all artifacts rely on all three contextual, textual-ideational, and interpersonal planes to support meaning making, different genres of artifacts seem to have a tendency to lean on one particular plane for the receiver to make sense of them. In the next section, I will present examples of three chosen genre of protest artifacts that seem to display such plane tendency (marked with the ">" symbol in brackets), including *Graffiti* (> the contextual plane);

Posters (> the textual-ideational plane); and *Built artifacts: Stonehenges, Post-its with Lennon Walls, Blank Lennon Walls* (> the interpersonal plane).

Graffiti (> The Contextual Plane)

Graffiti may have long been considered by some people or authorities a problem in cities (Fuller, 2005). The defacement of properties, be it the logo plates of public transport, tunnel walls, or signposts, has tended to be frowned upon by property owners and authorities responsible for maintaining public order. But graffiti can also be a form of self-expression (Valdez, 2007), artistic expression, and political statement (Awad et al., 2017). Figure 13.2 was captured in October. Perhaps the protest artifact had existed for weeks or months before I walked past the wall of the tunnel. Contextual clues are crucial for us to understand this artifact. Two incidents were possibly related to this artifact. On July 31, 2019, passengers were attacked by mobs at Yuen Long Station. Again, on August 31, 2019, passengers were indiscriminately attacked by the police in Prince Edward Station. MTR Corp initially refused to release comprehensive footage of surveillance camera recordings of both incidents. Protesters and citizens suspected a cover-up by the MTR company.

As for the textual clues, Figure 13.2 shows the defaced MTR logo with a Chinese radical "尸" sprayed (in black) above it to form another derogatory Chinese character "屎" (shit). By calling the company "shit," the sign maker called for people to boycott the public transport company.

The meaning potential of the road sign artifact in Figure 13.3 is highly metaphorical. The artifact was found on November 21, 2019. It was situated at the beginning section of a highway next to a pedestrian sidewalk in a residential area in Shatin. Considering the spatial element (i.e., the location) of the artifact, I assume that the intended audience could be drivers, pedestrians, protesters, or residents. On the textual level of the protest text, we only see the two spray-painted Chinese characters that mean "democracy" on a highway road sign. I can infer that one of the potential meanings of the text is that the sign cluster ("democracy" and the highway symbol) as a whole at the precinct (by the side of the road) denotes "the way/path to democracy."

Figures 13.4 and 13.5 show heavy "borrowing" of ideas from Western popular culture. Figure 13.4 was photographed in a street in Mongkok, near a regular protest site, on November 21, 2019. One contextual clue from only 2 weeks before the artifact was collected is that the slogan "Hong Kongers revenge" started to appear in social media and other graffiti after a university student was found falling from a multi-story parking complex on November 8, 2019. The death of the student was suspected by many protesters to be

Context	**Social context:** 2019 Nov 11-17 After the death of a university student, protesters occupy The Chinese University of Hong Kong, Hong Kong University, Baptist University, City University, and Hong Kong Polytechnic University. Police besiege all the campuses. Arrows, firebombs and objects are thrown at the police. Later, police retreat from CUHK after a weekend and arrest hundreds of demonstrators in PolyU. **Chronotope:** 2019 November 21. A road sign by a highway in Shatin.
Mode	Image—Spray-painted handwriting
Genre	Graffiti (to share)
Text	
Sign	Material form (signifier): Spray-painted "democracy" on the right bottom corner of a highway symbol on a road sign at the beginning of a highway. Meaning (signified): You/We are on the way to democracy
Audience	Drivers, pedestrians, protesters, residents
Possible Action(s)	To join protesters on the path to fight for democracy

Figure 13.3 Spray-painted "Democracy" on a highway road sign. Shatin. November 21, 2019. *Credit:* Author.

caused by law enforcement units who confronted the protestors nearby. The location where Figure 13.4 was taken, Mongkok, was also one of the protest sites where confrontations between protesters and police frequently took place in late 2019. Both signs were taken from the dystopian political action

Context	**Social context:** Same as Figure 13.3 **Chronotope:** 2019 November 21. A street in Mong Kok.
Mode	Image—Stencil-sprayed words and drawing on wall on a public utility construction
Genre	Graffiti (to share)
Text	 *[Image: Stencil-sprayed "IDEAS ARE BULLETPROOF" in black with a red "V" symbol in a circle]*
Sign	Material form (signifier): • Stencil-sprayed words "IDEAS ARE BULLETPROOF" in black • Spray-painted "V" symbol in red
	Meaning (signified): • Fights go on even after someone dies because ideas cannot be killed. • Vengeance
Audience	Pedestrians
Possible Action(s)	To take revenge, to resist

Figure 13.4 The Vendetta Graffiti in Mongkok. November 21, 2019. *Credit:* Author.

movie *V for Vendetta* released in 2005 (adapted from the original comic book under the same name published in 1989). It is not clear if the spray-painted "IDEAS ARE BULLETPROOF" slogan and Vendetta sign (a symbol from *V for Vendetta*) were made by the same graffiti artist(s). The meaning of vengeance in the artifact does not seem to be purely coincidental when I tried to make sense of the Vendetta-themed artifact.

I took the photo of Figure 13.5 under a bridge on the Shung Mun River in Shatin on November 21, 2019. On the other side of the river was The Chinese University. During November 11–17, 2019, the police brutally confronted protesters in the sieges of The Chinese University and a number of other tertiary institutions. The burning of objects by youth protesters and the firing of tear gas by the police in and outside university campuses were widely covered in the media for days. Figure 13.5 is another example of borrowing from a popular dystopian movie, *The Hunger Games* (Ross, 2012). *The Hunger Games* is a movie series adapted from the young adult fiction series under the same title. The catchy phrase "If we burn, you burn with

Context	**Social context:** Same as Figure 13.3 **Chronotope:** 2019 November 21. Under a bridge in Shatin.
Mode	Image—Spray-painted handwriting on tunnel wall
Genre	Graffiti (to share)
Text	
Sign	Material form (signifier): Sprayed words "If We Burn, You Burn With Us" in red
	Meaning (signified): Rebellion against authorities
Audience	Pedestrians
Possible action(s)	To rebel, to resist

Figure 13.5 *The Hunger Games* graffiti "If We Burn, You Burn With Us," spray-painted on a tunnel wall in Shatin. 2019 November 21. *Credit:* Author.

us" comes from the protagonist Katniss, who is a survivor-turned-fighter. The phrase in the movie reflects the fighting spirit displayed by Katniss in her rebellion against the elite class. Figure 13.5 features the same red color of the Vendetta sign in Figure 13.4. On the textual-ideational plane, red may represent the color of blood, of vengeance. The vengeance themes can be easily inferred from Figures 13.4 and 13.5 to the sieges of university campuses in mid-November. Thus, the temporal and geographical proximity sends a strong message to the pedestrians about the revengeful and resistant attitudes young protesters have towards the armed force.

From analysis of Figures 13.2 through 13.5, we can see that while multimodal details on all contextual, textual-ideational, and interpersonal planes contribute to the meanings conveyed through the protest artifacts, contextual cues related to social context and chronotopic context, including time and geographical locations where the graffitis were made and subsequently found (i.e., near public transport facilities, constructions, or protest sites), played a big role in enabling the audience (i.e., me as cultural geographer) to understand the signified meaning and the intended action(s), whether to convince them to join and support the cause or to encourage each other in the movement.

Posters (> The Textual-Ideational Plane)

Unlike graffiti, the posters to be presented in this part were all found on social media. Because I collected these posters on my mobile phone, the temporal information of the artifacts was immediately on my phone and its cloud collection. Being a digital image, they mainly circulated on social media, thus not bound to any geographical location, though sometimes people might print, glue or stick them on the streets, and inside shopping malls, buildings, and tunnels.

Figures 13.6 through 13.8 take us back to the relatively early stage of the protest moment when protests broke out. Figure 13.6 shows a typical example of a digital image collected on my Facebook page in 2019 June, when large-scale marches took place with up to one to two million people in attendance. The textual-ideational cues in this figure show that the text consists of two signs: the image of the German poet Goethe and the quote "None are more hopelessly enslaved than those who believe they are free" in Chinese. The quoting of the Romantic-era laureate and his ideas on enslavement and freedom encapsulate the civil/political value the 2019–2020 Hong Kong protest movement are against for: resisting political and legal suppression in pursuit of liberty.

Compared with the Goethe quote artifact above, Figures 13.7 and 13.8, also posters captured from the digital platforms, seem to embed more signs packed with more sophisticated complex meanings. They require more textual and ideational knowledge to decipher. Figure 13.7 was captured on August 18, 2019. To understand the meaning of the sign in Figure 13.7, readers may recall the contextual knowledge about the news of a first-aider who had her right eye injured by a bean bag round, likely fired by the police, just a week before, August 11. The most striking image in the center of the poster shows a female in a helmet with a wounded right eye. In addition to the girl with a wounded eye, we can draw a lot of meanings from the colors, smoke, and cityspace in the poster. The four primary colors carry political and semantic associations: yellow for pro-democracy; blue, support for the police and the government; black and white, metaphors in Chinese to mean right and wrong. Another textual cue is the smoke hanging over a

Post-it, Milk Tea, and Mini-Stonehenge • **307**

Context	**Social context:**
	2019 June 9 Third Anti-Extradition Law Amendment Bill (Anti-ELAB) march. Civil Human Rights Front (CHRF) organizes a white-cloth march. 1.03 million attend. Attendee number exceeded over one million for the first time after the 1.5-million turnout in 1989. More than double of the 0.5-million in the anti-Article 23 protest in 2003. After the protest, Hong Kong Chief Executive Carrie Lam decided to proceed to the second reading of the FOAB on 2019 June 12.
	2019 June 12 Protesters surrounded the Legco building complex, set up barricades to stop legislators from entering the building. Forces were used. Bricks and objects were thrown at police. Police use thousands of tear gas cylinders to disperse protesters. A police officer is videorecorded saying "Ask your Jesus to come down to see me!" when dispersing a crowd of protesters. The second reading is suspended.
	2019 June 15 One protester Leung Ling Kit commits suicide, wearing a yellow raincoat. Carrie Lam announces that the ELAB is "dead."
	2019 June 16 CHRF organizes a black-cloth protest to commemorate Leung. Two million people attend—the biggest ever protest in Hong Kong history.
	Chronotope:
	2019 June 22. Social media.
Mode	Digital image
Genre	Poster (to share)
Text	[Due to privacy concerns, Figure 13.6 cannot be printed]
Sign	Material form (signifier): • An image of Goethe against a dark background • A quote "*None are more hopelessly enslaved than those who believe they are free.*"
	Meaning (signified): Do not be willingly enslaved
Audience	Netizens
Possible action(s)	To share the post on social media to encourage to take part in the protest for freedom

Figure 13.6 A Goethe Quote. June 22, 2019. *Source:* social media image

blurred image of the central business district bathed in crimson color, possibly giving readers an impression of uneasiness on Hong Kong island. This may also remind reviewers of the tear gas that the police often used against protesters since 2019 June. The function is clearly stated on the poster: to invite the receivers (Netizens or any viewers of the poster) to join the march on August 18, 2019.

An incident that took place on June 12, 2019 (see Figure 13.6) is important to our analysis of Figure 13.8. When a police officer dispersed protesters on that day, he shouted, "Ask your Jesus to come down to see me!" His

Context	**Social context:** (See also Figure 13.6) 2019 August 11 Mass protests break out in many occasions. Photos are taken showing police brutally arrest protestors with unnecessary violence. A voluntary first aider is believed to be injured in her right eye by bean bag round. 2019 August 12–14 Flash occupy protests against police brutality took place in many locations. Massive arrests by police. Pepper ball guns are used to shoot protesters. **Chronotope:** 2019 August 18. Social media.
Mode	Digital image
Genre	Poster (to recommend)
Text	
Sign	Material form (signifier): • An image of a young-looking female with a wounded right eye and a helmet with "Give democracy back to me" slogan • "Yellow and blue are (about) political views. Black and white are (about) conscience." The four color-related Chinese characters are filled with their corresponding color. • Date and venue for 8.18 (August 18) march in Victoria Park. • An image of smoke hanging over some buildings that resemble Central, the central business district on Hong Kong island. Meaning (signified): • A young person has lost her eye for democracy. • Show your conscience by joining the march on August 18, despite the odds.
Audience	Netizens
Action	To join the march on August 18

Figure 13.7 The August 18, 2019 march poster. "Eye-injured girl reportedly safe: 'Thank you, Hongkongers. I will do my best to eat more, sleep more.'" *Credit:* Cookman (August 18, 2019)

Post-it, Milk Tea, and Mini-Stonehenge • **309**

words widely circulated in social media and triggered a lot of reactions from religious circles. Figure 13.8 is an invitation poster packed with textual-ideational cues. Like the colors used to stand for the pro-democracy stance in Figure 13.7, the light yellow used in the poster in Figure 13.8 serves as a similar textual-ideational cue. The title of the poster, entitled "Jesus Is Right Here Prayer Worship," may respond to an earlier remark made by the police officer. We can find a Biblical quote of Isaiah 41:10 in Chinese ("Do not fear, for I am with you, do not be afraid, for I am your God; I will strengthen you, I will help you, I will uphold you with my victorious right hand"). The use of hashtag mark ("#") in front of the phrases "religious assembly," "Christianity," "love," "justice," and "revival" helps to highlight the values behind the event. The hashtag may also serve to encourage viewers to share the invitation on social media.

The chosen examples in Figures 13.6 through 13.8 show that posters make an outstanding case in which textual-ideational cues play a distinctive role in conveying the meaning(s) of protest artifacts. With a quote by a

Context	**Social context:**
	Same as Figures 13.6 and 13.7
	Chronotope:
	2019 October 14. Social media.
Mode	Digital image
Genre	Poster (to recommend)
Text	[Due to privacy concerns, Figure 13.8 cannot be printed]
Sign	Material form (signifier): • An image of a nightscape of Hong Kong against a yellow background, accompanied with the title and details of the prayer worship to be held in Mongkok on 15 October, 2019 at 7 pm. • Invitation message "All are welcome." • Hashtags "religious assembly," "Christianity," "love," "justice," and "revival." • A quote of a biblical verse "Do not fear, for I am with you, do not be afraid, for I am your God; I will strengthen you, I will help you, I will uphold you with my victorious right hand" (Isaiah 41:10, New Revised Standard Version) at the bottom of the poster.
	Meaning (signified): • All are welcomed to an evening prayer worship. • Nature and values of the event • God be with participants at the event
Audience	Netizens
Action	To join the prayer worship on August 15; to share the invitation on social media

Figure 13.8 "Jesus Is Right Here Prayer Worship" Poster. 2019 October 14. Credit: Author's Telegram account.

Romantic writer, Figure 13.6 serves as an encouragement to motivate Netizens to offer their support to the protest movement. Through intentional use of colors, Figures 13.7 and 13.8 give clues to readers about their political stance. Figure 13.8, an invitation to an religious event, leverages the power of faith to promote the values and ideals they stand for in the protest movement, conveying a message of faith and courage to fellow protesters, believers, and perhaps any viewers who saw the artifact.

Built Artifacts: Stonehenges, Post-its With Lennon Wall, Blank Lennon Walls (> The Interpersonal Plane)

In my discussion of the last type of artifacts, I will focus on the interpersonal plane of multimodal meaning making of purposefully built physical objects in the environment, including Stonehenges, Post-its with Lennon Walls, as well as Blank Lennon Walls.

Stonehenges

Like graffiti, which uses the wall or pillar of a construction as the writing surface, objects on the streets were also used by sign makers to make protest artifacts. Figure 13.9 shows numerous mini-stonehenges made by bricks pried from the pedestrian walks nearby to form brick roadblocks to block or slow down police vehicles from advancing in protests during November 2019. The shape of the stonehenge might not carry any symbolic meaning, but the stonehenge did have a practical function. When a vehicle hit a stonehenge, the brick on top would fall and further buttress the two bricks below, thus strengthening the mini-roadblock and slowing down passing vehicles. In social semiotics, the use of the bricks for this function can be interpreted by the concept of affordance, which is defined as "the [potential use] of a given object, stemming from the perceivable properties of the object" (van Leeuwen, 2005, p. 273). The affordance of the shape of the brick arches served as roadblocks in this functional aspect. At the interpersonal level, in the eyes of the audience (be they pedestrians, drivers, or police), the artifact appeared to stand as a symbol of battlefield at the protest sites. This meant that the site in Figure 13.9 (i.e., an occupied road in a busy central business district) had been claimed by protesters as a battlefield, and vehicles should stay away from the street clashes during the protests.

Post-its With Lennon Walls

Continuing what Patsiaouras et al. (2018) call a "marketing method" observed in the 2014 Umbrella Movement in 2014, Post-it-note-filled Lennon Walls were commonly seen in public space like pedestrian pavements, shopping malls, and tunnels for protesters to share their ideas, propagate

Context	**Social context:** Same as Figure 13.7
	Chronotope: 2019 November. Des Voeux Road, Central.
Mode	Bricks (object)
Genre	Roadblocks
Text	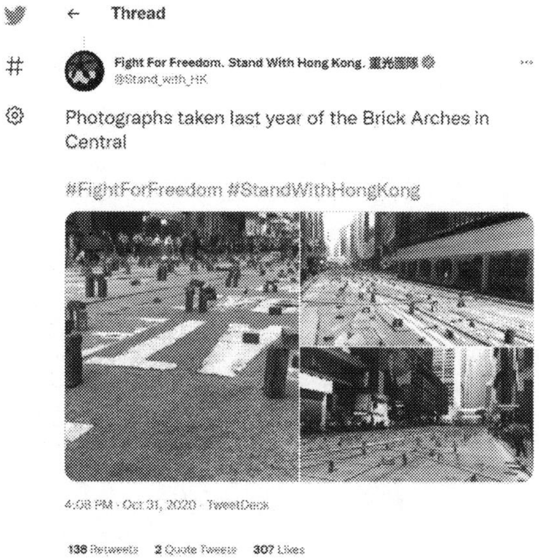 *[Screenshot of a tweet from @Stand_with_HK "Fight For Freedom. Stand With Hong Kong." reading "Photographs taken last year of the Brick Arches in Central #FightForFreedom #StandWithHongKong", posted 4:03 PM · Oct 31, 2020 · TweetDeck, 138 Retweets, 2 Quote Tweets, 307 Likes]*
Sign	Material form (signifier): Bricks stacked in stonehenge shape
	Meaning (signified): Barricade at the street battleground
Audience	Pedestrians, drivers, police
Possible Action(s)	To stay away from the barricades

Figure 13.9 Mini Stonehenges. Central in November 2019. "Photographs taken last year of the Brick Arches in Central." *Credit:* Fight for Freedom Stand with Hong Kong (2020, Oct. 31).

their reasons, and mobilize people to take part in the 2019–2020 protest movement. The Lennon Wall first started in Prague, Czech Republic in the 1980s. Young people put graffiti or put notes (sprayed or handwritten) and John Lennon-inspired lyrics on the Lennon Wall to express their complaints against the then communist regime, which banned Western pop music (Lonely Planet, n.d.). Lennon Walls first appeared in main Occupy sites of the Umbrella Movement in 2014 and Figure 13.10 shows one of

312 ▪ J. M-B. HO

Context	**Social context:** Same as Figure 13.6 **Chronotope:** 2019 July 12. A pedestrian bridge in Hunghom.
Mode	Handicraft, print–handwritten notes
Genre	Lennon Wall (to share)
Text	
Sign	Material form (signifier): • "Hunghom Lennon Wall" handwritten with marker pens • Carton board taped and tied to railing a pedestrian bridge • Post-it notes
	Meaning (signified): • Individual voices are invited to participate in the collective public display of ideas on the protest movement
Audience	Pedestrians
Action	To participate in the idea sharing, to grow support for the protest movement

Figure 13.10 Hunghom Lennon Wall. July 12, 2019. *Credit:* Author.

the Lennon Walls that could be found in various residential and commercial areas throughout Hong Kong in 2019. On the interpersonal plane, the Lennon Walls served as a protest message board that became a collective artwork that invited people to share their ideas and words of encouragement. The messages and meanings of the text on individual Post-it notes might vary. When pedestrians walked by a Lennon Wall, such as the one in Figure 13.10, it would not be difficult to find stacks of Post-it notes and pens placed nearby and be mobilized by the sign maker to share ideas and words of encouragement on the wall.

Blank Lennon Walls

Perhaps due to the Coronavirus outbreak, compulsory social distancing restrictions, and/or mounting political suppression of the protest movement since the beginning of 2020, protest artifacts that emerged since mid-2019 were increasingly erased from public view. Protest artifacts braced a change of wind when the new national security law took effect in Hong Kong on July 1, 2020 (see Figure 13.11). Figure 13.11 shows another creative form of protest artifacts could still be found in many shops at the time of writing. This artifact looked like the Lennon Wall in Figure 13.10, however this time, the Post-in notes were mostly blank as displayed in the store and on the shop window. Even though some notes might still have words on them, the content would either be irrelevant to any of the values and beliefs about the protest movement or encrypted in ways that would not show any resemblance to the previously known protest slogans. On the interpersonal level, the role of the sign maker and audience were different. While the Lennon Wall in Figure 13.10 invited pedestrians to participate in the making of the artifact, the blank one in- store did not. *Only* the sign maker designed and produced the artifact. The owner of this cafe in Figure 13.11, like many pro-democracy retailers in Hong Kong, appeared to be making a political stance in their creation of a so-called "yellow economic circle" (Shen, 2020). The intended function and meaning of the artifact was to show that the shop was displaying a kind of speechless resistance in the post-resistance era. If the audience understood the meaning of the artifact, they may choose to patronize at the cafe to show their solidarity. Amid the looming era of arrests of politicians and activists, dissolution of unions and civil society groups, and suppression of freedom of speech and press, the "silent" Post-it notes seem to make a powerful, yet speechless, metaphor for Hongkongers' resistance after mid-2020.

From the paper-form Lennon Walls to brick stonehenges, we can see how the sign-makers engaged with the audience in meaning-making, ranging from deterring drivers and police from advancing in or reclaiming their protest sites (Figure 13.9), to inviting others participate in making the collective protest message boards (as applied to Figure 13.10), and to telling the pedestrians or customers about the shop owners' political stance (Figure 13.11). They clearly show the importance of understanding the interpersonal relationship of the sign-makers and audience in making sense of the multimodal protest artifacts.

DISCUSSION

To answer my key question, "How do we make sense of the multimodal protest artifacts from the 2019–2020 Hong Kong protest movement?" I

Context	**Social context:** 2020 May 27 National Anthem law undergoes a second reading discussion in Legislative Council. It is later passed on June 4 and takes effect on June 12. People are banned from mocking, misusing or insulting the anthem. 2020 May 28 National People's Congress decides to promulgate national security legislation to be included in Hong Kong Basic Law. 2020 June 4 Despite a rejected application to organize June 4 vigil, a large number of citizens show up in Victoria Park to commemorate the 31st anniversary of the June 4 incident. Many chant June 4 and anti-extradition bill movement slogans, for the last time, legally in public. 2020 June 30 National People's Congress, the top legislature in the People's Republic of China, adopts the Hong Kong National Security Law. **Chronotope:** 2020 August 16. Outside a boba tea cafe in Causeway Bay.
Mode	Post-it notes (print) on an in-store Lennon Wall on a shop window (object)
Genre	Lennon Wall (to gain support)
Text	
Sign	Material form (signifier): Multi-colored Post-it notes stuck on a glass wall
	Meaning (signified): Speechless resistance
Audience	Pedestrians, customers
Possible Action(s)	To show support for the resistance movement

Figure 13.11 Blank Post-it notes on glass inside a Boba Tea Cafe. Causeway Bay. August 16, 2020. *Credit:* Author.

addressed three sub-questions that focused on how the protest artifacts make meanings on the (a) contextual, (b) textual-ideational, and (c) interpersonal planes. I have used three types of artifacts; namely, graffiti, posters, and built artifacts (e.g., Lennon Walls and brick mini-stonehenges) to show how each type of these artifacts relied on cues for the sign makers and audience to use and make sense of the contextual, textual-ideational, and interpersonal elements of the protest artifacts. As the samples presented above show, Blommaert's (2015) chronotopic context in which the protest texts were collected provided the reader valuable information to make sense of the artifact. If we are to understand how meaning is made in protest artifacts—be it protest graffiti, posters, or defaced road signs—we need to develop our skills in what Duncan (2021) calls "protest literacy." As Gee (2015) writes, "We cannot study literacy by itself. Once we remove it from its natural home in [discourses] and society, we have something akin to the black squares of a chessboard, but we no longer have chess or a chessboard" (p. 100). With protest literacy, it is important to understand the chess game itself (i.e., texts), black squares (i.e., geographical or virtual location), and chessboard (i.e., the social, cultural, and political context AND the temporal-spatial context) to form a better understanding on how sign makers use multimodality to make meanings and strive to remake the world as they want to see through protest movements.

Hybridity and intertextuality are also found when analyzing multimodal meaning making of protest artifacts. As The New London Group ([NLG]; 2000) explains regarding multiliteracies, multimodal meanings are made through hybridity and intertextuality. Hybridity demonstrates how creativity works through hybridizing "established modes of meaning (of discourses and genres)" and combining modes by crossing "boundaries of convention and creating new conventions" (p. 30). Graffiti artifacts contain borrowed texts or signs from other genres and modes to create new meanings for the protest texts through provenance. *Provenance* refers to the act that "signs may be 'imported' from one context (another era, social group, culture) into another, in order to signify the ideas and values associated with that other context by those who do the importing" (Kress & van Leeuwen, 2001, p. 23). In the case of Figure 13.3, provenance breathed new meaning to the road sign when the sign maker spray-painted "democracy" on it to invite the receivers to join the way of democracy. It also turned bricks (Figure 13.9) into a symbol of battle and resistance. Meanwhile, the Post-it notes on the in-store Lennon Wall (Figure 13.11) make meaning through intertextuality.

Intertextuality helps us to see how meanings are constructed through relating to other texts, text- types, narratives, and modes (NLG, 2000). Although the Post-it notes in Figure 13.11 were blank, viewers could "fill in the blanks" by piecing together other graffiti slogans they had seen before at other protest sites and Lennon Walls (like those in Figure 13.10) by recalling their viewer experience (their mental "view history," so to speak).

Moreover, such borrowing in the hybridization of meaning making in protest artifacts also involved translanguaging, which includes "all meaning-making modes" (García & Li, 2014, p. 29). The witty combination of spray-painted Chinese radical "尸" above the MTR logo (Figure 13.2) made an outstanding example of what Li and Zhu (2019) would call a "playful subversion" of Chinese characters in creative translanguaging practice. The complex design of posters like those in Figures 13.6 through 13.8 demonstrated the purposeful use of linguistic, digital, graphic, and other related modes in the production of such artifacts. Careful consideration must have been made in the use of font color (yellow and blue to represent different political camps), the choice of portrait (the image of Goethe to embody the ideas of a Romantic writer/thinker), and the use of hashtags (to highlight the universal values behind a public prayer worship and to encourage viewers to share the invitation with others). All these involve a mastery of sophisticated skills in the "multimodal nature of communication" (García & Li, 2014, p. 28) found in the local protest movement. Translanguaging can support our understanding of such multimodal nature. Li and Zhu (2021b) recently discussed how translanguaging supports creative linguistic activism, citing an example where the sign maker turns the Chinese characters of a popular protest slogan into abstract shapes to avoid being silenced by the newly introduced national security law.

PEDAGOGICAL AND RESEARCH POSSIBILITIES

In this chapter, I argue the complicated and sophisticated ways of meaning making involved in the design and interpretation of protest artifacts from the 2019–2020 Hong Kong protest movement. In the Hong Kong protest movement, we can see students' engagement in multimodal meaning making. Young people have demonstrated some mastery of multimodal protest literacy in their knowledge and experience of their social and virtual worlds. A protest literacy education can equip and empower students to fight for a world they desire.

Educators and researchers need to consider how to develop culturally situated and socially relevant pedagogical approaches and strategies to support students in their development of multimodal literacy, as Jewitt (2008) suggests. Magnusson and Godhe (2019) argue for the importance of recognizing multimodal meaning making in language education. Chun (2019) documents how she used multimodal social semiotics to help students critically examine family life and gender roles. The current research treats protest artifacts as objects of study, whether they are found on the streets, in shopping malls, on the public transport, or on their cell phones which students came across every day during 2019–2020. These artifacts reflect the semiotic tools and resources that students might have used to make their voices heard by their peers, local citizens, the media, and, certainly, the political authorities. Considering the potential of multimodal social semiotics in the classroom, one possible approach educators can consider is to adopt a reader-centered approach to engage students in reader reception analysis of multimodal protest artifacts. As Li and Zhu (2021a) suggest, teachers can invite students (as readers and viewers) to participate in multimodal analysis such the one that is discussed in this chapter, see how they respond to the signs and engage them in a critical discussion of the context of social, cultural, and political development in their community. Similarly, Liu and Lin (2021) propose using "multiple linguistic and semiotic resources to engage students to both gain access to and critically engage in the knowledge co-making" (p. 256) in the classroom through translanguaging and transsemiotizing. I believe the social semiotic approach as advocated here can enable educators to develop culturally relevant curriculum and practices to critically engage in co-making of knowledge about the word and the world. It is the duty of every educator, not just critical educators, to help students learn how to read the word and the world (Freire & Macedo, 1987).

Using a multimodal social-semiotic approach to exploring social justice issues would not only develop students' linguistic and semiotic competencies in communication but also enable teachers to develop repertoires in using critical pedagogy to address burning issues in society. Teacher research, for example, can become a form of resistance, questioning inequitable policies and resistance ideologies (Simon & Campano, 2013) by incorporating critical pedagogies in the curriculum and school practices. Activist and agitation literacy practices like those reported by Kynard (2013), Richardson and Ragland (2018) and Muhammad (2019) supported Black students in the United States to address and fight against racism as well as social and political inequality.

ENDING REMARKS

Some painters transform the sun into a yellow spot,
others transform a yellow spot into the stars.
—Pablo Picasso

At the time of writing of this book chapter, recent social and political developments may seem disheartening to many. Since the introduction of national security law on July 1, 2020, the annual June 4 candlelights—lit in the Victoria Park on the Hong Kong island every year since the 1989 Tiananmen incident—have been put out; politicians and activities have been tried in courts for various charges, or forced to exile for personal and family's safety; families have been forced to flee to other countries in search of freedoms and for a better future for their children. Against these odds, local Hong Kongers and overseas allies have not given up. Figure 13.12 is a digital image of a cartoon made by two Taiwan-based artists, titled "Taiwan and Hong Kong support Thai people" (in Chinese). The milk tea, a common drink of people in Hong Kong, Taiwan, and Thailand, makes an adequate symbol to represent the same spirit across people on different lands, to fight for a free world. The cartoonists, like Hong Kongers and their allies, continue to show the solidarity, creativity, and resilience demonstrated by the people who are united despite the difference in timespace. Perhaps it is through micro-resistance, fittingly symbolized by this small, harmless cup of drink, that people can exercise "the power of the powerless"—as Havel (2018) calls it in his fight for democracy for his country 4 decades ago. Perhaps our enriched understanding of the multimodal artifacts that

Figure 13.12 A digital image of Milk Tea Alliance. "Hong Kong and Taiwan Support Thai people." *Credit:* Jie Jie & Uncle Cat (October 17, 2020).

emerged from the 2019–2020 Hong Kong protest movement can help educators interested in multimodality, democracy, and social justice education to exercise a similar kind of solidarity, creativity, and resilience in various ways and modes.

NOTES

1. For more comprehensive collections of the 2019–2020 Hong Kong protest artifacts, readers can consult Museum of New Zealand's (n.d.) virtual "Hong Kong Protest Movement and Aotearoa" collection (https://collections.tepapa.govt.nz/topic/11038) or scholarly collections like the ANTIELAB Research Data Archive, hosted and managed by the University of Hong Kong's Journalism and Media Studies (https://antielabdata.jmsc.hku.hk/).

REFERENCES

Adams, R. (2022, February 18). Curbing political topics in English schools will harm minority students, say critics. *The Guardian: International Edition.* https://www.theguardian.com/education/2022/feb/18/curbing-political-topics-in-english-schools-will-harm-minority-students-say-critics

Andersen, T. H., Boeriis, M., Maagerø, E., & Tønnessen, E. S. (2015). *Social semiotics: Key figures, new directions.* Routledge.

Awad, S. H., Wagoner, B., & Glăveanu, V. P. (2017). The street art of resistance. In N. Chaudhary, P. Hviid, G. Marsico, & J. W. Villadsen (Eds.), *Resistance in everyday life* (pp. 161–180). Springer. https://doi.org/10.1007/978-981-10-3581-4_13

Bazerman, C. (2012). Genre as social action. In J. P. Gee & M. Handford (Eds.), *The Routledge handbook of discourse analysis* (pp. 226–238). Routledge.

Blommaert, J. (2015). Chronotopes, scales, and complexity in the study of language in society. *Annual Review of Anthropology, 44*(1), 105–116. https://doi.org/10.1146/annurev-anthro-102214-014035

Blommaert, J. (2019). Are chronotopes helpful? In S. Kroon & J. Swanenberg (Eds.), *Chronotopic identity work: Sociolinguistic analyses of cultural and linguistic phenomena in time and space* (pp. 16–24). Multilingual Matters. https://doi.org/10.21832/9781788926621

Blommaert, J. (2020, June 18). *Jan Blommaert on chronotope* [YouTube video]. https://www.youtube.com/watch?v=r4yluKPhTKE&list=PLE4sXy4xv8sO7zOVf6L_ioygxyzTsHYv4&index=11&t=51s

Chun, C. W. (2019). The intersections between critical pedagogy and public pedagogy: Hong Kong students and the Umbrella Movement. In. M. E. López-Gopar (Ed.), *International perspectives on critical pedagogies in ELT* (pp. 79–98). Palgrave Macmillan.

Cook, T. (2013). Fighting words: Canadian soldiers' slang and swearing in the Great War. *War in History, 20*(3), 323–344. https://doi.org/10.1177/0968344513483229

Cookman. (2019, August 18). *Eye-injured girl reportedly safe: "Thanks, Hongkongers, I will do my best to eat more, sleep more* [Online forum post]. HKGolden.com. https://forum.hkgolden.com/thread/7101508/page/5

Djonov, E., & Zhao, S. (2018). Social semiotics: A theorist and a theory in retrospect and prospect. In S. Zhao, E. Djonov, A. Björkvall, & M. Boeriis (Eds.), *Advancing multimodal and critical discourse studies: Interdisciplinary research inspired by Theo Van Leeuwen's social semiotics* (pp. 1–17). Routledge.

Duncan, J. D. I. (2021). *Researching protest literacies: Literacy as protest in the favelas of Rio de Janeiro.* Routledge.

Elnakkouzi, R. (2017). Strategic manoeuvring in Arab Spring political cartoons. In C. Hart & D. Kelsey (Eds.), *Discourses of disorder: Riots, strikes and protests in the media* (pp. 154–174). Edinburgh University Press.

Fight for Freedom. Stand With Hong Kong. 重光團隊 [@Stand_with_HK]. (2020, November 31). *Photographs taken last year of the Bricks Arches in Central* [Tweet]. Twitter.com. https://twitter.com/Stand_with_HK/status/1322450415032573952?s=20&t=VPAlkKks1qGInx69d-2yCg

Freire, P., & Macedo, D. (1987). *Literacy: Reading the word and the world.* Routledge and Kegan Paul.

Fuller, D. (2005). Graffiti. In R. W. Caves (Ed.), *Encyclopedia of the city* (pp. 212–213). Routledge.

Gee, J. P. (2015). *Literacy and education.* Routledge.

Gracía, O., & Li, W. (2014). *Translanguaging: Language, bilingualism and education.* Palgrave Macmillan.

Haoqingnian Tudushi [Corrupt The Youth 好青年荼毒室]. (2020). Dai Ben Zhexueshu Shangjie Qu [Take a book on philosophy to the street 帶本哲學書上街去]. Haoqingnian Tudushi [好青年荼毒室].

Hart, C. (2019). Metaphor and the (1984–5) Miners' strike: A multimodal analysis. In C. Hart & D. Kelsey (Eds.), *Discourses of disorder: Riots, strikes and protests in the media* (pp. 133–153). Edinburgh University Press.

Havel, V. (2018). *The power of the powerless* (P. Wilson, Trans.). Vintage Classics. (Original work published 1979).

Humphrey, S. L. (2013). Empowering adolescents for activist literacies. *Journal of Language and Literacy Education, 9*(1), 114–135. http://jolle.coe.uga.edu/wp-content/uploads/2013/05/Empowering-Adolescents.pdf

Jewitt, C. (2008). Multimodality and literacy in school classroom. *AERA Review of Research in Education, 32,* 241–267. https://doi.org/10.3102/0091732X07310586

Jewitt, C., Bezemer, J., & O'Halloran, K. (2016). *Introducing multimodality.* Routledge.

Jie Jie & Uncle Cat [@jiejie_unclecat]. (2020, October 17). *Hong Kong and Taiwan support Thai people* [Image]. Instagram.com. https://www.instagram.com/p/CGcJbVJHZtr/?igshid=YmMyMTA2M2Y=

Kasanga, L. (2014). The linguistic landscape: Mobile signs, code choice, symbolic meaning and territoriality in the discourse of protest. *International Journal of the Sociology of Language, 2014*(230), 19–44. https://doi.org/10.1515/ijsl-2014-0025

Kaye, B. K., & Sapolsky, B. (2009). Taboo or not taboo? That is the question: Offensive language on prime-time broadcast and cable programming. *Journal of Broadcasting & Electronic Media, 53*(1), 22–37. https://doi.org/10.1080/08838150802643522

Kong, T.-G. (2020). *Liberate Hong Kong*. Mekong.

Kress, G. (1993). Against arbitrariness: The social production of the sign as a foundational issue in critical discourse analysis. *Discourse & Society, 4*(2), 169–191.

Kress, G. (2009). What is a mode? In C. Jewitt (Ed.), *The Routledge handbook of multimodal analysis* (pp. 54–67). Routledge.

Kress, G. (2010). *Multimodality: A social semiotic approach to contemporary communication* [Kindle e-Book]. Routledge.

Kress, G., & van Leeuwen, T. (2001). *Multimodal discourse: The modes and media of contemporary communication*. Arnold.

Kynard, C. (2013). *Vernacular insurrections: Race, Black protest, and the new century in composition-literacies studies*. State University of New York Press.

Lee, F. L. F., & Chan, J. M. (2018). *Media and protest logics in the digital era: The umbrella movement in Hong Kong*. Oxford University Press.

Lee, F. L. F., Liang, H., Cheng, E. W., Tang, G. K. Y., & Yuen, S. (2021). Affordances, movement dynamics, and a centralized digital communication platform in a networked movement. *Information, Communication, & Society, 25*(12), 1699–1716. https://doi.org/10.1080/1369118X.2021.1877772

Li, W., & Zhu, H. (2019). Tranßcripting: Playful subversion with Chinese characters. *International Journal of Multilingualism, 16*(2), 145–161. https://doi.org/10.1080/14790718.2019.1575834

Li, W., & Zhu, H. (2021a). Making sense of handwritten signs in public spaces. *Social Semiotics, 31*(1), 61–87. https://doi.org/10.1080/10350330.2020.1810549

Li, W., & Zhu, H. (2021b). Soft power struggles: A diasporic perspective on the competing ideologies and innovative practices regarding the Chinese writing system. *Journal of Sociolinguistics, 25*, 737–753. https://doi.org/10.1111/josl.12535

Liu, G. [柳廣成]. (2020). *The fallen city: Hong Kong* [被消失的香港]. Geae Book.

Liu, J. E, & Lin, A. M. Y. (2021). (Re)conceptualizing "language" in CLIL: Multimodality, translanguaging, and trans-semiotizing in CLIL. *AILA Review, 34*(2), 240–261. https://doi.org/10.1075/aila.21002.liu

LonelyPlanet. (n.d.). *John Lennon wall*. https://www.lonelyplanet.com/czech-republic/prague/attractions/john-lennon-wall/a/poi-sig/401339/358835

Luke, A., O'Brien, J., & Comber, B. (1994). Making community texts objects of study. *Australian Journal of Language and Literacy, 17*(2), 139–145. https://www.semanticscholar.org/paper/Making-community-texts-objects-of-study-Luke-O%27Brien/a8fe6dafb296005e35ef1dc0a58676dff4393dfd

Magnusson, P., & Godhe, A.-L. (2019). Multimodality in language education—Implications for teaching. *Designs for Learning, 11*(1), 127–137. https://doi.org/10.16993/dfl.127

Montero, M. K., Bice-Zaugg, C., Marsh, A. C. J., & Cummins, J. (2013). Activist literacies: Validating aboriginality through visual and literary identity texts. *Journal of Language and Literacy Education, 9*(1), 73–94. http://jolle.coe.uga.edu/wp-content/uploads/2013/06/Validating-Aboriginality.pdf

Muhammad, G. E. (2019). Protest, power, and possibilities: The need for agitation literacies. *Journal of Adolescent & Adult Literacy, 63*(3), 351–355. https://www.jstor.org/stable/48556221

Museum of New Zealand. (n.d.). *Hong Kong protest movement and aotearoa.* Retrieved October 20, 2021, from https://collections.tepapa.govt.nz/topic/11038?fbclid=IwAR1dZsusmVvMFaKw5qlY6FPm84y_TS3jfMZuaoNb3wBfzvOWhc0y_9gDtmA

Ndi, G. S. (2017). On the aesthetics of mimicry and proliferation: Interrogations of hegemony in the postcolonial public sphere. *English in Africa, 44*(2), 93–115. https://doi.org/10.4314/eia.v44i2.4

Noddings, N. (2005). *The challenge to care in schools: An alternative approach to education* (2nd ed.). Teachers College Press.

Patsiaouras, G., & Veneti, A. (2017). The Hong Kong protest camps, political art and the emergence of emotions. In P. Reilly, A. Veneti, & D. Atanasova (Eds.), *Politics, protest, emotion: Interdisciplinary perspectives* [pp. 46–51]. Pressbooks. https://pauljreilly.pressbooks.com/chapter/the-hong-kong-protest-camps-political-art-and-the-emergence-of-emotions/

Patsiaouras, G., Veneti, A., & Green, W. (2018). Marketing, art and voices of dissent: Promotional methods of protest art by the 2014 Hong Kong's Umbrella Movement. *Marketing Theory, 18*(1), 75–100. https://doi.org/10.1177/1470593117724609

Purbrick, M. (2019). A report of the 2019 Hong Kong protests. *Asian Affairs, 50*(4), 465–487. https://doi.org/10.1080/03068374.2019.1672397

Reed, T. V. (2019). *The art of protest: Culture and activism from the Civil Rights Movement to the present* (2nd ed.). University of Minnesota Press.

Refaie, E. (2009). Metaphor in political cartoons: Exploring audience responses. In C. J. Forceville & E. Urios-Aparisi (Eds.), *Multimodal metaphor* (pp. 173–196). University of Connecticut. https://doi.org/10.1515/9783110215366.3.173

Richardson, E., & Ragland, A. (2018). #StayWoke: The language and literacies of the #BlackLivesMatter movement. *Community Literacy Journal, 12*(2), 27–56. https://doi.org/10.25148/clj.12.2.009099

Ross, G. (Director). (2012). *The hunger games* [Film]. Lionsgate.

Selander, S. (2017). Can a sign reveal its meanings? On the question of interpretation and epistemic contexts. In S. Zhao, E. Djonov, A. Björkvall, & M. Boeriis (Eds.), *Advancing multimodal and critical discourse studies: Interdisciplinary research inspired by Theo van Leeuwen's social semiotics* (pp. 82–93). Routledge. https://doi.org/10.4324/9781315521015

Shen, S. (2020, May 19). How the yellow economic circle can revolutionize Hong Kong. *The Diplomat.* https://thediplomat.com/2020/05/how-the-yellow-economic-circle-can-revolutionize-hong-kong/

Simon, R., & Campano, G. (2013). Activist literacies: Teacher research as resistance to the "normal curve." *Journal of Language and Literacy Education, 9*(1), 21–39. http://jolle.coe.uga.edu/wp-content/uploads/2013/05/Teacher-Research.pdf

The New London Group. (2000). A pedagogy of multiliteracies: Designing social futures. In B. Cope & M. Kalantzis (Eds.), *Multiliteracies: Literacy learning and the design of social future* (pp. 9–42). Routledge.

Valdez, L. M. A. (2007). *Graffiti art and self-identity: Leaving their mark* [Unpublished master's thesis]. California State University, San Bernardino. https://scholarworks.lib.csusb.edu/etd-project/3079

van Leeuwen, T. (2005). *Introducing social semiotics.* Routledge.

CHAPTER 14

DISRUPTING DISCOURSES IN PLACE

Youth, Space, and Activism

Amy Walker
Kent State University

ABSTRACT

In June 2020, in my rust belt hometown in the rural Midwest, over 100 residents stood on the grounds of the county courthouse and protested for Black Lives Matter. When students arrived, the nature and space of the protest shifted. Latinx and White youth led chants, held signs, and geographically repositioned the protest away from the courthouse and closer to the street. This rural town is considered part of the new Latino diaspora (Hamann et al., 2002), a region nontraditionally associated with an increased Latinx population; here Latinx families represent almost 30% of the population. Latinx residents have been historically marginalized in this community, yet Latinx youth were the de facto leaders of this protest. This research problematizes deficit notions and assumptions of rurality as homogenous, conservative, and uneducated while centering the intersectionalities and literacy practices of youth as they co-construct space in anti-racist activism.

Literacy practices and language are fundamentally multimodal and are situated across a variety of social contexts in addition to schools, such as community sites of recreation, homes, and professional institutions (Mills & Unsworth, 2016). Examining youth as activists expands the consideration of "learning space" by noticing the literacies students practice and the embodied and spatialized practices of their activism. Spatial justice (Soja, 2010) asserts that whatever is social is also inherently spatial, including justice. Considering spatiality and the power dynamics that influence a space's co-construction is crucial for noticing how youth meaned and resisted at this protest. Intersectionality is a spatial metaphor (Collins, 2019; Crenshaw, 1989) that foregrounds the relationships of race, class, geography, and age to consider how power relations are structured and constructed. This study uses spatial justice and intersectionality as frameworks to critically situate the social, cultural, historical, and spatial literacies of youth as they protest.

It is important to consider how students use semiotic resources to demonstrate knowledge and critical understanding of issues like racism and social justice (Siegel, 2012). Using geosemiotics (Scollon & Scollon, 2003) and social geography (Soja, 1989) as methodological approaches, this research analyzes publicly sourced photographs of the protest. This study also includes focus groups with both White and Latinx student protesters, during which they talk about racism, marginalization, their design choices, and activism. This chapter presents the literacy practices of students, the ways students re-semiotized school objects to call White community residents to anti-racist action, and how students used semiotic resources to co-construct space.

Vasquez et al. (2019) argue for new directions in critical literacy, including research that engages with spatiality and multimodality. Corbett and Donehower (2017) call for future research on rural literacies focused on material engagements. Meanwhile, there is also a significant gap in education research on resistance of youth in rural places in the United States (Woods, 2003). This chapter addresses these gaps in education research by centering the intersectionalities students navigate as they protest for Black Lives Matter, examining how semiotic resources work together to mean, resist, and co-construct in a space of protest.

DISRUPTING DISCOURSES IN PLACE: YOUTH, SPACE, AND PROTEST LITERACIES

In a small, conservative community in the rural Midwest, over 100 residents stood on the grounds of the county courthouse and publicly protested in support of Black Lives Matter. When students arrived, the nature and space of the protest shifted. Latinx and White youth together lined the front of the sidewalk, led chants, held signs, and geographically repositioned the protest away from the courthouse and closer to the street. Many of these teenagers were my former students. I was a resident of this community and former public school educator, and these young adults disrupted assumptions commonly made about rurality, civic engagement, and youth involvement.

Rural stereotypes of uneducatedness and deficiency are perpetuated in the media (Eppley, 2017), and the Midwest is often portrayed as conservative, uncultured, and uneducated (Sanchez-Jankowski, 2002). This study acknowledges the multiple ways in which, through protest, students disrupted the assumption of rural middle America as homogenous, monolithic, and uncultured.

This research examines the ways in which youth advocated for Black lives in their community, centering students' agential responses and literacy practices in a protest space by exploring the following questions:

1. How did students protest?
2. What discourses and literacy practices impacted students' conceptualization of racial justice and the ways they protested against it in their community?

LITERATURE REVIEW

Literacies are multiple and complex ways of being and doing in the world, encompassing one's perceptions and actions and bodies, and this viewpoint has the power to reposition students in learning environments (Thiel, 2015). Research suggests that youth learn more about the function of literacy and how to practice literacy outside of school than inside (Juzwik, 2004; Vasquez, 2000). Harste (2003) argues that, for students in the 21st century, to be literate is to be able to choose and articulate both the identity and position one wants to take on any given subject (p. 10). Moll (2000) states,

> The key point is that human beings and their social and cultural worlds are inseparable; they are embedded in each other. Thus, human thinking is not reducible to individual properties or traits. Instead it is always mediated, distributed among persons, artifacts, activities, and settings. (p. 265)

Looking at youth in rural spaces and practices of civic engagement extends the idea of literacy beyond traditional forms and spaces and asks researchers to explore the practices of youth resistance outside the classroom.

Rurality and Civic Engagement

Research examining rural literacies and civic engagement in community spaces shows that civic engagement is often tied to place and a sense of belonging, and that schools, families, and social media are primary factors in bolstering youth civic engagement (Hoffner & Rehkoff, 2011; Terman, 2020; Weinstein, 2014; Wiederhold Wolfe et al., 2017). Wiederhold Wolfe et al. (2017) found that youth often felt stigmatized and expressed a need for place-based identity in order to allow them to participate with others and engage in civic and community matters. Wiederhold Wolfe et al. (2017) also found that—in response to feeling stigmatized by place—young adults removed themselves to liminal spaces in the community, trying to reposition themselves in new ways to avoid being stereotyped as either an insider or an outsider. In Terman's (2020) research, young adults who are involved in their communities act as part of a larger network of others involved in activism, producing a collective place-based identity. Terman's findings suggest that young adults "with some marginalized identities seem to be particularly thoughtful about their relationship to place, which could, with institutional and symbolic support, foster elective belonging among less privileged groups" (p. 30). Zamudio et al.'s (2009) research supports this by looking at how Chicano students at the University of Wyoming joined high school students to organize protest events. Through these, Zamudio et al. determine that protests and political activism could influence the making and remaking of oneself, suggesting that social interactions and practices, then, "have a robust influence on our critical sense of identity and wholeness" (p. 109).

Spatialized Literacies

Spatialized literacies acknowledge space as complex and co-constructed by participants, possessing both positive and negative factors (Wohlwend, 2021). Space has an historic relationship with disciplines like geography and urban planning, but recent attention on space and educational research leads to spatialized literacies and newfound ways of thinking about space, literacy, and rurality (Corbett, 2015; Leander & Sheehy, 2004; Soja, 2010). Spatialized literacies conceptualize space as relational, active, and historical, not capable of being separated from activity (Leander, 2004; Lefebvre, 1991; Soja, 1996), and argue that place and the relationships in place make meaning and create and uphold boundaries (Wohlwend, 2021). Blommaert (2010) argues,

> Movement of people across space is never a move across empty spaces. The spaces are always someone's space, and they are filled with norms, expectations, conceptions of what counts as proper and normal (indexical) language use and what does not count as such. (p. 6)

Spatialized literacies examine socially constructed spaces and the production of power dynamics in order to make sense of the identities and relationships constructed in and with space (Leander, 2004; Lefebvre, 1991; Soja, 1996, 2010). Considering the relation of power dynamics, Jones et al. (2016) write, "Place and space-making for and with children and youth is a political act, and all educators and educational researchers are engaged in such politics" (p. 28). While objects in place and discourses in place reveal social expectations, embodied histories, and ideologies of practices within a place, looking at literacy spaces is a way to frame interactions in a place and see the ways in which such interactions are physically, socially, and spatially constructed. The dynamic relationships of space considers how actors and nonactors contribute to the co-production of space and history (Leander, 2004; Lefebvre, 1991; Soja, 2010). Space offers "valuable connections between the materiality of literacy and its flows in the new times" (Mills et al., 2013, p. 420).

Recognizing the balance among social, spatial, and historical literacies (Lefebvre, 1991; Soja, 2010) affords an understanding of the identities and complexities of youth in rural spaces—in essence, from the beginning, acknowledging and positioning youth as complex and disrupting stereotypes of a simple, nostalgic, or homogenous existence in the countryside. Viewing literacy as social, spatial, and historical considers not just the language but also the multiple modes interacting to make meaning, as well as the practices, histories, materials, emplacement, texts, and bodies that interact to produce discourses and reveal constructed ways of knowing, being, and doing (Leander, 2004).

Protest Literacies

Robust research exists about the classroom space promoting and building critical consciousness in response to social and political movements, including Black Lives Matter, through critical literacy practices and culturally sustaining pedagogies (Kinloch et al., 2020; Muhammad, 2019; Pennell, 2019). Kinloch et al. (2020) call for classroom pedagogy that de-centers Whiteness, promotes loving and humanizing interactions among Black communities and confronts public attacks against Blackness to dismantle racism and foster cultural equality. Muhammad (2019) shows such a classroom pedagogy in the form of agitation literacies, which she conceptualizes as reading and writing texts that disrupt systemic oppression. She argues for educators to engage in agitation literacies to promote critical literacy and identity development among youth in the classroom. Similarly, Pennell (2019) de-centered Whiteness in her classroom by using critical literacy, queer pedagogy, and social justice pedagogy to examine texts around Black

Lives Matter, arguing that confronting institutionalized racism in the classroom is a way to create better allies for racial justice.

Research also examines out-of-classroom literacy practices and civic engagement, focusing on the everyday practices of youth (Duncan, 2021; Kynard, 2013; Richardson & Ragland, 2018; Wiederhold et al., 2017). Duncan's (2021) extensive work in Rio de Janeiro studying reactions and protests in the favelas after policy changes examines the literacy practices developed and used to enact social change. Kynard's (2013) research also focused on protest literacies, examining how Black student protest literacies are a counterinstitution outside school spaces in which students engage in literacy learning (p. 30). Kynard examines protest practices of Historically Black Colleges and Universities from the 1920s to the 1960s and how students challenged the concepts of literacy and learning. Examining the literacy practices of the Black Freedom Movement, Kynard determines Black students enacted vernacular insurrections—not just a counter hegemonic response to dominant culture but rather new, emerging, culturally specific literacy practices and discourses. Richardson and Ragland (2018) also considered the Black language and Black literacies the Black community unapologetically performs (p. 52) in digital spaces and spaces of protest for the Black Lives Matter movement.

This research considers how students used literacy texts and knowledge of protests and anti-Black racism to situate their own activism. I examine the social, historical, spatial, and cultural practices students agentially enacted and how these practices disrupted power dynamics. This research positions community protests as literacy spaces from which education stakeholders can learn about the literacies students already have about systemic oppression in order to inform their own understanding and pedagogies on civic engagement in the classroom.

THEORETICAL FRAMEWORK

With the fluidity of emplacement and identity in mind, this study uses spatial justice (Soja, 2010) and intersectionality (Crenshaw, 1989) as two theoretical approaches. Combining intersectionality and spatial justice affords a framework for understanding the social and cultural categories as well as the power dynamics students navigate in a given space. I use intersectionality and spatial justice to consider how students are socioculturally situated and contextualized, how they co-construct space by connecting and joining to make meaning, and how their signs and bodies reveal an understanding about relations of power within place.

Spatial Justice

Soja's (2010) notion of spatial consciousness argues that social justice is a spatial issue by highlighting how geographies and places impact and contribute to inequity, oppression, and discrimination. Soja argues,

> [Geographies] are not just dead background or a neutral physical stage for the human drama but are filled with material and imagined forces that affect events and experiences, forces that can hurt us or help us in nearly everything we do, individually and collectively. (p. 19)

Referring to it as a critical spatial perspective, Soja sees geography as mutually constructed and the spatial and social as dialectically intertwined, maintaining that the inequities within a space could be changed by an awareness and recognition of space as a purposefully socially complex product. In this way, social movements could also be spatial movements, and such movements fought justice locally in connection with bigger organizations to foster equity and promote their own objectives, acknowledging that those who were oppressed and marginalized were, at some level, experiencing implications of unjust geographies (Soja, 2010). For example, Soja explains the resurgence of labor movements in Los Angeles and how, along with this resurgence of protest for economic justice was an increased consciousness of place-based politics, with neighborhood and community organizing efforts and local grassroots activism taking place. Change was a result of both economic and spatial justice, spurred by a consciousness "of how the regional economy significantly shapes local conditions" (p. 25).

Seeing social justice as an issue of space allows researchers to think differently about justice and action, perhaps cultivating new ways of knowing about space and justice and meaning making as tied to local histories and spatial understandings. This research uses spatial justice as a framework not to foreground spatial practices but, rather, to acknowledge the ways in which space is involved in social justice action and including it when analyzing the social and historical practices of youth within a space of protest.

Intersectionality

Intersectionality is a spatial metaphor (Collins, 2019; Crenshaw, 1989) that brings to mind a mental visual of place, relationships, and social experiences. In the late 20th century, Black feminists argue categories like race, class, and gender "were not stable and discrete but, rather, variable and changing constellations that are interrelated, co-constitutive, and simultaneous" (Tomlinson, 2019, p. 180). A framework of intersectionality examines these dynamics of sameness and difference across categories in relation to power (Cho et al., 2013; Crenshaw, 1989). Intersectionality "offers a window into thinking about the significance of ideas and social action in fostering social transformation" (Collins, 2019, p. 41). This research uses intersectionality to understand varying perspectives and positionalities as well as to conceptualize power relations in order to concretely examine the ways young people address anti-Black discrimination and police brutality at a Black Lives Matter protest. Intersectionality helps critically situate the positionalities of students as they participate in civic engagement in their rural community.

RESEARCH METHODS

Site

This research takes place in what I refer to as Crossroads, a rural town in the Rust Belt region of the Midwest (see Figure 14.1). Crossroads is the county seat in a county in which almost 70% of the population voted for Trump in the 2020 election. Twenty-five percent of families within the Crossroads town limits live below the poverty level (U.S. Census Bureau, 2020). Crossroads is also situated in locations within what is referred to as

Figure 14.1 Early on during the local Black Lives Matter protest.

the new Latino diaspora (Hamann, 2015), a region in the United States with an increased Latinx population in historically White areas. In Crossroads, Latinx families represent almost 30% of the population (U.S. Census Bureau, 2020). Nearly 29% of local students come from Spanish-speaking homes. Crossroads also has a growing population of undocumented residents, including unaccompanied minors, which has increased over the last 7 years.

Whiteness is embodied in the community's current, historical, and geographical framework. I had conversations with several long-term residents who told me of the signs that marked the boundaries of the community as a sundown town[1] well into the 1960s. As of 2019, Black families accounted for just 1.7% of the town's population (U.S. Census Bureau, 2020). As a former public school teacher, I was aware of local racial discrimination among students in my own classroom and reported several racially-based discriminatory offenses throughout my tenure as a teacher. A student complained that a teacher called him the N-word. A group of Latinx boys were asked by the head football coach if they had green cards; if not, he would not let them play (they were all U.S. citizens). A girl was prohibited by her bus driver from speaking in Spanish with her friends. While the town has become increasingly diverse, historic Whiteness and racism are prevalent among school and community spaces.

Positionality

My own positionality is grounded in the perspectives of race, literacy, and space. As a White woman who is also a long-time resident in this community, I have predispositions that situate my thinking, seeing, and acting. I have seen firsthand both the overt and subtle acts of racism and marginalization that affect the way we move in spaces. As a former teacher, I taught language arts and ESL in the local schools; many of these protesting youth are my former students. "White supremacy exists and, perhaps, thrives in our schools" (Tanner, 2019), and it was in these schools that I was routinely confronted with my own Whiteness as well as the historical White supremacy that was known to pervade this region. As one example, during the 2016 election season, some of the very students protesting at the Black Lives Matter event were in my classroom and witnessed racism in the halls and the cafeterias. White kids shouted to Brown kids, "Build the wall! Build the wall!" The air was thick with tension, and I did the best I could to stop it and stand against it as an educator inside and outside my classroom. A few Latinx students came to me after class that fall, crying, asking if I thought their families would be deported if Trump won. The day after the election, my co-teacher and I put our lesson plans aside and focused on empathy and restorative justice work (Winn, 2013), circling our chairs together and having honest conversations about biases and race and fear. For the rest of the school year, we implemented a project called "Empathy Fridays," a focus on learning from each other and celebrating our racial, cultural, and linguistic differences. Looking back, I wish I could say I had incorporated Whiteness into the discourse about race that school year. While we had hard conversations, I did not name Whiteness. I talked about equity and empathy and inclusivity and impacts of institutionalized racism, but during my tenure as a public educator, I was not aware of Whiteness enough to de-center it. In this way, I did not explicitly name racism or Whiteness as a White problem (Tanner, 2019).

Pauli Badenhorst (2019) writes about how White teachers must interrogate their own emotions and how anti-racist work "comes to be as much a work performed upon self as within the social spaces within which white educators work" (p. 2016). A Black Lives Matter protest, led by transnational Latinx and White youth, in a rural community space, featuring both educators and students, is complex and ultimately influenced by my own emotional responses, my desire to confront anti-Black racism as a White teacher, and my motivation to challenge cultural assumptions on rurality and youth as an education researcher and rural resident. I grew to learn the necessity of naming Whiteness and grappling with Whiteness and White racialized identities (Tanner, 2019). I also approach this research with the understanding of how space and social practices are both constructing and constructed. This research could not be done without exploring and noticing the literacy practices of youth—how they move and occupy space, how they emplace themselves and other literacy objects in space, and how they interact to produce social action.

Methodological Framework: Geosemiotics and Social Geography

This study uses geosemiotics (Scollon & Scollon, 2003) and social geography (Lefebvre, 1991; Soja, 1989) to consider how youth protested for Black Lives Matter, specifically with respect to where they were emplaced, how they were socioculturally situated and contextualized, how they connected across platforms to communicate and mean in place, and what their protesting reveals about power relationships and social positioning. Geosemiotics is a theoretical and analytical framework that viewed humans as "bundles of histories" (Scollon & Scollon, 2003, p. 16), people unconsciously navigating multiple social categories and performances situated and influenced by language, discourses, and experiences. Geosemiotics is rooted in the notion that signs placed in the material world are given meaning by social action and discourses in place.

Using geosemiotics considers not just the language but also the action that signs produced through their emplacement and social, historical, and cultural use. This requires researchers to examine how materials "are shaped by discourses and histories of practices that underlie our shared expectations" (Wohlwend, 2021, p. 12) while also looking at the systems that influence the signs' meaning-making process in specific places and times.

Geosemiotics is situated in the work of M. A. K. Halliday (1978) and other social semioticians, noting how all semiotic systems are systems of choice (Scollon & Scollon, 2003). These semiotic systems "operate as systems of social positioning and power relationship both at the level of interpersonal relationships and at the level of struggles for hegemony among social groups in any society" (p. 7). A geosemiotics approach reconceptualizes artifacts as identity texts that produce meaning and are read as assemblages of histories, discourses, practices, meanings, and modes (Wohlwend, 2021). This methodology considers how place semiotics and visual semiotics impact and index meaning of language, noting that "the cultural location or where a sign is placed is as important as the depicted meaning or what the print says" (p. 170).

Indexicality is a tenet of geosemiotics. Indexicality is the way signs make meaning based on their emplacement in the material world in a specific place and time, focusing not so much on indexicality of language but rather on how signs index other semiotic systems (Scollon & Scollon, 2003). Whittingham (2019) gives the example of how a stop sign means something different to a pedestrian or motorist when placed in an intersection compared to the meaning a stop sign makes when being on a truck en route to being placed at the intersection. Semiotic systems function as systems of power dynamics and social positioning "precisely because they are systems of choices and no choices are neutral in the social world" (Scollon & Scollon, 2003, p. 7).

Geosemiotics focuses on the interconnected relationships of three such semiotic systems: interaction order (Goffman, 1982), visual semiotics (Kress & Van Leeuwen, 2006), and place semiotics (Scollon & Scollon, 2003). Interaction order considers the ways humans form social relationships and produce interactions among themselves in a given space, noting how "our bodies make and give off meaning read by others because of where they are and what they are doing in space" (Whittingham, 2019, p. 55). When considering social action, interaction order looks at factors like body movement, position, proximity, sense of time, and posture within a space. While interaction order looks at social relationships, visual semiotics considers how signs visually represent various forms of social actions and relies on Kress and van Leeuwen's (2006) work to examine the ways in which pictures are produced for visual interpretation. Interpreting semiotic resources within a visual semiotics framework requires ethnographic attention, culturally specific visual observation, and documentation (Whittingham, 2019). Place semiotics looks at how place is a semiotic resource as well as an index to other semiotic systems. When explaining place semiotics, Scollon and Scollon (2003) state, "All we mean to indicate here is the huge aggregation of semiotic systems which are not located in the persons of social actors or in the frame artifacts of visual semiotics" (p. 8). The relationships among these three systems are the focus of geosemiotics.

Along with geosemiotics, this research also leans on social geography, which considers how space interacts with social, cultural, and historical practices to make meaning (Lefebvre, 1991; Soja, 1989; Whittingham, 2019). Geosemiotics allows researchers to identify social action rooted in social, cultural, and historical experiences, while adding social geography helps examine the significance of the co-construction of space. Whittingham (2019) uses the example of the printing of a world map: A world map printed in the United States foregrounds North America and Europe as the visual center, while a geographically accurate map visually orientates the continents differently. Soja (1989, 2010) uses the notion of the socio-spatial dialectic, which emphasizes how space shapes social life just as much as space is shaped by social life. This concept of space stems from Lefebvre's (1991) *The Production of Space*, which reconceptualizes space as socially produced, both real and imaginary. This concept of space considers space a powerful sociopolitical force, a mutable and dynamic target of power and action. Considering my own former students' signs as they emplaced themselves at a site of protest, this research considers the ways in which materials interact with bodies to make meaning in a specific time and space. This idea of place making and social geography in combination reiterates Soja's (1989) idea of the socio-spatial dialectic, a notion that spatial and social practices are relational.

Data Collection

In this study, I analyze publicly sourced photographs of the grassroots Black Lives Matter protest in Crossroads, focusing on students and their signs. I approach this analysis by first gathering photographs of the protest. I gathered photos by searching for a hashtag that indicated the geolocation of this event and also through local media posts. This led me to photos from local radio and news media sites as well as fellow protesters

Disrupting Discourses in Place ▪ **337**

with public social media accounts. I gathered over 30 photos. I then looked at photos concentrated on students as well as overall shots of the protest to analyze the ways in which students uniquely protested and emplaced themselves.

Because my attention was focused on students' multimodal literacies, I did my best to narrow down the photos to photos of youth, observing the emplacement of their signs and bodies in protest. As a former teacher in this small community and a fellow protester at the event, I had the affordance of recognizing many of the students across the photographs while also noticing their spatial patterns of gathering in place. Students geographically organized themselves together, so the photographs I gathered mostly concentrated on the presence of students at the protest. This narrowed the photos down to 10. This Black Lives Matter protest was a 6-hour event, so it was implausible that all students who were in attendance at the protest were captured in these photographs. This research is not about the number of students present but about the way students in rural areas showed up to protest. Figures 14.2, 14.3, and 14.4 are selected images from the analysis. I selected these images for analysis as they provide the depth necessary for a geosemiotics framework including attention to interaction order, visual semiotics, and place semiotics.

Figure 14.2 Students, signs, and the intersection.

Figure 14.3 Say their names.

Figure 14.4 Student leader with megaphone.

Disrupting Discourses in Place • 339

Data Analysis

Using a geosemiotics approach, I analyzed each photograph according to visual semiotics, interaction order, and place semiotics and identified all three sign systems across photographs, using a rubric to keep track of my observations. Tables 14.1, 14.2, and 14.3 are the geosemiotics analysis rubrics for

TABLE 14.1 Geosemiotic Analysis of Figure 14.2	
Geosemiotic Analysis	Description
Interaction Order	• Protesters are organized into lines. Index expectations and "rules" of protest. • Students near the intersection are separated from the other protesters but still in lines. • Arms and signs overlapping the two foregrounded. • Two on the left indicate a "with." The two in the middle indicate another "with." Together they all form the platform event of protest. Girl with camera = civil inattention. • The row behind this front row of protesters looks to be a row of students. They are formed toward the back edge of the large sidewalk. • The rest of the protesters gather in rows in the grass behind the sidewalk and up toward the courthouse. • Rows organized neatly. • No social interpersonal action happening in the frame in my perceived analysis. • All bodies facing forward. • Three protesters engage and look directly at photographer.
Visual Semiotics	• Three protesters gaze straight into the camera. • Participants in this photograph are turned based on the direction they are facing. • The two in the middle face center: Their stances align with the rest of their body. • The two on the right are turned slightly to the right, and their gaze and body movements align in that direction. • The boy on the left holds his sign straight forward but his body is shifted toward the direction of the camera. • The girl next to him looks down at her camera. • For the most part, the protesters on the grass face forward. There is at least one protester facing toward the camera. • The center of this photograph splits down the middle between the "Racism Is a Pandemic" sign and the sign with hearts. • Sign materials: • Mostly white posterboard. Sign with hearts looks as if white paper was glued or taped over the sign. 2 signs visible are cardboard. • Materials: mostly red and black markers. One sign in graffiti style. • Concentrating on sign with hearts: most salient is "OPPRESSED!"—outlined, bolded, and underlined. Also centered on the sign and

(continued)

TABLE 14.1 Geosemiotic Analysis of Figure 14.2 (continued)

Geosemiotic Analysis	Description
Visual Semiotics (cont.)	on its own sheet of paper. 6 hearts in red. 4 hearts frame the word "Oppressed" while the other hearts are placed over "No" and "Others" • Racism sign: "Is" is most salient. "Racism" and "a Pandemic" are written in red. Saturation of red and black and blue. "Is" is in the center of the sign, framed by dots and underlined several times. All capitals. • LGBT+ Sign: LGBT+ is most salient, underlined, largest word, in red. Protester wears a black shirt with words in multicolors: "We're all human." Each letter of human represents colors of a different LGBTQ+ flag. • All signs written in single strokes except the middle sign, which is written in single red stroke outlined in single black stroke. • Two signs in the middle held at eye level of a vehicle driver, along with cardboard sign to the left. LGBT+ sign held above head. • Three girls are emplaced in the intersection on the second busiest street in the downtown area. One foot slightly overlaps onto the road.
Place Semiotics	• Group of students stands out in front of the crowd. • Traffic pole shows they are at the intersection. • They stand together in a row, but the turn of their bodies suggest they may not all be together. • Signs are gripped on the sides for the two in the front; the LGBT+ sign holds hers with her first, her one thumb visible. • Postures are straight. Feet are planted. • Their proximity is closer to the road and further from the courthouse. • Middle of the day on a Friday. Flags in the background. • Suggests situated semiotics.

Green: Interaction Order; **Purple: Visual Semiotics**; **Blue: Place Semiotics**; Yellow: Social Action

Figure 14.5 Geosemiotic analysis of students, signs, and the intersection.

Disrupting Discourses in Place • **341**

TABLE 14.2   Geosemiotic Analysis of Figure 14.3

Geosemiotic Analysis	Description
Interaction Order	• Photograph is centered on one protester. • No interpersonal action that can be perceived based on the bounds of the photograph. • Seems to be single rather than with, but that is dependent on the photograph, not the actual scene or observation. • Three people stand near her—two behind and 1 to the left.
Visual Semiotics	• Gaze is off-centered; to the left. Arms extended up and out, holding the sign toward the bottom of each side. • Just visible in the bottom center of the photo is the image of Tupac Shakur on her black shirt. Sign indexes hip hop. • The sign is large in comparison to others. The sign has multiple materials: cardboard as a base and large white paper (it crinkles under her grip) glued on. Saturation. This suggests salience: white background with a list of names written in single-stroke black marker. • Sign is written in black and red marker. Mostly black. • The top of the sign: "USE" is capitalized. "NO" is capitalized. "Say Their Names" is in red and underlined. Periods between each word here indexes digital/text language and suggests emphasis. • Four rows are written the names of Black people murdered by police. • George Floyd is not the first name, but is the only name in red toward the upper left corner. • Hundreds is crossed out and the bottom right corner is capitalized, underlined, and says "Thousands More." • To the right in the frame of the photograph is a protester wearing what appears to be a multicolored religious stole. Indexes religious culture. Hands hold a sign that seems to read "Say Their Names" in black with smaller red words around it.
Place Semiotics	• Posture is straight. • Protester is in the front of some people. Hard to determine location but trees suggest she is in the front all the way on the opposite side of the courthouse. • Person next to her and two people behind her suggest rows again, which aligns with what the other photographs show. • Her body is turned in the same direction as her gaze. • Posture is straight. Arms are wide.

each of the included photos. I visually mapped photographs using Scollon and Scollon's (2003) geo-semiotic mapping process to show how these three sign systems interconnected to produce social action. These can be found in Figures 14.5, 14.6, and 14.7, noting that "the full utility of a geosemiotic analysis is only achieved when interaction order, visual semiotics, and place semiotics are attended to simultaneously" (Whittingham, 2019, p. 69).

As there are multiple social actions occurring in one site of engagement, and even in one photograph, these findings represent my own meaning

Figure 14.6 Geosemiotic analysis of "Say Their Names."

making process from my own positionality, an important distinction and clarification to make. Reading signs and photographs as texts "requires an understanding that signs and texts exist in relationship to other texts and contexts and that multiple, shifting, and competing readings are possible" (Baildon & Damico, 2008, p. 269). There are a number of social actions in each image. I focused on the action that was foregrounded in each photo. The mappings were created using Google Drawing. I also used Google Drawing to add masks on a few faces to conceal identity for safety and security measures.

My own design choices came into play during the analysis. Using geo-semiotics, it was a common practice to mark and annotate photographs with shapes and shading to indicate social action. As the designer of this research study, I intentionally chose pastel colors—green, purple, blue, and yellow—for the geo-semiotic mapping. Bolder colors encircling faces and drawing attention to students in the analysis felt harsh and dehumanizing. My attempt at noting social action was to highlight the action, not target any participants. To help make this distinction, I carefully chose colors I perceived as softer to keep focus on the collective social action rather than the participants.

Disrupting Discourses in Place • 343

TABLE 14.3 Geosemiotic Analysis of Figure 14.4

Geosemiotic Analysis	Description
Interaction Order	• Participant holding object stands in front of everyone else. Suggests single. • Social event • Platform event • With the exception of one protester, all protesters in photograph are gazing off-center and across the street. • Proximity of youth are much closer together than other rows.
Visual Semiotics	• Materials of posters are mostly posterboard. One sign in front is yellow, indicating saturation. Most are written with black and red marker except one sign. • Protester's eyes squint, and eyebrows are curled. Stands holding megaphone up near his chest, hand curled around the mouthpiece. Is he in the process of raising it? Lowering it? Action suspended as gaze reaches across street. • Protester in front is in the center of photograph.
Place Semiotics	• Signs are held overhead as well as at eye level. Almost all signs face the same direction, toward the front. Some signs overlap each other. • Grass is behind these protesters, indicating they are on the sidewalk (which other photographs support). • To the very right of the photo, a protester's mouth is open. Suggests shouting. • Protester in front is not talking during this shouting; interesting as this person holds the megaphone.

Green: Interaction Order; Purple: Visual Semiotics

Figure 14.7 Geosemiotic analysis of student leader with megaphone.

FINDINGS

Geo-semiotics analysis and social geography focus on the types of action supported or encouraged by this event in a specific time and place. I looked across photographs to note the movement and emplacement of students during the protest. I mapped each photo to identify and understand the social action and the ways in which youth at a rural protest positioned themselves to co-construct spatial systems in agentive ways and how material resources impacted their engagements in this space of protest. I elaborate my findings in three sections: place making and discourses in place, indexicality of power and emphasis in place, and indexicality of historical knowledge of protests and anti-Black racism.

Place Making and Discourses in Place

Geo-semiotics helps reveal the social meanings of the material placement of signs (Scollon & Scollon, 2003). Across photos, students had limited interpersonal action during the protest.

They seemed to stand with people they knew, based on how they emplaced themselves and the proximity and direction their bodies faced. The emplacement of bodies and signs faced the road, not each other. Across photos, students were engaged in what is referred to as a social platform event (Goffman, 1982). Students were not engaged with each other interpersonally but rather collectively for protest.

As a long-time resident, I was familiar with the organization of social justice events in this community. Historically, the few gatherings that were held on the courthouse lawn in the last decade were located back by the steps of the courthouse and the lawn right in front of the courthouse facing the side road. This Black Lives Matter protest faced the main road, which was something unexpected to me as a protester. Students pushed the protest even closer to the road by standing in the intersection and on the front edge of the sidewalk, garnering more visibility and attention. The sidewalk connected to two parallel sidewalks leading up to the main entrances of the courthouse. Early on during the protest, this front sidewalk remained empty. Most protesters organized themselves into rows on the grass closer to the courthouse. Once more students arrived, student protesters began to line that front sidewalk, near the intersection, as seen in Figures 14.2 and 14.4. Counterprotesters gathered across the street, and eventually youth moved and lined the entire sidewalk, facing the counterprotesters and the oncoming traffic. Students faced forward in these spaces, raised their signs both above their head and also at eye level with drivers of passing cars. This agential movement of students disrupted the protest discourse of geographic location. The spatial organization of students toward the front of the road suggested not just a gathering of showing support and solidarity, but of being seen and visible and communicating a message of social action.

Students used spaces like the intersection and front edge of the sidewalk to co-construct meaning; their signs and bodies made meaning differently at the front of the sidewalk, where driving cars (non-protesters) could see them, than back on the lawn or closer to the courthouse, where bodies and protest signs might suggest a gathering of support rather than a call to action. When students emplaced themselves along the sidewalk, they broke rank from the rows of adult protesters behind them in the grass and expanded the boundaries of the space of protest to now include the front of the sidewalk and intersection. They made a front line of the protest, shouting and chanting; and in turn, they became the de facto leaders of the protest. The intentionality of emplacement suggests that students intentionally shifted the purpose of the protest from gathering together to communicating with non-protesters, mainly the drivers of passing cars, as well as the counterprotesters.

All students co-constructed space in different and unique ways—from the girls who stood in the intersection, to the participant in Figure 14.4 who emplaced his body in front of all the other protesters, including the newly formed front line of students, to the protester who emplaced herself on the border of the sidewalk but all the way down on the other side. These were early formations but they indicate an agential purpose in where and how students placed themselves and decided to protest. The sidewalk was both a boundary and a sociopolitical wielding of power. Students stretched along the sidewalk, but kept the boundaries of protest rather than going into the road. Shifting the protest forward in this way gave them increased power in this space, as they stood in places of greater visibility and action.

Indexicality of Power and Emphasis in Place

Geo-semiotics and social geography together reveal the social action of a place as well as how the action in a particular place is an important indicator of its meaning. In Figure 14.2, the students held their signs in the direction of passing cars, emplacing their bodies and signs directly in the intersection. The student in the center of the photograph stood in the intersection crosswalk, indicated by the red tactile pavement—a sign itself in the community that indicated specific meaning at that place and time. Tactile paving here helped communicate to visually impaired pedestrians that a street was oncoming. In this image, the participant firmly planted her feet in the center of the tactile paving, a place communicating the ending of the sidewalk and the beginning of the road. She held the sign at the eye level of passing drivers. The sign held just below her shoulders emphasized the word "Oppressed." Whether the hearts were meant for the drivers that passed the protest or whether they suggested solidarity and empathy for Black lives, the hearts and placement of the hearts on the sign both emphasized and softened the protester's message. The use of hearts as semiotic resources indexed the use of emojis in text messages and social media spaces of discourse. In these spaces, emojis are often used to convey meaning, especially to add context to language in order to ensure the receiver understood the tone of the message.

Symbols as meaning makers is a ubiquitous form of communication, especially among young people. Hearts on this protest sign showed digital literacy and understanding of symbols and text, as well as literacy practices of understanding tone in written text.

Using visual semiotics (Kress & van Leeuwen, 2006) to analyze her protest sign, there was a seeming juxtaposition the center participant used. This sign centered, capitalized, and underlined the word "Oppressed," giving it salience on her poster. Two red hearts were placed on the sign above the words "No" and "Other," and four red hearts also clustered as a frame around the word "Oppressed." The materiality of her sign was a type of poster board on top of which she adhered two pieces of white paper; she dedicated one of those two white sheets of paper just to the word "Oppressed!" Her sign was not a call to action but rather a declarative statement emphasizing the oppression of the Black community by police brutality. Her emplacement of standing directly in the tactile paving further emphasized an intentionality, boldly declaring the oppression of the Black community to passing cars.

The protester to her right held a sign above her head that read, "LGBT+ Against Racism." What was interesting about this sign was that "LGBT" was underlined twice, not "Racism," as would be expected at a Black Lives Matter protest. This sign drew attention to the fact that the LGBTQ+ community was standing in support of Black lives at this protest. With her shirt indexing the LGBTQ+ community, as well as her emplacement in the red tactile paving, together this social action indexed a message emphasizing the LGBTQ+ community's support of the Black community in this space of protest.

Holding a megaphone rather than a sign and emplacing himself in front of the front line of protesters, the protester in Figure 14.4 solidified himself in a leadership role. A cheering mini-megaphone indexed a position of leadership and authority in chanting and cheering scenarios. The social action represented here, coupled with social geography, demonstrated how this student co-constructed space: He used a cheering megaphone as a symbol of power and leadership in this space, emplacing himself front and center, holding it with both hands, even when he was not actively chanting. The space did not dictate this student's movements; rather, he showed

Disrupting Discourses in Place • **347**

agential purpose in breaking rank to position himself in a place of power within a space of protest.

Indexicality of Historical Knowledge of Protests and Anti-Black Racism

Students as protesters demonstrate an extended knowledge of racial injustice and police brutality. In Figure 14.2, the protester to the left held a sign saying "Racism Is a Pandemic." She used blue dots to emphasize the word "Is," suggesting that she argued for the concept of racism as a global pandemic, bigger than just the murder of George Floyd. This protester's choice of words possibly indexed the legitimacy of COVID-19 being referred to as a pandemic while also calling racism a pandemic. At the same time of this protest, there was a lot of local tension and discourse among community leaders, schools, and families about the legitimacy of COVID-19. The use of the word "pandemic" on this sign suggested an indexicality to the discourse of COVID-19 as a pandemic while situating the idea of racism as an invasive problem affecting the entire world. "Racism is a Pandemic" was also a slogan used in photos of other protests on social media (Busby, 2020). This sign could possibly also index a knowledge of other anti-Black racism and police brutality protests.

The sign all the way to the left in Figure 14.2 showed several phrases associated with anti-Black racism and police brutality. The protester held a sign saying #Fuck12, #BLM, and Black Lives Matter, as well as George Floyd's name, the common phrase, "Say His Name," and phrases associated with the murder of George Floyd. These phrases all indexed a greater cultural awareness and depth of understanding of police brutality and the movements perpetuated through social media, evolving to resist and dismantle systemic oppression.

In Figure 14.2, the protester in the center also indexed a knowledge of protests. Her sign quoted a popular slogan seen often in recent protests: "No one is free when others are oppressed!" This quote, whose author was unknown, was used in recent marches like the Women's March in 2017 and other Black Lives Matter marches that took place before the one in Crossroads ("No One Is Free When Others Are Oppressed," 2017). Because of my residency over the last decade in Crossroads and my active involvement in the community, I knew Crossroads had not had a women's march nor held any rallies or events where this quote would have been known or seen locally. Therefore, the quote on this protester's sign indexed a broader knowledge of protests. Whether that knowledge was from participation or social media, the protester used a common quote associated with matters of resistance on her sign to demonstrate anti-Black racism and police brutality in her hometown.

In Figure 14.3, this protester emplaced herself at the very opposite side of the sidewalk, all the way down away from the intersection, the furthest sign on the other edge of the protest, which was confirmed by analyzing several photographs. She held the sign in different positions throughout photographs, mainly at eye level and above her head. She emplaced herself in a small cluster of people, away from most of the other protesters. In Figure 14.3, this protester designed a sign using multiple materials—a large piece of cardboard and multiple sheets of what looks to be 8 x 11 white paper. The sign listed 128 names of Black people murdered by police. The second name listed in the first column was George Floyd, right beneath Breonna Taylor, the only name written in red, indicating importance and significance (Kress & van Leeuwen, 2006). Listing 128 names of Black people murdered by police indicated a literacy practice of positioning this protest as an ongoing issue of systemic racism. Further, George Floyd's name was in red. One interpretation of this sign could be knowledge that while George Floyd was the catalyst for this protest, it wasn't the first. Also, she situated her own knowledge of the history of anti-Black murders when she crossed out the word "hundreds" and instead wrote "thousands." "Say.Their.Names" at the top was readable from the road. The purpose of the sign suggested that the importance was not to know each name but to show that anti-Black police brutality was rampant and not reduced to a singular case. This meaning carried a different message to non-protesters and protesters alike: not just Black Lives Matter but a reiteration of the institutionalized racism that existed among police. Using punctuation in between words indexed social media and texting literacies, as this was a popular written tactic across those platforms that the protester used here to index further importance and emphasis.

The social action in Figure 14.4 suggests the protesters' indexing knowledge of protests. He held a mini-megaphone and stood in front of the other protesters, most of whom held signs.

Triangulated by other photographs, his gaze was fixated on the counterprotesters across the street, and he used a mini-megaphone to amplify his message and to spread it among student and adult protesters, who followed and repeated his chants and calls of action. The use of an amplifying tool indexed a knowledge that at protests, people shouted in unison, and people were sometimes led in shouts and chants by a leader who stood in a place of visibility and authority.

DISCUSSION

Analyzing the ways students positioned their bodies and signs creates opportunities for understanding how students used space and semiotic resources to demonstrate critical understanding of issues like social justice and racism (Siegel, 2012). Noticing how students emplaced themselves at this site of protest illustrates the impact of space, both as a geographical practice and also as a literacy practice that dictates and shapes meaning. Students are agents of their own activism, breaking rank and moving forward from the grass to the edge of the sidewalk and even into the intersection, upturning the power dynamics and becoming the leaders of the protest. Students communicate social and cultural knowledge and histories through the combination of their signs, their emplacement of their bodies and signs, and the ways they interact with each other and the community during public protest. Their activism for Black Lives Matter helps elucidate the importance of studying youth activism and the numerous ways in which students resist in their towns. Furthermore, this study emphasizes the importance of considering place when observing youth and seeking to understand rurality and race relations (Lensmire, 2017).

This research is not representative of every geographically rural community in the United States, middle America, or in the Rust Belt. This research features one example of a protest in a rural community. Because of this, one limitation is that this research could seem singular and anomalous to rural culture. However, this study upturns deficit language and shows the complexities of youth as they protested and resisted against anti-Black racism and police brutality. In U.S. rural areas, protests are rare (Woods, 2003), and this was an opportunity to observe and study students as activists in a public space, focusing on the ways they exercised their own agency and multiple literacies.

The findings of this study illustrate how spaces of protest are sites of multiple literacies. The social action of student protesters show a decisive and agential purpose influenced specifically by place. Students pushed the protest and expanded the perimeter of the protest to the edge of the sidewalk and the intersection, closer to the community residents rather than the courthouse. Doing so also reconstructed the meaning of gathering. Rather than gathering together merely to express solidarity in numbers, the spatial organizing and social action of student protesters suggests that students positioned themselves in places of greater visibility in order to communicate and interact with the local community with their bodies and signs. Students co-constructed space as leaders, led chants, stood together, and called their community to anti-racist action.

Protesters' intersectionalities are visible in several ways at this protest. Students separated themselves from adult protesters. Students still kept themselves in rows, but they gathered together and grew in numbers over the duration of the protest, suggesting a navigation and attention to their age as an intersectional factor of protest. Students navigated sexual orientation, age, and geography as they positioned themselves as activists and co-constructed this space of protest. Their signs and bodies suggest that they used a knowledge of historical anti-Black racism and police brutality to situate their activism and meaning making. Students' protesting, through the use of symbols and hashtags, index digital and social media literacies. Students emplaced themselves in front of other protesters with signs in positions of leadership and power. These are just some of the ways local youth navigated space in this rural community.

Interrogating this particular space of protest using both geo-semiotics and social geography reveals the power relations and literacies that exist within a community space. A geo-semiotics approach supports the understanding of discourses in place, while social geography helps understand how space is co-constructed within a given social action. In other words, analyzing student protesters' positioning and how and what they protested by analyzing their protest signs and bodies in interaction with and among each other reveals the social and historical literacy practices students use to make meaning as activists. By examining the ways in which students' movements disrupt the origins of protest discourse, thereby implicating power dynamics, deepens an understanding of how students agentially protested, not just by leaving their house and being present at the protest but also by considering how they intentionally communicate and make meaning within the space of protest. This study brings critical attention to practices of youth that center them as co-constructors of their own meaning making rather than regarding them as responsive participants that adhere to expectations and norms set by adults. Understanding that these movements and positionings are both intentional and disruptive can afford researchers and educators the opportunity to (re) consider how youth make meaning in terms of movement as well as consider the sociopolitical knowledge youth may already have acquired outside of the classroom. Furthermore, this study emphasizes how spaces of protest are spaces of literacy and calls education stakeholders to learn from students' participation in civic engagement to discover how students make meaning, how they express their own ideas and beliefs about racial justice, and how they agentially and collectively stand together in purpose and intention.

This chapter seeks to answer recent calls in research for new directions in the field of critical literacy, including research that engages with multimodalities and spatiality (Vasquez et al., 2019). Literacy research on civic engagement, specifically in rural places, is often place-based but does not always include attention to how literacy practices are enacted in and with space. Research highlighting material engagements and rurality is relatively new and needed (Corbett & Donehower, 2017). For example, greater attention is needed toward the new Latino diaspora in the Midwest in order to understand cultural, historical, and social trajectories of anti-racist action in support of Black lives beyond this time and place, as well as how youth are responding, changing, and leading the action. Attention to spaces of protest in rural areas can further disrupt stereotypes of rurality as both idyllic and apathetic to racial justice while valuing the literacies of the space.

CONCLUSION

As Django Paris (2012) says,

> Our work as teachers and researchers is not about language and literacy learning or educational experiences in a mythical political vacuum. Our work as teachers and researchers has always been about struggles for language and literacy rights and human rights. (p. 9)

This chapter examines the spatialized practices of youth that contributed to the construction of literacy while emphasizing the literacies that emerge from spaces of protest and critically analyzes the ways in which youth in rural spaces agentially engaged in protest for Black lives. Students' signs and emplacement interacted and served as symbols that indexed meaning based on culture and place (Scollon & Scollon, 2003). This place in front of the courthouse was chosen by adult community organizers, but youth disrupted discourses in place in multiple ways. The social action of student protesters showed a decisive and agential purpose influenced specifically by place.

Students pushed to the intersections, closer to the community residents rather than the courthouse. Students emplaced themselves and their signs in front of their local community. Mapping social action and space reveal how youth protesters co-constructed space as leaders and used existing historical and cultural knowledge of racial oppression and police brutality to situate their activism. Educators, policy makers, and researchers must continue to find ways to value literacy outside of classroom spaces, learning from students' participation in civic engagement to find how students make meaning, how they express and situate their own ideas and beliefs about racial justice in the world, and how students use their agency to co-construct space in meaningful and powerful ways.

NOTES

1. Sundown towns were communities throughout the United States that historically excluded Black families from residing within city or town limits (Loewen, 2005). Mostly indicated by signs on the permitters of the town lines, people of color were allowed during the day and had to leave by sunset. Crossroads is historically known for being a sundown town

REFERENCES

Badenhorst, P. (2019). Raced encounter on a hilltop: A call for *soulful* justice alongside social justice work. *English Education, 51*(2), 200–208. https://www.jstor.org/stable/26797031

Baildon, M., & Damico, J. (2008). How do we know? Students examine issues of credibility with a complicated multimodal web-based text. *Curriculum Inquiry, 39*(2), 265–285. https://doi.org/10.1111/j.1467-873X.2009.00443.x

Blommaert, J. (2010). *A sociolinguistics of globalization.* Cambridge University Press.

Busby, M. (2020, June 12). This is a historic moment: UK anti-racism protesters on what needs to change. *The Guardian.* https://www.theguardian.com/us-news/2020/jun/12/black-lives-matter-historic-moment-protesters-on-why-they-have-been-demonstrating

Cho, S., Crenshaw, K., & McCall, L. (2013). Toward a field of intersectionality studies: Theory, applications, and praxis. *Signs, 38*(4), 785–810. https://doi.org/10.1086/669608

Collins, P. H. (2019). *Intersectionality as critical social theory.* Duke University Press.

Corbett, M. (2015). Rural literacies: Text and context beyond the metropolis. In J. Rowsell & K. Pahl (Eds.), *The Routledge handbook of literacy studies* (pp. 124–139). Routledge.

Corbett M., & Donehower, K. (2017). Rural literacies: Toward social cartography. *Journal of Research in Rural Education, 32*(5), 1–13. https://jrre.psu.edu/sites/default/files/2019-08/32-5.pdf

Crenshaw, K. (1989). Demarginalizing the intersection of race and sex: A Black feminist critique of antidiscrimination doctrine, feminist theory and antiracist politics. *The University of Chicago Legal Forum, 1989*(1), Article 8. https://chicagounbound.uchicago.edu/uclf/vol1989/iss1/8/

Duncan, J. D. I. (2021). *Researching protest literacies: Literacy as protest in the favelas of Rio de Janeiro.* Routledge.

Eppley, K. (2017). Rural science education as social justice. *Cultural Studies of Science Education, 12*(1), 45–52. https://doi.org/10.1007/s11422-016-9751-7

Goffman, E. (1982). The interaction order: American Sociological Association 1982 presidential address. *American Sociological Review, 48*(1), 1–17. https://doi.org/10.2307/2095141

Halliday, M. A. K. (1978). *Language as social semiotic.* Edward Arnold.

Hamann, E. T. (2015). *Revisiting education in the New Latino Diaspora.* Information Age Publishing.

Hamann, E. T., Wortham, S., & Murillo, E. G. (2002). Education and policy in the new Latino diaspora. In S. Wortham, E. G. Murillo, & E. T. Hamann (Eds.), *Education in the new Latino diaspora* (pp. 1–16). Ablex.

Harste, J. (2003). What do we mean by literacy now? *Voices From the Middle, 10*(3), 8–12. https://www.researchgate.net/publication/228828192_What_do_we_mean_by_literacy_now

Hoffner, C., & Rehkoff, R. A. (2011). Young voters' responses to the 2004 U.S. presidential election: Social identity, perceived media influence, and behavioral outcomes. *Journal of Communication, 61,* 732–757. https://doi.org/10.1111/j.1460-2466.2011.01565.x

Jones, S., Thiel, J. J., Davila, D., Pittard, E., Woglom, J. E., Zhou, X., Brown, T., & Snow, M. (2016). Childhood geographies and spatial justice: Making sense of place and space- making as political acts in education. *American Educational Research Journal, 54*(4), 1126–1158. https://doi.org/10.3102/0002831216655221

Juzwik, M. (2004). Towards an ethics of answerability: Reconsidering dialogism in sociocultural literacy research. *College Composition and Communication, 55*(3), 536–567. https://doi.org/10.2307/4140698

Kinloch, V., Penn, C., & Burkhard, T. (2020). Black lives matter: Storying, identities, and counternarratives. *Journal of Literacy Research, 52*(4), 382–405. https://doi.org/10.1177/1086296X20966372

Kress, G., & Van Leeuwen, (2006). *Reading images.* (2nd ed.). University of Chicago Press.

Kynard, C. (2013). *Vernacular insurrections: Race, Black protest, and the new century in composition-literacies studies.* State University of New York Press.

Leander, K. (2004). Locating Latanya: "The situated production of identity artifacts in classroom interaction." *Research in the Teaching of English, 37*(2), 198–250. https://www.researchgate.net/publication/246713710_Locating_Latanya_The_Situated_Production_of_Identity_Artifacts_in_Classroom_Interaction

Leander, K., & Sheehy, (2004). *Spatializing literacy research.* Peter Lang.

Lefebvre, H. (1991). *The production of space.* Basil Blackwell.

Lensmire, T. (2017). *White folks.* Routledge.

Loewen, J. W. (2005). *Sundown towns: A hidden dimension of American racism.* Touchstone.

Mills, K., Comber, B., & Kelly, P. (2013). Sensing place: Embodiment, sensoriality, kinesis, and children behind the camera. *English Teaching: Practice and Critique, 12*(2), 11–27. https://edlinked.soe.waikato.ac.nz/journal/files/etpc/files/2013v12n2art1.pdf

Mills, K. A., & Unsworth, L. (2017). Multimodal literacy. In *Oxford Research Encyclopedia of Education* (pp. 1–29). Oxford University Press. https://doi.org/10.1093/acrefore/9780190264093.013.232

Moll, L. C. (2000). Inspired by Vygotsky: Ethnographic experiments in education. In C. D. Lee & P. Smagorinsky (Eds.), *Vygotskian perspectives on literacy research: Constructing meaning through collaborative inquiry* (pp. 256–268). Cambridge University Press.

Muhammad, G. E. (2019). Protest, power, and possibilities: The need for agitation literacies. *Journal of Adolescent and Adult Literacy, 63*(3), 351–355. https://doi.org/10.1002/jaal.1014

"No One Is Free When Others Are Oppressed." (2017). Northeastern University Library. http://hdl.handle.net/2047/D20305969

Paris, D. (2012). Become history: Learning from identity texts and youth activism in the wake of Arizona SB1070. *International Journal of Multicultural Education, 14*(2), 1–14. https://doi.org/10.18251/ijme.v14i2.461

Pennell, S. M. (2019). Reading representations of race: Critical literacy and Ferguson. *English Journal, 108*(4), 68–75. https://www.jstor.org/stable/26670031

Richardson, E., & Ragland, A., (2018). #StayWoke: The language and literacies of the #BlackLivesMatter Movement. *Community Literacy Journal, 12*(2), 27–56. https://doi.org/10.25148/clj.12.2.009099

Sanchez-Jankowski, M. (2002). Minority youth and civic engagement: The impact of group relations. *Applied Developmental Science, 6*(1), 237–245. https://doi.org/10.1207/S1532480XADS0604_11

Scollon R., & Scollon S. (2003). *Discourses in place.* Routledge.

Siegel, M. (2012). New times for multimodality? Confronting the accountability culture. *Journal of Adolescent and Adult Literacy, 55*(8), 671–680. https://doi.org/10.1002/JAAL.00082

Soja, E. W. (1989). *Postmodern geographies: The reassertion of space in critical social theory.* Verso.

Soja, E. W. (1996). *Thirdspace: Journeys to Los Angeles and other real-and-imagined places.* Blackwell.

Soja, E. (2010). *Seeking spatial justice.* University of Minnesota Press.

Tanner, S. J. (2019). Whiteness is a White problem: Whiteness in English education. *English Education, 51*(2), 182–199.

Terman, A. R. (2020). Social identities, place, mobility, and belonging: Intersectional experiences of college-educated youth. *Journal of Rural Studies, 77*, 21–32. https://doi.org/10.1016/j.jrurstud.2020.04.033

Thiel, J. J. (2015). 'Bumblebee's in trouble!' Embodied literacies during imaginative superhero play. *Language Arts, 93*(1), 38–49. https://www.academia.edu/15211812/_Bumblebee_s_in_trouble_Embodied_literacies_during_imaginative_superhero_play

Tomlinson, B. (2019). Powerblind intersectionality: Feminist revanchism and inclusion as a one-way street. In K. Crenshaw, L. C. Harris, D. Martinez HoSang, G. Lipsitz (Eds.), *Seeing race again* (pp. 175–199). University of California Press.

Vasquez, V. (2000). Our way: Using the everyday to create a critical literacy curriculum. *Primary Voices K–6, 9*(2), 8–13. https://eric.ed.gov/?id=EJ617707

Vasquez, V., Janks, H., & Comber, B. (2019). Critical literacy as a way of being and doing. *Language Arts, 96*(5), 300–311. https://hilaryjanks.files.wordpress.com/2020/09/vasquezjankscomber-cl_as_a_way_of_being_and-copy-3-1.pdf

Weinstein, E. C. (2014). The personal is political on social media: Online civic expression patterns and pathways among civically engaged youth. *International Journal of Communication, 8*, 210–233. https://ijoc.org/index.php/ijoc/article/view/2381/1066

Whittingham, C. E. (2019). Geosemiotics <-> Social geography: Preschool places and school(ed) spaces. *Journal of Literacy Research, 51*(1), 52–74. https://doi.org/10.1177/1086296X18820644

Wiederhold Wolfe, A., Black, L. W., Munz, S., & Okamoto, K. (2017). (Dis)Engagement and everyday democracy in stigmatized places: Addressing brain drain in the rural United States. *Western Journal of Communication, 81*(2), 168–187. https://doi.org/10.1080/10570314.2016.1236980

Winn, M. (2013). Toward a restorative English education. *Research in the Teaching of English, 48*(1), 126–135. https://education.ucdavis.edu/sites/main/files/file-attachments/winn_rte13-1_toward_restorative.pdf

Wohlwend, K. (2021). *Literacies that move and matter: Nexus analysis for contemporary childhoods.* Routledge.

Woods, M. (2003). Deconstructing rural protest: The emergence of a new social movement, *RUST Journal of Rural Studies, 19*(3), 309–325.

Zamudio, M., Aragon, C., Alvarez, L., & Rios, F. (2009). Immigrant rights protest in the rural West. *Latino Studies, 7*(1), 105–111. https://doi.org/10.1057/lst.2008.58

CHAPTER 15

EPILOGUE

Mary B. McVee
University at Buffalo, State University of New York

AERA Discussant Remarks April 22, 2022 in session
Toward Critical Multimodality: Exploring Theory, Research, and Practice in Transformative Educational Spaces

As AERA has approached and I have revisited the proposal for this session and good work to be shared, I have had a growing sense that *not* being present in the room today means a considerable loss on my part—and a loss for anyone else not present. There is a power in the words on the page of the summary proposal originally submitted to AERA—I have no doubt that the enacted experiences and interactions today have been that much more powerful in person.

While I am not present in person, I am confident in predicting that this session will likely stand out for many of you, not just at this year's AERA conference but across many AERA conferences. The work is *that* compelling and unique.

Multimodality—the idea that there is more to communication or learning that just reading, writing, listening, speaking—is a powerful idea. It is represented in this AERA session through the diverse examples, contexts, artifacts, positionalities expressed by researchers and the modal expressions of research participants. This work is part of a longer tradition of multimodal scholarship and theories in social semiotics. Over the past few decades multimodal research has blossomed and spread across educational subdisciplines. As Mark Dressman (2008) observes, "The siren song of a good theory [in this case, multimodality, and social semiotics] can be hard to resist" (p. 95). Studies of multimodality themselves can be hard to resist. Oftentimes, such studies or presentations entice us with glossy digital media or other amazing artifacts.

Additionally, I would argue that there are increasing amounts of scholarship related to multimodality that use theories of multimodality or social semiotics in an applied sense, but are, in the end, largely repetitions of prior studies or studies in one subdiscipline of education now carried over into another (near replication with just a shift in discipline, context, and participants). Few current studies of multimodality evoke the energy or critical edge that is clearly, dynamically present in today's workshop. Today's presenters use theories of social semiotics and multimodality in ways that collectively press ahead to answer such questions as:

- What does it mean to engage in critical multimodality and social semiotics (CMSS)?
- What does this critical scholarship look like in practice?
- Where is it that studies of social semiotics and multimodality should be headed?

This session goes a long way toward providing excellent examples in response to those questions, and I suspect can prompt further deep discussions as well.

As I considered the topic and the various research projects in this session, I was also reminded of a powerful quote from Bettina Love. She writes, "Theory does not solve issues... but theory gives you a language to fight, knowledge to stand on, and a humbling reality of what intersectional social justice is up against" (Love, 2019, p. 132). Here, today we have eight projects that are attempting, in one way or another, to take action. Taken as a whole, the presenters today provide access to the voices of people from many nations as well as various linguistic, racial, ethnic, and geographic locales. These multimodal portraits discuss varied modalities from a transformative and dynamic stance to reflect the agenda and "humbling reality of what social justice is up against" but also what critical justice perspectives can envision when engaging with multimodal research. There is no single story here (Adichie, 2009) but instead the richest of stories—those of embodied lives in celebration, in struggle, in remembrance, in transformation. There is an intersectionality of theories here.

The presenters in this session make clear that theories are, as Dorothy Robbins (2003) says, not meant to be a "monolithic structure" (p. 76) to be imposed; instead, theories are "a living, flexible, tool" (p. 76). The vibrancy of today's session comes in part from the synergy across and between theories, but also from the stances of researchers who clearly privilege an agenda for research that centers people—and the purposes and agency of people—using various modes. This workshop helps us see the power and potential in theoretical pluralism. The session takes strides in exploring (and perhaps answering) questions such as:

- What do theories bring to our research?
- How do or how can theories humanize us and keep our research centered on what is not only important but life giving for our participants and ourselves?
- What further articulations of theory-research/critical theory-multimodality/critical theories-social semiotics do we need?
- How and what type of guidance is needed or helpful for scholars who are taking up these explorations and questions?

I greatly look forward to the forthcoming volume edited by Silvestri, Barrett, and Nyachae that has been represented in this session. It is a commendable body of work that will challenge, extend, elaborate, and expand critical theories of multimodality and social semiotics.

REFERENCES

Adichie, C. N. (2009, July). *The danger of a single story* [Video]. TED Conferences. https://www.ted.com/talks/chimamanda_ngozi_adichie_the_danger_of_a_single_story

Dressman, M. (2008). *Using social theory in educational research: A practical guide.* Routledge.

Love, B. (2019). *We want to do more than survive: Abolitionist teaching and the pursuit of educational freedom.* Beacon Press.

Robbins, D. (2003). *Vygotsky's and A.A. Leontiev's semiotics and psycholinguistics.* Praeger Publishers.

ABOUT THE EDITORS

Katarina N. Silvestri is an associate professor of literacy education at the State University of New York (SUNY) at Cortland. She conducts research pertaining to critical multimodal literacy practices, disciplinary literacies in elementary engineering, inquiry-based research in elementary schools, and online learning in higher education. Her work has been published in journals such as *Multimodal Communication, Elementary School Journal, Journal of Pre-College Engineering Education Research, Journal of Adolescent and Adult Literacy,* and *Theory Into Practice.* She has served as secretary for the New York State Reading Association and the American Educational Research Association's Special Interest Group (SIG), Semiotics in Education. She currently serves as treasurer for the Semiotics in Education SIG.

Nichole Barrett is the program director at the Rural Outreach Center in East Aurora, NY and an adjunct professor of literacy and English education at the State University of New York (SUNY) at Buffalo. Her current research and pedagogy focus on the ways that multimodal literacy practices can be utilized as a tool to not only engage youth in meaningful learning experiences, but how they can be utilized in conjunction with trauma informed care to positively influence social-emotional awareness among rural youth.

Tiffany M. Nyachae is an assistant professor of education and women's, gender, and sexuality studies in the College of Education at Penn State University. She employs critically conscious and humanizing research approaches to qualitative studies guided by various justice-oriented theories of race, Black girlhood, Black woman knowing/being/experiences, space, and becoming. Informed by her experiences as a middle school teacher, Dr. Nyachae's research portfolio includes: (a) ethnographic and multiple case studies on supporting urban teachers committed to social justice through "race space" critical professional development; (b) design-based research studies of learning, learning environments, and literacy development in social justice literacy workshops for youth of color; and (c) content and critical discourse analyses of extracurricular programs and curriculum for Black girls. Her publications have appeared in journals such as *Urban Education*, *Journal of Adolescent and Adult Literacy*, and *Gender and Education*. She is also a podcaster, educational consultant, creator, and founder of the Evolving Education Project where the educational joys, passions, interests, and inquiries of people of color are centered.

ABOUT THE CONTRIBUTORS

Earl Aguilera, PhD is an assistant professor in the Department of Curriculum and Instruction at California State University, Fresno. His research, scholarship, and teaching focuses on issues at the intersection of digital literacies, interactive media, and critical pedagogy. His work has been published in venues such as *Pedagogies: An International Journal*, *Theory Into Practice*, and the *Oxford Research Encyclopedia of Education*. Prior to earning his PhD, he has worked as a high school English/language arts teacher, K–12 reading specialist, and adjunct professor of literacy education.

Sara P. Alvarez is assistant professor of English at Queens College, City University of New York (CUNY). Her qualitative research focuses on the multilingual and academic writing practices of self-outed U.S. undocumented young adults. Sara is also interim co-principal investigator with CUNY's, first of its kind, Initiative on Immigration and Education (CUNY-IIE). Sara's works have appeared in *Literacy in Composition Studies*, *Journal of Adolescent & Adult Literacy*, among other journals and edited collections.

M. Isidora Bilbao-Nieva (PhD, Michigan State University) is a Chilean community psychologist. She has worked with artisan communities, exploring the use of crafts for building communities of women. Her research is focused on girls from Patagonia, using feminist critical discourse analysis to explore personal and collective discourses of well-being and specific contextual barriers that affect adolescent girls. She is an assistant professor of social community psychology and teaches in the psychology department at Universidad Alberto Hurtado based in Santiago, Chile.

Sara Cooper is an assistant professor of English at Murray State University in Western Kentucky where she teaches graduate courses in the Doctor of Arts in English Pedagogy program. Her research interests include multimodal composition, digital storytelling, handcrafted rhetorics, and feminist research methods. Her recent work can be found in the *Rhetoric Review* and the edited collection *Writing Changes: Alphabetic Text and Multimodal Composition* (Modern Language Association of America, 2020). In 2020, she was named the Kentucky Council of Teachers of English College Teacher of the Year.

William S. Davis is an assistant professor of world languages education at the University of Oklahoma. He teaches undergraduate and graduate courses in K–12 world languages pedagogy, emergent bilingual education, and cultural diversity in U.S. schools. His research examines autonomy and well-being in the world language classroom, the formation of multilingual teacher agency, and critical approaches in teacher education. He is an incoming president for the Oklahoma Foreign Language Teachers Association and an advocate for the Oklahoma Seal of Biliteracy.

Dr. Matthew R. Deroo is a former language teacher and teacher educator who spent 10 years in China ahead of his graduate studies. He is an assistant professor at the University of Miami. His interdisciplinary research centers around three lines of inquiry: supporting immigrant youth from a translanguaging perspective, multimodal and semiotic theoretical framing in teacher learning, and community engaged scholarship. Dr. Deroo serves as the co-chair of the Multilingual and Transnational Innovative Community Group for the Literacy Research Association and is the current awards chair for the Writing and Literacies Special Interest Group of the American Educational Research Association. Dr. Deroo is a Mandarin speaker committed to supporting teachers and students to draw upon their full linguistic repertoires in support of their learning.

Sarah M. Fleming is currently a visiting assistant professor of education in the Curriculum and Instruction Department at the State University of New York (SUNY) at Oswego, after having taught high school English for 21 years. Her research interests are in the use of young adult literature for the preparation of English preservice candidates, critical literacy, critical inquiry, and culturally responsive pedagogy. She is the past president of the Central New York Reading Council and the co-conference chair of the New York State Reading Association.

Andrea N. Franyutti-Boyles is a senior analyst of instructional design and development and currently resides in Elkins, West Virginia. She conducts research pertaining to L2 demotivation and has presented at the CCCC and

AERA conferences vis-à-vis multimodality and digital storytelling. She holds a Doctor of Arts in English pedagogy with a specialization in the English language, an education specialist degree in English as a second language, and a Master of Education in teaching English to speakers of other languages.

Angélica Galván is an assistant professor of counselor education at California State University, Northridge. She completed her doctorate in counselor education and supervision from The Pennsylvania State University. Angélica has a background in clinical mental health counseling and working with students with disabilities. Her research interests include multicultural counseling, the effects of language use on the counseling relationship, and building a sense of belonging for minoritized people through research and multimodality in higher education. Some examples of her work can be found in the *Journal of American College Health* and the *Journal of Creativity in Mental Health*.

ThedaMarie Gibbs Grey is an associate professor of literacy education in the Ohio University, Department of Teacher Education. She is committed to research, teaching, and community engagement rooted in equity and the honoring of Black youth. She enjoys mentoring preservice teachers of color, and Black middle and high school girls. Her work has been published in journals including *Equity & Excellence in Education*, *Journal of Language and Literacy Education*, and the *Journal of Higher Education*. One of her recent grants supported a mentorship program designed to combat inequitable school discipline for Black girls. She has also created a school-based yoga and literacy wellness space for Black girls.

Laura Gonzales is an assistant professor of digital writing and cultural rhetorics in the Department of English at the University of Florida. She is also the associate director of the TRACE Innovation Initiative at the University of Florida. Her work focuses on the intersections of language diversity, community engagement, and technology design.

Autumn A. Griffin is a postdoctoral research fellow in Georgia State's College of Education & Human Development. Having previously taught secondary ELA in Atlanta, Georgia, her research explores how Black youth use literacies as a means to heal from pedagogical and curricular violence, largely focusing on Black girlhoods, multimodal and digital literacies, and children's and young adult literature. Autumn's work has been published in the *Research in the Teaching of English, Urban Education, Equity and Excellence in Education* and she is currently awaiting the release of her book with colleagues Joshua Coleman and Ebony Elizabeth Thomas, entitled *Restorying Young Adult Literature: Expanding Students' Perspectives with Digital Texts*. Autumn is also the co-founder of the digital network Blackademia, a platform built to explore the historical and contemporary experiences of Black women in the academy and to support Black doctoral students on their journeys by offering community through its podcast, blog, and virtual book chats. In her spare time, Autumn teaches and practices yoga, loves to cook, and can be found anywhere there is live music.

Lynette D. Guzmán was formerly an assistant professor of STEM education at California State University, Fresno. She is currently a full-time content creator for her brand, WizardPhD, where she focuses on experiential and narrative elements in a variety of video games. She also reviews games and creates game guides for the entertainment media website IGN.

Jason Man-bo Ho (he/him/his), EdD, is currently a visiting scholar at EMI Development Center in National Pingtung University, Taiwan (R.O.C.). His research interests include content-and-language integrated learning (CLIL), critical sexuality literacy education, translanguaging, multiliteracies, and multimodality. He has been teaching English language, media communication, and cultural studies for over a decade. He has published articles on queer language education, creative writing, and multimodality, and has been a reviewer for *TESOL Quarterly*, *Critical Inquiry in Language Studies*, and *American Educational Research Association*.

Jeffrey B. Holmes is an instructor in film and media studies at Arizona State University. His research focuses on the changing landscape of teaching and learning in both schools and informal settings, in particular through video games and other digital media as parts of distributed activity systems.

Kyesha M. Isadore is an assistant professor of rehabilitation psychology at the University of Wisconsin–Madison. Her primary work centers on how intersectionality impacts mental health with special attention to race/ism, gender, and disability. Kyesha's current research includes examining therapeutic outcomes for marginalized populations, exploring the experiences of racially/ethnically minoritized college students with psychiatric disabilities, and enhancing multicultural and social justice competencies for counselors-in-training. Kyesha also conducts scholarly work on HIV, HCV, and other infectious conditions. She has clinical experience in mental health, substance use, school, and career counseling fields.

Davena Jackson is an assistant professor of urban education at Boston University. She focuses on English education, language, and literacy. A 20+ year veteran English educator, her research-practice partnerships have sought to disrupt anti-Blackness, anti-Black racism, and White supremacy in secondary English education classrooms and beyond. Also, her research interests include multimodal literacy practices, culturally responsive teaching theories, and justice. Her work has been published in journals such as *Research in the Teaching of English, Conference on College Composition and Communication, Journal of Literacy Research, Teachers College Record*, and the *International Review of Qualitative Research.*

Eunjeong Lee is assistant professor of applied linguistics and rhetoric and composition at the University of Houston. Her research examines politics of language, racialization, language and literacy practices of language-minoritized students, and decolonial and equitable writing education through ethnography, discourse analysis, and community-engaged teacher research. Her work has appeared in *Composition Forum; Journal of Language, Identity, and Education; World Englishes;* and *Journal of Multicultural Discourses,* and edited collections such as *Translinguistics* (Routledge, 2019) and *Crossing Divides* (University Press of Colorado, 2017). She has recently co-edited a collection, *Linguistic Justice on Campus: Pedagogy and Advocacy for Multilingual Students* (Multilingual Matters, 2021).

Dr. Vicki Mokuria teaches at Stephen F. Austin State University, primarily as a teacher educator. She is a lifelong educator/learner who worked as a high school teacher, as a parent educator, and now, on the college level. After graduating from Soka University of America's MA program, she earned her doctorate from Texas A&M University focusing on urban education. In addition to being a poet/scholar/author/educator, Dr. Mokuria is also a devoted mother and grandmother. She has published numerous articles in peer-reviewed journals and books. Research interests include anti-racism education, multicultural education, relational realms, and Soka education in Brazil.

Romina S. Peña-Pincheira, PhD, is an assistant professor of education at Gustavus Adolphus College. In her transdisciplinary research, she explores language as a multisemiotic social practice and sociopolitical relevant language education. She grounds her work in decolonial feminists, social semiotics, and critical applied linguistics in education. Currently, her research focuses on colonial entanglements in language learning and the decolonial possibilities in language education in the intersections of identity, memory, and sociopolitical contexts. Her work is published in *TESOL Journal, International Journal of Qualitative Studies in Education, Urban Education,* and *Educational Studies Journal.*

Grace D. Player's work is rooted in her experiences as a mixed-race Asian American woman, daughter, and sister. A literacy scholar, educator, and artist with a longstanding commitment to collaborating with communities of color, her work takes on a feminist of color lens to inquire into how girls and women of color mobilize their raced, gendered, and cultural knowledges and ways of knowing to forge sisterhoods that resist injustice and transform worlds. She is currently an assistant professor of literacy at the University Connecticut Neag School of Education.

Gregory Ramírez is an English instructor at Madera Community College. He earned his bachelor's and master's degrees from California State University, Fresno (CSUF) then earned his Doctor of Arts in English pedagogy from Murray State University. His research focuses on first-year composition theory, digital and multimodal composition, and equitable pedagogical practices. He has presented (or co-presented) at several conferences as well as published poetry in journals and anthologies throughout the United States. He lives in Clovis, California with his wife, Stephanie, and their two children.

Lau Romero-Quintana is a PhD in Hispanic cultural studies and an assistant professor of Spanish at Northern Michigan University. They specialize in Latin American women's writing, gender and sexuality studies, queer studies, and cultural studies. Their research interests include social justice, DEI practices, and Latin American Literature and cultural productions in the XX and XXI century.

Kelly M. Tran is a game designer, formerly an assistant professor of game design at High Point University (HPU) in North Carolina. Her research focuses on player communities, games and learning, and game design. She currently consults on a wide variety of games, including commercial games and educational projects, and writes for a number of tabletop roleplaying games (TTRPGs).

Jennifer D. Turner is associate professor of reading education and the College of Education ADVANCE professor at the University of Maryland College Park. Her research focuses on two interrelated areas: (a) Black youth's multimodal practices (e.g., photography, drawings, digital collage) for future making; and (b) literacy pedagogical approaches in P–12 schools that affirm the futures and cultivate the future making of youth of color. Her co-authored book, *Change Is Gonna Come: Transforming Literacy Education for African American Students* (Teachers College Press, 2010), received the Edward Fry Book Award from the Literacy Research Association. In addition, her research has been published in leading academic journals including *Research in the Teaching of English; Teachers College Record; Race, Ethnicity, and Education; English Teaching: Practice and Critique;* and *Educational Forum.* She recently served as lead co-editor of a special issue on young people of color and their multimodal future making for the *International Journal of Qualitative Studies in Education* that will be published in Spring 2023. She currently serves as awards chair for the American Educational Research Association's Special Interest Group, Social Semiotics in Education.

Amy Walker is an assistant professor in the School of Teaching, Learning, and Curriculum at Kent State University. Her research disrupts monolithic assumptions of students and geographies by examining the literacies students practice through resistance and activism. As a teacher educator and researcher, she works with educators and students to understand how space, movement, and power interact with meaning making in school and community spaces. She also serves as the social media liaison for the American Educational Research Association's Special Interest Group, Semiotics in Education.

Amy J. Wan (she/her/hers) is associate professor of English at Queens College and the CUNY Graduate Center where she teaches undergraduate and graduate classes on writing, literacy, and pedagogy. She is the author of *Producing Good Citizens: Literacy Training in Anxious Times* (UPitt Press, 2014). Her writing has also appeared in *College English*, *WPA Journal*, *Writing Spaces*, *Rhetoric Review*, *Literacy in Composition Studies*, and *Radical Teacher*, among others. Her current research analyzes how to create spaces for change and resistance within the global U.S. university through a historical and contemporary study of policies addressing access, diversity, race, and language.

Alexis Morgan Young is a doctoral candidate in teaching and learning, policy and leadership with a specialization in urban education at the University of Maryland–College Park. Alexis' scholarship centers the liberatory literacies of Black girls in elementary and middle schools. Her research speaks to the importance of seeing Black girls as whole, imaginative beings who are not passive actors in their education or in society. Above all, Alexis' work challenges us to (re)imagine a world where Black girls are seen as experts and change agents toward their liberation.

Printed in the United States
by Baker & Taylor Publisher Services